There Is No Me Without You

There Is No Me Without You

One Woman's Odyssey to Rescue Africa's Children

MELISSA FAY GREENE

BLOOMSBURY

Author's note: Where appropriate the names of some individuals
have been changed or modified.

Published by Bloomsbury USA, New York
Distributed to the trade by Holtzbrinck Publishers

All papers used by Bloomsbury USA are natural, recyclable
products made from wood grown in well-managed forests.
The manufacturing processes conform to the environmental
regulations of the country of origin.

Library of Congress Cataloging-in-Publication Data

Greene, Melissa Fay.
There is no me without you : one woman's odyssey to rescue Africa's children / Melissa
Fay Greene.—1st U.S. ed.
p. cm.
ISBN-13 978-1-59691-116-1 (hardcover)
ISBN-10 1-59691-116-6 (hardcover)
1. Teferra, Haregewoin. 2. Children of AIDS patients—Ethiopia—Addis Ababa—Social conditions.
3. Orphans—Ethiopia—Addis Ababa—Social conditions. 4. Children of AIDS patients—Services
for—Ethiopia—Addis Ababa. 5. Orphans—Services for—Ethiopia—Addis Ababa. 6. Child
welfare—Ethiopia—Addis Ababa. I. Title.

HV1344.5.Z8A334 2006
362.73'2—dc22
[B]
2006014088

First U.S. Edition 2006

1 3 5 7 9 10 8 6 4 2

Typeset by Hewer Text UK Ltd, Edinburgh
Printed in the United States of America by Quebecor World Fairfield

To Donny and our kids

PART ONE

I

AUGUST 2004

O N A D I M, clattering afternoon in the rainy season, I sat in a crowded living room in Addis Ababa, Ethiopia, stupefied by water. The rain drumming the tin roofs of the hillside district was deafening, as if neighbors on rooftops banged with kettles and sticks. The mud yard boiled and popped in the downpour. Through the wide-open front door, I watched arriving visitors leap across stepping-stones slick with clay. At the doorstep of Haregewoin Teferra's two-room brick house—an earthier, leakier dwelling than the modern two-story stucco house she'd once enjoyed—the men took off their hats and shook them and the women wrung out their shawls. Though Haregewoin was sliding further every day from her former middle-class standing, a dozen old friends opted to sit out the cloudburst with her—some as a sign of loyalty, some probably to see what she was going to do next. Despite misgivings about whom they might find among her guests, all entered beaming. They greeted everyone by handshake or raised eyebrows, dripped across the cement floor, and squeezed in to join the inactivity.

Ebullient and round, four foot eight, the hostess slapped across the wet floor in rubber flip-flops. Haregewoin Teferra (Ha-re-ge-*woin* Te-*fare*-uh) was a country-born, well-educated, bilingual woman in her late fifties. Her thick hair, bunched under a triangular kerchief, had sprung a few curlicues of gray. Her coffee-dark skin gleamed in the heat. She wore what she always wore: a long, leopard-print cotton skirt with an elastic waist, and a red, short-sleeve T-shirt. As each caller took a seat,

Haregewoin hurried back to her chair and pitched forward brightly to hear the news. When she laughed, she clutched her hands to her chest and leaned back; her eyes crinkled shut and her shoulders jiggled.

This was no special occasion or holiday. Some of Haregewoin's old friends had retired from work in retail or the professions; others were underemployed, simply unable—in Ethiopia's listless economy—to fill their days with gainful activity. Still others had hidden reasons for their freedom to visit in the middle of a weekday afternoon.

One guest practically dared new arrivals to sit beside him. "Let's see how far your good manners will get us" was the look on the face of Zewedu Getachew (Zoe-dew Ge-*tah*-chew) a once-handsome and affluent man. He had been director of construction for a French company and had taught engineering at Addis Ababa University. The shoulders of his khaki overcoat were angrily bunched up less against the rain, it seemed, than against the trick life had played him, the change in his health status that had cost him his job and good name.

Across the continent, people were lining up by the millions on one side or the other of a new binary system, being told they were "positive" or "negative" as if they had turned overnight into protons and electrons and everyone spoke of subatomic physics, rather than of who was going to live and who was going to be shunned, endure terrible suffering, and die.

Only Haregewoin, among many friends who had once hosted Zewedu, still welcomed him. He tilted far back on a metal-legged kitchen chair with his arms crossed on his chest, not expecting to be offered a handshake, nor offering one. Unshaved whiskers darkened his cheeks.

A humble and pretty young woman, wearing a long skirt, seated herself on a low stool to roast fresh coffee beans. She shook them in an iron skillet over a portable stove. Sara had been expelled from college during her sophomore year and denounced by her parents when her persistent cough had turned out to be not only tuberculosis (at which point her parents had bundled her up and raced around with her to the best doctors) but something unspeakable (when they evicted her). The lessons in subservience drilled into most Ethiopian girls did not prepare a young person for finding herself alone in the city; Sara was huddled in a doorway when Haregewoin found her. Haregewoin knew—even if Sara did not—that the college girl's options might soon be a choice between begging or the sex trade.

Thus, on this average weekday in East Africa, a rare scene: a house in which middle-class men and women untouched by the epidemic sat beside men and women who had crossed over the great divide.

The hard rain pummeled the roof, stirred up the courtyard, and sent herds of barefoot little kids galloping past Haregewoin's open door.

I was unhappily wedged in a love seat beside a fierce-looking old woman in a cocoon of homespun cotton. Her dark, pendulous skin and droopy eyes were pulled up and back by a head scarf, giving her an expression of alarmed disapproval. I didn't know if she was frowning against the upward yank of her face or because she had been stuck with me. Over the long hours, we became reluctant familiars, like strangers on an all-night bus trip. We secretly shoved each other over disputed millimeters of territory, but faced forward politely.

The wind sprayed mist through the open door. The whitewashed brick room seemed to dip and sway as if we rode a houseboat whipped by dark waves. The mummified dowager at my side slowly gained ground, as her long cotton shawls began to unwind.

It had taken me a few weeks to get the hang of this. On the long afternoons when the air fattens to water in Addis Ababa, the city's animal life—goats, sheep, donkeys, stray dogs, woodpeckers, catbirds, swallows—fall asleep standing up in crevices and bowers, or with their heads bowed in the deluge. That is when I long to trudge up the stairs to my room in the tidy Yilma Hotel, peel off my muddy shoes and socks, drink from a liter of bottled water, fall across the bed with Bahru Zewde's *History of Modern Ethiopia*, and sleep while the tall, sheer curtains drift into the room full of the scent and weight of rain.

But I was stuffed into a love seat in Haregewoin's common room and there was no getting out of it. The group inertia overwhelmed me. "Now?" everyone stirred and asked in bewilderment. "You want to go somewhere *now*, in *this* weather?" Some were thinking, I'm sure, "The *ferange* [white] has to go somewhere *now?*" My friend and driver, Selamneh Techane (Se-*lam*-nuh Te-*tchen*-ay), who was rolled forward with his head resting on his hands, sat up and looked at me with bleary confusion. Every time I tried to stand up, the materfamilias beside me sloughed off another layer of shawls.

Better just to sink down, everyone implied; we'll get through this together. So together we sank through the endless soft drone of the afternoon rains. The demitasse cups of coffee, thick with the sliding brown silt of sugar, somehow knocked one even faster into a somnolent state. The conversation, after we returned our empty cups to a wooden, four-legged tray on the floor, dropped off steeply. When the dim lamp flickered off, nobody thumped it. Nobody turned on the dusty television under its yellowing doily and vase of plastic flowers. (There was nothing to watch on TV: nearly all day, every day, the government-controlled TV station broadcast traditional dancers leaping and shimmying under harsh studio lights.) My impregnable seatmate, in an advanced state of coming unraveled, was snoring.

Haregewoin's cell phone rang and she answered with a crisp "Allo? *Abet?*" (Yes?) The coffee table was spread with papers, and there was a landline telephone, which often rang, too. Haregewoin Teferra was not weighed down by wind and rain and drowsiness. Things were happening in the city, even at this torrential hour, and she was deep in negotiations. Or perhaps the message she meant to relay to her old friends was "You see? I am still alive."

She put down the phone for a moment and looked out, calculating.

"What is it?" someone asked, as she knew someone would.

"It is the *kebele* [a local council, like a county commission]. They ask if I have room to take in a child."

Several visitors chuckled. Disbelief stirred under the surface. Ethiopians—especially the highlanders, the Amhara and the Tigray—are famously sarcastic people, so there probably were a few sly remarks, in a language and of a degree of subtlety impossible for me to understand even in translation. Centuries of living under tyrants have given Ethiopians the gift of double entendre. The hidden speech has a name: *säm enna wärq* (wax and gold): the *säm* is the surface meaning and the *wärq* is the deep or hidden meaning. Skilled practitioners are respected as masters of verbal artistry.

At any rate, of course Haregewoin had no room for another child: the two-room brick house, two small outbuildings, and rusted, bright blue boxcar with a door carved out of it overflowed with children and teens of every size, and there were wistful adult hangers-on, too.

She sat for a moment, holding the receiver against her chest and curling the fingers of one hand around her lips, counting. No one moved, nor did anyone offer to shelter the child in Haregewoin's place. Who knew what his condition would be? Probably sick, maybe contagious, certainly hungry and filthy; barefoot, uneducated, and hysterical. No thank you. While it was appreciated that the neighborhood's administrative unit, the *kebele*, took an interest, neither the *kebele* nor the federal government had a stipend to offer for the child's upkeep.

Haregewoin stood up. "I go," she said.

Thinking I'd caught the rhythm of the afternoon, I protested, "Now? You're going somewhere *now*?" I looked to the others for approval.

But one doesn't ask this of someone who actually *has* work to do, for real work is hard to find and always respected. Some now must have thought, "Now the *ferange* doesn't *want* to go?"

"May I come too?" I asked more humbly.

"Yes. *Ishi* [Okay]. Come. Please."

Selamneh Techane, the taxi driver, instantly alert, stood up, keys in hand. Haregewoin no longer had a car, much less the two cars of her married life. She gathered her *shamma* (thick, handwoven shawl) and black handbag and splashed cheerfully into the courtyard.

"Where are we going?" I asked, wading behind her.

"To pick up the child," she called over her shoulder, already hoisting herself into the front seat of Selamneh's tin blue taxi. I got into the back and off we backfired.

At the intersection of the mountain lane and a paved thoroughfare, we pulled over to pick up a woman in khaki slacks and a zipper windbreaker waiting outside her apartment building. She got into the backseat with me and introduced herself, shaking hands all around. Her name was Gerrida; she was a housewife, married to a police officer. It was she who had just phoned on behalf of the *kebele*.

"The little boy is Mintesinot [Min-*tess*-eh-note]. He is about two and a half years old," Gerrida said. He was growing up on a sidewalk near a busy intersection in town. Two months ago, his mother, Emebate (Em-eh-*bott*-ay) died of pneumonia (an opportunistic infection of AIDS); now his father was very sick, coughing all night, probably from tuberculosis (TB was one of the typical opportunistic infections of AIDS [OIA] invading immune systems weakened by HIV disease). It was evident to everyone in the neighborhood that the young father would soon die.

Gerrida had given charity to the small family over the years, she said, and many others in the district had also tried to help them. Finally, though, with the death of Mintesinot's mother, it was time: the boy required better care than what his homeless, terminally ill father was giving him in plain sight of the entire world, beside the gutter of a busy street, nearly under the hooves of urban herds of goats and donkeys.

"The child is so smiling face," Gerrida turned to assure me in English. "He is wonderful."

I wondered briefly why Gerrida didn't take in the little boy. But if he was indeed an orphan of the unspeakable disease, then she could not. The stigma of the plague crawled across its orphans, widows, and widowers, as if they, too, seethed with germs.

We wove through traffic and dashed across intersections without traffic lights, while packed vans, buses, and taxis raced, lurched, stalled out, crunched, and were pushed out of the way by crowds of onlookers hoping for tips. A line of donkeys laden with leafy branches skittered through the traffic; on the median strip, a solitary hump-necked cow grazed tranquilly, as if she stood knee-deep in a meadow and had nothing more to ponder than the clouds.

On her first trip to Addis Ababa, my twenty-four-year-old daughter, Molly Samuel, would say, "If I ever saw this many people in the streets of an American city, I'd think they were fleeing a disaster." The rain had stopped, followed by cool, cloudy sunlight. A man ran down the sidewalk holding up the hind legs of his goat, the animal pedaling as fast as it could on two skinny front legs with its rump in midair, the overall effect like a wheelbarrow. Wizened, kerchiefed, little ladies, bent double at the waist, struggled down the shoulders of the road under impossibly tall loads of firewood. Women in *hijabs* (Islamic head scarves) flowed down the crowded sidewalks, while other women veered around them, wearing heels and stylish pantsuits. Men of all ages walked the streets hand in hand, in heterosexual friendship; policemen, with rifles across their backs, stood at their posts holding hands. Young soccer players in glossy uniforms shouted to each other above the crowd; then a robed and white-bearded man cleared the way with his knotty walking stick, looking as if he had just arrived out of the biblical desert.

Older Ethiopian Orthodox women in long, white robes and shawls paraded under parasols quilted of shiny red, green, and purple fabrics, threaded with metallic gold, sprinkled with tiny gold ornaments, and swinging with red or gold fringes. Religious women will lift their parasols in a display of gratitude to God for answered prayers. Market stalls offered quivers full of the bright umbrellas, the sunlight dashing off them as if off broken glass.

"Why all the parasols?" I asked Selamneh on my first trip to Ethiopia, in 2001.

"They are . . .," he began. "Are they not . . . the umbrellas from the Bible?"

"The *umbrellas*? From the *Bible*?"

"Yes."

"*What* umbrellas from the Bible?"

"I don't know."

That night, from an Internet café, I e-mailed my family in America the question "Were there *umbrellas* in the Bible?"

The next day, my seventeen-year-old son, Seth Samuel, e-mailed back, "Well, Mom, it *did* rain for forty days and forty nights."

But a few days later, Selamneh remembered, "When King Solomon brought the Holy Tabernacle into Jerusalem, people sheltered it with umbrellas."

"Oh," I said. And why do middle-aged women in long, white robes—picking their way along the muddy shoulders of roads packed with traffic, cattle, and humanity—lift and twirl parasols in the air, fluttering in the wind like kites, other than for the pageantry? On the Orthodox holiday of Timket, the festival of Epiphany, why are umbrellas held aloft by the clergy while a Tabot, a replica of the Holy Tabernacle, is reverently displayed? Because Ethiopia was the biblical Abyssinia, the kingdom of the Queen of Sheba, who journeyed to Jerusalem (according to holy writ and legend) when the Tabernacle was young.

Standing like a mountain fortress above the Horn of Africa, near the confluence of the Red Sea, the Arabian Sea, and the Indian Ocean, ancient Ethiopia defied foreign conquerors for millennia and traded in slaves, gold, ivory, spices, gems, textiles, and animals with ancient Egypt, Persia, Arabia, the Roman Empire, and India. Five-thousand-year-old Egyptian hieroglyphs mention the preference of the pharaohs for myrrh from Ethiopia. For centuries, Axum, the highland Ethiopian kingdom of the Amhara people, was the dominant Red Sea power, builder of castles and massive stone monoliths, minter of gold, silver, and copper coins. Third-century CE Persian writings named the world's four great kingdoms as Rome, China, Persia, and Axum.

Sacred literature in both Israel and Ethiopia describes Queen Makeda's visit to the king of Israel. "The Queen of Sheba heard of Solomon's fame . . . and she came to test him with hard questions," reads I Kings, chapter 10, in the Hebrew Bible. "She arrived in

Jerusalem with a very large retinue, with camels bearing spices, a great quantity of gold, and precious stones."

"This Queen of the South was very beautiful in face, and her stature was superb," says the ancient Ethiopian holy text *Kebra Nagast* [The Glory of Kings]. "Her understanding and intelligence which God had given her were of such high character that she went to Jerusalem to hear the wisdom of Solomon." Makeda, known to the outside world as the Queen of Sheba, married Solomon, and they had a son: Menelik, founder of the Ethiopian kingship (thus, through the twentieth century, Ethiopian kings claimed Davidic descent).

The parasols, spinning like kaleidoscopes above the dusty crowded streets, sparkle with ancient secrets.

The traditional and the modern swirl together like this everywhere. A shepherd steers his ratty-looking sheep along the edges of the manicured, sloping lawn of the palatial Sheraton Addis Hotel. A hand-lettered sign in a shop announces WE RENT MOTORBIKES, CAMELS. On the road to Zoia, a motorcade of semitrailers is stopped by a proud, skittish procession of Afar camels and nomads: the men, with long curls knotted under bright head scarves, jog alongside their animals, waving sticks and yelling, oblivious to the trucks idling on the highway before them. On a hard-baked plain, a hundred miles south of electricity, a young goatherd stands in a field, holding a wooden staff and wearing a T-shirt with the Boston Red Sox baseball logo. And one day I glimpsed a shepherd and his sheep hitching a ride out of Addis on the top of an oil tanker. They straddled the silver missile and hung on for dear life, the man's hair and the animal's wool blown back in the wind.

Selamneh steered pell-mell through the wild traffic, throwing us from side to side in the backseat. Children roamed the streets, tapping on our car windows to offer packets of tissue, or individual eggs, or upside-down live chickens for sale. Nearly two thirds of school-age children are not in school in Ethiopia, nearly the worst record in the world, and only 41 percent of adults can read. Boys and girls in

V-necked maroon or sky-blue school sweaters (no matter how ragged) are the envy of dustier, unschooled children. The uniformed ones swing their notebooks and parade down the sidewalks in laughing, gossiping bunches, full of optimism and expectation, confident that their uniforms and notebooks will add up to something.

"They will feel happy until one-half year or one year after high school graduation," Selamneh told me. "Then they will begin to realize something is wrong." The urban unemployment rate here is also one of the worst in the world. Leaning against buildings and walls, sharing cigarettes, watching the horsing around of high school students only a few years younger than themselves, are listless young men, endlessly waiting, increasingly shabby, who finished school and then fell into an idleness from which there is no escape.

Adult beggars of every description tapped at the car windows. Nursing mothers did this, wordlessly indicating the babies within their dusty shawls; and a man with six fingers on each hand displayed his hands to idling motorists until they threw coins at him to make him go away. A man with leprosy displayed an arm that ended in a charcoal-like stump. Another turned a face disfigured by burns. A man lay on a sidewalk displaying a hugely swollen, gangrenous leg from which the foot had been amputated; it was huge as a fallen tree trunk, red and peeling. A woman at the car window showed a face swallowed by an eye tumor, and a young boy led his blind grandfather from car to car. It was a walking sideshow, a living testimony to the statistics: 81 percent of Ethiopia's people live on less than two dollars a day, and 26 percent live on less than a dollar a day, the marker of absolute poverty in the world.

A landlocked country (since 1993, when, by popular referendum, Eritrea became Africa's fifty-third sovereign state and Ethiopia became Africa's fifteenth landlocked state), Ethiopia's huge population, droughts and food crises, nonindustrial means of production, huge debt-service obligations, massive military spending, ongoing border disputes with Eritrea, and state ownership of land all foil and baffle development experts and keep the people rural, unemployed, and destitute.

The Ethiopian populace has struggled again and again to install democratic leaders who will promote industrialization, education, and civil equality; but the citizenry has been repeatedly disappointed.

In 1995, Ethiopia's first multiparty elections made Meles Zenawi prime minister and awarded his Ethiopian People's Revolutionary Democratic Front (EPRDF) a legislative majority. But the government—the first in Ethiopia's history with democratic pretensions—has been unable to steer a path toward industrialization, economic growth, and human rights. Recurrent cycles of drought, food shortages, and famine inspire critics of the government to call, in vain, for land reform and for agricultural modernization as stepping-stones to development.

"In a country where good governance does not exist and where the government is the land- and business-owner and the people are tenants, it is difficult to imagine that the private sector would prosper," said Lidetu Ayalew, secretary general of the opposition Ethiopian Democratic Party (EDP), last year.

"After fourteen years or so of leadership by the EPRDF, up to twenty percent of the country's sixty-five million people are not able to eat even once a day," said Berhane Mewa, president of the Ethiopian and Addis Ababa Chamber of Commerce.

Instead the administration has veered toward ethnic politics (the singling out for promotion of the Tigrayan people—the prime minister's ethnic group—as if others were rivals), saber rattling toward Eritrea, and the silencing of journalists and opposition voices. "Land will remain state-owned as long as the EPRDF is at the helm of the country's leadership," Meles has said. Border disputes with Eritrea spur massive military spending: the escalation into war in 1998 cost the government $2 million a day; in 2000, the defense budget exceeded $800 million.

Health and education budgets decline correspondingly whenever there is a military buildup. Funding for social and health sectors has expanded since 2000, but remains far below what is desperately required. Even across sub-Saharan Africa, health spending is about ten dollars per person per year, while, in Ethiopia, government spending on health, per person per year in 2002, was two dollars.

Thus victims of polio and malaria and HIV/AIDS and cancer, and the blind and the lepers, and the mentally ill and the malnourished, and the orphans and the dying, roam the streets of the capital city, or lie on its sidewalks, defeated.

Twice in the twentieth century, Ethiopia overthrew its authoritarian rulers: Emperor Haile Selassie was toppled by a Communist coup led by Colonel Mengistu Haile Mariam in 1974; and then Mengistu was overthrown by Meles Zenawi and the EPRDF in 1991. Both revolutions came with horrendous bloodshed.

To watch Meles's government turn dictatorial and martial is a source of momentous disappointment and discontent.

Neither the child nor the father was at home, we discovered. We also discovered that "home" was a pile of dirty rags and plastic bags on the sidewalk, a few feet from a bus stop. Scraps of corrugated tin and wood had been tied together to make a low fence around the filthy bedding. "He was born here, his mother gave birth to him *right here*," said Gerrida.

Gerrida spoke to a few passersby, and several pleasant soft-spoken guys, in jeans and T-shirts, jogged off; then they returned from around the corner with Mintesinot and his father.

How young and bewildered the father looked! He was thin, twenty-eight, with a light beard, wearing an oversize, beige, button-down shirt, maroon slacks, and a string necklace with a wooden crucifix. If *he* were the person in need of rescue, I wouldn't have been surprised. Gerrida told us that the young man, Eskender (Ess-*ken*-der), had trained as a metalworker beside *his* father, but both his parents had died years ago. When he got obviously sick with AIDS, he lost his job and house. He and his young wife, Emebate, also an orphan, had made a life here, on a square of sidewalk. When it rained, they lay flat and pulled a length of plastic over themselves and their baby.

Eskender held the hand of a swaggering stocky little fellow, his son, the crown prince of the neighborhood. Mintesinot had a square, shiny dark-skinned face, long curls, and endearingly sticking-out ears. He skipped as if he owned the world. He did own this stretch of sidewalk, everybody knew him. The name Mintesinot meant "What could he *not* do?" When Minty needed a nap, he climbed over the humble barricade protecting his blankets—it was like a play fort built by young children—and passersby tried to be quieter, reminding one another, "Baby is sleeping." When Haregewoin approached him, Mintesinot eyed her warily and drew closer to Eskender's side.

I worried that our assignment was to seize the child from his father and make off with him. I felt afraid for the young man.

Gerrida unfolded a packet of official papers from her handbag and held them out to Eskender. The young father read the orders and gave a sad smile. He held out his son's hand to Haregewoin.

"*Na* [come], Mintesinot," she said gently, but the boy pulled back like a pony yanked by the lead rope. Haregewoin bent over to make small talk with him, but he disappeared behind his father.

Selamneh decided to try. He squatted down and said, "Mintesinot, would you like to ride in my taxi?"

The pair of bright black eyes reappeared from behind the father's filthy shirttail.

"I will drive?" asked the boy in a clear, high voice.

Selamneh lost his balance in laughter. Sitting back on his heels again, Selamneh said, "Well, not this first time. Come on, I'll take you; we'll see if you like it."

"*Abate yimetal?*" Will my dad come?

"Let's go to the market and buy a package of biscuits for your dad, a present for your dad!" Selamneh invented on the spot. At this, smiling Mintesinot came out from behind his father, took Selamneh's hand, and allowed himself to be led to the taxi and given a boost up into the backseat. He waved to a few sidewalk admirers from his high perch.

I hurried back through the crowd to the father. "Does he know where we're going? Does he know where we're taking Mintesinot?" My hands were shaking for it seemed that everything had speeded up, that the taxi was revving to depart, that blocked cars were honking in protest, that people were running; distressed, I rummaged wildly through my backpack for a pen and a piece of paper and fumbled them into the air. One of the nice young men in the crowd caught them and wrote down, for Eskender, Haregewoin's phone number and address. The father thanked us with his infinitely sad smile and pushed the paper into his breast pocket.

Clearly this child was his whole life; he'd raised out of nothing, out of rags and refuse and handouts, a delightful and confident boy. But he knew this day must be coming. He grasped that people in good health had arrived to take away his son. He wearily lowered himself into his lonely knot of blankets. The whole neighborhood looked poorer as we departed with Mintesinot; the father had lost his only treasure, accepting, like a receipt, his son's forwarding address.

Mintesinot's smile disappeared the second the car doors slammed. *"Abi!"* he shrieked as the taxi jerked away. "Dad!" He lunged for the window. His curiosity about biscuits failed next to his panic at leaving his father.

"Let's go find biscuits for your dad!" Selamneh said again, but the boy whirled and knelt and pushed his worried face up under the back window. He was trying to memorize the route home.

"Minty, Minty," sang Haregewoin, turning around and clapping her hands. When he ignored her, she sighed and looked out the window again. The *kebele* had deputized her to do this degree of aid and nothing more; she could rescue the child; she could not save the father.

When we roared back inside the corrugated-tin walls of Haregewoin's compound, Mintesinot wailed, "This is *not* the market!" I remembered that somewhere in my backpack was a half package of Italian biscotti left over from a six-hour airport layover in Rome, Italy, a week earlier. I gave the rolled-down package of gourmet cookies to Mintesinot, unwittingly falling, myself, for Selamneh's fiction. *"Biskut!"* he yelled triumphantly. "Biscuits for my dad!"

"Let's clean you up, little man," said Haregewoin, turning him over

to Sara. Five minutes later there were screams of protest and terror.
Had the child ever been bathed before? But, half an hour later, here
came Prince Mintesinot, his dark curls glistening, tucked into a clean
T-shirt and dark blue, cuffed blue jeans, proudly wearing a used pair of
Power Rangers sneakers with Velcro closures.

When Mintesinot spotted Selamneh, he galloped over and threw
himself into the taxi driver's arms. "Let's go to my dad now!" he said
happily.

Selamneh bounced him on his knee. "I wish I could adopt this guy,"
he said. A gentle, square-faced man of high intelligence and intuition,
wearing a sparse mustache, Selamneh, thirty-seven, looked enough like
Mintesinot to be his father. In a different economy, Selamneh, who
favored khaki slacks, a plaid button-down shirt, and brown oxfords,
could have been a history teacher, a psychologist, or a journalist. But he
lived in his mother's house, underemployed and single. There was no
borrowing policy or landowning policy in this country; no college
loans, car loans, or house mortgages existed to enable an ambitious
person to climb the social ladder. And, regarding romance (with, for
example, a recent graduate of Addis Ababa University), Selamneh had
told me, "Parents with ambition do not prefer for their daughter to
marry a driver."

Wistfully, he let Mintesinot slide down his leg.

All this activity roused my rumpled fellow travelers. They exclaimed
over Mintesinot's good looks, while Haregewoin sat and answered her
phone again.

Suddenly she stood and said, "Another one. It's unbelievable. I'm
going."

Selamneh exited, jingling his car keys. Mintesinot bounced along at
his side, picking at his pants leg, singing about biscuits and Dad. Sara,
at Haregewoin's signal, hurried to detach Mintesinot from the taxi
driver; now there was true terror and kicking and screams of betrayal.
"Abi! Biskut!" He waved the Italian gourmet cookies in his fist.

Selamneh rolled down his window. "Later, Minty, we'll go later."

"But *will* you take him home later?" I asked, unable to keep the hurt out of my own voice, feeling that I tagged along plucking at Selamneh's side as Mintesinot had done.

"No."

"But will he see his father again?"

"Yes, he'll see him."

I returned to my seat in the humid room, too sad to go on another errand of child removal. I discovered that my seatmate, the matriarch, had decamped.

"Who *was* that anyway?" I asked crankily.

The dignified woman was a highly esteemed elder of the Ethiopian Orthodox Church and a relative of Haregewoin's late husband, I learned. She honored the household—nay, the neighborhood—by her visit.

I should have given her more of the love seat, evidently.

Sara led Mintesinot back into the house. Sobbing, he tucked the cookies deep inside his shirt, to protect them for his dad.

2

I WOKE UP the next morning in my hotel room into the crackling darkness of the mountain air. The minor-key prayer song was beginning from the Grand Mosque—*Allah, Allah*—soon joined by voices from Medhane Alem, the Ethiopian Orthodox cathedral *Halle-, Halle-, Hallelujah!* The nearly monotone chants were broadcast through static-filled loudspeakers. They were joined by the whinnying of donkeys trotting on dirt paths, the slap of the long shoes of solitary distance runners along blacktopped roads, and the fanfare of roosters as the city awoke.

By midafternoon, Addis Ababa would be choked in a haze of dust from thousands of hoofed cattle, smoke from outdoor cook-fires, powder from cement and brick factories, and car exhaust fumes. Prayers and curses alike would be swallowed in the cacophony of outdoor life—animal bleats and taxi horns and shouts from market vendors, and the commotion of hundreds of thousands of pedestrians. But in the early mornings, the highest-altitude capital in Africa was clean and bright and the morning prayers sailed far upon the sweet air.

Americans flatten, mispronounce, and syncopate the name of the city: *at*-tis a-*ba*-buh, we say, making it sound like a drink, or maybe a dance step, from the Harlem Renaissance.

Only the cognoscenti know to say: ah-*deece* ah-*bah-bah*.

I stood on the small cement hotel balcony, overlooking the next-door neighbor's miniature barnyard of goats and chickens, and felt amazed at what I'd witnessed at Mrs. Haregewoin's house the previous afternoon: the phone call, the launch of the child-rescue mission, the abandonment of the sick father, and the return home to find the coffee still warm in our cups.

I understood it to be an act of triage. Haregewoin couldn't save everyone—a million people had died of AIDS in its first two decades in Ethiopia, and the hardest hit were the men and women (especially women) between fifteen and forty-nine years of age: a generation and a half of *parents*. Haregewoin Teferra was trying to harbor a few of the children left behind.

Though I didn't know her personal story yet, I had a rough appreciation of the numbers behind it. I'd flown to Ethiopia for the first time in 2001 (and met Haregewoin in 2003) partly in an attempt to make sense of the statistics.

The data had hit me acutely for the first time one Sunday summer morning in Atlanta in 2000.

I was lounging by the sunny bay window, finishing my coffee, idly screwing in a pierced earring, as the Sunday *New York Times* spread its dark news across the kitchen table. I read, for the first time, the United Nation's description of Africa as "a continent of orphans." The human immunodeficiency virus (HIV) and acquired immunodeficiency syndrome (AIDS) had killed more than twenty-one million people, including four million children.

More than thirteen million children had been orphaned, twelve million of them in sub-Saharan Africa. Twenty-five percent of those lived in two countries: Nigeria and Ethiopia. In Ethiopia, 11 percent of all children were orphans.

And there was more.

UNAIDS (the Joint United Nations Program on HIV/AIDS) predicted that, between 2000 and 2020, sixty-eight million *more* people were going to die of AIDS (a disease of which few Westerners had died since the creation of antiretroviral [ARV] drug therapies in the late 1990s).

By 2010, between twenty-five million and fifty million African children, from newborn to age fifteen, would be orphans.

In a dozen countries, up to a quarter of the nation's children would be orphans.

The numbers were completely ridiculous.

Twelve million, fourteen million, eighteen million—how could numbers so high be answers to anything other than "How many stars are in the universe?" or "How many light-years from the Milky Way is the Virgo Supercluster?"

In the summer of 2000, my husband, Don Samuel, a defense attorney, and I had been married twenty-one years. We had two daughters and three sons, four by birth and the youngest by adoption: Molly had been born in 1981; Seth, 1984; Lee, 1988; Lily, 1992; and Jesse, 1995. In our forties, we were being driven cheerfully insane. We staggered through the middle-class blizzard of permission slips, soccer cleats, library books, musical instruments, dental appointments, science-fair projects, and college applications. In my pockets at night, I found things like somebody's chewed gum, or a small earring in the shape of a dolphin, or a one-armed Spider-Man action figure (or, on a different night, Spider-Man's missing arm). Once I was asked to empty out my purse at airport security and there was a life-size plastic banana at the bottom of it. I actually knew what the banana was doing there, but—since it didn't pose an immediate threat—I was waved on through without being asked to explain. Our front yard looked like a bicycle depot. There were bald spots in the grass from the badminton games.

On that summer morning, the children and their sleepover friends were yelling from room to room, and dragging sleeping bags and beach towels all over the house, and looking for small change so they could purchase Popsicles at the pool snack-bar. Someone got in the car and began helpfully honking the horn to urge the parents to *hurry*, despite the parents' repeated *clarification* that the pool outing would happen *in a little while*. That was the summer that five-year-old Jesse, adopted the previous fall from a Bulgarian orphanage, learned to swim in a single afternoon. When we asked, "How did you learn to swim so quickly?" he replied, "The shark that lives in the deep end taught me."

But suddenly here was this world beyond our house: twelve million orphans today. Twenty-five million orphans tomorrow. And those were just the numbers of AIDS orphans; if you added in the orphans from malaria and TB, you hit thirty-six million sub-Saharan orphans, and those numbers didn't include children deprived of the adults in their lives by war and famine.

Human beings are not wired to absorb twelve million or eighteen million or twenty-five million bits of information; our protohuman ancestors never had to contemplate more than about ten or twenty of anything. For a person who is not a mathematician, epidemiologist, demographer, geographer, social scientist, medical anthropologist, or economist—for a person, say, who barely *knows* anyone with one of those jobs (although, living two miles from the Centers for Disease Control [CDC] in Atlanta, I do enjoy carpooling to kids' soccer practices with the occasional epidemiologist), numbers with so many zeros are hard to fathom. Presumably you can make a variety of calculations and graphs with numbers like eleven million and twenty-five million, but hats off to anyone who can begin to imagine what this really looks like, what this *means.*

Who was going to raise twelve million children? That's what I suddenly wanted to know. There were days that Donny and I thought we'd be driven insane by five children.

Who was teaching twelve million children how to swim? Who was signing twelve million permission slips for school field trips? Who packed twelve million school lunches? Who cheered at twelve million soccer games? (That sounded like *our* weekends.) Who was going to buy twelve million pairs of sneakers that light up when you jump? Backpacks? Toothbrushes? Twelve million pairs of *socks*? Who will tell twelve million bedtime stories? Who will quiz twelve million children on Thursday nights for their Friday-morning spelling tests? Twelve million trips to the dentist? Twelve million birthday parties?

Who will wake in the night in response to eighteen million nightmares?

Who will offer grief counseling to twelve, fifteen, eighteen, thirty-six million children? Who will help them avoid lives of servitude or prostitution? Who will pass on to them the traditions of culture and religion, of history and government, of craft and profession? Who will help them grow up, choose the right person to marry, find work, and learn to parent their own children?

Well, as it turns out, no one. Or very few. There aren't enough adults to go around. Although in the Western industrialized states HIV/AIDS has become a chronic condition rather than a death sentence, in Africa a generation of parents, teachers, principals, physicians, nurses, professors, spiritual leaders, musicians, poets, bureaucrats, coaches, farmers, bankers, and business owners are being erased.

The ridiculous numbers wash over most of us. This is happening in *our* time? We, who have read the histories of the Armenian genocide and of the Holocaust and of Stalin's Gulag, who have lived in the epoch of the killings in Cambodia, Bosnia, and Rwanda, find ourselves once again safely tucked away. We may feel a vague sad tug of common cause with human misery on the far side of the Tropic of Cancer, but we are disconnected from it by a thousand degrees of space and time. This is true even in the hardest-hit countries, because even in the highest-prevalence countries of Asia and Africa, there are comfortable citizens—including elected leaders—keeping their hemlines above the rising waters.

The Berlin Wall is down, the Iron Curtain has fallen, but it is as if a pulsating wall of strobe lights, televised celebrities, and amplified music has gone up mid-Atlantic or mid-Mediterranean Sea. It is hard to look past the simulated docudramas, television "newsmagazines," and mock-reality memoirs designed to distract us in a thousand ways while making us feel engaged with true stories. America wrestles with its obesity crisis to such an extent that Americans forget there are worse weight problems on earth than obesity.

A few Westerners smash through. UN special envoy Stephen Lewis is one of these; the bow-tied, globe-trotting, charismatic physician Jonathan Mann, who died in a plane crash off Halifax, was another. Bill and Melinda Gates and former presidents Jimmy Carter and Bill Clinton are there.

How can the rest of us—normal citizens, steering along our paved streets between home and school, work and playground, mall and hardware store, holding open the front door with a foot while maneuvering inside with the mail, the grocery sacks, the purse, a paperback, the children's backpacks—how can the rest of us break through?

On that Sunday morning, as kids in swimsuits honked from the driveway for me to hurry up, I suddenly wondered, "Can you adopt one of the African AIDS orphans?" The notion of adoption gave me a way in, a way to look behind the big numbers with all the zeros. Before I went to Ethiopia as a journalist, I went as an adoptive parent; Ethiopia was one of the few countries in Africa permitting foreign parents to adopt.

Going to Ethiopia as an adoptive mother turned out to be the best possible introduction to Haregewoin Teferra. Mothers were endangered where she came from, so a mother willing to care for children not hers by birth was praiseworthy indeed.

I wouldn't end up adopting a child from Haregewoin's compound, but I found my way to her through the chain of men and women—Ethiopians and Americans—handing orphans one by one out of Ethiopia to adoptive families in the West.

Adoption is *not* the answer to HIV/AIDS in Africa. Adoption rescues few. Adoption illuminates by example: these few once-loved children—who lost their parents to preventable diseases—have been offered a second chance at family life in foreign countries; like young ambassadors, they instruct us. From them, we gain impressions about what their age-mates must be like, the ones living and dying by the millions, without parents, in the cities and villages of Africa. For every orphan turning up in a northern-hemisphere household—winning the spelling bee, winning the cross-country race, joining the Boy Scouts, learning to rollerblade, playing the trumpet or the violin—ten thousand African children remain behind alone.

"Adoption is a last resort," I would be told in November 2005 by Haddush Halefom, head of the Children's Commission under Ethiopia's Ministry of Labor, the arbiter of intercountry adoptions, "Historically, close kinship ties in our country meant that there were very few orphans: orphaned children were raised by their extended families. The HIV/AIDS pandemic has destroyed so many of our families that the possibility no longer exists to absorb all our Ethiopian orphans.

"I am deeply respectful of the families who care for our children," he said. "But I am so very interested in any help that can be given to us to keep the children's first parents alive. Adoption is good, but children, naturally, would prefer not to see their parents die."

Far too little medical aid from the West reaches Africa. Today, in 2006, 4.7 million people in Africa are in immediate need of the lifesaving AIDS drugs and only 500,000 have access to them. Sixty-six hundred Africans are dying every day of AIDS. The most recent UNICEF report states that, in Zimbabwe, a child dies of AIDS or is orphaned by AIDS every twenty minutes.

There are victories. The anti-AIDS medicines are so powerful that dying people regain their health and return to work within two months of starting treatment. Africans who receive the lifesaving AIDS drugs adhere to the strict drug regimens much better than do their American or European counterparts, research shows; their success rate is about 90 percent. In countries like Uganda and Senegal, public education campaigns, community outreach, and drug treatment are beating back their epidemics.

But Africa lacks the resources it needs to win the war against AIDS. UNAIDS (the Joint United Nations Program on HIV/AIDS) has estimated a cost of about $20 billion per year by 2007 to control the pandemic. But the world's richest countries contributed less than $5 billion to fight global AIDS in 2003.

Broader interventions—fair trade, alleviation of unjust debt, the sharing of medical discoveries, and the support of the Global Fund to Combat AIDS, Tuberculosis and Malaria (the Global Fund) by our rich governments—are the indispensable steps toward generating fewer orphans in the first place, and, so far, the affluent world has not stepped up.

Although I didn't know her well, I understood why Haregewoin existed. The disease crawled across the land, wrecking families. It was a tsunami in slow motion, the dying calling and reaching their arms out for help before going under, children swept from their parents' embrace. Haregewoin was an ordinary citizen, a middle-class, middle-aged woman, who suddenly found herself toe-to-toe with the worst epidemic in history, the only disease ever to be labeled a global security threat by the United Nations Security Council, the first to be the subject of a UN General Assembly meeting, the only disease to earn its own cabinet-level U.S. ambassador, the disease bringing down governments and altering the relationships between nations.

And I knew that people like Haregewoin Teferra were interesting to the epidemiologists, economists, and sociologists grappling with the HIV/AIDS pandemic. From their panels and conferences in Washington, Paris, and Geneva, the global experts tried to imagine, to graph and to chart, what life looked like on the ground with orphans everywhere. The Reverend Dr. Gary Gunderson, a director of the Rollins School of Public Health of Emory University in Atlanta, told me, "Although governments can and are providing billions of dollars, the only hope, for the vast majority of the twenty-five million orphans, are thousands of people like Haregewoin Teferra. It is crucial that we understand the miracle of her life so that we can know how to come alongside her and lend our strength. A dozen global conferences will not shed half the light that her life does."

But why was Haregewoin Teferra intervening in the epidemic? Why did refugees cram into her modest compound, rather than into the more generous compound up the road? Why choose her two-room brick house instead of the three-story villa across the valley?

On the street it was rumored that *Waizero* [Mrs.] Haregewoin had tested positive for HIV.

The great appeal about this explanation—to those who offered it—was it suggested Haregewoin welcomed and helped people stricken by HIV/AIDS only because she was one of them. Haregewoin didn't shriek insults, throw rocks, spread ash on their footprints, or shake a broom at HIV-positive sufferers and slam the door in their faces, because she shared their fate. This explanation freed up her HIV-negative friends and acquaintances to remain uninvolved. *As long as we haven't been caught by the pandemic, we can continue to pretend it's not happening.*

"Well, it's not true about her," *Ato* (Mr.) Zewedu, Haregewoin's old friend, told the gossipers. (An engineer and college teacher, he got involved with the plight of AIDS sufferers only after a blood test told him he had joined their ranks.) "Of course, you won't believe *me*."

But Zewedu was correct: Haregewoin was HIV-negative. The presence of a deadly virus in the blood evidently was not the secret ingredient that inspired a person to step to the front lines. (The blood test has not yet been invented to measure that kind of thing.)

So how does it happen that—while most people instinctively try to save themselves and their families from a catastrophe—a few slow down, look back, and suddenly reach out to strangers? Instead of fleeing in the opposite direction, a few wade into the rising waters to try to yank the drowning onto higher land. What made Haregewoin one of those?

In the coming months and years, I would learn that—just as there is no blood test to identify who will jump into the fray—there is no simple biographical arc either. No résumé can predict why this man or woman, at a safe remove from a crisis, suddenly announces, "This is *my* fight."

In the *Pirkei Avoth*, the Jewish ethical compendium from the third

century, it is written, "In a place with no people, try to be a person"
(2:6).

And Haregewoin tried.

The hardest thing I learned as I drew close to this story was,
Haregewoin Teferra was no Mother Teresa.

At first I was crushed by this news. I had thought I would write a
hagiography, a chapter for *Lives of the Saints*.

But calling a good person a saint is just another way to try to explain
extraordinary behavior. She must be sick! She must be righteous!
Whatever she is, she's moving on a different plane of existence from the
rest of us, which means we are off the hook. Since most of us onlookers
are neither one nor the other—neither saints nor survivors—no one
will expect us to intervene.

I would watch Haregewoin's reputation rise and fall like sunrise and
sunset. As she blended her life with the lives of people ruined by the
pandemic, she became a nobody, like them. Then, she began to be seen
as a saint. Then some cried, "Hey! This is no saint!" and accused her of
corruption. Or maybe she started out as a saint, became a tyrant, then
became a saint again. Or was it the reverse? The story line changed. But
in every account, no middle ground was allotted to Haregewoin: either
she was all good, or she had gone bad. Those who watched, judged her.

Zewedu, her old friend, saw who Haregewoin was: an average
person, muddling through a bad time, with a little more heart than
most for the people around her who were suffering and half an eye
cocked toward her own preservation. But most observers failed to
reach this matter-of-fact point of view, and *Ato* Zewedu probably
would not live much longer.

But then I heard, to my delight, that some people say even Mother
Teresa herself was no Mother Teresa.

3

THE MORNING AFTER the rainy afternoon during which Mintesinote was fetched from the streets, Selamneh picked me up in front of the little hotel. We scraped along in his blue taxi up a steep dirt road, then parked and went on foot. We tramped beside endless seven-foot walls and fences. Family life in Addis Ababa takes place in compounds hidden from the street by high walls of corrugated tin, piled stones, cement blocks, or wooden or bamboo poles. You never know what awaits you on the other side of a wall. It may be a mud-and-straw hovel, a brick house like Haregewoin's, or a stylish Mediterranean mansion with indoor plumbing, satellite TV, a washing machine, Internet connection, and—from its upper balconies—an airy view of the cool Entoto Mountains.

Scores of children scampered down the dirt lane that ran beside Haregewoin's compound. Some chased wooden hoops with sticks, a game unseen in America since colonial times. Some carried younger children on their backs. Their clothes were mismatched, ill-fitting, and dusty. Even on hot days, many wore wrong-gender, ill-sized winter coats complete with fuzzy hoods or mittens clipped to the sleeves. Evidently some kind North Americans or northern Europeans had packed up used clothing for AIDS orphans and a box of parkas and ski pants had landed in this hot, dry East African neighborhood.

Rich countries and their global organizations and multinational drug companies have been reluctant to share the antiretrovirals, the anti-AIDS medicines. The World Trade Organization, with the backing of the United States, has placed intellectual property rights (such as the molecular composition of AIDS medicines) above the human right to health care, thus the brand-name medicines shimmer expensively out of reach of most of the people dying for lack of them.

But shipments of secondhand clothing arrive dependably despite plague, famine, and war. Within the psyches of first-world populations is the urge to box up used clothing and ship it to Africa.

Like most houses, Haregewoin's was walled off from the teeming city of three million by a seven-foot corrugated-tin fence, jammed and wired together. She unbolted the heavy compound door anchored between two cinder-block pillars, swung it inward, and greeted Selamneh with a kiss to each cheek. She pulled me down toward her into a warm four-handed handshake and two sets of kisses. At five feet eight, I towered over her. I always felt like Major Gangly White Woman next to Haregewoin. Her posture was erect and straight-shouldered, her head tilted back a bit defiantly, I thought; or perhaps she was simply always prepared to make conversation with persons much taller. She had the knack of making it seem that everything happening at her altitude was normal, while, at my height, the goings-on were rather outlandish.

She turned and swept us behind her into the brick house. Selamneh and I sat side by side on the low, loose-bottomed sofa in the common room.

Haregewoin called to Sara, the ex–college student disowned by her parents, to prepare in my honor the traditional "coffee ceremony," a ritual of hospitality and of enjoyment of *buna* (coffee).

Sara entered, dressed in a handwoven white dress trimmed with colorful embroideries. She was carrying a sheaf of long, fresh-cut grasses; she tossed the sweet-smelling grasses onto the cement floor. She left again and returned with a small charcoal stove, which she placed on the grass carpet, and she sat before it on a low three-legged stool. She began to roast fresh coffee beans on an iron skillet, shaking it to rattle the beans free of the husks. When the pan smoked with coffee-bean oil, she carried it by the handle toward us; Selamneh and Haregewoin fanned the smoke toward their faces, savoring the aroma,

and I copied them. Back on her stool, Sara ground the blackened beans
with a pestle and mortar, then brewed the coffee in a shapely
handmade black urn. She poured out the rich *buna* into tiny china
cups heaped with sugar. It was traditional for guests to nibble popcorn,
as well, or the dry-roasted barley called *kolo*.

Suddenly, with a whoop, Mintesinot flew through the front door
and into Selamneh's arms.

"Will we go to my dad today?" asked the boy.

"Hmmm, not today, but soon. Do you still have the biscuits?"

"Yes!" he shouted, and pulled the flattened bag with a few surviving
crumbs from his pocket.

"Minty, *na* [come]," said Sara. "Let's see what the other children are
playing." He took her hand, but looked over his shoulder at Selamneh
as he departed.

After a swallow, Haregewoin set down her coffee and turned in her
chair to face me. She spread her hands, palms up, as if feeling for rain,
and smiled her crinkly smile at me. She was inviting me to ask. But she
was unhappy about it. The centers of her eyes were coal black. The sad
creases between her eyebrows gave a different invitation, a caution.

The story of her life was not a pretty one, so she turned, smiling, away
from me and toward every interruption, eager to break the narrative.
The cell phone would ring, or the landline, or an office assistant would
step in to ask her to sign some paperwork, or a visitor would ask for a
word with her. She turned to each (but not to me) with a kind, rosy,
smiling face. When Haregewoin looked back at me, she shrugged, with
a helpless smile, to indicate "You see? It is impossible to find the time
to tell this useless story, which is, in any case, very old news and not of
interest to anyone."

When she allowed herself to be drawn into a protracted telephone
conversation in rapid Amharic, requiring much leaning back, patting of
chest, and hard coughing laughter, I set down my demitasse cup and
stepped outside. The radiant morning air sparkled with high-altitude
light. Children loitered in the dirt courtyard. A happy little girl caught

my eye: she flounced about barefoot in gray sweatpants under a frilly, puffy pink dress and, on top of the dress, a too small boy's winter coat. I watched her seat herself upon a flat stone with her queenly petticoats arrayed around her. She showed great pride of ownership and was reaching around as best she could in her winter parka to smooth the stiff tulle. I saw her cast her soft eyes around to see if anyone was noticing how pretty she was today.

I noticed. I stepped over and stroked her warm little head, her hard, dry little braids, and murmured an incomprehensible compliment in English. I startled her, but then she understood: her lips turned down in a pleased, flustered smile.

I didn't know who took care of this little girl in pink—maybe a grandparent, maybe a not-much-older sister or brother—but I saw that she remembered being mothered. A longtime orphan would not expect anyone to compliment her pretty dress.

Haregewoin came for me. "We talk," she said.

A pair of elderly women had found their way to her common room from the road and bowed low to me, from their chairs, when I reentered. She wasn't going to tell her deep history in front of them. We'd start with the lighter stuff.

She was the firstborn (born around 1946) of a rural district judge, Teferra Woldmariam, in the village of Yirgealem. (An Ethiopian takes the father's first name for a last name: Woldmariam's son Teferra is Teferra Woldmariam; Teferra Woldmariam's daughter Haregewoin is Haregewoin Teferra. Women do not change their names after marriage.)

The judge and his first wife had two daughters, Haregewoin the eldest; after a divorce, the judge remarried and his second wife gave birth to eighteen children. Haregewoin lived with her father and stepmother. "Every year a child, sometimes twins," she said, laughing. Haregewoin turned out to be very short, but bossy. She wore her hair in two long braids and stood hands on hips, with a skeptical tilt of the head, when hearing—then waving away—every sort of accusation, plea, whine, and alibi offered by the swarms of her younger siblings. In the only cinder-block building in town, Judge Teferra presided over civil and criminal cases with similar kind bemusement.

"I was laughing always," Haregewoin told me. "I was the happiest girl. My father was a great believer in girls' education; he wanted for me to be able to support myself. He insisted that I sit down and study, but I was restless; I liked to jump up."

In her teens, Haregewoin was sent to the capital to attend a good secondary school; she lived with an uncle and aunt. In 1965, at nineteen, attending a friend's wedding, she met a man who used to teach at her grammar school. He was the bridegroom's brother, Worku Kebede.

"He hadn't been my teacher, but I remembered him," she told me. "Now he was having a mustache. He smoked cigarettes." Tall, quiet, and serious, Worku was twenty-nine, a high school biology teacher with a graduate degree from Alemaye University in Harar, Ethiopia. Haregewoin was a flibbertigibbet. Worku's somber mien broke into surprised delight when she approached him and accused him, with a wagging finger, of not remembering her.

"I was so innocent," she told me. "He laughed at me."

He did more than laugh. "He sent people to tell to my father that he would like to marry me. But my father refused. He said, 'He is a teacher. I cannot give my daughter.' To me he said, 'A teacher will never be a husband. A teacher will always be like a father, even more than me.'

"Then a friend of Worku's father called on my father, representing Worku's family. It took my father two months to agree, but finally he approved." In 1966, at the ages of twenty and thirty, they married. "Our wedding was very beautiful, in a church; I wore a white bridal dress, in the Western style. He wore a black suit and a white tie. We had music and dancing in the evening."

They rented a two-story cement house in Addis Ababa, behind a busy neighborhood of dress shops, bakeries, and barbershops. In the first year of their marriage, 1967, Haregwoin gave birth to a daughter,

Atetegeb (Ah-*teh*-te-geb). Two years later, Suzanna was born. When the girls started school, Haregewoin took a secretarial job with the federal highway department. She later moved to a better position in the accounting office of Addis Ababa University, and then to the Burroughs Computer Company, an American corporation. Worku was promoted to principal of the high school. "We were very happy together," she said. "Both of us loved reading, the same hobby. I liked novels by Danielle Steel. He loved biology and history. We always felt very happy to be together."

Worku loved books and was fastidious with those he was fortunate enough to own, handling them with clean hands, turning the pages with the tips of his long fingers. Atetegeb grew into a book lover like her father; from a young age, she was content to snuggle into a chair near Worku's desk and read by his lamplight. Worku brought home books from his school for her, and she sat solemnly stroking the illustrations of dinosaurs or planets or whales.

Suzie inherited her mother's ebullience, easy laughter, and scurrying gait; dashing out the door to join her friends, she called to Atetegeb to join her, but the older girl—oval-faced, shapely, with wavy, shoulder-length hair and naturally dark-outlined eyes—declined without raising her head from the book. As the girls entered their teens, Haregewoin fretted over this—"You're a pretty girl!" she assured Atetegeb—but Worku intervened, saying, in Amharic, *"Teyat"* (Let the child be).

4

O N S C H O O L H O L I D A Y S, Worku filled their German-made
Opel with gas, and Haregewoin loaded a hamper with fruit,
lentil stew, corn stew, *injera* (the national bread, a spongy
sourdough pancake), and carafes of water, and the four of them drove
into the countryside. They headed south out of Addis toward the town
of Debre Zeyit and descended into the Rift Valley along the chain of
lakes. Around the shores of the platinum-blue crater lakes, there were
cuckoos and orioles, bee-eaters and swallows. More than eight
hundred species of birds have been identified in Ethiopia, including
fourteen endemic species.

The family drove across the sunlit grassland of the savanna. Beside
cultivated fields of teff, the national grain, the family glimpsed families
living in the old way, the country way, in *tukuls*, round straw huts. A
small child steered a family's few ducks or geese to a pond and back
with a whip of soft weeds. Hard, little oranges grew in ancient
orchards. In the middle of a scorched plain, a thorny acacia tree
offered a frayed bit of shade to a passing nomad.

Dik-diks and zebras, hartebeests and kudu, gazelles and baboons,
hung on in the wild places. At Lake Ziway, hippopotamuses loitered
waist-deep in the green water among the reeds, gargling their baritone
hums. Occasionally one surfaced, water cascading off his enormous
rubbery black gourd-shaped, bug-eyed face—and yawned his enormous
mouth at the others, then sank and turned away. A pink-white cloud of
flamingos turned back and forth across the bright water in the distance.

Forty-five different tribal groups occupied lands south of Addis
Ababa, including the famous Mursi people, who inserted plates into

their lips, and the body-painting Karo. Some of the southern peoples understood they'd been colonized by the highlanders and had started to participate in the rough processes of nation-building; others had never heard of "Ethiopia" or of the late-nineteenth/early-twentieth-century king, Menelik II, who had conquered them and claimed their lands.

The bedrock of Ethiopia is Gondwanaland, the earth's first continent, six hundred million years old. Ancient seas washed over it, followed by eons of dry air; sediment was deposited and baked atop the hard old continent for epochs, then millennia of wind and rain scattered the sediment. Today, write historians Graham Hancock and Richard Pankhurst, "Gondwanaland stands once again exposed, glittering with the ineffable fire of ancient minerals like gold and platinum."

Hidden up in the clefts of the dry hills, archaeologists emerged from their camps once every few years to announce the discovery of bones of astounding antiquity. Humankind evolved on this landscape. The National Museum of Ethiopia preserves the bones of the three-million-year-old hominid Dinkenesh, or Lucy, discovered by American anthropologist Donald C. Johanson in 1974, fabled to be the mother of humankind.

One of natural history's beguiling mysteries—"Where are the head-waters of the Nile?"—is half-answered in the northern Ethiopian highlands: Lake Tana is the source of the Blue Nile, which joins with the White Nile from Lake Victoria on the Uganda-Tanzania-Kenya border to flow north across Sudan into Egypt. The Blue Nile Falls are known in Amharic as Tisissat, "Water That Smokes." Lake Tana is dotted by islands occupied by fifteenth-century monasteries. Inside are monks, studying medieval religious manuscripts written in the ancient ecclesiastical language of Ge'ez on goatskin and horse-skin parchments. They pore over the fourteenth century Ge'ez epic *Kebra Nagast*, "The Glory of Kings," which describes the journey of Queen Makeda of Axum to Jerusalem.

Another of the great mysteries of history is "Where is the Ark of the Covenant?" The Ark—or Tabernacle—is believed to contain the first, broken, set of the Ten Commandments, or the second intact set given by Moses to the people of Israel at Mount Sinai, or both. It traveled with the ancient Hebrews in the desert of Sinai and through the conquest of Canaan. King David transported it to Jerusalem, and King Solomon oversaw the building of the Temple as a permanent resting place for the Ark in the tenth century BCE.

In 586 BCE, the Temple of Solomon was destroyed by the Babylonians under Nebuchadnezzar. What happened next to the Ark is unknown and has been asked for fifteen hundred years. It may have been looted by the Babylonians, but the conquerors made careful lists of their bounty and the Tabernacle is not on it. King Josiah may have buried it on the Temple Mount (now under the Dome of the Rock, off-limits to archaeologists). Or King Solomon may have set aside a cave near the Dead Sea in which the Ark was to be hidden in case of disaster.

Ethiopians, however, believe they know where the *Tabot* (Amharic for Tabernacle) is: it is in the ancient capital of Axum and has been ever since King Menelik brought it there during Solomon's time. In a small granite building on the grounds of Saint Mary of Zion Church, a monk known as the Keeper of the Ark stands guard.

Any Ethiopian can tell you this.

Not many people ask them.

Modernization of the country and expansion of its administrative region across neighboring lands began in the late nineteenth century. In the 1880s, after Italy established a presence on the Red Sea coast, King Menelik II—with territorial designs of his own—allied himself with the European power and signed the Treaty of Uccialli. He accepted Italy's right to Eritrea and to northern lands around the cities of Keren, Massawa, and Asmera (in the region that would become Eritrea) in exchange for money and weapons, including thirty thousand muskets and twenty-eight cannons.

But there were two versions of the Treaty of Uccialli, with the Italian version implying a more subservient role for Ethiopia than did the Amharic version. Italy declared to the world that Ethiopia had become an Italian protectorate, while Ethiopia understood no such thing.

In 1890 Menelik II denounced Italy's claim and, in 1893, he repudiated the entire treaty.

Italy chose to respond militarily. The Italian commander in the Eritrean colony was ordered to win a decisive victory over Ethiopia's army; he promised to return triumphant, with the Ethiopian ruler in a cage.

At the end of February 1896, the Ethiopian king set out from Addis Ababa with 100,000 troops, accompanied by his wife, Empress Taytu. "His army was remarkable not only for its size but also as an eloquent demonstration of national unity," writes historian Bahru Zewde, professor of history at Addis Ababa University. "There was scarcely any region in Ethiopia which had not sent a contingent."

The Italians had occupied high ground at Amba Alage, a natural fortress; the vanguard of the Ethiopian army attacked and fought its way uphill against entrenched and better-armed troops. The Italians were routed and their commander was among the casualties.

The second phase of the campaign was a siege against the Italian fort of Maquale, forty-five miles north, during which the Italian troops ran out of supplies and water and eventually surrendered.

On the night of February 29, 1896, the Italian general, Oreste Baratieri, anticipating an easy victory, launched a surprise three-column advance. "News of his march had preceded him," writes Zewde, "and was greeted with great relief by the Ethiopians, who were waiting eagerly for a decisive engagement."

The armies met at Adwa on March 1, 1896.

Professor Zewde writes: "The root of Italian disaster lay in the failure of the three columns to coordinate their action. Through faulty map-reading, [General Matteo] Albertone's brigade found itself isolated, the target of the combined fury of the Ethiopian troops. Trying to come to the rescue of Albertone, [General Vittorio] Dabormida made a fatal swerve to the right instead of to the left. The outcome was that, although Ethiopian losses were not negligible, the Italians were routed. By midday of I March, the Battle of Adawa was practically over. Italian colonial ambition was dead. Independent Ethiopia survived."

When the news reached Italy, there were riots in the street, and the defeat led to the downfall of the prime minister. The new Italian government acknowledged the independence of Ethiopia.

"The battle at Adowa [sic] was, at the time, the greatest defeat inflicted upon a European army by an African army since the time of Hannibal," writes Greg Blake in *Military History*, "and its consequences were felt well into the 20th century. As an example of colonial warfare on an epic scale, it cannot be surpassed. As an example of the twin follies of arrogance and underestimation of one's enemies, it should never be forgotten."

The Ethiopian script and alphabet, the Ethiopian church, the Ethiopian calendar, the Ge'ez script (the first written language in Africa) and Ethiopian literature, the illuminated Ge'ez Bibles, the Ethiopian clock, Ethiopian holidays, and indigenous styles of architecture, painting, oral poetry, dance, and tapestry survive uncompromised, undiluted, unique on the planet.

And the handsome, slender, prideful Ethiopian people know it, too.

What is the quality of all these things, these rare Ethiopian things? Perhaps it can be judged by the fact that Ethiopia gave coffee to the world. The berries were first harvested in the forests of Kaffa.

For how many millennia were the Abyssinians sitting up there on their rocky plateau, discussing literature in coffee shops, while, in barbarian Europe, less evolved of the *Homo sapiens* clubbed each other with rocks and rode warhorses and lofted spears at each other? For how many thousands of years have the subtle Ethiopians known the source of the Nile and the resting place of the Holy Tabernacle, speaking and writing of such matters in ornate languages no outsider could read or understand?

* * *

As they neared small towns and villages, Worku slowed the car. Ping-Pong tables were set up along the dirt shoulders of the road. Men played and children watched. Boys kicked soccer balls made of plastic bags and string. Roadside merchants offered fresh coffee beans, mangoes, pumpkins, and eggs, displayed upon cotton sheets spread over the dirt. Beekeepers sold fresh honey from washed-out plastic jugs hanging from poles. All this washed over the family in the hot wind as they bumped along, windows down, plastic seats baking, Haregewoin and Suzie drowsing, Atetegeb in the backseat with a book.

In the little towns, barefoot children rushed up, offering to sell flip-flops, bars of soap, clutches of eggs, tree branches heavy with nuts, or colorful baskets. Those with nothing to sell asked permission to wipe bugs off the windshield. The dusty country girls wore their hair knotted up with bits of cloth, their faces burned nearly black from the hot, open sky. Colorful wooden hotels and tin shops dotted the country villages, smoldering with aromas of fresh local coffees and meat stews. The city family pulled up at a café with a tree-shaded brick patio to order Coca-Colas and to splash water on their faces in the tiled bathroom. They sat under an umbrella and watched country boys drive donkey carts pell-mell down the main road. Boys of eight or ten stood up in the wagons, flashing the reins, hollering and racing. Others rode bareback through the dust, scattering the goats, chickens, and pedestrians. Atetegeb and Suzie laughed to watch the helter-skelter parade of boys, carts, and livestock; they felt a little envious of the wild country childhood, so like their mother's, so unlike their own.

Once, Haregewoin had worried about the fact that she and Worku had only two children. She had assumed they would raise a huge family of ten or fifteen children. She thought it was what people *did*. But Worku relished a peaceful home. He felt the soft tumult of two girls to be sufficient. So she'd fretted: would two children be enough to see them through? But the girls' infancies had not been easy—Suzie had been a sickly baby—so Haregewoin agreed, "Two is enough." Surely her anxiety was nothing but a carryover from the rural experience of high infant and child mortality. There was good sense in raising two modern, well-educated city children: there were music lessons, vacations, and birthday parties. The urban middle-class arrangement promised health and stability. Surely her small family's good fortune would last forever.

5

WORKU AND HAREGEWOIN knew that darker truths lay behind the sunny rural scenes. In the mid-1970s, Ethiopia was in the grip of a palace coup that was turning corrupt and murderous. The populace was intimidated; the country lived from day to day with a knife at its throat.

Emperor Haile Selassie, "the Lion of Judah," had ruled Ethiopia throughout their lives and the lives of their parents. Even as he grew elderly and disoriented, the King of Kings made no plans for the country's future leadership other than his own longevity. The heavenly aura he'd drawn about his person seemed to hint at immortality.

Born Tafari Makonnen in 1892, he had advanced through connections, marriage, and statecraft to being named *ras* (duke) of Harar in 1913. In 1930 he was crowned the 111th emperor in the succession of King Solomon and took the royal name Haile Selassie I (Might of the Trinity). Selassie immediately authorized the writing of Ethiopia's first constitution, which established the holiness of his person and his birthright to the legendary throne of Menelik the First, the almost mythic son of the Queen of Sheba and King Solomon of Israel. Selassie was a diminutive, soft-voiced man, with melancholy eyes and a pointed beard; urban legend tells of a minister of the pillow, who rushed in, whenever the emperor was seated, to place a satin pillow under his feet, so that the tiny man's legs would not be seen swinging like a child's. Still, he strode like a giant across the world stage. He was the outstanding visionary and elder statesman of Africa; he swashbuckled through the capitals of Europe with his entourage of nobles; and he was a hero throughout the African diaspora. Soon after his coronation, a sect of Jamaicans began to worship him as divine; they took his earlier title *Ras* Tafari, for the name Rastafarianism.

Elegantly and eloquently, Haile Selassie represented Ethiopia. At home, he promoted himself as a loving father to all his subjects. He was the world's only free black African king.

As in ancient times, Ethiopia's promontory above the Red Sea made it a valuable piece of real estate, especially after the opening of the Suez Canal in 1869. In modern times, the empire faced the territorial designs of an industrialized Europe. Selassie and his predecessor, King Menelik II, found themselves hemmed in by British, French, and Italian colonies, influences, and expansionist intentions.

In 1896, at the Battle of Adwa, King Menelik II had delivered a blistering defeat to the Italians, the first military defeat of a European army by an African one since the time of Hannibal. In the following century, Italy would return. On October 3, 1935, with Selassie on the throne, Fascist Italy invaded Ethiopia without a declaration of war. The Italians intended not to be humiliated again; they decimated the Ethiopians with superior arms and chemical warfare and, after seven months, reached Addis Ababa.

The Emperor traveled to Geneva, stood before the League of Nations, and demanded justice from the world community. No African monarch had ever defended his country in the sort of gilded chamber of power from which colonial adventures had been launched during the "Scramble for Africa." He protested "the unequal struggle between a government commanding more than forty-two million inhabitants, having at its disposal financial, industrial, and technical means which enabled it to create unlimited quantities of the most death-dealing weapons, and, on the other hand, a small people of twelve million inhabitants, without arms, without resources, having on its side only the justice of its own cause and the promise of the League of Nations."

He spoke in defense "of all small peoples who are threatened with aggression." Citizens all over the world were stirred by his words, and Americans called him a hero. But no nation intervened to free Ethiopia.

Selassie spent the war years in Britain, while resistance to the onslaught continued on the ground at home.

Restored to his throne by the British after World War II, Selassie grew increasingly autocratic. He was a potentate, a pharaoh. Petitioners knelt or lay facedown in the presence of the emperor; his word was absolute. Men were promoted and rewarded, hanged or shot, at an unimpeachable word from the King of Kings. He brought modernization to Ethiopia, but without altering the chain of command: himself at the summit, a circle of entitled property-holders he'd created, and the vast countryside of subsistence farmers. No road was paved, no school or hospital or factory was built without his initiative, and all constructions were named after him. His face was on all currency. He decreed that Ethiopia should have industrial development, so there was industrial development, but there was no political or economic reform. He established a newspaper, but did not give permission for a free press. He oversaw the creation of an air force and airline; he was a founder of the Organization of African Unity (OAU) and made Addis its headquarters; but the good energies he spent on foreign contacts and diplomacy were not equaled by attention to the underpinnings of life at home. He founded Haile Selassie I University (today Addis Ababa University) and paid for his best students to study abroad, but felt hurt when they returned and criticized the archaic land-tenure system, the primitive means of production, and the absence of democracy.

Agriculture, the foundation of the economy, was practiced as in earlier centuries: man- and beast-driven, denaturing the soil, the farmers taxed and tithed by their landowners. The almost medieval social inequalities allowed the emperor to move in a gilded realm of the finest jewels and robes, of ballrooms and banquets, of a fleet of Rolls-Royces; he enjoyed a life of abundance and travel, of strolls through his private zoo on the palace grounds. He fed steak to his lions. He tossed grain to his peacocks. When he and his palace guard rode out in a fleet of limousines, crowds lined the streets praying for a nod or a gesture from him and felt blessed if the royal eye fell upon them. But millions were suffering.

The monarch did not protect the country's woodlands, which were consumed in the clamor for housing materials and fuel; the deforested lands grew parched; lands already subject to periodic droughts grew drier; topsoil blew away and eroded into the once-clear streams. When the main rains failed in the once-forested highlands of Wello and Tigray provinces in 1972, famine in those regions was imminent.

Famine might have been averted: other provinces realized normal harvests that year and the government received American aid sufficient to purchase surplus grains for the needy. But acknowledgment by the emperor that a famine was brewing in his northern provinces would be taken as an admission of failure; Ethiopia would fall in the world's esteem; and citizens outside the famine regions might lose faith in the image promoted by Selassie of himself as an omnipotent and caring father.

So there was a palace cover-up: of crop failure, of famine. A migration of hundreds of thousands of living skeletons began to descend from the highland villages. They left behind, in their houses and on the roads, the dead and dying skeletons of their elders and children, their husbands and wives. Ryszard Kapuscinski, Polish correspondent from Africa, stumbled upon an alley full of the dying in the small town of Debre Sina:

"On the ground, in the filth and the dust, lay emaciated people . . . The drought had deprived them of water, and the sun had scorched their crops. They had come here, to the town, in the desperate hope that they would be given a sip of water and would find something to eat. Weak and no longer capable of any exertion, they were dying of hunger, which is the quietest and most docile kind of death. Their eyes were half-closed, lifeless, expressionless. I could not tell if they saw anything, whether they were even looking at anything in particular . . .

"The government could, of course, have intervened, or allowed the rest of the world to do so," wrote Kapuscinski, "but for reasons of prestige the regime did not want to admit that there was hunger in the land."

Professors from Haile Selassie I University broke the story, visited the provinces, returned with photographs of thousands of starving people. University students demonstrated, demanding government aid for the starving, and raising supplies from among themselves; soldiers were sent to fire into the student demonstrations, killing some, and the professors were dismissed. A British journalist, Jonathan Dimbleby, snuck film footage of the famine out of the country; when it was shown on British television as a documentary entitled *The Unknown Famine*, a shocked world began to send aid.

The public revelation of the famine was the beginning of the end for the emperor. In response to increasingly difficult economic hurdles placed before them by the government, the taxi drivers struck in protest of gasoline taxes, then teachers struck in protest against low pay, then—in barracks across the country—soldiers struck against low pay, lousy food, contaminated water, and abysmal living conditions. It was evident to all that the monarchy was wobbling.

In 1974, a committee of 120 junior officers stepped in and began to take charge. They broadcast, on Ethiopian television, Jonathan Dimbleby's footage of the famine, interspersed with scenes of a palace feast. They drained the palace of servants, gold, and bureaucrats; when finally they came for the eighty-two-year-old emperor, he went with scarcely a protest. He was asked to squeeze into the backseat of a Volkswagen Beetle and was driven away from the palace forever.

The ruling Coordinating Committee of the Armed Forces, Police, and Territorial Army, the Derg, tightened its grip on the reins of power. One of the leaders of the revolution, Colonel Mengistu Haile Mariam, plotted and murdered his way to the top of the Derg by eliminating his fellow officers. Eighty of the original 120 army officers of the revolt were executed on the orders of their former comrade. Mengistu ordered the execution of sixty of Selassie's senior officials, the patriarch of the Ethiopian Orthodox Church, and, in time, the elderly emperor himself. An early flurry of multiple parties was suppressed; a brief "spring" of hope, after the overthrow of the feudal state, was crushed by the brutality of the new dictator.

Colonel Mengistu's greatest challenge came from a rival Marxist organization, the Ethiopian People's Revolutionary Party (EPRP), which advocated democracy, and self-determination for ethnic minorities. It argued that the military officers of the Derg, having fulfilled their historic mission, should step aside in deference to elected civil leaders.

Mengistu responded with what he called, in honor of Soviet precedent, the Red Terror. He required citizens to report all suspicious activity to local governmental units called *kebeles*; he armed petty authorities loyal to the Derg and deputized them to execute traitors. Opponents of Mengistu and suspected opponents of Mengistu (especially intellectuals, students, and teachers) were executed—some point-blank, by their own neighbors—in the hundreds of thousands.

Ethiopia became another Cold War battlefield.

The United States and its allies shored up racist and repressive regimes in Angola, Mozambique, and Rhodesia (Southern Rhodesia is today Zimbabwe and Northern Rhodesia is Zambia) and supported rapacious dictators such as Joseph Mobutu in Zaire (Democratic Republic of the Congo) in the name of resisting Communist infiltration into Africa.

Soviet arms flooded the continent in opposition. When the USSR backed Somalia against Ethiopia, the United States armed Ethiopia; when a land war over the Ogaden region began in 1977, the USSR armed Ethiopia and the United States fortified Somalia.

Ten billion dollars in arms and financial support flowed from the Soviet Union into Ethiopia, until even Mikhail Gorbachev grew disgusted with Mengistu and cut him off. In the last years of the military regime, the defense budget was nearly a billion dollars a year, or 14 percent of GDP. Ethiopia had more than enough tanks, guns, artillery, cannons, rockets, grenades, and missiles to arm every man, woman, child, and cow, though millions could not find enough to eat on any given day.

✳   ✳   ✳

And there was a deeper and equally cruel reality, one that would kill more people than Mengistu did and outlast him.

Worku and Haregewoin could not see this one coming.

It had no name in Ethiopia, yet.

Between the mid-1970s and 1980—not yet in Ethiopia, but in Uganda and Rwanda and the Congo, along the shores of Lake Victoria and beside the banks of the Congo River—a highly contagious, debilitating, and fatal disease began to move. It was a virus (meaning the organism was incapable of reproducing independently—it invaded a human cell and converted the machinery of the cell to the job of replicating the virus). It was a retrovirus (meaning its genome consisted of two RNA—rather than DNA—molecules; inside each host cell, an enzyme (reverse transcriptase) rewrote the virus genome as DNA to infiltrate the host's genome). And it was a lentivirus, a slow virus, meaning it took a long time to produce adverse effects on the body.

Each virus particle is one ten-thousandth of a millimeter in diameter. In magnification, each looks like a child's plastic ball covered with suction cups, of the type you throw against a window and it sticks. Like a water balloon, each suction-ball is filled with liquid. Enzymes dot the viscous liquid, and a large object is suspended in it, too: a soft-sided triangular wedge (resembling a waterlogged slice of pizza). Two threads of genetic material swim within the translucent wedge. Thus: strands of RNA within the wedge within the suction-ball. A cluster of the HIV particles looks like a deposit of frog's eggs.

An HIV particle cleaves onto a larger, human white blood cell (the CD4 or T-helper cell) and fuses its membranes with that of the human cell. Its genetic material invades the nucleus of the conquered white blood cell and forces it to churn out HIV particles. Even diagrams of this process look scary: the innocent T-helper cell disfigured by the parasite; the march of the little HIV particles—each containing a pizza-shaped wedge—through the cell membranes and out into the blood system.

About half of people infected with HIV experience flulike symptoms—fever, fatigue, rashes, sore joints, headaches, and swollen lymph nodes—in the first two to four weeks after infection, but then the disease falls quiet, sometimes for many years.

"Slim disease" was the early name given by Ugandans to the infection that devastated sufferers with violent diarrhea wasting.

In the late 1970s, when Haregewoin's family was young, most of the world was unaware that this monster was astir. But it had begun to show itself—a fin here, the gleam of a canine tooth there.

Its first appearances were these:

Slim disease in Kinshasa, Zaire (late 1970s)

Slim disease in Uganda and Tanzania (early 1980s)

Esophageal candidiasis in Rwanda (from 1983)

Aggressive Kaposi's sarcoma in Kinshasa, Zaire (early 1980s)

Aggressive Kaposi's sarcoma in Zambia and Uganda (from 1982 and 1983)

Cryptococcal meningitis in Kinshasa, Zaire (late 1970s to early 1980s)

"The dominant feature of this first period was silence," wrote the late Dr. Jonathan Mann, one of the great early AIDS researchers and advocates for the ill. "The human immunodeficiency virus was unknown and transmission was not accompanied by signs or symptoms salient enough to be noticed . . . During this period of silence, spread was unchecked by awareness or any preventive action and approximately 100,000 to 300,000 persons may have been infected."

By 1990, sixty-one thousand children had been orphaned by AIDS in Ethiopia, the third-highest number of such children in the world, after Uganda and Democratic Republic of the Congo.

6

ONE MORNING IN 1990, Haregewoin picked up the phone and could barely make out that something had happened to Worku.

A woman caller shouted that Worku had just collapsed at a local meeting of the *kebele* (a benign unit of administration, post-Mengistu). He had presented a school issue; he sat down; he pitched forward. Everyone rushed to his aid. Haregewoin must hurry—*hurry!*—to meet them at the hospital. The caller sobbed and hung up.

Haregewoin hung up the phone, froze in confusion, then picked it up again to make a call. But whom was she calling? Oh! Worku, she was about to call Worku, in his office at the high school, to tell him something. Normally she didn't like to disturb him at work, but in an emergency . . . Wait . . . No. Beginning to shake violently, she made herself pick up her car keys, step outside, lock the door, start the car, back out, and veer in and out of traffic; she was blind, she was not breathing, she was not thinking; she simply drove. A crowd met Haregewoin in the parking lot at the hospital, standing near a stretcher. She was too late, they said. He was already gone, he had just died. They stepped away from the stretcher, indicating that it was Worku's body under the cloth.

"I came right away," she protested, making her way across the cement. "He was not sick at all. He was never even sick."

She stood over the covered body, which perhaps was not, after all, Worku's. Perhaps this very evening they would laugh a chastened laugh about the terrible mistake, about how badly it had scared her. Someone peeled off the sheet.

"He had a heart attack," someone said.

"He never even complained of headaches," Haregewoin objected.

"Maybe from smoking?" someone asked.

"He was only fifty-four," Haregewoin retorted, ready to debate anyone who persisted in telling her that her husband was dead.

Haregewoin had grown up in the country; no one in the countryside was unacquainted with death. Death is a village elder. But here? In the city? In the middle of the school week? He was the high school principal! They still had two young-adult children at home. (They had only two children!) Death was a murderer. She had to let other people take her home. She couldn't remember the way.

"He was my brother, my husband, my friend; he was everything to me," she told everyone.

The urge to phone him with the news that something large had happened did not abate for many weeks. The impulse to speak at night from her pillow, sensing he also lay awake thinking, did not abate. The funeral affairs, guests, and arrangements took up most waking hours. If she made a move toward her bedroom for a moment of privacy, several kinswomen sprang up to speed her way—they bustled ahead to freshen and turn down her bed, they offered her glasses of water, they offered to make tea. Her father was too old to travel, but when she phoned him, he cried. It didn't seem so long ago that Worku had begged Judge Teferra for his daughter's hand in marriage. Now the judge had outlived him. "I did not want to see you become a widow," he said.

Suddenly everyone seemed to feel the ceremonies of solace were concluded and they returned to their homes and villages.

Haregewoin was not sure what she was supposed to do with herself now. Only because she, Suzie, and Atetegeb were obliged to sleep, to bathe, to dress, sometimes to speak, did their bodies shuffle around in the house. They acted like old people. The sounds inside the house were muffled, while the noises coming from outside seemed garish and screeching.

Atetegeb, twenty-three, worked for the World Food Programme, the UN's global antifamine agency, as the dispatcher of trucks to famine areas. She was religious and tried to accept her father's death as ordained. "God has called him home," she said. Suzie was a university student. After a few weeks, she went out again with friends, but she let herself out the door quietly now, rather than letting it slam on her heels and giddy laughter. Atetegeb read in her bedroom in the evenings. But Haregewoin felt some resistance starting within Atetegeb; her pliancy seemed to have been for her father; with her mother, she began to show obstinacy and disagreement over the smallest matters; it was enough for Haregewoin to prepare this dish rather than that for Atetegeb to say she'd have preferred the other, or that the spices somehow seemed insufficient. She had been advanced academically, Haregewoin thought, but a late bloomer socially. She began to slip out at night; given her lack of experience, there seemed something unnecessarily sly about it. Having not been accustomed to dance down the sidewalk in a circle of girlfriends like Suzie, surrounded by male supplicants, she lacked the ease of an extrovert. She did everything with intensity. She didn't know how to flirt, how to string along, how to jilt. Though Haregewoin knew all Suzie's friends, she knew none of Atetegeb's, including the shadowy man who, it was becoming increasingly clear, was Atetegeb's boyfriend. This time would Worku have said *"Teyat,"* let the child be?

Suzie ran into them on the street and thus met a man we will call Ashiber (*Ahsh*-shee-bear). "I don't like him," she said.

"How does he look?" asked Haregewoin.

"Old. Very tall, very big, light skin. He is full of himself."

"Maybe she will break up with him."

"She won't," said Suzie forebodingly.

For Suzie, if it's not a good man, then it's "Good-bye! Here's another!" thought Haregewoin. *Atetegeb is a different person. But I always tell the girls, "I will not choose husbands for you. You must choose your own person. Find someone who will be good to you."*

She hoped Atetegeb's good heart would guide her. Since childhood, she'd been boundlessly generous. "She'd reach into her pocket for a birr for a beggar," Haregewoin told me, "and if she pulled out a hundred-birr note by mistake, she gives that. 'Why do you give away such money?' I'd say, and she answered, 'Who says the poor shouldn't have one hundred birr?' She comes home with one half or one quarter of her salary; she'll have given the rest away."

The three of them were still close, but they didn't go on weekend trips anymore. They had a small TV and often turned it on while they ate dinner. At the office, Haregewoin chatted and smiled during her work hours, but she did so by rote; there was a flatness in her eyes and voice. At home at night, when Suzie went out, Atetegeb retired to her room to read, but later slipped out alone. Haregewoin was absorbed by her grief. She got into bed at night and sat staring at the opposite wall, dumbfounded.

If someone had shot Worku, she thought, *that would make more sense than this.*

7

"**M**OTHER, I'VE MET SOMEONE," Atetegeb finally told Haregewoin, although her mother had surmised the whole story already, including the fact that twenty-four-year-old Atetegeb's boyfriend was in his mid-thirties.

"I'm happy for you, dear. When can I meet him?"

Their swaybacked sofa sighed the night Ashiber plumped himself onto it and stretched out his legs into the room, making himself at home. Above his well-padded cheeks, his eyes scanned the room for offense. He wore a holstered sidearm, and the muscles of his big shoulders and upper arms strained against the thin black fabric of his uniform. It was hard for the mother to see past the tough-guy exterior. The gun suggested that a single stray iron molecule of armed might had fallen near this fellow and he had seized it. Was he intending to impress Haregewoin by wearing the sidearm into their house? If so, he certainly blundered; as for soft-spoken Atetegeb, he had already conquered her.

At dinner, looming over their small table and embroidered table-cloth, occupying the chair that had been Worku's, Ashiber enjoyed every bite of the repast. He laughed hard at his own remarks, while seeming bored with the conversation of the women. But he was not, for all that, such an important man, Haregewoin noted: he worked in security for a private company.

But what could a mother say to a beloved daughter who believed she was in love, and for the first time? Especially a studious and hopeful girl with no experience of life? Maybe Ashiber appeared to Atetegeb as a romantic protagonist from one of her girlhood novels. Probably she believed she saw something kind and good behind the self-satisfied cheeks, the mightily shifting biceps, the hair so oiled and curled that outside in the bright sun it looked metallic.

Atetegeb's father had been a gentle man; of course she did not detect an authoritarian streak in her boyfriend. Atetegeb scarcely knew such traits existed, outside of books.

Suzie knew. Haregewoin's and Suzie's eyes met as the housekeeper cleared away the dishes.

"He's . . . he's not bad-looking," Haregewoin offered later to Suzie, grasping for a bit of optimism. "He's a nice-looking man."

"She is far too quiet when she is around him," Suzie replied.

In the night, Haregewoin twisted awake with a stitch in her side she had been mistaking for grief. The pinch had troubled her for months. She'd assumed it was stress, and fear of the future, and that it would fade over time. Instead she crumpled around a wrenching cramp several times a day; at work, she had to lean over her desk, supporting herself on her arms, to get through the pain. She stirred the paperwork with one hand to fool her officemates.

As she lay sleepless, silently weeping, pale light entered through the wooden shutters and lay in stripes on her blanket. Of a morbid turn of mind since losing Worku, Haregewoin concluded that she must have cancer and was dying. *It's my turn,* she thought. After Worku's unexpected death, many people said to Haregewoin, trying to ward off her look of bottomless confusion and despair, "It was God's will." Wailing and covering her face with her shawl, Haregewoin failed to see the sense in it. The injustice, the *waste,* of his sudden death shocked her.

Awake in the night, gripping her side in pain, she considered her options. The health care services available to Ethiopians were among the worst in the world. Neither Haile Selassie nor Mengistu had invested in public health. Decent sanitation facilities eluded 90 percent of Ethiopians. Seventy-five percent lacked access to clean water. Ninety percent of laboring mothers gave birth without any medical assistance (compared to 66 percent in the rest of Africa south of the

Sahara). Fewer than half the population lived within ten kilometers of a health facility, and those health stations were decrepit and without adequate equipment and essential drugs.

In 1991, Haregewoin decided to withdraw money from her bank account, buy a plane ticket to Cairo, Egypt, and check into a hospital there.

Sorrowfully she gave notice at her job at Burroughs Computer, and one Friday afternoon—wishing she were home in bed—she thanked everyone warmly for the small farewell reception. Truly they were sorry to see her go. Having grown up the eldest of twenty children, Haregewoin had maintained her tolerant recognition of shenanigans and a penchant toward clapping her hands for order in the midst of anarchy. Though her officemates towered over her, they enjoyed that she treated them like pesky younger brothers and sisters, scolding and laughing in the same sentence. They would miss her.

Her daughters drove her to the airport. Three short, round, and pretty women stood hugging for a long moment in the parking lot, heads tilted together, hair swinging forward, arms interwoven. It was decided that Suzie would stay behind to finish college, that Atetegeb would stick with her job at the World Food Programme, and that Haregewoin would go on to Egypt alone. The girls promised to visit as soon as they had vacation time. The three wept in their embrace. What if it was for the last time? The young women pawed briefly, like younger children, at their mother's cotton shawl as she was forced to disengage, wincing in pain.

One issue remained unspoken: Ashiber. As Haregewoin pulled herself up the concrete steps to the Addis Ababa airport, turning to watch her little blue car zip back into the road, she wondered whether Atetegeb was thinking, *I'm free!*

Finally a word of good news: the Egyptian physicians found only a benign uterine cyst. Haregewoin lingered in the sun-flattened baked-mud city to recuperate, then decided to stay in Cairo. She would live happily there for seven years. A large middle-class expatriate Ethiopian community had gathered in Egypt, escaping the Communist oppression at home. Haregewoin found a job within an Ethiopian Orthodox church as a caterer and event planner. First she lived in a room lent to her by the church, then she moved to her own small apartment. Atetegeb and Suzie visited, and Haregewoin did her best to convince them to stay. Suzie said yes and moved there permanently. But Atetegeb explained that she loved her job with the World Food Programme in Addis and wanted to return to it.

Haregewoin didn't waste her breath in pointing out that Cairo, too, was an excellent home base for famine relief programs.

Colonel Mengistu Haile Mariam was toppled in 1991, while Haregewoin lived in Cairo.

His forcible rural resettlement policies had generated famine, and just like the late emperor, Mengistu attempted to cover it up. The reappearance of the walking skeletons refuted his denials.

"A million people died in Ethiopia during this time, a fact concealed first by the emperor Haile Selassie, and then by the one who took his throne and his life," writes Kapuscinski. "They were divided by their struggle for power, united in their lies."

Nobel Prize–winning economist Amartya Sen has observed that there has never been a famine in a country with a free press.

A free and informed electorate does not keep in office a president or prime minister on whose watch hundreds of thousands of people die of starvation.

The living dead spoke. They relayed a bitter oral poetry that circulated, for years, among their people, though outsiders failed to hear it until recently.

> Oh, this cruel day, it used me so cruelly
> It reduced me to a cowherd,
> It gave my sister to the vultures. [Couplet 18]

> I have quarreled with God
> For nothing else,
> But for just a piece of Bread,
> "Why do You refuse to give me?
> You can't eat it Yourself,
> You have no stomach." [Couplet 56]

Professor Fekade Azeze of Addis Ababa University has gathered the words of the "anonymous poets" who created and transmitted verses about their famines. The terrible words are not without wry humor and insight:

> Clouds faded from the sky,
> And rain vanished from the earth,
> As if angered by the braying committees. [Couplet 3]

> I wish God descended down to earth,
> And I told Him about all His doing.
> For He thinks I am happy because I praise Him. [Couplet 55]

> Even husband and wife
> No longer feed each other by hand,
> Because each one is saying,
> "Save me, Lord! Oh Lord!" [Couplet 12]

Meanwhile, with the disintegration of the Soviet Union, Mengistu lost his backers, his bank account, and his arms supplies. The Ethiopian People's Revolutionary Democratic Front (EPRDF) and the Tigrayan People's Liberation Front (TPLF) invaded Addis and deposed the Derg. With relief, feeling liberated themselves, Mengistu's barefoot and starving soldiers walked back to their homes across the country. Mengistu fled to Zimbabwe.

Rebel leader Meles Zenawi was named Prime Minister and the EPRDF the ruling party.

Half a million innocents had perished in the Soviet experiment.

And the number of AIDS orphans had reached 294,000, fourth in the world after Uganda, Democratic Republic of the Congo, and Zimbabwe.

The toppling of Mengistu inspired tremendous hope. Twice in seventeen years, Ethiopians threw off the yoke of a despot.

Africans everywhere were repelling their colonizers and oppressors; the foreign governments that robbed them of oil, copper, gold, uranium, diamonds, coffee, chromium, labor, and human equality. Angola, Mozambique, Namibia, Zimbabwe, and South Africa waged wars of liberation; the rest (excluding Liberia and Ethiopia—never colonized) fought political battles.

From Libya in 1951 to South Africa in 1994, the colonial powers fell. As the Soviet Union receded, Cold War military investments in African battlefronts diminished. This was a moment for Ethiopia to join with the postcolonial African nations on the adventure of peace and democracy, education, women's rights, health, and economic development.

Instead, by every measure—because of the hidden enemy, the one without tribal identification or politics; and because of first world trade and financial policies imposed on the young governments—the "development" clock began to turn backward.

"Terminology like 'developing countries' [gives] the impression that the whole world is moving in the same direction, albeit at varying rates," writes Mark Heywood of the AIDS Law Project of the University of the Witwatersrand in Johannesburg. "The whole world is not moving in the same direction. Many so-called 'developing countries' are more accurately described as undeveloping countries. They are going backwards. On a whole range of vital indicators, development is now being reversed. In South Africa in 1992 two decades of progress in reducing infant mortality were put into reverse thrust. Infant mortality is on the rise again. Adult life expectancy is going down. Poverty is increasing."

These markers were all true for Ethiopia as well. The engines of social collapse included not only the HIV/AIDS pandemic, but the structural adjustment policies imposed by the World Bank and the International Monetary Fund. Beginning in 1980, loans to developing countries were made conditional upon the borrowers' transformation, instantly, into free market economies. This so-called structural adjustment (also known as shock therapy) required the slashing of public sectors like health and education. School fees were established across Africa to get governments out of the role of school provider; clinic and hospital fees were imposed to reduce government costs. The new policies chased away the poor from health and education.

Free market economies evolved int he rich countries over centuries of trial and error, but history did not deflect the outside experts from their utopian mission, which has since proven disastrous.

When, in 2005, the UN appraised the health, longevity, education, and standard of living of people in 177 nations for its Human Development Index, Ethiopia was ranked 170th. The UN's Gender-Related Development Index, capturing inequalities in achievement between men and women, ranked Ethiopia 134th out of 140 nations. The UN Human Poverty Index evaluated 103 nations and ranked Ethiopia 99th.

Human happiness and health were in free fall.

8

AN AMERICAN GREEN-CARD marriage is a sought-after transaction in many countries; while in Cairo, Haregewoin learned of a young Ethiopian-American in Maryland who was open to negotiations. For a price, he agreed to fly to Addis Ababa, marry Atetegeb, and whisk her away to the United States. Atetegeb, by long-distance telephone, said she would consider it. A few days later she called her mother back and said yes. Haregewoin didn't deceive herself: she assumed that Atetegeb planned, once she found her footing in the United States, to divorce the green-card husband, marry Ashiber, and bring him across. What she *hoped* was that once her daughter was settled in the United States, loosed from the bonds of Ashiber, the security guard would be forgotten.

However, before an immigration-inspired wedding ceremony could be performed (and Haregewoin *hurried*), Ashiber intervened. Atetegeb phoned again. This time she announced her engagement to Ashiber: the wedding was just a few weeks away! Haregewoin gave the man credit: he was prescient. Clearly he'd pictured the same outcome that she herself had imagined: Atetegeb as a modern American woman severing her connection to the hometown boyfriend.

The crackling phone line—pulled aslant across eastern Sudan parallel to the Red Sea—altered the mother's yelp of pain and whimper of protest, conveying it to the girl as a squeal of surprise and congratulation. Then the connection disintegrated. The mother's wail of sorrow fell short, leaked out the frayed cable, and evaporated instantly, no more than a drop of moisture in the ocher furnace of the Nubian Desert.

Haregewoin declined to fly home for the wedding. She mentioned work, the expense, a bad cold. The truth, as she told Suzie: "I don't want to see him. I do not wish to see him with her." Ashiber and Atetegeb were quietly married by an Orthodox priest. Maybe it would be okay, this marriage, hoped Haregewoin from afar.

Then her delicate daughter's letters grew briefer, and rarer. It wasn't easy to phone, but Haregewoin did.

"Tell me," she said.

"Nothing, Mother. I'm fine."

"Tell me, dear."

"Just tired. I'm just feeling really, really tired."

"Is he treating you well? Is he being good to you?" demanded the mother.

"Yes, Mother! He's fine. He's sweet. It's not like that. I have to go now. I love you."

Haregewoin and Suzie wrote weekly to Atetegeb: "Come to us! Just come for a visit!"

"My husband would not enjoy my absence," came the somewhat stilted reply.

Here and there, in Atetegeb's letters, were hints of illness: fatigue, depression, a persistent cough, and on some mornings a lassitude so great she could barely get up.

"Please see a doctor," wrote Haregewoin, enclosing cash to cover the price of an office visit.

"Please do not worry so much about me," Atetegeb wrote back. "I send you both all my love."

One evening after work, Suzie opened the mail and screamed.

"What on earth? My dear!" snapped Haregewoin.

Suzie held out the letter. "She's pregnant."

They hastened to reply, posting many letters over the next several days. "But are you well enough for this? Is this why you were so tired? Was it the early stage of pregnancy?"

"It must have been her first trimester making her so tired!"

celebrated Haregewoin at dinner. Suzie quietly counted months on her fingers and doubted it.

Haregewoin flew home for a visit. Pale, hollow-eyed, Atetegeb reached out her arms.

"Sweet one!" cried Haregewoin, enveloping her.

Ashiber was in high spirits: a married man, an expectant father, master of his own house. Haregewoin tried to like him; when his laughter boomed out over the dinner table, she tittered unhappily. She made out that he meant to impress her; in case he was failing to do so, he avoided eye contact, abruptly excused himself from the table, and went out.

Haregewoin stocked Atetegeb's cabinets with groceries and vitamins. In a drugstore she studied the box of an American shampoo that promised "radiance" and bought it. At the end of two weeks, she called a taxi to take her back to the airport. She hugged her daughter goodbye, murmuring, "Come to us. We have room for you. Come and have your baby in Cairo, then come home."

"Leave my husband?" cried Atetegeb in surprise.

"No, not leave your husband; just let us help you with the baby. Just come until you're feeling strong again," said Haregewoin, stroking her daughter's head.

In the taxi, choked up, she rolled down the window and called, "I love you so much." Hands suddenly shaking, she undid her wallet and passed a roll of bills, her travel money, to her daughter. "Just for you. Use this for yourself."

Six months later, a healthy baby boy was born. Haregewoin heard the relieved happiness in Atetegeb's voice in one brief phone call. Even Ashiber got on the line to shout, *"Selam, Ayateh!"* Hello, Grandma! Haregewoin raced around Cairo buying baby gifts to ship home, immeasurably grateful and relieved to have dodged what catastrophe she didn't know.

But once the presents were sent and silence stood between them, Haregewoin again felt the prick of dread. She woke up at night in a sweat of foreboding, like the months during which she thought she had cancer. She inventoried her body, curled quietly in bed, to detect the source of the worry—was it some new pain or illness announcing itself? But she found no purchase here. No, it was Atetegeb.

"Shall I come to you, to help with the baby?" she wrote.

"Yes, but not right now. Later you will come," Atetegeb replied.

"Shall I go?" she asked Suzie.

"I don't know, Mother. Shall I?"

"Well, your sister loves to have money. Better we should keep working and help her out on the side. I don't know how much money he gives her. Besides, if I moved back to Addis, where would I live— with *them*?"

"With Ashiber?!"

But several days later, as if she hadn't just settled the question, she asked Suzie again, "Should I go?"

She telephoned Addis Ababa. Ashiber answered, was gruff. "She's sleeping," he said, and hung up.

She phoned a few days later and got him again. She threw her voice into a high octave, trying to sound like nothing more than a giddy grandma. "How's the baby? How's my daughter?"

This time he said, "She's out."

Now the grind of her stomach told her once or twice an hour, *Something is wrong.* Maybe something was wrong with the baby. It was decided: she must go. She flew home, told no one she was coming, and took a taxi to her daughter's house.

9

WITH A SUITCASE full of gifts, she waited outside the door of the compound. A woman she didn't know opened it, a maid, middle-aged, with the two-month-old baby resting against her shoulder.

Haregewoin stepped onto the cement drive and reached for the little boy. "I'm the grandmother," she said. She leaned her face into the sweet-and-sour chamber of his presence. In an instant the baby became the fourth part of her life, along with Worku, Atetegeb, and Suzie. A gorgeous boy with flawless skin, wide-open round eyes, and plump dark lips; he was smooth as soap, solid and pleasant. Curly wisps of hair fluttered from his head; his eyebrows were feathery and gave him an expression of curiosity.

"Where is my daughter?" she called, whiplashed by the speed at which her fact-finding mission had swerved into joy. Waiting outside her daughter's closed bedroom door for the housekeeper to announce her, she felt as if she held a young emperor and stood outside the throne room of the queen mother.

"Hello, sweetheart! It's Mom!" she called through the closed door. She basked in the ivory light of her grandson's face. His eyelids fluttered, a tiny snort came from the small nose, he shivered briefly, sighed, snoozed. As his warm little hand uncurled its grip on her finger, Haregewoin overthrew the life she'd built in Cairo. Would she even leave the baby to fly home to pack her things? No, Suzie could ship them. Surely she could find a house to rent in the neighborhood. She was flying with happiness.

The housekeeper opened the door. "Come in, madam."

✳   ✳   ✳

Tall wood shutters darkened the room. The air was thick with the smell of medicine; bottles—syrups and capsules—crowded the dresser top. Lost in a jumble of sheets lay a gaunt woman with chopped-off hair and chapped lips. One cheek bore an oblong wart. Her bony bare legs restlessly moved and pushed at the blankets. Her eyelids were raised only halfway.

". . . Atetegeb?" whispered Haregewoin, looking in confusion to the maid. "Where is . . .?

"Atetegeb?" she asked again, creeping closer. She handed the baby to the maid, suddenly dizzy and afraid she would drop him. Her eyes were riddled by dotted light and her mouth went dry; she stumbled and caught hold of a chair.

"Sweetheart? Atetegeb? It's Mother."

Her daughter's face remained flat, but the fingers of the hand nearest Haregewoin opened and strained. Haregewoin caught her daughter's hand in both of hers and moved to sit on the bed beside her. She could feel the fever through the bedcovers.

"Darling! Oh my God, what happened to you?"

"Mother. I'm sick."

"But sick how? With what?" Again she looked to the housekeeper.

The housekeeper—a silent type, in her forties—smiled sadly and withdrew with the baby, quietly closing the door behind her.

"Why didn't you tell me?" Haregewoin wept.

After a long silence, the young woman said, "I didn't want you to suffer."

Her words led to a spasm of feeble coughs. Atetegeb tried to shut her eyes, but her eyeballs protruded and prevented the frayed fabric of the eyelids from closing. Atetegeb's fingers gestured again. On the night table lay a dry washcloth, curved to the shape of her forehead.

"Shall I wet it?" whispered Haregewoin, and Atetegeb nodded. With infinite tenderness, Haregewoin smoothed the dampened cloth over her daughter's face. The bony fingers untensed; she seemed to sleep, though the dry eyes still gazed out under half-closed lids.

✳   ✳   ✳

Haregewoin blew out of the room like a hurricane. She called the Black Lion Hospital, the major teaching and tertiary-care hospital in Ethiopia and the one affiliated with the Addis Ababa University medical school. She called a taxi (ambulance service was nearly nonexistent). She browbeat the housekeeper, who knew nothing, least of all that there was a concerned mother in Egypt all this time.

"Why wasn't I told?" bellowed Haregewoin. "Where is that Satan of a husband? Where is Ashiber?"

The housekeeper blinked once in the direction of a closed door, then said, "He is at his job."

Haregewoin threw open the closed door and beheld a well-appointed bedroom. She understood—he slept apart from his wife.

"Where does the baby sleep?"

"With me," said the maid, indicating a pallet on the floor of the kitchen.

Atetegeb meekly gasped, "No," only once when the taxi driver, paid extra by Haregewoin, lifted her from the bed. Haregewoin was shocked at how skeletal her daughter looked. She rushed to throw a bedspread over her. The bright light hurt her daughter's eyes. She was shrunken and pale as an underground creature suddenly unearthed. In the hospital, Atetegeb was given a corner bed in a big, high-ceilinged old ward. She was given a blood transfusion, fed intravenously.

"Doctor, please! What is it?" cried Haregewoin in the hallway.

"It may be leukemia," said one physician. "She is completely wasted."

"It is certainly pneumonia," said a nurse.

"She has tuberculosis," pronounced an attendant.

"That is a skin cancer," said a technician.

Haregewoin sat on a chair beside Atetegeb's hospital bed, wringing her hands, swaying back and forth.

A course of Bactrim brought the TB to heel, allowed Atetegeb to breathe a little more easily. But no sooner was one threat ameliorated than another arose. For several weeks, Haregewoin slept in the chair beside the hospital bed at night. Every few days she returned to Atetegeb's house for a few hours to shower, nap, and cook. She brought baskets of food into the hospital, broke off and rolled up small balls of *injera*, and brushed her daughter's lips with them. But Atetegeb did not want to eat and cried in protest.

"In the name of heaven!" Haregewoin accosted Ashiber one night. "What were you thinking?"

"We saw a doctor," he said. "I bought medicine. What do you want me to do? I hired a full-time servant to help her. You want me to stay home? If I stop working, we'll end up on the street."

"Why didn't you tell me?"

"My wife wrote to you every week. There was no end to the phone calls from you. How is it possible you didn't know she was sick?"

"She didn't tell me," said Haregewoin, crushed.

"Well then."

At four months, the baby was a smiling fellow quite attached to the housekeeper. "He is a fat one, and very smart," Haregewoin praised the baby to Ashiber one night, and Ashiber lit up and said, "He is! I know! I know! A fine boy!" In a lower voice, he asked, "How is Atetegeb?"

"You should visit her at the hospital, you know."

"Someone in this family actually has to work—and to see our son," he snapped, reminding Haregewoin that he, too, was under great strain.

Aware that her stay in Addis Ababa would be of indefinite length, Haregewoin rented a brick house with two bedrooms, an indoor kitchen, an outdoor brick latrine, and an outdoor shower faucet. The front yard was packed dirt within tin walls, but flowers could be grown there, she thought, to delight Atetegeb in the spring. She purchased a few pieces of furniture—armchairs and a sofa—from a roadside kiosk and paid a taxi driver to deliver them. Nonsensically, she felt happy; she was eager to prepare a bedroom for Atetegeb to enjoy.

The patient plateaued. She was a listless vessel of diseases and hospital products. But the doctor pronounced her stable enough to go home.

"I'm taking you to my house," she told her daughter.

"Ask Ashiber," said Atetegeb.

Haregewoin phoned her son-in-law. "I'm taking her to my house."

"You should bring her here," he said.

"No. You are the husband, but I am the mother. You can marry again someday. If I lose her, I will never find her again."

She moved Atetegeb to the fresh sheets and clean room of the hillside bungalow. Green figs were fattening on the wild fig tree outside the window, and green pigeons fluttered among the leaves.

Haregewoin left early one morning by taxi and returned with the baby. "Look who is here to see his *amaye*," she crooned, waking her daughter midmorning. He was seven months old now, plump and warm as fresh bread. His light brown hair was like the fluff of a dandelion. Atetegeb was too weak to hold him, so Haregewoin scooted behind her on the bed to prop her up, while holding the boy in front of her, Haregewoin's arms encircling both mother and child. He opened his eyes wide and smiled. Two baby teeth shone from his lower gum. Both women laughed.

"He remembers me!" cried Atetegeb.

"Yes, my darling," said Haregewoin.

When Atetegeb was too tired to sit up and smile anymore, Haregewoin rode home with the boy. Ashiber stood in the driveway with his arms crossed. The child's babysitter, in a panic, had phoned her boss at work. "Never, never, never," he warned Haregewoin, "never again do you take my son from this house. My son stays here."

"She is his *mother*."

"He stays."

"She is his mother, Ashiber," said Haregewoin wearily. She handed over the jolly, wet-bottomed boy, strode into the house, picked up a few of Atetegeb's things, and returned to the waiting taxi.

"Do you hear me, *Waizero* Haregewoin?"

"She is his mother."

She allowed herself one last look at the child, sitting high on his father's chest, then slammed the car door closed and rode away.

Now it was Suzie writing from Cairo: "Mother, shall I come?"

"No, my dear, you are the only one of the three of us working. I do not expect help from Ashiber. God only knows if you could find work here."

Haregewoin tore recklessly through her inheritance from Worku and her savings; she was purchasing time for her daughter, she was buying hope. At a slender rumor of a new drug, she bought a case of it; she telephoned health agency workers. She made overseas phone calls. Five times in ten months Haregewoin hired a taxi driver to pick up her daughter, trying a different hospital or clinic each time.

Ashiber visited their house just once. Fresh air billowed behind him like a cape; his manly health and bulk, polished shoes, deep voice, and smell of aftershave were foreign to this house of women and sickness.

"Please, Ashiber, let me see our son," croaked Atetegeb, gaunt and yellow-faced, from her pillow.

"I will bring him tomorrow," he said, surprisingly conciliatory.

But he broke his promise. He didn't bring him the next day, or the next, or the next. Haregewoin phoned. "I will come to your house tomorrow morning to pick up the baby; we'll have a nice visit and I'll bring him home by lunchtime."

But the next day she found the house dark and locked.

"He is afraid we will kidnap the baby," said Atetegeb. "The baby is the only person in the world he loves."

But Haregewoin thought, *He fears the baby will catch his mother's disease.*

Atetegeb's diarrhea was relentless, and she had bedsores; her small strength ebbed. Haregewoin alone turned her and washed her and changed her, stripped off the sheets, washed the bedclothes by hand in a galvanized tub in the yard. She found a small bit of contentment in remembering how she'd once washed diapers this way when her girls were babies. Atetegeb was lost in memories of her son. In her unhappy, restless daylong sleep, she sometimes pulled a pillow to nestle at her side, like a nursing baby.

Ashiber did not visit again.

Bland stews, nutritious soups, nourishing breads, chunks of mango, of watermelon—all the baby-food-like treats concocted by Haregewoin in the small kitchen, offered lovingly to her daughter spoonful by spoonful—were refused.

"It's no use to eat, Mother," Atetegeb sadly said, turning her face away. "The food ravages me. It tears me apart and I make a mess for you and I don't want it. I'm tired."

In the kitchen, scraping off the plates, Haregewoin cried aloud. She couldn't trick more than a teaspoon of sugared tea past her daughter's lips.

"Sweet one, forgive me," she cried as she opened the door once again to a taxi driver and had Atetegeb, in agony at being disturbed, driven back to the hospital.

This time she stayed only a week. Doctors observed her, made notes, chatted in the hall outside the door to the ward. Any thought of saving the patient was long gone from everyone's mind except Haregewoin's. She couldn't help it: every time a doctor, nurse, orderly, janitor, approached Atetegeb's bed, Haregewoin looked up from her chair, eyes bleary with hope.

Atetegeb slept all the time. Haregewoin sat with her head bowed, sometimes watching her daughter's heart pulse feebly in her wrist. Her daughter was leaving her. The small bit of warmth that sometimes flared up in Atetegeb's face was precious to Haregewoin, even though she knew fever drove it.

"Mother," spoke Atetegeb clearly one evening, startling Haregewoin awake in her chair. "It's time for me to go home. Can you take me home?"

A mix of hope and fantasy crumpled Haregewoin's face again. Had the fever broken?

Atetegeb smiled, raising her arms a little, indicating the tangle of plastic tubes.

"Enough," she said. "It's enough. It's time."

WHERE HAD HIV/AIDS come from?

Cats, sheep, horses, and cattle are prone to lentiviruses, but monkeys and chimps carry the lentiviruses closest to the human immunodeficiency virus (HIV); researchers call them simian immunodeficiency viruses (SIV).

An Old World monkey found in the West African forests of Guinea Bissau, Gabon, Cameroon, Sierra Leone, and Ghana was the sooty mangabey: long-toothed, long-tailed, long-fingered, and slender, with pale eyelids in a dark face. Sooty mangabeys were carriers of sooty mangabey SIV (SIVsm), which would turn out to be the genetic precursor of the lesser of the two HIV epidemics: HIV-2, which has rarely been seen in humans outside West Africa.

In the tropical forests and mountain forests of Central Africa, there are three subspecies of common chimpanzees. Between the Niger River and the Congo River roam the Pan troglodytes troglodytes. Some carry chimpanzee SIV (SIVcpz), which was discovered, in 1999, to be the genetic ancestor of HIV-1, the virulent human virus that is the source of the world pandemic.

But why and how did a monkey immunodeficiency virus and a chimp immunodeficiency virus give rise to two human immunodeficiency viruses, in two far-removed different regions of Africa, and at the same time?

Why did the benign simian virus that kills its animal host about 1 percent of the time change into a voracious, frequently mutating human virus that kills its host 99 percent of the time?

Numerous hypotheses have been proposed; none yet has been proved.

The first might be called the *genocidal* theory.

Africans have an unhappy history with Western medicine, especially with the pharmaceutical industry: they have watched their countries become dumping grounds for uncertain and outdated drugs, and people often win access to treatment only by consenting to test new products, sometimes to the detriment of their health. Thus, in villages that began to witness decimation by AIDS, rumors spread that Western powers had deliberately infected Africans with it.

An Africa purged of humanity, or peopled only by weakened sufferers, would once again invite plunder of its rich natural resources by outside powers.

Haregewoin's old friend Zewedu, the former engineer and college teacher, privately gave the genocidal theory a great deal of consideration. As an educated man, he was more aware than most that the industrialized nations had invented a treatment for the disease that was killing him. Even if the West hadn't deliberately infected Africa, the West inarguably stood by now as Africans perished by the millions.

A nonconspiracy theory of the origin of HIV suggests that HIV is a zoonotic disease, or *zoonosis:* a human disease that originated with animals and jumped the species barrier. While some infectious diseases are species-specific, others are caused by bacteria, viruses, or other organisms shared between animal species. "In some cases, zoonotic diseases are transferred by direct contact with infected animals, much as being near an infected human can cause the spread of an infectious disease. Other diseases are spread by drinking water that contains the eggs of parasites. The eggs enter the water supply from the feces of infected animals. Still others are spread by eating the flesh of infected animals. Tapeworms are spread this way. Other diseases are spread by insect vectors . . ."

The *hunter* theory supposes that a zoonosis, HIV, crossed the species barrier and infected human hunters and consumers of monkey and chimpanzee meat. An African hunter or butcher, with an open cut on his hand, handling a newly killed monkey, assimilated the blood-borne virus into his own system. Similarly a child, playing with her pet baby monkey.

In 1987, a University of California virologist, Preston Marx, noted the ubiquity of live and dead sooty mangabeys in villages in Liberia and Sierra Leone: dead animals were sold in markets for meat, young ones were kept as pets. He drew blood samples from household pets, then from villagers. The monkey blood tested positive for SIVsm; and the human blood occasionally tested positive for both SIVsm and HIV.

The results were important, but did not explain the whole story. Humans in these regions have hunted, captured, tamed, and butchered monkeys for millennia. SIV DNA is thousands of years old. The villagers whose blood tested positive for both SIVsm and HIV showed little sign of illness and did not transmit the virus through sexual contact. "All of the primates that carry these SIVs have been in close contact with humans for thousands of years without the emergence of epidemic HIV," Marx would write, with co-researchers Phillip G. Alcabes and Ernest Drucker.

"[One] is trying to explain why several different strains of the human immunodeficiency virus that causes AIDS appeared in roughly the same period of time in Africa in mid-century," Dr. Ernest Drucker, professor of epidemiology and social medicine at the Albert Einstein College of Medicine, told ABC radio. "The simians—the monkeys, the chimpanzees, and others that carried the progenitors to this virus—had been around for hundreds of thousands of years, living *with people* for hundreds of thousands of years, and the people had been exposed to these viruses. So why, suddenly, in mid-century, in the 20th century, do we see several different strains of HIV that come from several different strains of simian immunovirus?"

✻   ✻   ✻

The *social upheaval* theory builds on the concept of HIV as a zoonosis: it explains the mid-twentieth-century explosion of the disease out of central Africa as a result of the movement of populations during the independence struggles of the 1950s and 1960s. "Under that hypothesis," reports *San Francisco Chronicle* staff writer William Carlsen, "the epidemic emerged as roads were cut through the rain forests and strict colonial travel prohibitions were lifted. This enabled HIV carriers, who had been infected by monkeys and had previously lived in isolated rural communities, to crowd into cities, where they spread the virus through less restrictive sexual practices."

And yet the social upheaval theory fails to address: Why now? Between 1450 and 1850, at least twelve million Africans—and possibly twice that number—were forced into captivity and taken as slaves across the notorious Middle Passage of the Atlantic to colonies in North America, South America, and the Caribbean. People were uprooted from regions in West Central Africa in which the relevant monkeys and chimps were at large, and where the plague now thrives. Why didn't the AIDS epidemic emerge between the fifteenth and nineteenth centuries, spread by enslaved Africans?

The social upheaval theory yields to the argument that something *new* must have happened fifty or sixty years ago to upset the balance between benign simian viruses, their animal hosts, and their occasional human hosts.

Theories of *iatrogenic* origin ask whether AIDS was launched inadvertently, by medical treatment or experiments.

"Gentlemen and ladies, people of the town. I wish to make an announcement. AIDS is a man-made disease," began an article by former BBC radio reporter Edward Hooper. Entitled "The Story of a Man-Made Disease," it appeared in the *London Review of Books* in 2003. "It is now all but certain that it was human hands (and, in particular, those of the doctor and the scientist) that started the AIDS pandemic, which now represents the worst outbreak of infectious disease the world has ever seen."

In his book *The River: A Journey to the Source of HIV and AIDS*, published four years earlier, Hooper laid out his argument that HIV can be traced to the development and testing of an oral polio vaccine given to hundreds of thousands of people in the Belgian Congo in the late 1950s.

A Polish émigré scientist, Hilary Koprowsky, of the Wistar Institute in Philadelphia, raced against Jonas Salk and Albert Sabin to perfect a vaccine against polio. The Wistar Institute cultivated the vaccine in the kidney cells of organs harvested from African and Asian monkeys and chimpanzees. The Central African villages where the Wistar vaccine was tested between 1957 and 1960 later produced the first terrible eruptions of HIV/AIDS.

Had the monkey or chimpanzee kidney cells, in which the Wistar vaccine was cultivated, come from animal carriers of SIV?

Did the campaign to inoculate against polio simultaneously infect thousands of people with HIV?

Experts recruited by the Wistar Institute disputed the theory. It was unlikely any SIV particles could have survived the vaccine tissue-culture process, they argued; at any rate, such tiny concentrations of SIV that survived would have been too low to transmit disease. Furthermore, oral delivery of SIV particles would be much less likely to spread disease than introduction of the particles directly into the bloodstream. And surviving vials of the vaccine showed no traces of SIV. Finally, Wistar protested, the same vaccine tested in the Congo had been administered in Poland and in the United States, with no resultant AIDS outbreak.

And there was the indisputable fact that two distinct AIDS epidemics—HIV-1 and HIV-2—arose a thousand miles apart, the first related to a chimp virus, the second to a sooty mangabey virus. The Wistar vaccine could not be held accountable for both.

Hooper's intriguing theory of contaminated oral polio vaccine does not cover all the bases and remains unproven.

But, in the 1950s, in the regions of Central Africa now seen as ground zero for HIV/AIDS, there were other medical campaigns besides polio vaccine tests. Another compelling *iatrogenic* theory examines the mass immunization crusades that swept the continent without due attention to the use of sterile equipment.

In the postwar era, "a period of swashbuckling medical optimism," notes Carlsen, the World Health Organization (WHO), the United Nations, and other relief agencies launched unprecedented and ambitious inoculation and treatment programs against congenital syphilis, tuberculosis, and yaws (a tropical disease of the skin, bones, and joints that is spread by gnats and that targets children). "The campaigns were a medical intervention on a scale never seen before on the African continent," reports Carlsen, "but the noble goal of eradicating disease was compromised by a widespread failure to ensure sterile injections, and the consequences of that failure could be staggering."

Hypodermic syringes had been invented in 1848: they were expensive and highly prized medical instruments, individually handmade from glass and metal. They could be sterilized. In 1920, only 100,000 syringes were manufactured worldwide. After World War I, as more uses were discovered for them (like injecting insulin), syringes began to be mass-produced. By 1930, two million units a year were manufactured and seventy-five million by 1952. Their prices steadily declined. Their greatest role came with the appearance on the scene of penicillin.

Discovered in 1929, penicillin was a wonder drug; but, by 1941, it had only been produced in quantities sufficient for the treatment of two hundred people. During World War II, mass-production techniques were designed (leading to Nobel Prizes for the scientist who discovered penicillin and for the two scientists who first produced it on an industrial scale). Between 1949 and 1964, U.S. production of the antibiotic increased from 76,000 pounds to 170 million pounds, and the price decreased from $1,144 to $49 per pound. Penicillin therapy was synonymous with injections, since oral antibiotics had not been perfected.

The manufacture of injectable antibiotics and the manufacture of injecting equipment scaled up simultaneously. Between 1950 and

1960, glass-and-metal syringes were largely replaced by disposable plastic ones. Production increased a hundredfold to one billion units a year in 1960.

The mass-produced penicillin joined hands with the mass-produced syringe, and off they traveled to Africa to do good work.

UNICEF describes the historic "enthusiasm for dealing with disease through technical interventions":

As the 1940s gave way to the 1950s, the predominant motif in international public health campaigns generally was the struggle to control or eradicate epidemic disease. These campaigns were among the first, and certainly the most spectacular, extensions of non-war-related international assistance . . . New drugs and vaccines were becoming ever cheaper and, for the first time in history, offered a genuine prospect that age-old scourges could be swept away without waiting for the spread of doctors, hospitals and health centres. Used on a mass scale, and following a systematic geographical plan and timetable, the new techniques could—theoretically—force a specific disease to relinquish its hold over a whole population.

The disease that succumbed earliest and most dramatically to the mass campaign was yaws. This painful condition, spread by a micro-organism, could lead to total disability. It was found in tropical, poor and remote rural areas and was contracted through broken skin. In the early 1950s, there were thought to be around 20 million cases worldwide . . . The invention of penicillin transformed the prospects of cure. One shot cleared the ugly pink lesions, and a few more cleared the disease from the body.

Injections were quickly accepted throughout the continent as the sine qua non of medical treatment. Any doctor who did not offer an injection in response to an infection, a fever, fatigue, or the common cold was regarded as short-changing his patients. Traditional healers and indigenous practitioners quickly adapted the new technology to their repertoires. Studies in the 1960s indicated that in 25 to 50 percent of sub-Saharan households, someone had received an injection within the previous two weeks. By the 1990s, injections were being administered at 60 to 96 percent of outpatient visits.

In the 1950s congenital syphilis was common in Africa and injectable penicillin was the drug used to combat it. At the same time, chloroquine was being injected to fight malaria. The United Nations International Children's Emergency Fund (UNICEF) administered over twelve million injections of penicillin between 1952 and 1957, and thirty-five million injections by 1963.

In London, in September 2000, at a Royal Society conference on the "Origins of AIDS and the AIDS Epidemic," Drs. Preston Marx and Ernest Drucker presented their paper "The Injection Century: Consequences of Massive Unsterile Injecting for the Emergence of Human Pathogens," the theory of unsterile needles as the *progenitors* of AIDS. Marx and Drucker pondered the possibility that reused unsterile syringes not only *spread* HIV/AIDS but *fathered* it, in a process similar to one practiced by lab researchers, known as *serial passage*.

Developed as a lab technique by Louis Pasteur in the 1880s, serial passage makes possible the speedy mutation of a virus by injecting it into host A, giving it time to incubate, injecting host A's virus into host B, host B's virus into host C, and so on down the line of the petri dishes. The virus adapts to each host's immune system and changes before it is extracted and inserted into the next host. Carlsen writes: "The process had already been witnessed in monkey experiments, Marx told his colleagues. Simian viruses became a thousand times more pathogenic as they were 'serially passaged' through as few as three monkeys."

The *serial passage* theory is that the relatively harmless monkey or chimp SIV, found in the blood of a few hunters or consumers of monkey meat, could have been transformed—through tens of millions of unsterilized injections beginning in the 1950s—into the monstrous pandemic.

"If you take a weakly pathogenic virus, the monkey virus," said Drucker, "and infect the human with it, that virus may survive for a few days or even up to a few weeks while it tries to adapt. And it begins to adapt to the human host, but the human host beats it back.

"But if—during that period while it's still trying to adapt—you were to share some of the person's blood (which is basically what a dirty injection does) you *passage* some of that partially mutated virus to a second person. And that second person picks up where the first one left off. The virus is now partly adapted to humans, and it's able to live a bit longer. So that second person moves it forward a little closer to HIV. And then you do that one more time and one more time . . . and each time you passage the virus it gets more and more pathogenic, it adapts to the new host. And by four or five or six passages later, you have one that actually is adapted to the human host; it begins to replicate, it begins to shed off viral particles, [it becomes] infectious to another human being."

Dr. Preston Marx, Dr. Ernest Drucker, and Dr. Christian Apetrei of the Department of Tropical Medicine of Tulane University questioned the very identification of AIDS as a zoonosis in the first place. "Based on findings demonstrating the simian ancestry of HIV, AIDS has been reported to be a zoonosis," they wrote in 2004 for the *Journal of Medical Primatology.*

However, this theory has never been proved and must seriously be questioned. Several arguments show that HIV-AIDS is not a zoonosis. (i) If AIDS were a zoonosis, there must be evidence of AIDS being directly acquired from an animal species, as is rabies, a disease that is directly acquired from animals. (ii) Despite long-term and frequent human exposure to SIV-infected monkeys in Africa, only 11 cross-species transmission events are known, and only four of these have resulted in significant human-to-human transmission . . . If AIDS were a zoonosis that is capable of significant human-to-human spread, there would be a plethora of founder subtypes and groups. (iii) Human exposure to SIV is thousands of years old, but AIDS emerged only in the 20th century. If AIDS were a zoonosis that spread into the human population, it would have spread to the West during slave trade. (iv) Experimental transmission of SIVs to different species of monkeys is often well controlled by the new host, showing that the virus and not the disease is transmitted. Therefore, we conclude that cross-species transmission of SIV does not in itself constitute the basis for a zoonosis.

"All HIVs do derive from simian species," the authors explained, "but AIDS does not qualify as a zoonosis and this explanation cannot in itself account for the origin of AIDS epidemic."

The simian viruses, the SIVs, provided the building blocks of the human virus, but the conversion process is a mystery. For these scientists, the inadvertent serial passaging of harmlessly SIV-tainted blood from person to person to person to person, from hunter to farmer to merchant to child to seamstress to midwife to teacher, through the infinite reuse of unsterilized needles, created a new thing, a killer disease, a pandemic.

"It's striking that the first cases of AIDS that we know come out of Central Africa—Zaire, the Belgian Congo—at that time," Drucker said in 2000. "In about 1959, we know we have the virus in the Congo. And that was the area of some of the first . . . mass campaigns for penicillin, the yaws eradication . . . By the 1960s, penicillin and other kinds of injection campaigns are going on through Africa, throughout the developing world, India as well.

"People turned a blind eye to this for a number of different reasons. WHO, which was distributing hundreds of millions of doses of vaccine, were often distributing many, many fewer needles to go with them, with the recommendation that these needles be sterilized, and providing some sterilizing equipment to do so. But in reality, anyone who worked in the field in Africa in the fifties and the sixties and the seventies, knew perfectly well that most sterilization did not take place. Indeed these disposable plastic syringes are not really sterilizable."

"We hypothesize," wrote Drs. Drucker and Marx, "that the massive increase in unsterile injecting in Africa associated with the introduction of antibiotics in the 1950's was the modern 'event' that allowed several weakly pathogenic simian virus, long native to Sub Saharan Africa, to increase in pathogenicity and complete their genetic adaptation to human hosts, emerging as the first epidemic strain of HIV by 1959." The doctors believe that Hepatitis B and C were spawned in the same way.

"The norm," said Drucker, "was to simply give these injections, to sterilize the needles in a very cursory way; there's one case where a doctor did five hundred people in two hours using six needles, and [the syringes] were just thrown into a bath of alcohol. Because, in all fairness, the penicillin and the other drugs that were being used were seen as so important and lifesaving, and the downside—the kinds of contaminations that might take place, [like] hepatitis, were not seen as particularly lethal, because we didn't know about hepatitis C then. So there was a lot of very, very sloppy procedure, even within medical practice. And then *outside* of medical practice—in what were called 'country clinics' and 'bush medicine'—needles were all over the place, penicillin was all over the place, other injectibles were there, and just a huge, huge number of injections . . . Between 1950 and 1960 the production of needles goes up from ten million to a billion needles. And today there are forty billion needles produced in the world each year; many of them stay in the system.

"AIDS isn't the only new disease, is it?" asked Drucker. "We see other diseases happening all the time—like mad cow disease—which are a product of technologies that we didn't really understand the implications of. Cows weren't meant to eat animal protein; they have no mechanism to protect themselves. There wasn't meant to be a device that would carry blood from one person to another when [the blood] might carry an animal infection. All of our viral diseases are crossovers from animal species, and what we've done with the unsterile injecting campaigns, and the massive use of unsterile injections in the world . . . [is to] provide a mechanism for taking weakly pathogenic animal viruses and helping them evolve into pathogenic human viruses that will be with us. And I think we're at the beginning of this story, not the end."

The story is just beginning, Drucker believes, because WHO estimates an ongoing global rate of thirty billion to fifty billion unsterile injections a year. Forty percent of injections in 2000 were performed with reused needles. In some countries, perhaps three out of four injections were unsafe. WHO estimates that unsafe injections result in 80,000 to 160,000 new HIV-I infections every year, eight to sixteen million hepatitis B infections, and twenty-three to forty-seven million hepatitis C infections worldwide (this figure does not include transfusions).

Even under the auspices of WHO regional immunization programs, which constitute 10 percent of all mass vaccination campaigns, an estimated 30 percent of injections are done with unclean, re-used syringes. As recently as 1998, WHO *recommended* reuse of syringes up to two hundred times in vaccination programs, relying on sterilization routines that WHO's own studies show are usually not followed.

Insufficient supplies of syringes and needles are the major cause. Equipment is often reused, sold, or recycled because of its commercial value.

The technology exists to prevent this hazardous reuse of needles: single-use autodestruct disposable ("auto-disable") syringes have been invented; after one injection, the needle retracts back into the barrel. Syringe makers are prepared to mass-produce them, but they're costly. Global health experts agree that safer needles are a crucial step toward eradicating the iatrogenic spread of diseases, but where will the funding come from? WHO's budget is insufficient and the big donors are not coming forward.

Joel Schoenfeld, chairman of auto-disable-syringe maker UNIVEC of Farmingdale, New York, hails the serial passage theory presented by Drucker and Marx: "These respected experts confirm our call for the exclusive use of auto-disable syringes in mass immunization programs and for clinical use . . . Why does the world's medical community continue to ignore [this]? What it should do is stop the practice of allowing multiuse syringes in every immunization and clinical program the world over. Only when we adopt an auto-disable syringe policy, to be mandatory in all mass vaccination programs, will we contribute significantly to the scourge of disease around the world."

Epidemiologists studying the HIV/AIDS pandemic from a different angle (for example, the charting of "sexual networks"—who is sleeping with whom? how soon after infection [the time of highest contagion] is there further sexual contact?) have been stymied by the big numbers. Unsafe injections open an intriguing theory of corollary transmission.

"Since the late 1980s, the dominant hypothesis has been that HIV in Africa is transmitted primarily through penile-vaginal contact," says Dr. Richard Rothenberg, editor of *Annals of Epidemiology* and professor of infectious diseases at the Emory University School of Medicine. "But the available survey data do not fully support that hypothesis. There may be important elements that are being missed which would help account for the trajectory."

For example, there are regions in Africa in which public health campaigns have significantly increased safe sexual practices and condom use, rates of other sexually transmitted diseases are falling, yet HIV infection is increasing. There are case histories of children testing HIV-positive when neither parent has the disease; of wives testing seropositive when their husbands do not, and vice versa, in cases in which attestations of fidelity appear to be reliable. The accusations and violence following such results can scarcely be imagined. But the children and the wives and the husbands may have been infected by unsterile injections.

The paradigm in popular culture—that rampant promiscuity and hypersexual behaviors launched and continue to stoke the African AIDS epidemic—may be an extraordinarily cruel example of "blaming the victim."

The serial passage hypothesis—that AIDS is not a zoonosis that leapt the species barrier, but is a new virus, created by the technology of the hypodermic needle and the mass inoculation campaigns of the mid-twentieth century—has not been firmly established, but research continues.

"We know the source," says Marx, "but not the spark that ignited the epidemic."

11

T HEY RODE HOME from the hospital in the back of a taxi, Haregewoin cradling Atetegeb. She asked the driver to help her carry the patient into her bedroom. He raised his eyebrows in question. Fear of contagious disease is typical in tropical and subtropical countries. Inhabitants of temperate zones fail to appreciate the extent to which their steel and glass civilizations are built upon the bedrock of annual winters, while those in tropical zones are bedeviled to death by contagious parasites, viruses, insects, and bacteria that are never beaten back by ice or cold. Was the woman dying of tuberculosis, of malaria, of measles, of polio, of hepatitis, of sleeping sickness, or river blindness, of the horrendous new wasting disease people called *aminmina* (slim)?

"Cancer," Haregewoin told him.

That night she phoned Ashiber. "She's going. This is the end." Perhaps fearing for his own health, he stayed away.

"I love you so much," Haregewoin told Atetegeb. She had her tucked in warm and snug. She noted the bare windowsill, where the next day she would place flowerpots. "You are so precious to me."

"I love you, too," Atetegeb garbled.

In the night, the gaunt young woman's gasping for air kept Haregewoin awake in the bed beside her. *Worku was lucky*, she thought. Atetegeb's hair was nearly gone, her face was pockmarked, her lips cracked, her eyes blind, but to Haregewoin she was still beautiful. "My poor child," she cooed in the night, gathering insensible Atetegeb to her. Her daughter's life was as small and frail now as that of a premature baby's. Haregewoin's very first hours with newborn

Atetegeb mixed into the sensations of her last hours with Atetegeb, the disorientation of sleeplessness, the joy of intimacy, of climbing into bed at night and finding the warm, small body waiting for her.

"Live," breathed the mother into her ear as Atetegeb flitted in and out of consciousness.

Haregewoin collected the random sticks and thorns of her daughter's limp body to her, gathered the bedspread around her to swaddle her, and rocked her gently, weeping a small lullaby. It was like trying to keep an ember lit on a windy mountaintop, all the forces of nature arrayed against her. "Atetegeb," she whispered. But the joints came unhinged, the strings of the muscles went slack, and the tiny flame of life was blown out.

It was April 1998.

Ashiber showed up.

"I will bury my wife," he offered.

"Take her," wept Haregewoin.

Her grief for Worku was a normal emotion compared to this.

Haregewoin staggered through the rooms of the small house wild-eyed, uncombed, unzipped, with a terrible face. At the burial she shrieked and clawed her cheeks. Suzie, having flown home, drove Haregewoin to the little house and tried to put her to bed, but her mother was insane for several days. The mother's tears hardened into a glaze; she stared uncomprehendingly at anyone who spoke to her as if she were behind thick glass. She had crept for so long beside her daughter so close to death—it was stunning that Atetegeb had found the falling-off place, tumbled over it, and left her behind.

Suzie was also staggered by grief. "She was my sister, my closest friend," said Suzie to visitors, bowing and shaking her head, allowing her hair to fall forward to screen her; she had nothing else to say to anyone except her mother.

Haregewoin sat staring out the window into the bushes. A crow—a butterfly—even a cricket possessed the secret recipe for life she couldn't concoct for her daughter. She could barely squash an ant now, knowing that its tiny machinery was something the most brilliant scientists could not build, nor the greatest doctors restore. She was exhausted from having tried to preserve for her daughter what even a worm took for granted: the gift of inching along, alive.

It hurt most of all to see how blessed were all other mothers. They kept their daughters in life, while to her eternal shame she had failed hers at the only thing that mattered.

Old friends, officemates, neighbors, and families of Worku's students wafted in carrying smoky stews smelling of *berbere* (red pepper), green peppers, and onions. "Haregewoin!" they cried, kissing her on both cheeks, willing her to look them in the eye, to eat their food, to say what her plans were.

"But my daughter," she whimpered, too ashamed to meet their eyes.

12

S HE BEGAN THE winter of her life. Her characteristic smile
had fallen and could not be lifted. Her eyes sagged with tears
and her cocky shoulders rolled forward. Her body shriveled and
did not fit into her pantsuits. She wore only black anyway, a cotton,
calf-length skirt with an elastic waist and a pullover tunic of T-shirt
material, belted over her slack belly.

Her money was nearly depleted—she'd thrown it onto the bonfire
of Atetegeb's illness. She needed to find a job, but she couldn't think of
it yet. Meanwhile Ashiber vetoed the shaping of a life around her
grandson. Atetegeb was a "chapter" of his life that he was "putting
behind him." He severed his connection to the family of Atetegeb
Worku. He turned instead, for help, to his sister who lived in
Germany. He visited her often. In time, she returned to Addis to
help him raise his son. The child grew up believing that his aunt was
his mother.

Haregewoin encouraged Suzie to return to her life in Cairo, where
she had friends and interests to distract her; but Haregewoin felt
incapable of doing the same. After Suzie left, she became her mother's
greatest prop—emotionally and financially.

Haregewoin collected the sickroom detritus into cardboard boxes for
the dump. She bagged up Atetegeb's nightgown and sheets. She opened
the windows, so that the empty bedroom took part in the bright
mountain seasons; the single bed and mattress and the wooden bedside
table grew warm in the sun like the fig tree branches tangling in the
yard, lacking only the starlings and green pigeons.

The emptiness and cleanliness of the little house strangled her. She couldn't eat in such solitude. She could chew but not swallow. She carried her plate across the courtyard and yanked open the metal door a crack. She ate standing up, looking down the road. The air was smudged by wood smoke and truck exhaust; down the lane, someone was grilling meat and onions.

She got in bed when the sun set and simply lay there. One night she thought, *What became of all the books from Atetegeb's childhood?* She sat up, then fell back, thinking, *No, I don't want to read!* Novels were full of feeling, she remembered, and she had too much feeling in her life already. She wanted nonfeeling, the absence of feeling. At sunrise, she got up, giving up on the hope of sleep; she showered behind a bamboo divider under a cold trickle of water from the outdoor nozzle. She wrapped herself in black, pulled on socks and sandals, avoided a glance in the mirror, and drove to the cemetery. She spent the day seated on a granite bench near Atetegeb's grave. "Mother's here, sweetheart," she said to the mound. When she curled forward and cried, it was out of pity for Atetegeb, cut off from her baby and her mother and her sister. When she talked to herself, it was also half to Atetegeb: running out the door without her purse, she'd hurry back, clucking her tongue and scolding, "If Mother can just get organized, she'll be on her way!"

Probably she snoozed in the long afternoons, slumping forward. The big-headed bougainvilleas drooped, too; only the razzmatazz of the cicadas and crickets never faded. When she jerked awake, she saw that the gold hillside light had thinned into silver stripes on the branches and leaves. At dusk, sighing, her knees creaking, she rose and shuffled back to her car. She drove slowly, for no one waited for her in the cold house.

Often, on the way home, she pulled into a church to pray. There were many churches and mosques in Addis Ababa, even a Jewish prayer compound; though she was Orthodox, she no longer cared which Christian denomination she visited. (Ethiopia is one of the oldest Christian countries, having converted to Christianity in the fourth century. Slightly less than half the population is Christian, most of those Ethiopian Orthodox; while more than half is Muslim. Islam reached Ethiopia during the lifetime of the prophet Muhammad. Some of his disciples found refuge in Axum; the Prophet later commanded his followers, "Leave the Abyssinians in peace." In southern and western regions live practitioners of indigenous religions; in the northern highlands, clustered around Gondar, are the followers of an ancient and unique form of Judaism.)

All churches lead to God, Haregewoin thought. Without realizing it, she began to impress other regular churchgoers and clergy as a devout woman.

If strangers asked, she told them, "My daughter has died in childbirth."

In this way, a year passed.

Each day she made a circle from mattress to stone bench, from stone bench to church pew, from church pew to kitchen chair, and from kitchen chair to mattress. Even such minor circumnavigation wearied her. Her own maintenance cost too much money and effort. She started sleeping in her clothes to save on the energy required to remove them at night and put them back on in the morning. Food so little interested her that she mashed it nearly down her throat, bypassing taste.

Worst were the days when reason told her—from the moment she opened her eyes in the morning—that Atetegeb no longer existed in any realm, and that none of her actions ferried her any closer to her daughter. On such a day, she left her car at home and tried to lose herself in the packed city. She pulled the black shawl half over her face, bowed her head, and joined the multitudes trudging along the dirt shoulders of the city streets. She was borne along by the hordes of people, her head bowed so low that sometimes she nearly missed the uphill turnoff to the cemetery. Old women draped in black pedaled up and down this nearly vertical short road: old crucifix-wearing widows of a familiar type, known in Greece, in Italy, in Ireland, in Ukraine. She was one of them now. Her back would grow humped like theirs; her teeth would yellow and blacken; strange incantations would enter her speech. This was the career open to her now.

Occasionally she ran into an old friend on the street. She shook her head, trying to ward off the approach. "My dear!" a lipsticked woman in a pantsuit would begin, but Haregewoin would put up her hand.

"You must join us at least for coffee. Please!"

"I'm sorry, no, I can't."

She didn't want the solace and the distractions offered by her old friends, for grief was the last tether between her and Atetegeb.

If people persisted in asking, she told them humbly, "My daughter was very near to me. I liked her very much."

13

THE SHAGGY HILLSIDE cemetery was dotted with round huts. Each was like a tiny church, with a wooden cross attached to the peak of a grass-covered roof. In the huts lived squatters who'd fallen out of the world. The Ethiopian Church permitted seekers and beggars to enter monklike seclusion in cemeteries. Some were wild holy men, bearded, with manes of matted hair and leathery bare feet. Maybe they were seers, maybe they were just lunatics. Others were solitary men or women in deep mourning or in the grip of terrible repentance. They prayed, rocked, knelt, wept, and then slept on the cold mud floors. They ate no meat. Some subsisted on water and on figs from the trees in the churchyard. Others accepted handouts from church volunteers. Once a day, a priest descended to sprinkle them with holy water.

Haregewoin knew her true place was here, among the mourners, the penitents, and the dead. It was October 1999, eighteen months after Atetegeb's death, and she still felt unable to perform the words and gestures of normal human commerce.

Everything everywhere is ruined for me, she thought. *I am* mena (useless, without value).

She prepared to present herself to the Orthodox priest and ask to be taken into seclusion. She would request a hut near Atetegeb. She would store or give away her last possessions; she would give up the house.

I must tell a few people that I am taking leave from the world, she thought.

She would wait until the last minute to write to Suzie, when the opportunity for debate had passed. There was no neighbor to tell, nor any old friend she could face. She had no energy for their protests or helpful suggestions. But she would make the round of churches one last time to tell the benevolent clergy and laypeople her plans.

She ran into an obstacle at her favorite Catholic church. The director of MMM, the Catholic charity, didn't want to let her go.

"Oh, *Waizero* [Mrs.] Haregewoin, I am very sorry to hear that."

"No, it is for the best," she said, surprised by his reaction.

"But, do you know, we were just talking about you this morning?"

"About me? What have I done?"

"Well, the priest suggested you might do us a favor."

"That *I* might . . . but you know I'm not Catholic."

The round-faced, smooth-headed man chuckled. "That doesn't concern us!"

"What could I do for the priest?"

"You know our organization, MMM, helps poor families in the neighborhood?"

"Yes?"

"*Waizero* Haregewoin, we are simply overwhelmed with children, with orphans."

It was true, Haregewoin thought; children were everywhere, filthy and barefoot, shyly begging, scattering at the approach of police. They darted across thoroughfares, narrowly avoiding getting hit by vans and taxis. School-age children carried toddlers in their arms or tied upon their backs; toddlers dragged one-year-olds. Sometimes she opened the door of her compound in the morning and surprised sleeping clutches of children, nesting in the bushes.

"Why do you tell me this?"

"*Waizero* Haregewoin, we have an urgent case. The priest wondered if you would help us. He knows you are a devout woman."

"What is this case?"

"Her name is Genet [hard G: gen-net]. She is fifteen. Her parents have died. She has been living on the streets; she sleeps in people's doorways. No one will let her in because she has become a little bit wild.

"She was delivered to us for the first time," he said to Haregewoin, lowering his voice, "after she was raped. We are feeding her, but she has no place to sleep. *Waizero* Haregewoin, is it possible you could house this girl?"

Now my friends will really think I'm crazy, Haregewoin thought. *Let me think what I must do.*

I could go into seclusion at the cemetery; there I will sit and I will pray. Maybe it is better not to go into seclusion but to help somebody. Atetegeb always said, "Mother, you like children so much!" "Mother, if you had not had children, you would have gone crazy." One time she said, "Mother, you should run a kindergarten!" It is true I like children very much. If this is what God wishes for me, I will do it.

She bowed her head.

The man misunderstood her silence. "*Waizero* Haregewoin, before you say no, maybe you could meet this girl. I will bring her here. Then you can decide if it would be possible for you to help her.

"Of course, perhaps you would like her to be tested," he rushed to add. "We do not know if she is positive or negative—you know, she has lived on the streets, she has supported herself . . ."

"Yes."

"Yes, you will meet her?"

"Yes. I will meet her. And I will help her. And I know what all this means—'positive' and 'negative.'

"I will come tomorrow to meet her, and if she wishes, she may come home with me."

The man grabbed both Haregewoin's hands with both of his and bowed deeply, nearly touching his forehead to the cross-stitch of their hands.

14

A T HOME, SHE opened the door to Atetegeb's room.
The open window had allowed the trees and bushes in the
yard to toss their dry chaff onto the windowsill and floor.
Haregewoin swept and dusted, then made up the bed. That night, for
the first time since Atetegeb's death, she picked up the telephone and
called a few old friends. They were thrilled to hear from her. Their
cascade of invitations extended until the moment she revealed her new
plan: to take in this girl from the streets.

"*What?* Haregewoin, have you lost your mind? I thought you'd want
to go back to work," said one. "I thought maybe you'd travel a bit—it
would be so good for you," said another. "Won't you be returning to
Cairo?" asked a third. "Haregewoin, you do not have to do this," said a
fourth, speaking most emphatically. They were the collective voices of
the still-secure middle class, women focused on keeping themselves
well above the waterline of the disaster seeping into the country.

"This girl is no good," they all said.

"Well, let me see," she told them. "If she is no good, I will let her
go."

Genet was short and thick-boned, scarcely taller than Haregewoin. Her
young skin and broad nose were light and freckled; she had a high,
wide forehead and almost invisible eyebrows. Her light brown eyes had
shards of gray; the unusual color glittered like misgiving. Her face was
downcast, her manner disconsolate. She wore a man's big yellow T-
shirt, big khaki trousers, rubber flip-flops, and, incongruously, a little
girl's blue-jean vest with lace trim squeezed over her strong shoulders.

Her brown hair was fuzzy and haphazardly yanked back. Upon being introduced, she fell to the ground and kissed Haregewoin's shoes.

As a fifteen-year-old, orphaned Ethiopian girl, Genet was at risk for HIV disease on every front. Girls in Ethiopia received less education and had fewer job prospects than boys, and they had no property or inheritance rights. An orphaned girl lost the protection of her father; if she had lost her parents to AIDS, she might find herself turned out from her house, school, and village, as well. "Orphaned girls are at the absolute margins," said a UNICEF spokesman. "They are the very bottom of the barrel. They are much more likely to engage in risky behavior just to survive." Steep gender inequality across Africa and Asia empowered men to summon, to deceive, to compel, to purchase sex from, to rape, to marry young, to marry multiple, and to cheat on girls and women. A survey by French epidemiologists of young women in cities in Kenya and Zambia showed 6 percent of women were infected with HIV by age fifteen, 13 percent by sixteen, 20 percent by seventeen, 24 percent by eighteen, 30 percent by nineteen, and 40 percent by twenty.

Haregewoin helped her up. "It's all right, it's all right," she murmured. "Do you think you would like to stay with me for a while?"

"Yes, please, *waizero*," said the girl, looking down.

"You are being given a wonderful opportunity, Genet," the man from the Catholic charity told her. "You must be a good girl. You must respect *Waizero* Haregewoin, you must help her."

The girl's eyes sliced across Haregewoin's face just once, in jaded skepticism.

Genet was a mix of fervor and paralysis. One moment she bounded about like a puppy; the next, she was silent and afraid. Up close, Haregewoin saw that her face was dotted not just with freckles but with small, pale skinny scars; her thick hands and strong arms were flecked with pale scars, too—perhaps from a cook-fire? Many country children got burned by toddling close to open flames. She balked at the doorstep of Haregewoin's house, unable to enter. Noting the girl's fear, Haregewoin rummaged through her purse, juggled the grocery sack, handed the groceries to Genet, made harmless bustling noises. "Help me, dear," she said, pretending she couldn't manage to both hold her purse and open the door.

"Who else lives here?"

"I'm all alone here."

"You have this whole house?"

"I have two daughters, but they . . . they don't live here now. Here, you may use this bedroom."

Genet entered Atetegeb's room slowly, sliding her feet forward. The girl was afraid even to touch the bed, afraid to presume. "You'll sleep there," said Haregewoin crisply.

Genet owned nothing.

Haregewoin found a floor-length, pullover cotton dress that had belonged to one of her girls. She shooed Genet toward the outdoor shower stall, saw the bewilderment, put a bar of soap in the girl's hands, pointed out the bottle of shampoo on the cement floor, then reached in and turned the nozzle herself. Later Haregewoin sat on a kitchen chair with the clean-smelling girl sitting cross-legged and barefoot on the floor in front of her. She chopped at the hair with a hairbrush. She kneaded conditioner into it, and little by little, like carding wool, she separated out tufts, rolled them between her fingers, and braided them into tidy cornrows. When she was finished, Genet bolted away, but glanced back once over her shoulder at Haregewoin.

"Last thing," said Haregewoin, luring her back and pumping a drop of moisturizing lotion onto Genet's palm.

A clean-faced freckled girl sat humbly over her plate of food. Haregewoin reminded her to wait for the blessing, then nodded that they could begin. Genet dropped her face down into the plate and began shoveling and gobbling and swallowing so fast and noisily that Haregewoin looked up in shock. Genet devoured everything in sight; she choked down the *injera, dinich wat* (potato stew), *doro wat* (peppery chicken stew), and an orange-hued, stew-soaked hard-boiled egg, and another egg, then most of a sliced mango. She pushed back from the table, belched, laughed, jumped up, cleared the table, washed the few dishes, and skipped off to her room.

Haregewoin slowly registered what she herself had done: she'd compelled the teenager to grocery shop, move in, shower, have her hair done, and even bow her head in prayer—and all the while Genet was hungry.

She would never make that mistake again. In case she ever hosted such a person in the future, she would know: when in doubt, feed first.

Genet lunged at every chance to leave the compound with Haregewoin in those first few weeks and exulted in being let loose in a food market or pharmacy or bakery, practically sprawling down the aisle in her zeal. She didn't ask for anything, but squinted her light eyes at an item—a plastic hairbrush, a pair of cotton sneakers, a watch—and sometimes at something ludicrous, such as a camera or a pair of binoculars, and stood as if hypnotized, mouth open, feet apart, dramatizing her desire so that Haregewoin would notice and buy her the gift. Haregewoin found the behavior grating.

When Haregewoin saw Genet's hand dart out to pocket a lipstick, she grabbed the girl by the shoulder and steered her out the door. Genet sulked all the way to the car, smacking the flat of her feet down hard, her forehead in knots. When she stormed through the house and slammed the door of Atetegeb's bedroom behind her, Haregewoin made a pot of tea and sat at the kitchen table, chuckling into the steamy cup. She was not rattled by Genet's shows of temper; *I had* two *teenage girls once,* she thought.

On Sundays, Haregewoin ordered the girl to get up, get dressed, and come to church. For the first few weeks, while the teenager was still in an endearing mode, she went unprotestingly. Suddenly she began to balk at following orders, refused to make conversation in the car, and silently fumed in the wooden pew of the Catholic cathedral. (Since the Catholic charity MMM had rescued Genet, it seemed proper to Haregewoin that they worship together there.) Genet defiantly raised her chin when other worshippers bowed their heads in prayer. Haregewoin rolled her eyes. Perhaps, in time, affection would grow between them.

Then one Sunday morning Genet hopped out of bed and got dressed willingly. She slicked back her hair and applied some color to her cheeks and lips (where had Genet obtained makeup?). She seemed actually to pray during the service, clasping her stubby, freckled hands in prayer. When she asked to be excused to wait for Haregewoin in the church courtyard, it seemed innocent, but she had reasons.

MMM helped poor families all over the district, so beggars and orphans tended to gather in the courtyard, hoping for a bit of food or a birr from a parishioner. A week earlier on the church steps, Genet had spotted her old comrades, emancipated orphan girls as desperate as she had been two months ago. They were the lowest rung of the sex trade: without even the permission of beer or wine shop owners to wait on customers, they were simply "street girls." Now, when Genet tap-danced down the church steps, her friends squealed and ran to her. She floated like a celebrity among them: even the touch of lip gloss wowed them; that she wore slip-on shoes rather than flip-flops made her a fashion queen. When she flounced away, summoned by Haregewoin, and got into the passenger seat of the car, she waved good-bye like any teenager in the world taking her leave of girlfriends at the mall, riding home with her mom.

"Come back to us," the girls urged on a subsequent Sunday. "Or do you like living with *her*?"

"It's okay," said Genet, distributing bread rolls she'd brought for them.

"Well, just come see us."

"I really can't. She doesn't let me go out at night."

"You mean you're her *prisoner*?" gasped the girls.

They clucked their tongues in pity. Suddenly their envy and admiration turned to superiority. It was so unfair! She couldn't bear it. Genet—so beat-up, humble, and defeated six months earlier—now seemed to recall selectively her lost freedom. Forgetting occasional rough treatment, forgetting the attack by one scofflaw that had landed her at MMM in the first place, ignorant that she risked her life every time she engaged in unprotected sex, she began to moon about how it felt to have money. Why shouldn't she have the best of both worlds— Haregewoin's roof, food, and bed, *and* the fifty cents a week a few trysts would bring? She would sneak out at night and she'd be back before dawn, with the old lady none the wiser. Then the girls wouldn't call her "prisoner."

The first problem was that wily Haregewoin locked the compound door at night and slept with the key. Genet made a couple of attempts to scale the corrugated tin wall, but scraped her knees when the ivy she clung to came loose. Nor could she sling herself up into the lowest branches of the eucalyptus tree in order to drop over the wall, as she could have done as a child; she scraped her thighs trying. So she offered to run errands in the evening, hoping to get outside the walls. "Shall I go buy us some tea for the morning?" she'd ask like a good daughter.

"No, dear, I have tea."

"I'd love a glass of milk! Do we have any milk? I don't think so."

"We have milk. Go to bed, Genet."

"We need rice!"

"Go to bed, Genet."

"I'm dying for a cigarette!" she blurted one night. But that may have been a mistake, for it provoked a long over-the-top-of-the-reading-glasses gaze from Haregewoin, which was at once appraising and troubled.

15

SIX WEEKS AFTER Genet's arrival, the director of the Catholic charity phoned Haregewoin again. "There is another child," he said.

Haregewoin didn't understand. ". . . Another child?"

"Can you take in a boy?"

"Oh!"

"He's also an orphan. He's about Genet's age."

"Uh-oh."

"He's got no one . . . He's been sleeping on the sidewalk."

She had to think for a minute. She slept in one bedroom, Genet in the other—the one that had been the sickroom. There was an outbuilding with a cement floor and no furniture; better to move Genet into her own bedroom and give the boy Atetegeb's room. Genet wouldn't be happy to share Haregewoin's bed, but it could be done.

"Bring him over."

Abel was bone-thin, tall, and slope-shouldered, and his first unshaved mustache lay in a tuft on his upper lip. He came from the countryside, from Harar. No way was he fifteen, thought Haregewoin; he was seventeen or eighteen. His shirt was too short for his arms and his pants stopped above his ankles. He gruffly said hello to Haregewoin and Genet in a basso profundo voice so low it made them both laugh; he shook their hands limply; his upper lip recoiled briefly to show the ridges of protruding upper teeth—perhaps that was a smile; then he slouched into Atetegeb's bedroom, fell facedown on the bed with his long feet dangling off, and slept for two days. One morning Haregewoin smelled smoke coming from under the door, pushed it open, and beheld Abel finally awake, reclining on his pillow, one arm behind his head, enjoying a cigarette. He tapped the ashes onto the floor.

"*No, no, no*, this will *not* happen," she barked, rushing across the room. She shook him, the sheets, the cigarette, the ashes, all out of bed at the same time. "Put that out. Clean yourself up. This room *stinks*." She yanked up the window and fanned the air with her hand, in the useless and immortal way mothers have annoyed sons for generations. She practically hurled him by his belt loops across the courtyard toward the shower stall. "Clean yourself up. Then we'll talk." Genet looked up in amazement as Abel flew through the living room.

Haregewoin served Abel breakfast. He ate, but not ravenously. His movements were slow.

"Do you go to school?"

"No, I finished."

"What grade?"

"Third."

"Do you work?"

He shrugged.

"What are you planning to do?"

He shrugged.

"Well, you need to go to work." She told him the address of a small nearby brickworks factory. She packed him a lunch. "Go ask them to put you to work. The owner is a friend of mine."

With long, angular strides as if he walked on stilts, he left the house. He came back late at night, swooning and red-eyed. He was high on something.

"Did you get a job?"

He shook his head.

"Did you ask them for a job?"

"Who?" he asked in annoyance.

"At the brickworks."

"Oh. I couldn't find it." He headed for his room.

"Abel!" she snapped. He stopped in his tracks, but didn't turn around.

"What have you been smoking?"

"Nothing."

"I'm not stupid, Abel. You've been smoking *tumbaco*. Is that what you've been doing all day? I smell it on you."

"No," he said, and entered his room and closed his door. *Tumbaco* was a form of hashish; it thrived in Abel's native region of Harar and was sold on the black market all over Addis Ababa.

She shook him awake late the next morning, after he'd been asleep for sixteen hours. "Aren't you hungry?"

"No, *waizero*," he said rather nicely. He got up, got dressed, and headed for the door.

"Eat something, Abel!" she called, feeling remorseful they'd gotten off to such an unfriendly start.

"I'm okay," he called back. "Not hungry."

The drug canceled his hunger, she realized. Many poor people smoked it for that reason; it was cheaper than food.

He stayed out that night and the next. When he returned two days later and wobbled down the hall to his room, she knew she couldn't let him out of her sight.

"Stop!" she commanded the next day when he began to slide out the door. He was a beanpole. His head was bony and angular and his front teeth poked forward earnestly. She could see the nice young man he was born to be, but he was headed for an early grave. If powerlessness made vulnerable the girls of Ethiopia, hopelessness made vulnerable the boys.

"You can't go out today," Haregewoin told Abel.

"What does that mean?"

"That means if you're going to live with me, you're going to stay in the compound today."

"And do what?"

"Wash the car." She handed him a bucket. He shrugged and ambled out to the courtyard. Soon she heard voices and laughter and realized

Genet was out there with him. So what was funny? Haregewoin looked out the window and saw Genet standing with her arms crossed over her chest, giggling. And Abel? He was kneeling beside the car. He had his face pressed up against it. Oh, Lord, he was inhaling fumes from the gas tank.

"Abel!" she screamed. Even on his knees, he was tall; he swayed backward with a stupid smile while Genet chuckled at his antics, finding his insurrection delicious.

"Abel, what will I do with you? Are you addicted to this stuff?"

He shrugged dreamily.

16

"WE HAVE TWO more children," said the Catholic charity director when another six weeks had passed. He spoke quickly into the phone, as if fearing Haregewoin would hang up at the sound of his voice.

"Oh, heavens no! I wouldn't survive more teenagers," cried Haregewoin. "You'd better call someone else."

"*Waizero* Haregewoin!" he said, hurt. "I *have* no one else to call."

She was taken aback and could not think what to reply.

"These are two little girls. They're each about six years old."

"Two? *Six?* What happened to their families?"

After a pause, the man murmured in a low voice, "*Aminmina.*"

Soon she would learn not to ask.

"Haregewoin, don't do this thing," pleaded her friends when Haregewoin phoned to tell them she was getting two little girls. It was one thing to help rehabilitate teenagers, the friends felt; that was a good outlet for her, a continuation, in a way, of her late husband's having been a high school teacher and principal. But to bring orphans of AIDS into her home was reckless and dangerous. It was of another order of risk.

In the year 2000 in Ethiopia, it looked like the most dangerous thing a person could do.

Nineteen years earlier, in the spring of 1981, eight gay men in New York City had turned up in doctors' offices with bizarrely aggressive forms of Kaposi's sarcoma (KS)—a cancer usually found, in a benign form, in the elderly. On June 5, 1981, the U.S. Centers for Disease

Control (CDC) reported that five young men, all active homosexuals, had been treated for biopsy-confirmed PCP in Los Angeles hospitals; that two of the patients had died; and that all five had cytomegalovirus (CMV) infection and candidal mucosal infection. The report marked the dawn of recognition of AIDS in America.

Meanwhile, also in Los Angeles, five gay men presented with a rare lung infection, Pneumocystis carinii pneumonia (PCP).

On July 4, 1981, CDC reported that twenty-six cases of KS had been diagnosed in the previous thirty months, all in gay males.

Researchers at the National Cancer Institute in Maryland, with a brand-new device called the Fluorescent Activated Cell Sorter, tested the blood of fifteen apparently healthy gay men from the Washington area. The results showed half the men to have such severe abnormalities in their immune systems that the researchers concluded the brand-new machine had malfunctioned.

The first cases of AIDS in Haiti were recognized in 1978 and 1979, coinciding with the earliest reports of AIDS in the United States.

Researchers in Sweden would determine that HIV was introduced into the gay male population of Stockholm between 1979 and 1980.

The bewildering nexus of symptoms gained several appellations in medical and mainstream media: *gay cancer, gay plague,* and *gay-related immune deficiency* (GRID).

Those who fell ill were victimized by an onslaught of bizarre and painful symptoms—which would come to be known as the opportunistic infections of AIDS (OIA)—and by opportunistic moralizing, as well. A virus passed from person to person through the most intimate contact—a fatal sexually transmitted disease—seemed to some to carry the weight of dark meaning and penalty within it.

"AIDS is God's punishment," the Reverend Jerry Falwell preached. "We do reap it in our flesh when we violate the laws of God."

"The poor homosexuals," clucked Patrick Buchanan, aide to President Ronald Reagan. "They have declared war upon Nature, and now Nature is exacting awful retribution."

Ronald Goodwin, director of the powerful Moral Majority, said, "What I see is a commitment to spend our tax dollars on research to allow these diseased homosexuals to go back to their perverted practices without any standards of accountability."

Gay men were chased from shops and restaurants in California by people hurling epithets like "Disease leper!"

But then a few hemophiliacs presented with PCP and KS, and a few drug addicts, and a few Haitians.

So a new name was coined: *acquired immune deficiency syndrome*— because the condition was acquired rather than inherited; because it destroyed the immune system; and because it was a syndrome, with a number of manifestations, rather than a single disease.

In 1982, CDC linked the disease to blood. The published risk factors were male homosexuality, intravenous drug abuse, Haitian origin, hemophilia.

Because of the fringe populations implicated in the epidemic, the Republican administration of the United States stood back. From June 1981 to May 1982, less than $1 million was allocated with which to investigate the first two thousand cases of AIDS, including a thousand deaths. In the same year, $9 million was spent on Legionnaires' disease, a type of pneumonia that had struck an American Legion convention in Philadelphia in 1976. It had killed fifty.

Then, in December 1982 in the United States, a twenty-month-old child, who'd received multiple blood transfusions, died of AIDS-related infections. Dr. Harold Jaffe of CDC called the toddler's death a turning point. "Up until then it was entirely a gay epidemic and it was easy for the average person to say, 'So what?'"

January 1983 brought reports of AIDS in non-Haitian, non-drug-using, non-blood-transfused women. Could women catch it through heterosexual sex?

Two different types of HIV epidemics seemed to emerge in Europe. In France and Belgium, infections occurred in immigrants from Central Africa. In England, West Germany, and Denmark, gay men presented with the symptoms, especially those who reported sexual contact with American men.

South Africa's first AIDS patients were diagnosed in 1982, and the epidemic surfaced in Uganda, along the shores of Lake Victoria. Doctors and public health researchers in Zambia and Zaire noted the emergence of a new, aggressive form of Kaposi's sarcoma in patients with no history of blood transfusion, homosexuality, or intravenous drug abuse, suggesting a "strong indication of heterosexual transmission." One study concluded, "African patients with KS [Kaposi's sarcoma] seem to have an immunological and virological profile similar to that seen in American patients with AIDS."

Nevertheless, world attention was captured by AIDS as a disease of gay white men. It was widely assumed that the disease originated in America.

In November 1983, the World Health Organization confirmed the presence of AIDS in the United States and Canada, Australia, fifteen European countries, seven Latin American countries, Haiti, and Zaire, and with two suspected cases in Japan.

Fear of AIDS and AIDS carriers grew rampant. Hemophiliacs were reported by the press to be "innocent victims" of AIDS, while gays and drug users were seen as having brought the disease upon themselves. Holiday-makers on the *Queen Elizabeth* evacuated upon learning an HIV-positive passenger was on board. Churchgoers feared sipping from a common Communion cup.

On April 23, 1984, U.S. Health and Human Services secretary Margaret Heckler announced at a press conference that an American scientist, Dr. Robert Gallo of the National Cancer Institute, had discovered the cause of AIDS: a retrovirus he named HTLV-III (human T-cell lymphotropic virus, type 3). The same virus had been isolated the year before by Luc Montagnier of the Pasteur Institute in Paris, who called it LAV (lymphadenopathy-associated virus). Jay Levy at the University of California/San Francisco and a group of CDC researchers were zeroing in on the same virus.

In March 1985, it was established that LAV and HTLV-III were the same. Drs. Gallo and Montagnier vied bitterly for the claim to be the sole discoverer of the virus, with exclusive patent rights and naming rights, until their governments mediated and gave equal credit to both. The International Committee on the Taxonomy of Viruses ruled that the virus should be known as human immunodeficiency virus, HIV. In December 1985, the Pasteur Institute filed a lawsuit against the National Cancer Institute to claim a share of the royalties from the NCI's patented AIDS test.

In 1985 in the United States, thirteen-year-old Ryan White, an "innocent victim," a hemophiliac, was barred from school after testing positive for the virus. That year, the first report appeared of a case of mother-to-child transmission through breast milk. The first case of AIDS in China was confirmed, meaning the epidemic had reached every region of the world. American movie idol Rock Hudson revealed that he had spent his life as a closeted gay man and that he had AIDS. He died on October 2.

By the end of that year, twenty thousand cases had been reported worldwide, of which nearly sixteen thousand were in the United States.

CDC quietly removed Haitians from the list of AIDS risk groups.

Although AIDS appeared in the medical literature and in the popular media in 1981, President Ronald Reagan did not officially address it until October 1987, by which time in the United States 59,572 AIDS cases had been reported and 27,909 people had died.

President Reagan did, at least once, enjoy a joke about AIDS. In 1986 in the New York harbor, at the centennial rededication of the Statue of Liberty, a distinguished crowd included the Reagans and French president François Mitterrand and his wife. Bob Hope was onstage. "I just heard that the Statue of Liberty has AIDS," said Hope, "but she doesn't know if she got it from the mouth of the Hudson or from the Staten Island ferry." Television footage shows that, while the Mitterrands appeared shocked, the Reagans laughed.

Paul Monette, a National Book Award–winning nonfiction writer, wrote, "It was often remarked acidly in West Hollywood that if AIDS had struck Boy Scouts first rather than gay men—or St. Louis rather than Kinshasa—it would have been covered like nuclear war."

As Western public health scientists looked closer at "slim disease," reported in Uganda since 1982, the similarities to AIDS seemed more striking than the differences. Researchers reported, "[Evidence] suggests that slim disease cannot be distinguished from AIDS and ARC [AIDS related complex] by extreme weight loss and diarrhea. Thus slim disease may not be a new syndrome but simply identical with AIDS as seen in Africa."

Could AIDS be older and far more entrenched than anyone had imagined? Rather than a new syndrome cropping up among Western homosexuals and drug abusers, its origin might be African. Dr. Halfdan Mahler, director of the World Health Organization, warned in 1985 that it was not impossible that ten million people were already infected.

As the point of origin and locus of victims seemed to shift from New York and Paris to Uganda and the Democratic Republic of the Congo, AIDS fell further from popular interest. That *most* AIDS patients were not gay but *African* completely failed to capture the hearts of the Western public or the resources of the rich. The disease edged no higher on the agenda of any government, including—with few exceptions—African governments.

(The exception was Uganda. Soon after the 1986 coup that placed him in office, former guerrilla leader Yoweri Museveni sent sixty of his top officers to Cuba for training. "Several months later," reports the *New Republic*, "Fidel Castro approached Museveni at a conference in Zimbabwe with a staggering bit of news: medical exams in Cuba had revealed that 18 of the 60 officers were HIV-positive. 'Brother,' Castro told Museveni, according to the version of the story the Ugandan leader has shared with many visitors, 'you have a problem.'"

The threat to his army was a powerful wake-up call for President Museveni. He personally mobilized the country against AIDS in a program nicknamed ABC for "Abstain, Be Faithful, or Wear a

Condom," but most famous for its slogan of marital fidelity—
plastered on billboards all over the country—"Zero Grazing.")

HIV/AIDS rampaged across Africa through heterosexual (penile-
vaginal) more than homosexual activity, through mother-to-child
transmission, and through unsterile medical procedures—inoculations,
blood tests, labor and delivery, and transfusions.

But the popular consensus remained the same as in the early years in
America: it must be a disease of sinners (the religious view) or of the
oversexed (the secular view) or of promiscuous sinners (a combination
view).

By 1999, UNAIDS estimated that 33 million people around the
world were living with HIV/AIDS and that 16.3 million people
worldwide had died of the disease. The *Independent* (London) reported,
"At least 30 million Africans are expected to die from AIDS in the
next twenty years."

"It exploded at the end of the 1990s," Stephen Lewis told me. He is
the UN secretary-general's special envoy for HIV/AIDS in Africa,
former Canadian ambassador to the UN, and former deputy
executive director of UNICEF. He is irascible and probing and
impatient, the horn-rim bifocals sliding down the nose, the wiry salt-
and-pepper hair flying about as if in high wind or alarm. With his
wife, feminist thinker and columnist Michele Landsberg, he shares a
shady, book-lined, comfortable house in Toronto's Forest Hill
neighborhood, but he rarely touches down here. His father was
the late David Lewis, leader of the New Democratic Party of
Canada; his brother-in-law is the architect Daniel Liebskind; his
daughters, Ilana and Jenny, and his son, Avi, are all politically
engaged left-wing high achievers working in foundations, documentary film, and television; his daughter-in-law, Naomi Klein, is the
author of *No Logo*, a bible of the antiglobalization movement; and
there are two grandchildren. In short, there's plenty to stay home for;
you could cocoon in this house forever, sinking into these soft
couches, sliding handsome tomes in English, French, Swahili, or

Yiddish off the wooden shelves, drinking tea, rattling the news-papers. The people shucking off their icy galoshes on the mat and sliding in socks across the dark hardwood floors are inevitably the best people, the top people, and the most interesting, the ones who care about humanity and governance; they argue war and oil over dinner and head for the guest bedrooms at night carrying along arcane texts on trade and debt relief. African art is on the walls, African sculpture on the shelves.

Even if Lewis never left home, a certain steady light would beam from this address, an intelligence, a moral clarity. Beautifully crafted journal articles would originate here; his crisp voice—angry at the world, yet, at the same time, modestly self-deprecating—would be carried on public radio stations.

But he doesn't stay home and he has never stayed home. Lewis has gone on extended jaunts to Africa since the age of twenty-two.

"Immediately pre-independence and postindependence," he told me, "what a magically generous and human environment it was. Ghana, Nigeria, Guinea-Bissau, and Kenya . . . such lively and musical worlds, such a hopeful time. How decent and generous the people were. It's all still true, but so often now impaired by hunger, poverty, disease, and despair."

UN special envoy Stephen Lewis is on the nonstop world tour. In loosened necktie, rolled-up shirtsleeves, and wrinkled khakis, squint-ing into the beastly sun of the treeless plains, sneezing into the gales of the rainy seasons, hunching in twin-engine prop airplanes guttering low across the Matobo Hills of Zimbabwe, he plays to packed houses in South Africa and Swaziland, in Botswana and Angola, in Sierra Leone and Rwanda. But the scheduled stops on Lewis's world tour are death wards, hospices, orphanages, and cemeteries. The crowds he greets are dying two and three to a cot. The children who line up on dirt yards and sing for him sometimes sob between breaths. (He's come too late for them; their parents are already dead.) The UN special envoy is losing constituents faster than any other official on earth.

"Everyone was dimly aware that this was a problem that would have to be faced," he said, "but *no* one understood the extent, *no* one appreciated the carnage that was coming, because the incubation period was so long. By 1999 when I left UNICEF, I had come to understand that this thing called AIDS was increasingly undermining everything we wanted to do in Africa—all the elements of UNICEF's mandate were being undermined by this virus. I should have been more responsive. I guess in a way I mirrored the delinquency of most of the Western world. We were engaged with child survival, child soldiers, child labor; we were dealing with land mines, with child sexual exploitation; I was worried about arsenic in the wells in Bangladesh and maternal mortality in India and the education of girls in Vietnam and the teenage guerrillas in Bogotá, but AIDS was . . . well, AIDS was quietly incubating all that time.

"Honest to God, outside Uganda—where Museveni realized that if he lost his army to AIDS, he'd lose the source of his power—nobody did a hell of a lot until about 2000. I wish I had been more prescient, and more ferocious."

Ethiopian patients were first diagnosed with HIV in 1984; the first full-blown AIDS case was reported in 1986. ("Full-blown AIDS" means that, in addition to testing positive for HIV, a patient has seen his CD4 [T-cell count] fall from the normal adult range of 500 to 1,500 cells per cubic millimeter of blood to below 200 or has been afflicted by one or more of about two dozen "opportunistic infections of AIDS," which vary by region [PCP, KS, CMV, toxoplasmosis of the brain, pulmonary tuberculosis, etc.])

"I first saw the full horror of it in adult hospital wards in Ethiopia in 1999 and 2000," said Lewis, "and I became more and more personally frantic about what was happening and what was *not* happening. The hospital wards were filled with the rancid smells of feces and urine and rotting food and death. There were people lying on the concrete floors, on top of the beds, under the beds, everyone dying. I visited a fifth-grade class in Harare, Zimbabwe, and eight out ten kids were composing school essays about their parents' death. I suddenly understood that their lives were consumed by funerals, that everyone around them was dying."

In a speech on World AIDS Day, 2005, Lewis said, "I have the deep impression that if only we could galvanize the world, we'd subdue this pandemic. We need a superhuman effort from every corner of the international community. We're not getting it. At the present rate, we'll have a cumulative total of one hundred million deaths and infections by the year 2012. [And] we call ourselves an advanced civilization."

The news was slow to reach most Ethiopians (the majority—illiterate and without electricity—could not be informed by television, radio, posters, or brochures) that HIV/AIDS was transmitted only in five ways: engaging in unprotected sexual intercourse with an infected person, sharing needles or body-piercing equipment with an infected person, allowing infected fluids to get into a cut or sore on the body, receiving a transfusion of infected blood, or being born to or breast-fed by an infected mother. And people tended not to tell anyone they'd tested positive for HIV in their blood until they were in the grip of full-blown AIDS, so death by AIDS looked rapid: the time between announcement and death was short. Because AIDS had invisibly spread for many years, when it finally surfaced, it surfaced everywhere at once, as if easily spread by coughs, kisses, sneezes, used tissues, shared food dishes, toilet seats, swimming pools, rivers, wind, and mosquitoes.

In the absence of real information, the urban myths flourished. People said that if an HIV-positive man discarded a used condom on the ground, and grass grew from it, and a cow ate the grass, the cow's milk could kill you. People said that if you bought meat from an HIV-positive butcher, the virus could travel into your kitchen inside the raw meat. Customers avoided shopkeepers, barbers, and dressmakers suspected of having HIV. Most pervasive of all was the belief that AIDS was God's punishment for sinners, and that HIV/AIDS in children was the result of the sins of the parents. Some clergymen preached that only fasting and holy water could lift the evil decree.

AIDS widows, widowers, and orphans were rejected by their families and communities lest they spread contagion and the shadow of divine punishment. In Ethiopian societies traditionally devoted to sustaining widows and protecting orphans, the refusal and paralysis surrounding the AIDS survivors was strange and terrible.

Around the world there were AIDS-related attacks and "shame killings." In 1987, arsonists destroyed the Florida home of a family with three hemophiliac sons, all of whom had been infected with HIV through blood transfusions. On World AIDS Day, 1998, in South Africa, a thirty-six-year-old activist, Gugu Diamini, mother of one son, appeared on Zulu-language radio and television and revealed her HIV-positive status. She encouraged sufferers to come out of the closet and urged the citizenry to cease persecuting the sick. That night a mob of her neighbors kicked and beat her to death.

Shame and stigma were intense; people spoke in lowered voices and pseudonyms such as *gizeyaw zamamu beshita* (the disease of the times), *kesafi beshita* (the disease that kills) or, simply, *aminmina* (slim). The cause of a person's death was concealed. He died of lung disease, mourners said; she died of a cold. TB was mentioned, or diarrhea, or a nerve problem. In the West, obituaries famously reported, "He died after a long illness."

"HIV/AIDS" was almost never pronounced except by those who were HIV-positive. Magical thinking stopped the uninfected—or those who hoped they were uninfected—from saying it aloud, as if even the syllables could contaminate the tongue and lips. Only a person like Zewedu, whose magic had run out, felt listlessly free to call the disease by any name he liked.

By 2000, he was one among two million of his countrymen. Ethiopia had the world's third-largest HIV/AIDS-infected population, trailing only India and South Africa.

Of every eleven people in the world living with HIV/AIDS, one was Ethiopian.

✳   ✳   ✳

In the year 2000 in Ethiopia, the decision by a healthy, safe middle-class widow to open her home to children orphaned by AIDS looked—to the widow's closest friends and former colleagues—dangerous and foolish.

"Haregewoin, I cannot think why you are resolved to lower yourself in this way," said one old friend. "I try to understand, but I cannot."

"I'm afraid you will end up completely alienated," said an old friend of Worku's. "You could be shunned. You must be careful, please. This is not a matter to treat lightly."

"It is already decided," said Haregewoin.

"You could be evicted. You could lose the house," moaned Suzie on the phone from Cairo. "I worry about you."

"How can a child live without a mother?"

"I'm afraid that people will think *you* are positive," whispered the daughter.

"What can that matter to me?" cried Haregewoin. "Let them think what they want to think."

"Mother! What do your friends say?"

"They say . . ." Haregewoin had to think for a second how to phrase it. "They say that I have lost my mind."

"Surely it would have made more sense," the friends were saying to each other, "if Haregewoin had gone into seclusion."

17

S O, O N O N E S I D E, contagion, deformities, horror, secrecy, stigma, shame, killings, and panic. A new elite world class of disease experts. A new world underclass of untouchables. Another reason for Africa to founder. A human landslide.

And, on the other side, two little girls.

Within a few days of each other, Selamawit and Meskerem were dropped off at Haregewoin's house. The first to arrive—a round-faced, large-boned girl—had been distracted, by hunger, from the business of throwing herself into life and ferreting out everybody's gossip and news. For Selamawit's first year with Haregewoin, whether it was getting close to mealtime and what was on the menu were her chief concerns. With a full tummy, she was a jolly girl, fearless and honest, sociable and silly. Haregewoin marveled, she was another Suzie!

Selamawit had been shuffled about from place to place for a long time, but she held on to memories of her mother.

"I had happy times with her, especially at holidays," Selamawit told Haregewoin. "We had fun, danced, and ate popcorn. I took care of my mother when she got sick, such as feeding her and making coffee for her, while neighbors and relatives would not come close to her."

Having had her prospects ruined at a young age, with the death of her mother, Selamawit had bravely accepted whatever small kindnesses fell her way. Out of bits and pieces of transient attention, she had pieced together what felt like a supported life. If someone knit springy braids all over her head, she wore them; if not, she banged back her thick hair with a hairbrush. She felt full-hearted interest in other people, assumed others felt the same toward her, and met them more than halfway. At night, in her dreams, her late mother visited and reassured Selamawit that she no longer felt pain.

Later that same week, Haregewoin saw six-year-old Meskerem for the first time, alone and forlorn on the ripped leather seat of the Catholic charity van. Thick black eyebrows had been sketched as if in charcoal upon the classic oval Ethiopian face; huge round eyes midface were full of intelligence and melancholy. The girl was encased in filthy sacklike clothing, which she picked at with long, elegant fingers. "Come to me," Haregewoin said, opening her arms, and Meskerem stooped to exit the van and allowed herself to be hugged. So thin! Over Meskerem's back, Haregewoin raised her eyes questioningly.

"She was living alone with her mother when her mother died," said the MMM staff woman. "She moved to her father's house, but she was very unhappy. Her older half brother brought her to us."

It was early evening. Slender and tentative as a fawn, Meskerem tiptoed into the house and peered around, but then her grief drowned out her curiosity; her brown lips trembled and turned down at the corners; she threw her arms across her face and wailed. Genet, flipping through an old magazine in the front room, was bored by the display, as if she couldn't *believe* she was supposed to spend her evening listening to this.

Selamawit's first impulse was to pick up Meskerem and give her a grand welcoming hug; but the thinner, grief-stricken, same-age girl would have none of it and fought her way free. Meskerem was newly orphaned and was holding on to a tiny bit of hope that her mother, Yeshi, would recover and come find her. Everyone and everything else in the world—Haregewoin, Selamawit, Genet, the house, the car, the compound—screamed to her that they were not Yeshi and had never belonged to Yeshi. They didn't exist for her.

Haregewoin drew Meskerem into her own bedroom, dressed the child in a flannel nightgown, tucked her into her own bed, and brought her a hot cup of tea. Genet loudly sighed with restlessness every time Haregewoin hurried past on missions of mercy for Meskerem.

Selamawit bounced in and out of the room, excited to have been given a new friend. "What happened to her mother?" she asked loudly.

"What happened to her father?

"Why couldn't anyone else take care of her?

"Is she going to stay here forever?

"What's wrong with her?"

"Genet!" called Haregewoin in desperation, and the sullen older girl drew Selamawit away from the bedroom.

Finally Abel came home and the two teens made themselves something to eat in the kitchen, with plenty of laughter and cigarette smoke. Selamawit now annoyed *them*: "Are you boyfriend and girl-friend? . . . Are you going to get married? . . . Who's older, him or you?"

In the night, Meskerem woke up missing her mother. She began crying before she was even awake, a high nasal sound like a siren in the distance. Her anguish woke up Haregewoin and made the old lady cry, too. In the darkness she found and stroked the child's head. Meskerem's hair was a glossy and tangled mass like seaweed. Haregewoin pushed herself up against the wall and took thin Meskerem into her arms; she rocked her there in the bed, singing softly to her. She could smell on the child's breath the sweet grapes she'd eaten at dinner and the sugar she'd dumped into her tea. When Meskerem relaxed back into sleep, Haregewoin rolled her onto the pillow, but was left wide-awake. Carefully, so as not to wake Meskerem and Selamawit, and not to disturb Genet on the bedroll on the floor, she slipped off her bed.

She pulled her cotton shawl from a chair and wrapped it around her, then stepped out the front door. She breathed in the mountain air and closed her eyes. "Thank you," she said to the universe. Hadn't God, hadn't Atetegeb, sent her these children? Another Suzie, another Atetegeb? A replica of the daughter she had, a replica of the daughter she had lost?

Meskerem had entered straight into her heart of hearts, her holy of holies. Meskerem looked to her just like Atetegeb.

✵   ✵   ✵

Suddenly there were errands to run, pencils and notebooks to buy for school, and socks and sneakers and toothbrushes. Meskerem and Selamawit rode with her in the car.

"Call me *Amaye*," Haregewoin urged both little girls.

Selamawit complied immediately, with a huge smile.

But the request made Meskerem's eyes fill with tears. The word *amaye* belonged only to Yeshi; she would never speak that word again unless to her own poor mother.

My lungs are filling with air again, Haregewoin thought. She grew rotund again. She used a hair dye to restore a shiny blackness to her head, befitting a mother of young children. She visited the neighborhood school, introduced herself to teachers. She chatted with other mothers in the lane. She bought knickknacks, doilies, dolls, to make the little house cheerier. She started over.

Like any proud new mother, she invited her friends, "Come see my children!"

Nervously, fearful of catching AIDS, fearful of finding Haregewoin in too pathetic a state, the old friends and colleagues crept to the door of the compound and peeked in. Whatever grim scenario they'd imagined—perhaps a black-draped woman weeping beside ghastly waifs—was not what they found. They found Haregewoin invigorated, planting a vegetable garden, while Meskerem and Selamawit jumped rope on the driveway.

"You see?" Haregewoin said, laughing.

Well-reared girls, Meskerem and Selamawit politely extended their hands to shake hands with Haregewoin's friends. Most of the women laughed nervously and found ways to avoid skin-to-skin contact. One clapped her hands together, enthusing over the garden, and turned away; another rewarded the outstretched little hand with the gift of a mango. No one, on a first visit, would accept a bite to eat at this house.

"Are *they* sick?" someone asked bluntly.

Haregewoin knew the prim questioner meant "Aren't you worried they'll *infect* you?"

The question rattled Haregewoin terribly from the moment it was

Haregewoin's family, November 2003   AARON ROSENBLUM

Haregewoin approaches Eskender and his son, Mintesinot, August 2004

An HIV-positive child came to Haregewoin's compound from this Addis Ababa house.

The rocket balloons! AARON ROSENBLUM

Two dozen children
enjoyed school classes
and three daily meals
inside a used container
on the compound.
AARON ROSENBLUM

A typical morning in Haregewoin's compound AARON ROSENBLUM

A newly arrived child
at Haregewoin's
compound,
November 2005
AUTHOR PHOTO

An orphaned child feels shy upon arrival in
the compound; soon he will be running and
yelling with the others. AARON ROSENBLUM

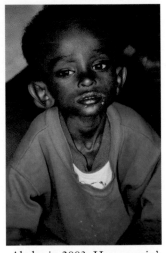

Ababu in 2003. Haregewoin's
friends warned her not to take
this child; he looked too sick
to survive. AARON ROSENBLUM

Baby boy whose
mother died
moments after
handing him to
Haregewoin
AARON ROSENBLUM

Singing songs under the canopy of Haregewoin's compound
AARON ROSENBLUM

Chanting the Amharic alphabet inside the container AARON ROSENBLUM

Haj Mohammed Jemal Abdulsebur (left rear) beside Zewdenesh Azeze and Fasika Addis, bringing Mekdes (front row left) and Yabsira (beside her) to live at Haregewoin's compound AARON ROSENBLUM

Mekdes, who was orphaned by AIDS, is distraught after being left behind by surviving family members too poor to raise her. AARON ROSENBLUM

Mekdes AARON ROSENBLUM

Mekdes being comforted by Selamneh AARON ROSENBLUM

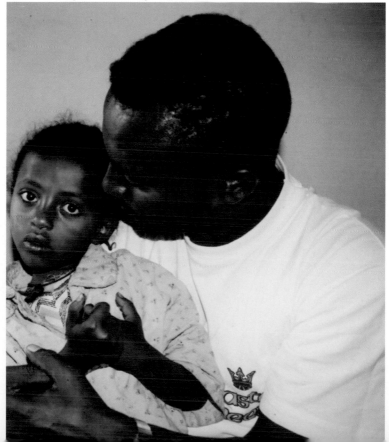

Meskerem growing up at
Haregewoin's compound
COURTESY OF HAREGEWOIN TEFERRA

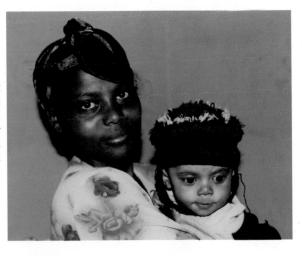

A caregiver at
Haregewoin's
compound
with a newly
orphaned child
AARON ROSENBLUM

Lunch and schoolwork in the container AARON ROSENBLUM

asked. Not because she feared for herself! She feared for the *children*. She tried to unhear the question, to forget that she'd heard it, but she could not. They didn't *look* sick.

That's what she kept returning to: how healthy they looked. They bounced out of bed in the morning; they peppered her with questions—about people, about birds, about dogs (could they have a puppy?); they were eager to have uniforms and to start school.

She assumed their mothers had died of AIDS; it couldn't be known for certain. Could the virus be snaking through their veins at this very moment, while they sat in the sunshine playing jacks with small stones and laughing?

And if they *were* infected . . . oh, God, it meant she had taken leave of her senses to love them; she had moved far too quickly and had placed herself at risk. She should have listened to her friends, not for their reasons (they believed that orphans of AIDS were dangerous to your health), but because if Meskerem and Selamawit were sick . . . well, she didn't think she could go there again.

She'd been joyously captured by the little girls; were they now going to haul her, their willingly captive new mother, to places she never wanted to see again?

In 2000, there were no anti-AIDS drugs in Ethiopia outside the black market.

If Meskerem and Selamawit were infected with HIV in 2000 in Ethiopia, they were going to die of AIDS.

18

THE HOSPITAL CLINIC phoned for Haregewoin to come in and receive the results of the children's blood tests. It had been three months since their arrival at her house. As she edged forward in a slow line into a packed waiting room, which overflowed into an outdoor courtyard, she joined the truly wretched of the earth.

Waiting in a clinic for the result of an HIV blood test, or for a child's blood test, is the archetypal experience of modern Africans.

The patient waiting for results may imagine that the outside world—the industrialized democracies of the West—once alerted to the terrible situation here, will ride to the rescue. Because how could people *know* and not help?

A few may suspect that the outside world *has* been fully informed, for there is no shortage of experts. In fact, extensive documentation has been collected and collated, graphed and disseminated.

Stephen Lewis calls the voluble hobnobbing of experts on the subjects of global health and orphans "speakathons"; they "give credence," he writes, "to the proposition that if you talk about something for long enough, the illusion will be created that progress is being made . . . And I suppose there has been some progress in the world of reports, analyses, figures, tables, diagrams, and at least a thousand PowerPoint presentations, not to overlook throbbing intellectual rumination, but very little progress that's discernible in the lives of orphaned and vulnerable children on the ground."

The African patient, waiting for test results, discovers that the outside world, while not completely indifferent, is not going to intervene in time to save his or her life, or the child's.

Around the world, a few fantastically popular television shows strike me as bizarrely playful versions of contemporaneous darker scenes.

On *American Idol* and its many knockoffs, singing contestants wait for verdicts issued by seated judges. "Yes, you go on to the next round," they may hear; "See you tomorrow," or "No, your competition is over," "America has voted," "Your journey ends here." Viewers phone in votes for their favorites. In other shows, individuals fight for survival on island expeditions until they are voted off the show, off the island, by their erstwhile comrades. The last man or woman standing is crowned "the survivor."

These programs are "reality shows."

In Africa, by the hundreds and thousands and millions, but one by one, a person sits in a clinic waiting room, jumpy or still, feeling fine or feeling nauseous, coughing or not coughing. Or she squats outside in the dirt yard, holding her head in her hand, occasionally looking up and calling to her children not to wander too far. Each waits to hear his or her name called. Inside the examining room, a doctor or nurse or nurse's aide examines a slip of paper and looks up. The eyes speak first.

Negative: You advance to the next round. See you tomorrow.

Positive: America has voted. Your journey ends here.

There are no television cameras.

No viewers at home are cheering or weeping.

No viewers at home phoned in their individual votes. Most never knew anything was at stake.

"I have heard there are treatments," a woman will whisper.

"Not in our country," the doctor will say with a sad smile.

"Does it mean I will die soon?" a man will ask.

"Yes, I'm afraid that is what it means."

"I thought perhaps I just had a cold."

"No, I'm afraid not."

"Some say . . . well, I am not a believer, but I have heard . . . that there is holy water which is effective?"

"No. That is a myth."

"As I supposed. Thank you, Doctor."

Driving to the hospital, Haregewoin was now beyond thinking "Why did I put myself at risk like this again?" and "Will my house turn into a hospital ward again?" She was numb. She shuffled forward in a long line, until it was her turn.

The nurse opened the file, read the results, reread them, and looked up from her desk.

"Selamawit is negative," she said.

She closed that file carefully, methodically picked up and opened the next one.

"Meskerem is negative," she said.

Benevolently, Haregewoin continued to structure Genet's and Abel's lives with kind discipline. But her second life as a mother began with Selamawit and Meskerem.

She was again, miraculously, a middle-class woman with children.

PART TWO

19

THE MMM DIRECTOR did not lose Haregewoin's phone number. He phoned again a few weeks after placing Selamawit and Meskerem at Haregewoin's house in early 2000. "*Waizero* Haregewoin!" he enthused when he heard her voice.

"No!" she laughed. "What could you possibly want with me?"

"Mrs. Haregewoin, there are more children here and—"

"No!" she cried, laughing again. "What are you thinking? I have four children here, I am fine now, really, I am fine. Perhaps I have neglected to thank you? I feel quite restored. Meskerem and Selamawit are wonderful girls. Truly they are godsends to me. You were right, you were absolutely right about everything. It was foolish of me to think of withdrawing from the world when there were children who needed me . . ." On she chirped.

"No, Mrs. Haregewoin!" he hastened to answer. "It is we who thank you."

"Yes, very good, thank you so much for calling."

"No, wait . . ."

This was the beginning of the end of Haregewoin's self-centeredness. She had believed that Abel, Genet, Selamawit, and Meskerem were offered to her as a balm. In reaching out to others in pain, her own pain was lessened. The priest, in his wisdom, had not allowed her to retreat to a life of prayer and mourning but had invited her to aid a couple of lost children. This she had done. A parable of healing. It was a transaction as old as humankind, yet it seemed each soul in agony had to find the way to it anew. She had been broken and now she would put the knowledge of that to good use, to repair others, to bring

Selamawit and Meskerem back to life. "Mrs. Haregewoin," said the director, "we have Meskerem's brother now. Half brother, I should say. He is the son of her mother and her mother's first husband."

"*What?*"

"He is seven, maybe eight."

"Oh my."

"And—"

"Yes?"

"And a little pair of twins, they are about four. Helen and Rahel. Their mother has just died. She was very very poor, very poor."

She stood confused.

"And—are you still there, Mrs. Haregewoin?"

"I'm here."

"And a five-year-old girl also, named Bethlehem. Also her mother has died."

Haregewoin leaned against her doorframe, gazing onto her courtyard where Meskerem and Selamawit were playing house in the shade of the eucalyptus tree. They'd dug bottle caps out of the dirt, washed them, and now arranged them for a coffee ceremony.

"And you want me to *choose?*" breathed Haregewoin, knowing already she would take one, already rearranging beds in her mind. "How can one choose among orphans? Perhaps I should take the brother?"

"No, *Waizero* Haregewoin!" He laughed heartily. "We wish you to take *all* the children."

"I don't understand what is happening."

"It is very bad out there now, Mrs. Haregewoin. Please, may we bring the children?"

"Yes. Of course."

Two days later, the MMM van pulled into the courtyard and four forlorn, bewildered, snuffling children looked sadly out the windows. Meskerem's brother Yonas, with sad red eyes in his triangular face, looked almost Armenian; he would prove to be a gentle and intelligent boy. The scrappy twin girls looked nothing alike, but they kept their fingers twiddling each other's clothing at all times. Bethlehem, with no place else to hide, simply covered her face with her hands.

Meskerem greeted Yonas by shaking his hand and kissing his cheeks politely, but the two had grown up apart—she had lived with their mother, he had lived with his father. "Come, children," clucked Haregewoin, leading the silent children behind her into the kitchen and hastily setting food before them. She sat between the twins and fed first one, then the other. She laughed a lot, sang fragments of children's songs, looking deeply into the eyes of all the children, willing them to be unafraid, to draw near to her.

Haregewoin heard Genet slam into the main room. "Genet, come look!" she called with delight, but Genet did not share this delight.

"Where will *they* sleep?"

"I'll put that one on the floor of Abel's room," she said, nodding toward Yonas.

Genet puckered her lips and crossed her arms, waiting to hear the rest. "These twins and that girl in my bed with Selamawit and Meskerem; you and I on blankets on the floor."

"No thanks," said Genet.

"Genet, my dear, what can I do?"

Genet shrugged and turned away. "I'm not going to be staying here much longer anyway," she muttered.

Indeed she was becoming ever more blatant in her misbehavior. She smelled of cigarette smoke when she came in from school, if she even went to class. Sometimes she wore a different blouse in the afternoon than she'd left with that morning. Then she began to come home late, after dark. She was returning to the streets.

Abel managed to spoil his welcome, as well. He came and went in a daze, at all hours. At one moment he was indifferent to the children—which they initially mistook for kindness—at the next moment, coming down off a high, he would slap or kick at them. "Be careful," Haregewoin warned him more than once. "You've got to behave around these little ones."

So she was probably the most disappointed of everyone the night they found Abel in the driveway carefully siphoning gas from her car and inhaling it from a bucket while Yonas and several little girls studied the situation close at hand. Yonas asked questions as if he were observing a science project. "How will the car drive without gas?" came the boy's high voice.

Haregewoin was obliged to phone her friends at MMM the next morning. "You've got to come get Abel. I can't do anything for him."

"Yes, *Waizero* Haregewoin, I understand," said the director. "Actually I was going to call you today anyway."

The van that arrived that afternoon to pick up Abel dropped off a little girl named Rahel Jidda, so newly orphaned that she still looked up sharply, full of hope that it would be her mother, whenever someone entered the room.

Abel scissored slowly on his knobby knees and ankles out the front door without looking back, carrying nothing. "*Ciaou,* Abel!" called Genet as Abel folded into the van. "See you soon!" she added, to irritate Haregewoin. Then she sulked for the rest of the afternoon and evening. "Old witch," she muttered. She grabbed her pillow and blanket off Haregewoin's floor and hurled them back into the second bedroom, reclaiming it as her own.

But Haregewoin hurried after the van as it began to back out, slid open the door, and leaned in to kiss Abel good-bye on each cheek. Despite her disappointment in the young man and in her failure to help him, she was dismayed at his departure.

Then there was Genet. After Abel's departure, Haregewoin tried to soften toward Genet and not fail her as well. But she feared the teenager was tormenting the little kids. She heard Genet scolding them and wondered if muffled punches and arm-twists accompanied the reprimands. The children, who had accepted their status as the nobodies of the earth, took it quietly, as their due. They dropped their heads, their tears fell silently. When Genet came home in the afternoon, the kids rapidly stopped whatever they were doing around the compound and congregated near Haregewoin.

"No!" roared Haregewoin the first time she saw Genet's fingers twist the skin of the upper arm of Rahel Jidda, the newest girl. "Genet, this must stop. This is absolutely not allowed."

"Then tell her to stay out of my stuff."

An American nurse on a long-term church mission to Ethiopia had been introduced to Haregewoin by MMM and had fallen into the friendly habit of visiting once a week. She was white, in her forties, with sunburned skin and a likably practical manner. She seemed to feel that Haregewoin was too strict with Genet. "Perhaps you expect too much from her?" she offered one day as they visited in the common room. "She's just a child."

Haregewoin sputtered into her tea.

"I like her very much," said the nurse.

Haregewoin arched an eyebrow at her, waiting.

"I live alone, you know, in a two-bedroom apartment. I've never had children.

"Haregewoin," she said suddenly, turning in her seat to face the Ethiopian woman. "What would you say to my taking Genet? What if I became her foster mother? Do you think MMM would permit it? Would you mind terribly giving her up?"

For Haregewoin, it was proof that God sometimes answers prayers. "She's a handful," she said, laughing. "You think you can handle her?"

"I was a teenager once! Can we tell Genet?"

"Please," said Haregewoin.

Genet packed up her things and cockily moved out at the end of the week, as if she'd known all along she was destined to move up, as if she'd just been biding her time until her big opportunity. Haregewoin held her hands for a long time, looking hard into her eyes, but Genet sniggered, flipped a beaded strand of hair off her forehead, and looked away, tapping her foot. "Be a good girl," Haregewoin pleaded, realizing she sounded just like the MMM director who'd sent Genet to her in the first place.

After the nurse drove away with Genet in the front seat, all the little kids jumped up and down and yelled their happiness at being freed from the oppressor.

Haregewoin had one color photo of Atetegeb holding her baby. She enlarged this photo until its lines turned all pastel and soft. She framed it and centered it on the wall above the sofa. She framed a smaller black-and-white photo of Atetegeb and Suzie as teenagers laughing together. Under the glass she placed a slip of paper upon which she'd typed the words from a pop song: "There is no me without you."

A child cannot live without a mother or father. A mother or father cannot live without the child.

Although, at least once a day, she caught her breath in a quick sob of missing her late daughter, Haregewoin was content in her pond of children. The older four went out the compound door each day in red pullover school sweaters and walked to school; the three youngest played in the compound. She read them stories, taught them songs, had them take off their shoes and socks and stomp around with her on the soapy clothes in the metal laundry tub. With children, even laundry was funny.

When they first arrived, all had worn the same face: stunned, empty, blank. One or another would freeze in the yard, bewildered and cautious, like a child in a dark hallway unable to find the way back to bed. But Haregewoin was everywhere now, hunching down to eye level, encouraging each child's tiniest attempt to smile—or at least not to cry—with huge promising smiles of her own. When, in grief and terror in the night, they raised anguished cries for *"Amaye!"* she ran stumbling to respond, even though she knew she was not the *Amaye* for whom any of them called. She lavished hugs and tickles on them; she snuggled them back to sleep. She washed and braided their hair, she taught them their letters. She laughed often now, savoring her life. Within a month or two, the calls in the night often were for Haregewoin; at least it seemed that, when a frightened child focused on Haregewoin's face looming out of the darkness, the child didn't startle or cry out, but relaxed with relief and sleepy gratitude.

Suzie sent money to the compound every month. Haregewoin's friends helped out, too.

She took in accounting jobs she could do late at night or early in the morning, at the kitchen table by lamplight, with a cup of tea, while the seven children slept.

But Haregewoin was not to be permitted to retreat back into the simple pleasures of child-rearing. The most terrible epidemic in human history was knocking at the scraped metal door of her compound, politely at first, but with persistence, and then it was banging with fists.

20

S HE WAS BEING watched.
Word spread out from Haregewoin's compound and across the neighborhood that the woman was taking in AIDS orphans.

By 2001, there were 989,000 AIDS orphans in Ethiopia, second in the world after Nigeria.

One morning, amidst the bustle of kids getting ready for school, Haregewoin heard a knock at the outer door of the compound. In flip-flops, housedress, and uncombed hair, she called, "*Abet?* Yes?" through the door.

"Police," said a man's voice, so Haregewoin swung open the heavy door.

Two officers stood there in uniform. In the arms of the shorter man there was a wiggly bundle. This he held out to Haregewoin. She leaned in to see, pulled back the blanket, and found the scrunched-up mad expression of a baby outraged at the indignity of having a blanket thrown over its face.

"Who is *this?*" Haregewoin cried in surprise.

"We found her," said the taller officer. "She was left on the road, under a bush."

Haregewoin covered her mouth with her hand.

"Will you take her?" asked the short policeman, acting as if he were having trouble maneuvering the bundle and needed Haregewoin to catch it.

"Me? Why do you bring it to me? The poor thing! You must take her to the *kebele!*"

"We took her to the *kebele* and they told us to bring her to you," the officer said, holding the child still farther from his body.

"But what about Mother Teresa's?" asked Haregewoin. "They have a home for orphans."

"They're full there, can't take any more."

She'd thought there was room there for hundreds of children; later she would try to decipher what this meant, that Mother Teresa's was full.

"If you could just watch her for a few days, they'll probably figure out what to do with her," said the shorter officer, again miming for her the difficulty of hanging on to the rolled-up blanket. It began to grunt.

"No one asked me, no one phoned," said Haregewoin vaguely, her mind racing. "I'm not set up for a baby here."

"Aren't you the woman taking in AIDS orphans?" questioned the taller. He took a slip of paper from his breast pocket. "Forgive me. Are you *Waizero* Haregewoin Teferra?"

"I am," she said. "All right, if the *kebele* wishes me to take her, give me the baby. But someone should have phoned me. I don't even have a bottle here."

The officers nodded in thanks; the shorter one poured the flailing bundle into Haregewoin's hands. They turned on their heels and walked to their car as the baby fought to untangle itself.

"Wait! What is her name?" said Haregewoin.

The policemen looked at each other, then the taller yelled, "You name her!" She closed the door.

"Children, come see!" she called. "You have a baby sister!"

The baby was pleased to see daylight again; she ceased thrashing and her angry purple color calmed to café au lait. When children started leaping around her, she stuck out the tip of her tongue and chortled.

Haregewoin named the discarded baby Menah, a form of the word *mena*: useless, unwanted, a person without value. It was the word she'd applied to herself a few months earlier as she dragged herself to and from the cemetery.

Nobody called, in the next day or two, to tell Haregewoin what to do with Menah, nor in the next month, nor ever. No one ever asked about the baby at all.

Now, thought Haregewoin, *I really am finished. Life is good.* She bent forward at the waist, balanced the baby high on her back, and looped a shawl around the two of them. When Haregewoin stood up, sparkly eyed Menah peeked over her shoulder at the children and laughed a silly baby laugh.

Despite her name, she was no longer a worthless one!

Neither was Haregewoin.

21

THREE YEARS AFTER Atetegeb's death (it was now the spring of 2001) Haregewoin still dressed in black.

One afternoon, an official of the *kebele* knocked on the gate for a visit. He wanted to see her small operation. He walked around frowning, his hands clenched behind his back, poking here and there, shaking hands with a few of the eight children quite formally, making them giggle. Then he smiled, straightened his jacket, and pronounced himself pleased. "You are a good woman, *Waizero* Haregewoin," he said. "It is time to take off these black clothes. You are a mother to these young people and they will prefer to see you in clothing not of a mourner."

She followed his advice.

Two days later he sent her four new children.

One night, Haregewoin was awakened by an insistent tapping on the steel door of her compound. In her nightgown, barefoot, she crept to the steel outer door and listened. The African night was jazzy with street dogs and goats, baboons on the distant hillsides, and hyenas and jackals on the plains beyond. The metallic mountain air of the capital was cold, which made the rough cement of the courtyard feel warm to her feet. A tall thin man swayed on the road. He wore a wool sports jacket and tie. His eyes were bloodshot and his mustache unkempt. She thought he was forty-five, and intoxicated; later she would learn he was twenty-nine and a nondrinker. A tiny girl slept in his arms.

"My wife has died. I am Theodros. This is Berti."

Haregewoin unstuck her tongue from the roof of her mouth several times in the Ethiopian sound of empathy.

Betti was four, he said.

Haregewoin pulled her flannel nightdress closer around her and stood on tiptoe to look. "So small?" she asked.

"Here," he offered with sudden enthusiasm, "you may see how she was, before."

He maneuvered one hand away from the blanketed bundle to his pocket and pulled out several wallet-size portraits of Betti. Taken one year earlier in a photographer's studio, they showed a bright-eyed, pigtailed child in a yellow satin leotard and tutu. Her round tummy stuck out and her hands were raised above her head in a ballet position. Haregewoin examined each of the four different poses, the photos soft and well-worn as an old deck of cards.

"I am a builder," he began anew, returning the photographs to his empty wallet. "I have a college degree and a master's degree from Addis Ababa University. But since my wife died and my daughter got sick, no one will give me a job. I can't feed her. I can't buy medicine.

"I can design and oversee construction. Perhaps there is some small job you are planning?"

"You wake me up at this hour of the night to ask for work?" asked Haregewoin.

"People will not shake hands with me. Just to look at the child, they know. She is positive."

He said nothing about his own health status, she noted. But it was obviously the same as his child's.

"When I take her into the hospital, people stand far from us and won't help me. One time when she was playing outside, a sore on her hand started bleeding and the neighbors ran to gather their children— 'Betti is here, quick, come inside!' Now she won't try to play with the other children.

"Please, madam, I heard that you are helping the children.

"It would only be for a short while."

Until that moment Haregewoin had thought the thin gentleman was asking for a handout, for food or money or a job. And she would have scurried to provide him with something, if no more than a sack of

teff (an endemic grain) from her larder. Now she understood that he
needed her to take his daughter.

She accepted the sleeping girl from the father. He bowed deeply to
Haregewoin and stayed angled forward, hands clasped. As she pushed
the door shut with her foot, the father cried out, "I will visit on
Sunday!" and, again, from beyond the locked door, "It is only
temporary!"

Haregewoin carried Betti back to bed with her, but the four little
girls already sleeping there had squirmed over and taken her warm
spot. She nudged the children with her knee and hip to squeeze herself
and sleeping Betti onto the mattress edge. She half reclined and fell
asleep with the new girl in her arms.

When Betti sat up in Haregewoin's bed later that morning and
found herself in a tangle of girls instead of at home in her cot, beside
which her father slept on the floor, her lower lip poked out. Other
children cooed to her, eager to carry her about in their arms like a
toddler, and Betti did not protest and was borne out into the crowded
courtyard.

As usual, it was busy. The minor-key notes of grief were being
drowned out by the percussion of childhood: hopscotch, hand-
clapping games, the *oof!* of a deflated soccer ball kicked into the
air, wet clothes slapped across the laundry lines, plastic soup ladles
clicking against plastic bowls, and the slide and whack of jump rope. A
eucalyptus tree stirred in the hot wind beside the fence, its small, dense
leaves making a high-pitched rustling noise.

The following Sunday afternoon, Theodros knocked on the steel
door for his visit. Betti ran to cling with both fists to his pants leg.
Theodros gestured for her to run and play with her new friends, but
she refused: she was afraid to turn around and find him gone. Thus
he was deprived again of a father's pleasure in seeing his daughter
play among children. She stood hanging on to his leg while he
gently stroked her head, and together, with somewhat bewildered
smiles, they watched the healthy children career around the court-

yard in chaotic games of soccer accomplished with shoving and argument.

Theodros returned every Sunday and took his leave in the evening. Betti didn't cry when her father went out the door, but she sucked her thumb hard until all you could see of her face—over the shoulder of the child carrying her to dinner—was the inserted fist and the huge, worried eyes above it.

One Sunday, Theodros did not come. He sent word to Haregewoin that he was in the hospital.

He came again a month later, moving slowly, his legs bending in an angular, careful way like those of a grasshopper; wearing the same wool sports coat, but without the tie, he nodded and smiled to all, as if the slow motion were a form of gallantry.

This time Betti, who was also growing sicker, did not scamper to him. She pushed one foot forward and then the other, sliding over the rough ground until she reached his arms.

To Haregewoin's surprise, Theodros took Betti away with him and they lasted several months. She later learned that he had placed Betti at Mother Teresa's orphanage for part of that time. Still later she learned that he'd hoped to find anti-AIDS medicine for children at Mother Teresa's, but they didn't have any. There would be no anti-AIDS drugs for children in Ethiopia until 2005.

But Theodros couldn't know that. He refused to see the end in plain sight; he persisted in believing their luck was about to change, if only he could think his way through to a new angle, a different strategy.

Theodros came for his visit one Sunday afternoon. The skin was pulled tight over his cheekbones; he bobbed his head as if to show that his smiles were of a friendly nature rather than the grimaces of enormous effort. He gingerly made his way to a low ledge of concrete and seated himself; and Betti allowed herself to be carried over by a friend and propped against her father's leg.

Both turned, as was their habit, to watch the healthy children play in the courtyard. Theodros stroked Betti's hair. And she, who had stopped growing, who barely had the strength to lift her arms in her long-ago fifth ballet position, if she even remembered it, was content to lean against him, the two of them still and peaceful in one another's company in the assembling twilight.

22

I T W A S P E R H A P S Haregewoin's own chronic mourning that compelled her to hesitate, to hold her door ajar, when strangers materialized in the lane and asked for her help. She instantly recognized the pain of fellow mourners and would not abuse them.

Sometimes it felt as if she, too, waited for someone.

This slight gap in the impenetrable landscape—door after door closed to the afflicted, clergy preaching against them, their own families stonily denying them—had been discovered. Somehow the untouchables had found this woman who did not shriek insults, throw rocks, or shake a broom at them before slamming the door in their faces. Now they rode by bus or by donkey, they hiked or they limped, toward the brick house of Haregewoin Teferra, in a rickety hillside neighborhood of Addis Ababa.

Adults stood on the rocky road outside Haregewoin's gate, politely knocked, then waited in the rough-cut shade of a juniper tree, holding the hands of frightened children.

"Please, I am sick; I cannot feed him."

"Please take them, we will not live much longer."

"I cannot bring him up, I have no money, and his father is dead."

"I found them in my yard—I don't even know who they are."

Some ragged children were given a rough shove in Haregewoin's direction by the neighbor or distant relative in a hurry to be rid of them; others were petted and wept over by grandparents too poor and frail to keep them.

"Please," some said.

"Take her, I don't want her!" said others.

Haregewoin saw the small, pinched faces, the heads hanging so low on the chests they seemed to have been unpinned from the necks. Like sacks of grain, the children were transferred to new ownership. They shuffled forward without looking up, ashamed.

One day a driver from a village fifty miles away honked outside Haregewoin's gate. She pulled open the door and the dented van rumbled over the stones of the courtyard. The man descended and shook Haregewoin's hand, slid open the side door, and gestured for children to hop out, as if this were a class field trip to the science museum. The kids emerged filthy and runny-nosed, their scalps itchy, molluscum contagiosum nodules sprouting like mushrooms around their lips and eyes. There were toddlers too small to get from the van's running board to the ground by themselves. "Wait, which one are you?" the driver called to a small boy.

The boy froze, then said with surprise, "I am Natnael!"

He was the only person left who knew that.

Sometimes a newly arrived child made a woeful sound of abandonment, hoarse from calling its mother's name, beginning to horribly suspect that Mother wasn't coming, but unable to stop calling, *"Amaye. Amaye."* Haregewoin crouched beside the child and whispered, *"Ishi, ishi, ish ish ish ish,"* which meant, "Okay, okay, shh shh shh, I know, I know, okay."

Sometimes when Haregewoin opened the door of her compound, she discovered that the adult who had banged for attention had already fled, leaving behind a small child besieged by flies, squatting in soiled diapers.

Haregewoin's old friends continued to act scandalized. She was choosing *foster care* instead of office work or genteel semiretirement?

But by then the plague was all around them, orphans as numerous in the city as pigeons. Orphans hitchhiked into the capital from every direction. New ones were produced, underfoot, with every wail of an ambulance, with every shriek of a woman dying in childbirth, with every hike to the cemetery of a newly bereaved family. The few orphanages in the city were overflowing, as were the hospitals and schools. Orphans were tucked away in wards for the mentally ill, in paupers' hospitals, in cemeteries, in garbage dumps. Some lingered outside the schools they could no longer attend; once they had flown out the door after school and sprinted home; now there was no home, and—with no one to pay school fees and buy uniforms—no more school. A four-year-old girl was scavenging alone in an alley, outside the kitchen door of the hotel where her late mother had worked. Hotel workers left food for her beside the garbage cans.

"I take the small children thrown in the streets," Haregewoin told her friends. She had no clue that epidemiologists were culling statistics; she had no idea that anyone was aware of the crisis, other than the MMM director and a few other kind souls. She was scarcely aware that what she was seeing *was*, technically, a "crisis."

"They are found near churches, near police stations," she told her friends. "I cannot say no."

How can a child live without a mother?

There is no me without you.

"They're *healthy*, aren't they?" some friends continued to ask.

"Yes, yes, they're healthy!" cried Haregewoin, sick to death of the question. "You couldn't catch the disease from them even if they had it!"

But with *that* insight, she was years ahead of general knowledge. Better to wave her hands at the herd of children in the courtyard and assure her friends, "Healthy, healthy, healthy!" than to discuss the finer points of HIV/AIDS transmission with her proper middle-aged, middle-class ladies.

So her friends resumed visiting; they sat in her common room on rainy afternoons; they drank coffee; and they left small gifts of money. Old friends of Worku's came, too; and couples with whom Haregewoin and Worku had once played cards. They had all reached late middle age now; they had steered most (not all) of their family members to safety through the rise and fall of emperors and dictators, past the falling axes of war and famine; they'd earned a rest now, a peaceful time. They were entitled to fantasize that Meles would prove to be an enlightened leader, that Ethiopia would again stand in the forefront of nations. The news that an unspeakable disease threatened to unravel Ethiopia's health and productivity was devastating, thus they wished to be permitted to enjoy a state of denial a little longer. In visiting, they signaled their grudging acceptance of Haregewoin's project, though some made a show of pretending to regard her as an eccentric, and they didn't want to be trapped into actually *touching* one of the children.

One afternoon there was a feeble scratching at the metal door of the compound. "I think someone is here, *Emama* (Grandmama)," called a child to Haregewoin.

Haregewoin greeted a spectral young woman in a dusty skirt. Her face was drained, her eyes were dilated, and she seemed disoriented. With an abrupt move, she displayed a pretty curly-haired boy nestled within her dirty shawl.

"Please keep my baby I'm going to die he is twenty days old," she said breathlessly.

Haregewoin accepted the baby and prepared to ask the girl —no more than nineteen or twenty—to come into the house and have a cup of tea. Perhaps she could be assisted in keeping her child; with just a little help, a few coins, some food, she might gain a footing in the neighborhood. But the girl turned away instantly and dropped. Her breast had burst open, Haregewoin saw in horror. She fell sideways onto the rocky road. Haregewoin screamed for help. The two oldest boys ran to lift her (she weighed nothing!) and bring her into the compound. She was dead.

Having made arrangements with the *kebele* to collect the body, Haregewoin sat that evening with the baby in her lap. He had bright eyes, shiny ringlets, cherry-dark lips, but no name. The dying mother had given every cell of her being to the baby, but had been too weak to speak his name.

✳   ✳   ✳

The horror was becoming domesticated, so ordinary that only something truly bizarre invited comment. "You see that one?" whispered Haregewoin to Zewedu one day, indicating a bushy-haired little girl of about six sitting at the table waiting for lunch. Her name was Nurit. She had her head bowed low, waiting for someone to say grace.

"She was an only child. She and her parents shared one bed. She slept between them. She woke up one morning and discovered that both her mother and father had died in the night."

"Is this not a cold war against us?" Zewedu asked Haregewoin.

Every day and every night, the death toll mounted, and more children staggered out of their houses and villages in fright and hunger and grief. Behind the ghoulish depletion—of families, of villages, and of farming communities by AIDS—the well-known grim reaper of *famine* leered. Famine was made more dangerous and powerful by communities too weakened by illness to prepare for it and to survive it in the old ways.

Haregewoin stood on her outer threshold early one morning, drinking a cup of coffee while surveying the pleasant green-and-silver hillside patchwork of tin roofs and grass huts, plots of corn and walls of bamboo, flights of yellow canaries and moving herds of belled goats. The mud-and-straw hovels and wooden lean-tos borrowed nothing in design or material from modernity, other than the pieces of metal or plastic tarp scavenged in the slapdash assembly. The random, lazily drooping electrical and telephone wires reflected the country's haphazard supply of public utilities to the citizens. A white-chested, red-tailed buzzard stood on the top of a telephone pole, ready to spring.

Then Haregewoin glanced down and discovered a cloth-wrapped sleeping newborn beside her wall.

She was flabbergasted. "Oh, dear God, oh, dear God," she cried, gathering the child. "Thanks, God, thanks, God," she said, discovering the child was still breathing.

In the coming months and years, she would find another newborn outside her door, and another, and another, and another.

23

S O F A R , N O N E of the children delivered to Haregewoin looked to be near death. But a very sick one was headed her way.

In one of the poorest neighborhoods of Addis Ababa lived a destitute girl with a tiny, bald, discontented baby. The girl wrapped herself and the thin baby in a shawl and slept on whatever mud floor they were pityingly offered. Sometimes they were given a piece of plastic to spread beneath them as a sheet. Rain filtered through the gaps between the mud wall and the tin roof. By day, the girl begged in the streets. She spent every birr instantly, trying to feed herself. When the owners of the shanty realized she would contribute nothing to the household, they asked her to move on.

She was too thin and hungry to produce enough milk to nurse the baby, who seemed always to be disappointed and angry. When he turned his head away from her chest and screamed in frustration, his face turned beet black and his eyes bulged and he raved with his small fists. Even when she managed to squeeze a thin stream of milk from her breast, he wasn't satisfied. She offered him a stick of sugarcane to chew; he tried to shape his gums around it to suck, found nothing, scowled, then wailed in dismay. He slept fitfully like an old man, bitterly muttering against her in his dreams. He rarely even wet himself, as if he couldn't trust her to keep him clean, or refused to give her evidence that she was doing something correctly. She felt the baby didn't like her. In her village, she'd always been liked; a wide-cheeked, smiling girl, she'd had plenty of friends, plenty of laughter in her life. She'd never made anyone as miserable as she made this baby. She bent her head over him and cried huge tears. The premature death of her father had disrupted the normal course of things. Now she was ashamed that she'd left her home for the city, ashamed that she'd slept with a man who had lied in saying he would marry her, mortally ashamed that she had a baby and no husband, and ashamed that she did not know how to make the baby feel good. She felt the mad baby, Ababu, was thinking, *How unlucky am I, to get this incapable girl for my mother instead of a nice plump married village woman.*

In shame and hunger, she visited the lean-to of her grandmother—a cranky old woman as dry as the sticks of kindling with which she earned her living. The girl put Ababu on the straw mat on the floor of her grandmother's three-sided shelter—smaller than a bus stop—then knelt and asked her grandmother's permission to slip away for an hour to the river to wash her clothes and bathe. She bowed her head, knowing the old woman would shout at her "*Why* did you bring this unneeded baby upon us? *Why* didn't you stay in the village? What possessed you to think you would find a better life in the capital? You see? You see?" The ruined girl knelt, waiting for the weak blows of the old woman's knotty fists to pummel her shoulders and head, and they did. She took this as permission. She gave Ababu a kiss on the top of his hard, bald head and fled. Instead of going to the river and then back to her grandmother's lean-to, she ran barefoot straight up into the hills.

By dawn the old woman knew she had been stuck with the skinny baby, her great-grandson. She also knew this meant the ruin of her feeble subsistence. Twelve hours a day, every day, she hiked up the steep hills ringing the city in search of firewood, then practically crawled back down with a pile of sticks three times her own height piled on her bent back. She was a human burro. She and her kind had deforested the city; the government frowned upon it, but it was the only work she knew. And it was not as if a million slum dwellers had a *choice* between cooking and heating with wood fires rather than with modern electric or gas stoves and furnaces. Meanwhile, the disappearance of the great forests chased away the rain and further impoverished the already denatured soil.

The calories the old woman expended to earn the daily five birr barely translated into a plate of boiled beans to replenish her concave belly at night. The margin of life was so thin that she was just a few calories ahead of staying home and starving to death. She did not have the strength to wear Ababu on her back during her desperate scavenger hunt for firewood, nor could she carry him in her arms when she trudged back down into the city at dusk, laden with sticks. So she took the young girl's place on the streets as a beggar, wearing the emaciated Ababu in a shawl on her back. She did not have the smooth, pretty face of a young mother to entice handouts (or more intimate contact) from a tourist or a businessman. She was an exhausted old woman. She had asked nothing of the world but a few bites of something at bedtime; for her trouble, she now had this burden.

Ababu, perhaps eighteen months old now, didn't complain or whimper anymore, expected nothing. He looked out from his great-grandmother's back with huge, worried eyes in a shrunken head. He weighed nothing, he said nothing. Food came as a great surprise when it arrived. The food came to him straight from the old woman's mouth into his: she chewed up boiled kidney beans twice a day and transferred them into Ababu's mouth. It was his baby food. It was her only food, and his. He lay listlessly on her lap and opened his mouth. His dull eyes looked nowhere. She bent over him, pecking and emitting like a mama bird. She liked him well enough. But she doubted he would live.

Poking along one day, scanning the sides of the dirt road for anything that could be eaten or sold for a paper birr, she passed Haregewoin's open door and glimpsed children in the courtyard. "Is that a school?" she asked another passerby.

"A lady who takes in orphans," she was told.

She stood outside the gate watching. She saw round little Haregewoin whistling to make a path through the children like a farm wife shooing her way through a yard of chickens.

She crept to the bottom of the driveway and hooted to catch

Haregewoin's attention. She yanked Ababu off her back, dashed bravely a few feet up the drive, shouted, "This is Ababu! There he is! Take him!" Then she set him on the ground and scrabbled away down the road.

"Wait! Tell me your name!" cried Haregewoin.

"Good-bye! Good-bye!" shouted the old lady without looking back.

"You know her?" Haregewoin asked the people in the lane.

"Yes. She lives in Ketchene. *Enchut teshukemah* [a wood carrier]."

Haregewoin looked down at the child, who had fallen over sideways in the driveway without a whimper. She practically flung Ababu into the air when she lifted him, so light was the boy. His big head bounced back and forth on his skinny shoulders.

"The old beggar woman did not kiss him," Haregewoin told her friends. "She did not tell him good-bye. She is fed up with this boy. She sets him on the ground—*BOOM*—like that; shouts, 'It is Ababu! There he is!' and runs away.

"He didn't cry. He didn't do anything or say anything. He did not even say 'Mommy' or 'Daddy.' He could not say anything. When you give him food, you will see that he has been starving for a long time."

Such a child shakes with anxiety when you put food in front of him.

Haregewoin knew the special recipe for a starving child. She crushed beans and seeds into milk and fed it to Ababu every few hours, followed by a bottle of cow's milk. He made pitiful whining sounds in the night. She heard him, got up, mashed the food, made the bottle, and fed him twice a night.

He has diarrhea, she noted. *He is still starving, I think.*

"Oh, did everyone make a fuss when I took in Ababu," she told me. "Everybody was shouting at me, 'This boy is dying! Why are you taking this boy? Give him to the *kebele*.' I said, 'God has a reason to bring him here. I will keep him.'"

Once she had thought she could not do this again—attend the deathbed of a dying child of hers—now that it was upon her, she saw that she *could* do it. Because the alternative was even worse: to drop off Ababu at one of the city's underfunded, understaffed, underequipped, overcrowded hospitals would mean that the boy would die anyway, but alone and unloved.

All the big action of the household—the scores of healthy children breezing in and out, the outside play, the young caregivers swishing about—swept past Ababu like storm winds. He couldn't partake in the life the other children enjoyed, other than to be blown over by it. But he had a small bit of life all his own. When Haregewoin handed him a roll, he gnawed on it. When she scooped him up and showered him with endearments, he purred.

Ababu sat hunched over in a patch of sunlight on the floor until the sheer exertion of trying to sit up exhausted him. Haregewoin carried him back to his crib; he rode in her arms as limp as a stuffed animal, with glassy eyes. As she put him down, he strained upward with his skinny neck at the last moment, expecting—and receiving—her kiss.

24

"**D**OES YOUR PROGRAM have a name?" asked an official with the *kebele*.

"My program?" she asked vaguely, unsure what he meant.

"Well, you have a foster home now. It would be a good thing for you to name it."

So she named it: *Atetegeb Worku Metasebia Welage Aleba Histanet Merj Mahber.*

The Atetegeb Worku Memorial Orphans Support Association.

Haregewoin invited a gap-toothed, gangly, elderly fellow from the neighborhood to act as *zabania* (house guard) for her compound, in exchange for meals and a tin shed in which to throw down his shawls, prop his staff, and sleep at night.

Beginning in 2002, making use of her administrative office experience, Haregewoin opened a case file on each arrival, including whatever few details attached to a child. She arranged the folders in a metal file cabinet in chronological order of arrival:

Baby boy, 3 months, found on Churchill Road, brought by police. Given the name Yonas.

Newborn girl found on street, brought by police. Named Yemisrach.

Masresha Mesfin, 9, brought by his grandmother after mother died; father died already.

Esublew Abayneh, 8, sister Betelhem, 3, dropped off by a kebele *administrator after they were discovered living alone.*

Mihret Tadesse, 10, brought by her mother who was very poor and very sick with AIDS.

Haregewoin had seven children living with her, then twelve, then fifteen, then eighteen. There were four bedrooms now: two in the main house, two in the larger outbuilding. She had a rusty boxcar towed to her compound. With a door cut into the side, it served as a dining hall and as a classroom for the younger children. Haregewoin slept in the babies' and little girls' room, with any number of them in bed with her and more joining them throughout the night.

She preserved the spot closest to her for baby Menah, whom the police had given her. A giggly baby, Menah liked to snuggle and play before falling asleep. Sometimes, in the near darkness, with the warm, sleeping children heaped all about them, Menah and Haregewoin made deep eye contact; Haregewoin then closed her eyes, pretending to fall asleep, and suddenly whipped them open. Menah laughed out loud, a gurgling baby laugh. Haregewoin had to shush her, lest she wake up the whole crew, and she hugged her tight, laughing, too.

By 2003, Ethiopia had more than a million AIDS orphans, Haregewoin had twenty-four of them living in her house, and more children were headed her way.

Mekdes Asnake [*Mek*-dis Ah-se-*nah*-kee] was five years old and lived with her grandfather Addisu, her young aunt Fasika, and her little brother, Yabsira, [*Yab*-sira] in a hut on a shared dirt compound outside the capital. The walls of her house were a hard mix of mud and straw; the windows were open squares cut into the walls. Sometimes the family had firewood; when they did not, the circle of ashes on the floor was black and the hut was cold. They subsisted, year-round, on eggs.

The children's late father, Asnake, had been a day laborer in coffee processing. One day when Mekdes was three or four years old and waiting impatiently for him to come home and play with her, she saw a strange thing: he approached the house but suddenly knelt and lay full length on the dirt courtyard for a while, before getting up and coming inside.

Later, when her father got sick, Mekdes felt he must have caught the bad sickness that day, from the dirt. He got thinner and thinner over the next few months, with a look of surprise in his brown eyes. Then thick black blisters erupted on his skin and he cried out from the pain during the day and groaned with it all through the night. Mekdes thought he would get better. She was shocked when she woke up one night to the haunting sound of her mother, Mulu, howling over Asnake's wasted body.

Mekdes had not recovered from the horror of Asnake's death when her mother began to get the same disappointed, surprised look on her face. At night under the blankets, Mekdes and Yabsira snuggled close to their mother. By day, Mekdes, then four, chatted busily to her mother so she would be happy again. She told her news about the chickens in the yard or the children in the lane. Such stories once made her mother laugh. But Mulu grew still; blisters encroached on her body, too; her eyes protruded and did not blink often; her voice grew hoarse. Even though she was frighteningly bony, she turned away from food.

Mekdes helped her mother by running to neighbors with important messages, and by taking care of Yabsira, twenty months younger. Though he weighed more than half what she did, she carried him on her hip as her mother once did. When she fed Yabsira, she set food by her mother's side, too, and removed the untouched plate later. At bedtime, her mother barely returned Mekdes's enthusiastic hugs and kisses; her eyes were open but she didn't react. Then one night Mulu did not move at all and Mekdes understood that her mother had died.

Yabsira remained the same funny fellow as always. When he escaped from the hut naked, Mekdes and Addisu pursued him, and all three hugged and laughed together. Yabsira had nearly forgotten his father, and his mother had been bedridden as long as he could remember. Mekdes, however, forgot nothing.

One November morning in 2003, Mekdes found her grandfather in a somber mood. Aunt Fasika, their late father's sister, was oddly quiet, too. When their other young aunt, their late mother's sister Zewdenesh, suddenly entered the hut, the children brightened, but she, too, was subdued.

Mekdes's hair had been braided into pigtails several days earlier by Fasika; Addisu ran his hand fondly over Mekdes's head. He was a wiry man with a thin, unshaved face; he wore a floppy fishing hat, a plaid shirt, colorless trousers, and a gray wool poncho. Mekdes was wearing the clothes she'd slept in—a striped T-shirt and striped leggings. They were the only clothes she owned, other than a blue cotton blouse. Addisu gestured for Mekdes to put on her blue blouse because the air was cold and she was going out.

The grandfather patted down each of the children, giving small, aimless tugs and tucks on their clothing; he bent and kissed Mekdes hard on each cheek, then stooped and tried to do the same with runny-nosed Yabsira. Each aunt took a child's hand and the family stepped into the mud yard.

An elderly religious leader, Haj Mohammed Jemal Abdulsebur, was waiting for them. He wore a pressed khaki shirt and khaki slacks and a cream, hand-crocheted, round Muslim cap. The two old men—the official and the grandfather—shook hands in the respectful style of holding the right forearm with the left hand, as if the very honor of the handshake were weighty. Haj led the two young women and two children onto the mud lane. Mekdes did not call good-bye to her grandfather. She did not know she was leaving him. The group headed downhill, in the direction of a paved street with a bus stop.

I was in Haregewoin's courtyard that afternoon, surrounded by shrieking children, because I had brought them a surprise from America: rocket balloons! The balloons were long, curly blimps, hard to blow up; when released, they buzzed horizontally overhead and made blubbery noises. A rocket balloon would suddenly sputter up into the branches of a tree or shoot onto a roof or pelt someone on the back. Wherever it landed was hilarious to the children. Sometimes one fizzled out in the dirt after buzzing around the children's feet. They screamed with happiness, running wildly around the compound after each balloon. They danced in mock fear when a balloon nose-dived and snuffled around their ankles. When a balloon popped, the children ran to gather the pieces. To possess even a rubber scrap from a rocket balloon was the closest most had come to owning a toy.

At this moment of general hysteria, a small, downcast group entered the courtyard and stood with stiff formality near the washtubs and laundry lines. Haj Mohammed and two pretty young women in modest kerchiefs and long skirts waited with two children. The stiffness and formality of the group told me something solemn was happening: I suspected the children were about to be left here.

Haregewoin hurried across the courtyard to greet them, wiping her hands on her apron as she ran.

Mekdes was awed by the crowds of children streaming in play back and forth across the cement yard. Was this a school? She wanted to go to school. But the children were not in uniform. She felt frightened; she hunched down and tried to hide behind the round head of her brother.

After handshakes and kisses all around, and commiserating talk among the adults, Haj and the young women began to depart. Mekdes felt the air at her back, suddenly aware that her aunts were no longer behind her—they were walking toward the exit! Mekdes shrieked and ran after them. How would she find her way home to her grandfather? Aunt Fasika and Aunt Zewdenesh turned around; they stroked Mekdes's face, kissed her many times, and told her good-bye.

Haregewoin stepped up and took Mekdes's arm, restraining her as the aunts slipped out the metal door to the street and pulled it shut behind them.

Mekdes turned inside out with grief and terror. She understood: she was being abandoned! She arched her back in protest. She pulled out of Haregewoin's grasp, fell backward to the ground, and writhed there, beginning to shriek.

Then she stood up and ran after the departing adults. She ran straight at the metal door of the compound, without slowing down, and hit it with a bang; it threw her back onto the dirt; she was up again in an instant, running straight at the door again. *Bang*. Berserk, she screamed and ran in circles. She whirled and cried in high *aii aii*

aii whoops. She dodged the elderly compound guard and aimed full tilt at the door again, determined to run straight through it and all the way home. *Bang.* It knocked her back. In the dirt, she went through all the prostrations of grief; she knelt facing the door, bowed forward till her head touched the dust, brought up fistfuls of dirt, and dropped it on the back of her head and neck as she cradled her head. She moaned and rocked and reached her hands out beseechingly toward the metal door.

I slipped out the door myself to see what had become of the adults who'd dropped off the brother and sister. I thought I'd spot them at the top of the dirt hill, heading home, but they were right there, right outside the door of the compound, and they, too, were grief-stricken. Two pretty young women in their twenties had covered their faces with their shawls and were rocking and moaning, too; *"Aii aii aii,"* they cried. One held out her hands palms up as if asking God for answers. Elderly Haj Mohammed's eyes looked red and hurt. People in the street gave them wide berth. Then we all heard *bang* and knew Mekdes had flown into the door again; then again *bang.* I began sobbing, too. I rummaged through my backpack. "I have two hundred dollars," I told my driver and friend Selamneh. "If I give it to them, could they take the children home again?"

"No," he said. "Let it be. They are too poor to raise the children."

The adults looked at me with their red eyes and I looked back at them the same way. *Bang!* went the door. There was nothing to say. Head bowed, I stepped back inside.

The elderly guard picked Mekdes up from the dirt and carried her toward the house. She went limp and fell backward in his arms as though she had fainted. When that didn't make him stop, she began kicking and screaming again, the passion and terror unabated. Haregewoin approached and took the thrashing child. Mekdes twisted and flailed and cried, and Haregewoin, with squinting eyes, averted face, and strong arms, absorbed the blows.

Haregewoin was used to this.

❉   ❉   ❉

As I left Haregewoin's compound that day, Mekdes stood near her, looking dazed, coated with dust, her eyes at half-mast. I'd traveled to Ethiopia with duffel bags full of toys and school supplies for several orphanages, but I'd given out the last of them that morning to the children in Haregewoin's yard.

I desperately wanted to give a gift. I rooted through Selamneh's taxi frantically, but it looked as if all the toys were gone. Finally, in the trunk, I found a stray toy: a three-inch, plastic Madame Alexander bridesmaid doll given for free to customers of McDonald's. Mortified that it wasn't something more, I held it out to Mekdes. She seized it with a lightning-fast grab. When other children tried to see the doll, Mekdes elbowed them out of her way like a linebacker. As I backed out of the compound, bereft Mekdes stood watching, expressionless. Her family was gone, but she had a plastic McDonald's Happy Meal toy in her hand.

I would say it was the most inadequate gift I'd ever offered anyone, had I not given a poorer one earlier that hour.

As the children uproariously screamed and chased the rocket balloons, Haj Mohammed Jemal Abdulsebur watched from the side-lines with a wistful smile. He had stepped back into the compound after Fasika and Zewdenesh had begun their trek home. He suddenly tapped on my shoulder, held up two fingers, and pantomimed two small heads at his side. I understood that he was expressing his desire for balloons for two children he had at home, perhaps his grand-children. But I felt jealous for Haregewoin's children, who had no kind grandfathers and no homes. So I fished out just one balloon for him, figuring his children could share it. He thanked me by holding his hands together prayerfully as he bowed to me.

Later that day I learned that Haj, in his home village, ran a hole-in-the-wall orphanage like Haregewoin's. He was a surrogate grandfather to about eighty older boys.

I gave that nice man a balloon.

25

THE DAY AFTER the tumultuous arrival of Mekdes Asnake, I traveled to Haregewoin's compound again, with Selamneh, to see the sad little girl. Zewedu was there.

"They have no education, they have nothing," Zewedu said bitterly, about the orphans in the yard. "Of course their parents died for lack of medicine; most of their parents never even had enough to *eat*."

For Zewedu, his ruin and Ethiopia's were entwined.

"The EPRDF [Ethiopian People's Revolutionary Democratic Front] has held power since 1995, and we have still twelve million people in this country not sure they will eat once a day," he said. "They must choose: shall we eat breakfast today or shall we wait until dinner? The government and a few elites are the landowners and the people are tenants. We are peasants. We are sixty percent illiterate. There can be no development in such a case."

Zewedu had founded an organization, Dawn of Hope, for HIV-positives like himself, so that sufferers who still had energy could care for the weak and dying. The organization was crippled from the start by the high mortality rate of its membership. People joined Zewedu's group only when their AIDS became too obvious to conceal. The life expectancy of new members was measured in months and weeks.

Zewedu had hoped he could launch a campaign like that of South Africa's Treatment Action Campaign (TAC), a grassroots movement of HIV-positives that had gained powerful leverage against the government, demanding treatment and affordable medications, pushing back against the taboos and hysteria expressed by the ill-informed public. Zewedu had read newspaper reports of demonstrations in

South Africa in which hundreds of people wore TAC T-shirts screen-printed with the words HIV POSITIVE. Even Nelson Mandela donned one, in solidarity.

But it wasn't happening here. The people who joined his group—men, mostly, with nothing left of them but bones and agony—had been humiliated by the familial and public response to their infection.

Zewedu sat with drooping eyebrows staring out upon the bright day.

Haregewoin led reluctant Mekdes into the room. The little girl seemed almost afraid to put one foot in front of the other. She had a vacant expression, as though she were not fully awake. She wore the same dusty clothes and same braids as the day before, but her face had been washed. With enormous tenderness, Selamneh lifted the thin child to his lap. Mekdes was so shy she could barely speak. She wanted to bury her face in his chest, but didn't know him well enough to do so. Thus she sat frozen, exposed on all sides.

Three-year-old Yabsira dashed into the room looking for Mekdes, saw her, let Haregewoin hug and kiss him, then turned to the toys scattered on the floor and started banging. As long as his sister was nearby, he felt cheerful; it was five-year-old Mekdes who had to navigate the empty new world for the two of them.

"Does she remember her father?" I asked.

"Do you remember your father?" Selamneh gently asked in Amharic.

In the flat face, vacant of feeling, Mekdes's lips moved, but there was no sound. Instinctively all the adults in the room bent closer to catch the threads of a whisper so small it consisted mostly of air.

"My father's name was Asnake Addisu," said the statue of a girl.

"My father died by herpes zoster. I was there. In the nighttime."

"What does she remember about her father?" I asked, and Selamneh translated.

"I never will forget my father," Mekdes whispered.

Though her eyes were flat, she sat in Selamneh's lap wringing and wringing her hands. She scratched at the palm of one hand with the nails of the other.

"Do you remember your mother?"

"My mother's name was Mulu Azeze," said the soundless voice. Her face showed no feeling, her brown eyes were lifeless, and still she wrung her hands. "After my father has died, my mother is sick and she suffer. And, after that, she died."

"Do you remember your mother before she fell sick?"

In a voice too small to be called a whisper (but a word for the smaller sound does not exist), she said, "I remember my mother by calling her name."

"When do you call your mother's name?" Selamneh whispered back.

After silence, the chapped lips moved again in the still face. "When somebody hit me, I call my mother's name."

"Mekdes, aren't they nice to you here?" Selamneh asked.

After a long pause, Mekdes whispered, "Yes, but they have a regulation here I do not like."

"What is it?"

Everyone leaned forward to hear.

"I never watched television before last night," she whispered. "Last night I liked watching it, but there is a regulation here." She gave a small sob before continuing. "You must turn off the television and go to bed at eight o'clock. Yet I did not feel finished."

When every adult in the room shouted with laughter, Mekdes jumped. We all felt reassured that, despite all the terrible things that had happened to Mekdes, she was a normal kid who preferred watching television rather than going to bed.

Even Zewedu looked up sharply, brightened, and then laughed.

26

IN ETHIOPIA, WITH the second-highest concentration of AIDS orphans in the world, motherless children were tumbling out of apartments and hovels in the cities, and from traditional circular dwellings (*tukuls*) in the countryside; they crossed the great golden valleys barefoot or in flip-flops; they dodged cars and buses in the cities and towns to tap on car windows with outstretched hands. In rags, they labored or begged to earn their meals; they were highly vulnerable to becoming sex workers and physically or sexually abused house servants or fieldworkers. Children the age of middle schoolers found themselves suddenly the heads of households, responsible for younger brothers and sisters, including babies. When the babies died of AIDS or malnutrition, the older children were crushed by guilt. On dirt floors, in shacks and huts across beautiful Ethiopia, children sat cross-legged together, quietly starving.

Experts dubbed them "child-headed households."

UNICEF noted that the "survival strategy" of the child-headed households was "eating less."

A brother and sister pair ran into Haregewoin's bedroom one afternoon with furious accusations. Both were crying hard. Both had gleaming black eyes, raven-black skin and curls, and the muscular legs of runners. The boy, about nine, accused his sister of smacking him. Haregewoin sat on her bed and listened.

"He is ordering me around!" cried the sister, eleven. "I am the elder! He must not boss me!" She stomped her foot in frustration.

"She is a *girl*," said the boy. "A boy is the man of the family. I am the man of the family now. The man is the boss."

"You are not the man of the family. You are a stupid little boy," said the girl.

"You must do as I say!" shouted the boy.

"No!" she interrupted, crying from aggravation. "I am the elder. I am his elder. He cannot order me."

They were too angry to look at each other. They stopped shouting and glared at Haregewoin.

"You are the only two left of your entire family?" she asked.

They nodded.

She removed her glasses, held the bridge of her nose for a moment, then looked up and said, "You must treat each other with respect and kindness. You must treasure each other. Yes, you are the boy, and that is important, but she is the elder. She is your mother now. You must do as she says. When you are bigger, you will be strong and you will help her. She is your sister *and* she is your mother."

The children stared in amazement at Haregewoin, too stunned by this judgment to speak. They'd really only anticipated that one or the other would get a scolding or a spank. They turned to look at each other, in shocked silence. Moments passed without resolution. Suddenly the boy dove onto the floor at his sister's feet, cradled her sandals, and kissed them, begging forgiveness.

"Go on now," Haregewoin said. They turned and ran out, back to their games.

Unchecked sibling rivalry was not the worst risk to children left behind, alone.

On another monotonous, drippy afternoon in the rainy season, a phone call came for a girl named Kedamawit (k'-*dahm*-a-wit). Haregewoin's houseguests that day were two elderly ladies in traditional white robes and shawls. One wore her reading glasses on a beaded chain. Both were drinking their coffee in the comfortable semidarkness. When the house phone rang, Sara, the HIV-positive ex–college sophomore being sheltered by Haregewoin, answered it, then went to the door to yell for Kedamawit. If Haregewoin had answered the phone, maybe she would have handled the call herself.

A skinny, unkempt girl in a ripped T-shirt and too small jeans tore into the room, followed by her frightened little sister, Meseret (mes-*er*-ett). Eight-year-old Kedamawit picked up the phone and almost instantly began to rock and shriek and cry; she hit at her face with the flat of her free hand, smacking a cascade of tears. The child was panic-stricken, anguished; her mouth was a huge oval, wailing. Her dry, scratchy hair stuck straight out; her skin had white patches that seemed to glow as she howled. She threw the receiver down on the table to hold herself and rock. Meseret, the little sister, made her mouth an oval of fear and wailing, too, though it wasn't clear if she'd absorbed meaning from the phone call or was echoing her big sister's distress. Haregewoin tore into the room, picked up the receiver, and shouted into it. When she hung up, she took both little girls in her arms and stroked them. Kedamawit shrieked and tore at her hair; Meseret pawed at her and at Haregewoin in fright and confusion.

The older women turned to each other in distress: had the children just learned of the death of their mother?

Haregewoin quickly shook her head at her friends. She murmured to the girls, then sent them into the adjoining bedroom where stacks of donated used clothing were piled against the wall. "Go find something new to put on," she told them, and they ran flat-footed, pigeon-toed, wailing again, into the bedroom and slammed the door. Sara let herself in the room after them, to help.

Their mother had not just died. She had died half a year earlier. It was almost worse than that.

Kedamawit and Meseret, at seven and five, lived alone in a one-room cinder-block house, which their parents had rented. It faced a hard-dirt courtyard shared by other cinder-block houses. There was a common cook-fire in the middle of the courtyard and a common latrine with walls of tin and a roof of tree branches. Old women in long skirts tended the fire in the courtyard, shaping bowls from wet clay for sale in the Mercato.

When the children's father died of AIDS, and then their mother, their bodies were collected by strangers from the *kebele*. There were hurried condolence calls by neighbors and distant relatives; plates of food were left on the wooden table; someone donated a blanket; then everyone went away again. Nobody told Kedamawit and Meseret what to do or where to go, so they stayed in their house alone. The woman next door brought in food once a day, their only meal. An old lady in the courtyard always greeted them happily, with black and missing teeth, and sometimes handed them chipped cups of tea. Their school did not expel them, so they held hands each morning and walked down the lane to class.

After school they came home to their empty house, ate the cold food left by the neighbor, draped their uniform skirts and sweaters over the two wooden chairs in the house, put on oversize T-shirts as nightgowns, and got into bed. They buffered themselves against the crisp mountain night and the scary noises by wrapping their arms around each other. They cried for their parents, but letting their tears splash onto each other as they whimpered *"Amaye! Abaye!"* made them feel worse instead of better. So Kedamawit tried to act more like a mother to Meseret; she sang fragments of songs she remembered her mother singing and petted Meseret's head as their mother had done. That made them feel a little better. When they felt scared—of intruders, of hyenas, of wild dogs—Kedamawit got up and wedged a chair against the door, then sprinted back to bed. They tried to fall asleep at the same instant, so neither would be left alone.

There was an uncle.

The *kebele* told the uncle to supervise the children. "Will you bring them to your house?" he was asked.

"No, sirs, honestly I cannot," he said. "I have a wife and children of my own."

AIDS, he implied.

"Then you must supervise them and give them money."

One night the uncle knocked at the door of his late half brother's house and ducked inside. "All right, all right," he said in a jolly voice. When he opened his arms, the little girls jumped from bed and ran to hug him. He sat down and jiggled them on his lap, tickled them under their arms, and rubbed his rough cheek against their faces; they felt shy—they didn't know him well—but they giggled and tried to feel happy.

"Do you know me?" he asked.

"Uncle," they said.

"There you go! Do you need anything?"

They shrugged. They studied his face, looking for a trace of *Abaye*. They looked into each other's eyes and smiled excitedly.

"All right, all right," he said again after a few minutes. He stood, sliding them from his lap, and watched as they got back into bed. He pulled out some paper birr from his pocket and put it on the wood table. Kedamawit ran to the neighbor the next morning and gave the money to her. The woman put it in her apron pocket. That afternoon, beside the usual cloth-covered plate of food, two shiny apples stood on the wood table. The round, red apples lit up the room, bright as electric lights. It looked like a holiday. The children had never tasted fresh apples before. They decided to eat one and save the other. They took turns nibbling at the peel, then breaking through to the spraying sweetness. They ate it all, leaving only the stem. Then they agreed to eat the other one.

The next afternoon, they found two bananas.

And the next afternoon, on a tin plate, a big bunch of red grapes. The uncle returned.

When he returned, it was past midnight. The compound was asleep. He didn't knock. At the bed of his nieces, he shook Kedamawit's shoulder. "Get up," he ordered. Sleepily she got out of bed. He sat down on the chair and pulled her by the waist toward him. "Take off your clothes."

"I don't understand."

"You heard me. I said take off your clothes. Here, I'll help you, take off the shirt."

Sleepily she thought he had brought gifts of new clothing. He was eager for her to try on something. She lifted her arms and let him pull the big T-shirt over her head. She was startled when he pulled down her underpants.

In the morning, she saw he had dropped money on the table again.

Two nights later, he returned. He had to shove the door hard to knock the angled chair out of the way. It took several moments of banging struggle and he was angry by the time he entered. This time he found Kedamawit wide-awake, already trembling. He dragged the chair to her bedside. "Get up," he said. She moaned and didn't obey. "I said get up or I'll wake *her* up. Is that what you want? It doesn't matter to *me*." She got up.

Afterward, when he left, throwing just one birr (nine cents) onto the table, he said, "I don't expect to find that chair in the way the next time. Keep it where it belongs: *here*." He shoved it hard under the table, nearly toppling the chair. "This place is a pigsty," he complained as he exited. "Clean it up."

He came once or twice a week for many months. One time he visited on a Sunday morning, bringing his own small sons, the girls' cousins. He made a big show of greeting all the neighbors, shaking hands, accepting condolences. He had a covered plate with him, food his wife had prepared, which he held aloft so all could see he was making a generous delivery.

"Why does Uncle visit late at night?" Meseret asked Kedamawit. Kedamawit knew by the way she asked the question that Meseret woke up in the night and saw.

"Tell *her*," said Meseret, referring to their neighbor. And it was a good idea.

Kedamawit tugged on the woman's skirt as she was hanging laundry on the line. "My uncle is pulling down my pants," she said.

"What?!"

"What did she tell?" asked Meseret when Kedamawit ran back into the house.

"She called the police and they told us what to do," said Kedamawit. "Tonight I am to wear all our clothes to bed. And if Uncle comes, I am to scream for our neighbor and she will come and she will bring all her friends."

The idea was that the extra layers of clothes would slow down the uncle as he undressed the child, allowing time for her to scream and for the neighbors to come.

She put on Meseret's school uniform under her own, with her mother's long brown dress and cotton shawl on top of that. Both girls laughed as fat Kedamawit waddled around the room. In bed, Meseret hugged her, with her eyes closed, smelling Mother's dress and remembering.

Their uncle didn't come that night, or for several nights. The neighbor peeked in each evening and said, "You call if you need me, okay? Everyone is ready."

Kedamawit began to imagine that it was over, that somehow the clothes kept her uncle away. Then he came. She was deeply asleep and awoke with a violent start when he poked her shoulder.

"Get up," he said. "Hey, what are you doing?"

"I was cold," she said.

"Get undressed."

Her throat somehow closed up, she was too scared to scream.

"Hurry up," he said.

She tried to nudge Meseret as she got out of bed, to wake her so *she* could scream, but Meseret didn't wake up.

Kedamawit's hands shook and she began to fumble at her buttons, feeling her uncle's hungry eyes on her. He pushed her down onto the mud floor and began to yank open the clothes himself. As she descended, she sucked in a great desperate breath, closed her eyes, and screamed. It was a full-throated, tremendous scream—she hadn't known she had it in her. Meseret instantly sat up in bed and screamed, too.

The neighborhood women ran barefoot across the courtyard, burst in the door, raised their lanterns, and found the grown man straddling the child on the floor.

"What are you doing?" they roared.

"You better die than be doing this!" bellowed one.

"You better be thinking, 'If my mother could see me now,'" shrieked another.

"I was just checking if the children are sleeping properly," the uncle stammered, shielding his head against the blows of their fists. He ran out, tugging up his pants, while the women whipped out their cell phones, calling the police. Meseret started to cry. Kedamawit did not cry but watched in amazement.

The next-door neighbor took the girls to her own house that night, and the next morning she marched them to the police station. The police phoned Haregewoin—"Will you please take these children?"—and she did.

The uncle had run away to the countryside, where he hid himself for a long time. He learned that the girls had inherited village land from their parents. He wanted this land for himself, but he needed the children's signatures.

"He came back to Addis crazy to get control of the children again," Haregewoin told her friends. "He needs their signatures in order to sell their land. Last week he came here.

"The first time he came, we did not know him, but we turned around and the children had run to hide. So we knew he was the uncle."

The next time he came, Haregewoin refused to admit him.

"Why have you come?" she shouted through the door.

"To see the children."

"You didn't bring the children here; the police brought them."

"They're mine. The *kebele* said for me to bring them to my house."

"The police are looking for you. I am calling them now."

The man ran away and hid in the countryside again.

The phone call that terrified the girls that afternoon came from their old next-door neighbor.

The neighbor saw the uncle snooping around their house, so she phoned Kedamawit to warn her to be careful, that the uncle was back in town.

The children emerged from Haregewoin's bedroom in clean clothes and dry faces. Still catching their breaths with intermittent sobs, holding hands, Kedamawit and Meseret went back outside to play.

"What will you do?" asked the ladies gravely.

"Oh, I've done it already," said Haregewoin. "I told the police where he is. They'd better go pick him up. The uncle is a very bad man. I will never let him near these children. I will find a new home for them and he will never find them again. I will find new parents for them who make sure the children get their money. The uncle doesn't scare me."

I started to wonder what might happen back home if the adult guardians and protectors of children began to disappear from our pretty neighborhoods.

If a plague began erasing mothers, fathers, school principals and crossing guards, pediatricians and coaches, teachers and clergy, band directors and PTA presidents, would the children of North America, Europe, and Oceania be safer than their vulnerable age-mates in Africa and Asia? Would our children still do their homework and have good bedtimes, play their high school sports and their musical instruments, observe their religious holidays, drive safely, graduate with honors, apply to colleges and universities, launch careers, choose the right spouses, and capably raise their own children if they had to do it all on their own?

Someone told me once about a public-service TV spot on AIDS in Africa. Though I never saw it myself, I began to imagine it in great detail: a towheaded, white American kid, in blue jeans, T-shirt, and sneakers, rides his bike down the sidewalk, turns in at his driveway, drops his bike in the grass, and jogs up the steps to the front door. It's a clean and comfortable house with art on the walls, bright pillows on the sofas, umbrellas in a brass stand—but it is silent. "Mom?" he calls. "Mom, are you home? Dad? Hey, is anyone home?" He walks through all the rooms; the kitchen counters are gleaming, the dining room table has a vase of flowers, sheet music is opened upon the piano. But no one is home. The commercial fades out as the boy starts up the stairs, still calling, "I'm home! Hey, where is everybody?"

And a deep voice-over says, "This has happened to twelve million African children. What would you do if it were your own neighborhood?"

But I don't know if there actually *was* such an awareness campaign or if I imagined it.

27

H AREGEWOIN WAS CONFIDENT in her ability to protect
the sisters from their predatory uncle.
     She was confident in her ability to protect and nurture
them all, all the children being brought to her on foot, by cart, by taxi,
by van; or, at least, she was confident until the sheer raw numbers of
children—more than thirty in 2003—began to dwarf her ability to
mother them.

     (Lately, one strategy in the AIDS orphan crisis in the ancient
sixteenth-century walled city of Harar was for a social worker to gather
a bunch of children, borrow a van, drive all day to Addis Ababa, and
drop off the children at Haregewoin's. Sometimes she had only a few
hours' notice that they were on their way.)

     Haregewoin was an untrained volunteer. She received no govern-
ment assistance for the upkeep of orphans—not at the local level, not
at the federal level.

     She knew nothing about the repercussions of sexual abuse on a
child. She offered Kedamawit the chance to pick out a nice outfit from
the mountain of used clothing and she promised to keep the uncle
away. End of intervention strategy.

     No social worker, nurse, or psychologist was assigned to her house,
nor was she ever provided with a course in basic principles of foster
care, counseling, child development, or health care. She knew everything about grief—she was a practiced hand at grief—but no one
offered to teach her modern principles of how to support children
stunned by the deaths of parents and siblings. She knew nothing about
childhood trauma.

She was offered no training in business management. No one measured the square footage of her house and compound and assigned children according to capacity, number of beds, and budget.

She was given no supervisor, no administrator, no mentor.

The only kind of punishment she knew about in her country was a swat, administered with a hand or with a switch ripped from a tree.

She received no advice in menu planning. Someone had told her that HIV-positive children needed green vegetables, so she stocked up on canned green peas and sprinkled them over the rice of the children who seemed sickest.

No one offered Haregewoin guidance on how to choose staff. No one fingerprinted or did criminal background checks on applicants for positions that paid pennies a day. It never crossed her mind that children who'd made it to the safety of her compound could still be vulnerable in any way.

The government gave one thing only to Haregewoin Teferra: a foster-care license. That they gave her for free.

Professionally speaking, Haregewoin Teferra continued as she had begun: she was a nice neighborhood lady.

Inspired by the direction her life was taking, increasingly purposeful, she asked the elderly guard to paint the name *Atetegeb Worku Metasebia Welage Aleba Histanet Merj Mahber* in white on a piece of tin. He was illiterate, so one of the big boys in the house did it for him. Haregewoin then asked the guard to hang the sign by a wire to the outside of the tin compound wall.

He warned her, "This will make it easier for people to find you."

"If the children aren't left with me," she snapped, "where in God's name will they end up?"

Bamlak, a boy, age 4, father died, mother dead. Came from Harar.
Miret, girl, 20 months. Father died, mother sick. Came from Harar.
Edlawit, 3 years, girl. Father died, mother died. Harar.
Roto, 1 year, mother died, nobody will take him. Harar.

But a few onlookers began to wonder like the guard, with concern, whether their old friend was not extending herself too far.

At night, Haregewoin began to pray to God for food.

Sometimes her prayers were answered. A farmer detoured on his way into town in an ancient truck and dropped off a sack of potatoes, grain, or eggs. At the Mercato, a knowing vendor offered her bruised fruit or not-quite-rotten vegetables at a steeply reduced price. A popular local singer sent word to Haregewoin that she would pay salaries ($18 a month) for several young women in the neighborhood to work as caregivers. Suzie faithfully shared her paycheck with her mother, and Haregewoin's old friends slipped her folded bills out of their household allowances. At each gift, Haregewoin closed her eyes, held her hands palms up, and said, "Thanks, God."

She sold off everything that wasn't of practical use, including almost all her clothes. Every trinket, every book, every bracelet, every record album, was sold. With the coins, she bought beans. She didn't know whether to laugh or cry when remembering—while ankle-deep in a galvanized tub in the yard, treading on little shirts and underpants and socks—that she and Worku had once owned a washing machine.

None of her austerity measures was sufficient. She and the children were living on collard greens, lentils, and weak tea. At night, when the children complained of stomachaches, she sent them to bed, sometimes with a harsh tone or an angry word, which she regretted later.

Scowling, squeezing her fists in the night, Haregewoin began to swear at herself, *No more children.* She struck her own leg in emphasis. *You cannot take in one more child. We will starve if you keep opening the gate.* She prayed that she had not misinterpreted her mission. She was willing for children to be assigned, to be housed, elsewhere, but she had reached the same observation once made to her by the MMM director, when he'd pleaded, "*Waizero* Haregewoin, there *is* no one else." Well, there were a few, but all shelters, like hers, were overcrowded.

Haregewoin and Worku once enjoyed two cars, a fine house with an indoor bathroom, a gas oven, a telephone and a TV. Now she began to fear she'd plummeted too far and too fast, gotten herself in trouble, become responsible for too many children. People praised, "Oh, you're so good, such a Christian woman." But she feared they lied and that in fact they thought, "But this is a foolish lady. She will end by doing more harm than good."

Too many children slept in every bed and in every room.

Every day, new children waited hopefully outside her gate. From the countryside, elderly people started out by oxcart or on foot with young children in tow, aiming toward the place in the capital where AIDS orphans were not shunned. Every day she greeted with open arms the new arrivals—every child was made to feel wanted, as if his or her presence were the very element missing from the house's happy chemistry. She stooped and tried to win a smile from the child or, at least, a cessation of tears. Every night she lay awake stunned in the tangle of young arms and legs on her bed.

Is anyone out there?

Does anyone know what is happening in our country?

An angry banging on the door of the compound, late one night, lacked the hesitant sound of a grieving adult about to surrender a child.

"Yes?" Haregewoin said hoarsely, standing in her nightgown inside the walls.

"This is Ahmed. You have my daughter in there!" shouted a man.

"Who is your daughter?"

"Meskerem Ahmed."

"Why do you come so late?"

"She must return to my house."

"You did not bring her here, MMM brought her to me. Go get a letter from MMM."

She waited, but he did not reply. He had gone away.

He returned the next afternoon, waving his letter. "At least you come by daylight this time," she said snippily, opening the gate to him. "Meskerem!" she called. "You have a visitor!"

But Meskerem—the deep-browed girl, one of the first young

children given to her by MMM—did not race across the courtyard to embrace her father. She hung back, watching from the threshold of the house.

"Come, Meskerem," he called. "It is time to come back home."

"No!" shouted the graceful girl, astounding everyone. No one had heard Meskerem raise her voice before. She was gentle, an excellent student. She clutched the hand of her best friend, Selamawit, for protection.

"Come, Meskerem," he repeated. "Be a good girl."

"No!" she yelled again. "Why do you look for me now? Why didn't you come to see my mother before she died? How do you think I lived all this time?"

Haregewoin listened openmouthed. Meskerem was eight now; who knew she was capable of rage?

"Did your wife get a child?" taunted Meskerem from the doorway. "You need help in your house? You need me to carry water? Why didn't you look for me before now?"

"He didn't expect this," Haregewoin marveled. "Even me, I did not expect."

"I will take her by force," Ahmed told Haregewoin.

"No, you will not take her by force," said Haregewoin. "If she wants to go, here she is."

"Meskerem!" he said again.

"I think you'd better leave, Ahmed," said Haregewoin.

"I will go to the police," he said.

"Go then."

A police officer phoned the next day, asking Haregewoin to bring Meskerem to the police station for a meeting with her father. They walked in with arms tightly linked. "Who is this woman?" Meskerem was asked by the officer to whom Ahmed had appealed for custody.

Clutching Haregewoin's hand, Meskerem said, "She is my mother."

The officer looked back at his paperwork. "It says your mother died."

"Yes, she died, but I got a new mother. I am like her own child to her. I better die right now than leave this woman."

"MMM placed her with me," said Haregewoin. "It was the wish of her mother's oldest son, Meskerem's half brother."

"What do you say?" the officer asked Ahmed.

"She belongs with me," he said.

"If the child does not wish to live with you, you must not force her," said the officer. "If she wishes to live with you, she may go. Otherwise she will stay where her mother's son has placed her. Do you have a complaint with the foster mother? No? Then you must not harass your daughter." He obliged Ahmed to sign a paper relinquishing custody to Haregewoin.

On Meskerem's birthday, Ahmed's young wife showed up at Haregewoin's house with a gift of freshly baked bread for Meskerem. "Why do you do this?" snapped Meskerem. "Can you not see the party my mother has made for me?"

"I didn't expect her to talk like that!" thought Haregewoin again.

As the stepmother set down the bread, all could see that she was pregnant.

"Aha!" yelled Meskerem, pointing. "This is why you wanted me."

So Meskerem stayed, though anxiously, afraid of being ripped away from Haregewoin's house. And Haregewoin worried about her in a different way. Meskerem was a smart and wonderful girl. What future did she have here? Girls and women lived lives as backward in this country as anywhere on earth. Female genital mutilation was practiced by many families; girls were denied education and given in marriage while still children. Their illiteracy, their poverty, their relentless childbearing, their early deaths, brought great suffering. Haregewoin felt pity for the young wife of Ahmed, who now, indeed, would have no help, who was little more than a girl herself, who would do all the child-rearing and housekeeping and most of the wage-earning for her household without even the small arms of an eight-year-old girl to help her.

And Haregewoin berated herself for not having done better by

Meskerem, the child who'd felt like a third daughter to her. "If I'd stopped with her, if I'd taken in only Meskerem and Selamawit, I could have raised them like Suzie and Atetegeb," she thought. "Instead, look what I've done to them." The girls, though happy, were ragged and unschooled.

"I save them from the streets for what?" Haregewoin thought angrily. "Stop. Stop, stop, stop. *No more children.*"

"Please, no, *please,*" groaned Haregewoin, trying to follow her own midnight resolutions and close the door in the face of the old couple from the countryside, standing on the dirt road with a small girl.

"I can't take any more. Honestly, I can't," Haregewoin pleaded, trying to avoid looking at the child.

"She ain't ours," they said in rural grammar.

"Who is she?"

"Her family lived in a *kojo* [grass hut] on our farm," said the woman. "Her father died last year I guess, I don't really know, and the mother died last week. We've been feeding her, but she can't stay alone and we have no room for her. Our own daughters died of it and we have our own grandchildren to raise. But this one," she said, pointing to her, "keeps turning up at our door. No sooner than we take her home than she's back."

Listening but resistant, Haregewoin absentmindedly reached into her apron pocket and pulled out a roll. She offered it to the dusty little girl, who grabbed it, instantly squatted down on the road, and began gnawing. She was about four. Her name, they thought, was Ruhima.

"Aren't there grandparents?"

"There may be, but we don't know the people."

"Do you have a grandmother, Ruhima?" asked Haregewoin.

"*Ow*"—yes—she said with her mouth full.

"What is her name?"

The girl looked up for a moment, considering, then offered, "*Ayatie*" (Grandma).

The adults met each other's eyes with involuntary smiles.

"Listen," said Haregewoin. "Truly I have no place for her. There is nowhere for her to sleep."

The couple looked down, now too ashamed to make eye contact. The husband was chewing the inside of his cheek. They were thin and ragged.

"Did you try to find grandparents?" asked Haregewoin.

"We asked all around," said the woman. "No one knows the child."

No, the truth is that no one is willing to claim the child because of how her parents died, thought Haregewoin.

"Well, we'll take her to the *kebele* here then," said the man. "They'll do more than ours."

"Oh, for God's sakes," said Haregewoin. "The *kebele* will send her here."

"Yep," said the man. "That's as we thought."

Haregewoin took Ruhima.

"Can we live with you?" sang a choir of fresh voices outside her compound door when Haregewoin opened it. She no longer flung it open, lest she be mowed down by a herd of neighborhood children. She opened it a crack and kept her grip on the door. Surely they didn't *all* mean it—some must have living parents—but some were sincere in their appeal.

"No, no more room, I'm sorry."

"Please, *waizero*, please! Please!"

"Please give me what to eat!" one might say, then they all took it up. "We are hungry, missus!"

If she scolded, "Go home to your parents for your meal!" she would be sorry, for a roar would return "They are dead, *waizero*! My father and mother have died, madam!"

She sent her own dozens of children out the door to the public school every morning, with Suzie and with her old friends covering the cost of their uniforms and school fees; in the afternoons, interlopers hidden among them tried to squeeze back through her gates. She stood guard at her compound door, blocking entry to the neighborhood children while summoning her own children to squeeze in under her arm.

Sometimes the bakery gave her bags of second-day rolls, and she shared them with the neighborhood children. She was happy to visit them, unless it resulted in a stampede. One day, as she said good-bye and tried to end the visit, she nearly slipped and fell. "Mother, please, Mother! Mother!" cried the mob, hanging on to every part of her flesh and clothing, kissing her hands, stroking her arms, falling to the dirt to kiss her shoes. "I am very good boy, Mother!" a big boy said, and she saw a small boy in the lane close his eyes and raise his arms, thinking she was about to fetch him.

"I can't, I can't," she said, backing away, peeling them off, angrily dabbing away her tears with the sleeve of her sweater.

"Madam!" cried a small girl. It was the little girl in the frilly, pink Sunday dress I'd met in the lane one day; her pretty dress was bedraggled and torn now; she took no further pride in it. She flew to Haregewoin's side, wishing to kiss her good-bye. Haregewoin hesitated, then bent over for her kiss. The child nuzzled her face deeply into Haregewoin's cheek and lingered there, with her eyes closed, breathing in, and then she insisted upon having a go at the other cheek, where she again kissed the tired face most earnestly and lingered there. She wasn't asking to be taken into the compound—she seemed to understand that she couldn't have Haregewoin as her own mother—she was only asking to be allowed this opportunity to kiss the mother.

28

T HERE WAS A problem with Mintesinot, the little curly-haired prince from the sidewalks. He was hoarding his food. His bedmates complained that it smelled bad and the bed was lumpy and ants were coming. Haregewoin watched him at dinner: sure enough, he put a few bites into his mouth, the rest went into his lap. She watched him smuggle it later into the outbuilding crammed with metal beds. When she inspected his bed, she found crumbled, moldy pieces of *injera* as hard as cardboard, a few pebbly morsels from last month's meat stew, an antique chicken drumstick, several bottle caps, and a slimy tangle of spaghetti, all nesting on a spreading circle of mildew.

"Mintesinot! *Na!* [Come here.]"

"*Abet?* [What?]" He ran in.

"Minty, no," she said, indicating the compost heap.

"For my dad!" he yelled.

"But this is unclean, we can't leave this here, your dad doesn't want this."

She began tugging off the sheets.

"Yes, he does, yes, he does!" he screamed, tugging back, trying to preserve his mound of decayed food and found objects.

"Minty, please."

"For my dad, for my dad, *formydad!*" he screamed, and pitched into hot-faced despair, eyes shut, arms windmilling against her.

She worked around him while she cleaned up the mess—the mattress was now stained; she took the soiled sheets out the door and came back to find him on his back on the floor, throwing his head from side to side, stomping his feet and screaming, "*Abi!* [Dad!]"

"Mintesinot! Mintesinot. Listen to me," she said, sitting on the mattress. "Mintesinot, do you want to visit your father?"

"Yes!" he snuffled. "Yes! Yes! Today!"

"Let me call the nice woman who knows him. Let me find out when."

He stood up and came to her, laying his hands on her knees. "Today!"

"It's too late today. It's bedtime."

"The day after today?"

"Maybe."

"Selamneh take me?"

"I'll ask Selamneh. *Ishi?* [Okay?]"

"*Ishi.*"

Haregewoin phoned Gerrida, the woman from Eskender's neighborhood, the next day.

"I meant to call you, Haregewoin," said Gerrida. "Eskender died last week."

In 2004, when Mintesinot's mother, Emebate, died and his father, Eskender, fell ill, they were two of twenty-six million men, women, and children in sub-Saharan Africa living with HIV/AIDS. Perhaps 4 percent of them had access to the lifesaving antiretroviral medications (ARVs) that reduced HIV/AIDS from a terminal to a chronic disease and rendered infected individuals less contagious.

In 2004, a quarter million HIV-positive Ethiopians reached the critical stage of the disease requiring ARV treatment to avert rapid deterioration and death. Only 4 percent—ten thousand people—had access to the medicine, which restored the lives of patients in wealthy countries.

Where were the drugs?

The first ARV was approved in the United States in 1987. It was zidovudine, commonly known as AZT.

The AZT molecule had been synthesized—as a potential cancer medicine—in 1964 by Jerome P. Horwitz, a chemistry professor at Wayne State University in Detroit, in conjunction with the Michigan Cancer Foundation. It proved ineffective against cancer. In the 1980s, Duke University researchers discovered AZT's potential to slow HIV in test tubes and in early clinical tests.

A pharmaceutical company, Burroughs Wellcome (later Glaxo Wellcome), had purchased the rights to the interesting molecule prior to confirmation of its impact on HIV. (There are two types of drug companies: research-based or "innovator" firms, which conduct original research, pioneering and patenting new medicines; and generic firms, which produce and sell versions of existing drugs.) The private firm, Burroughs Wellcome, filed for patent protection as the sole inventor of AZT and was licensed as such by the U.S. Patent Office. When AZT proved effective at slowing the growth of HIV, Burroughs Wellcome hit the lottery.

Given exclusive marketing rights to the first and only ARV (in a year during which more than four thousand Americans would die of AIDS), Burroughs Wellcome brought AZT to market under the proprietary (or brand) name Retrovir and set the cost at $10,000 per patient per year.

When public protests against AZT's extravagant price tag ($16,000 a year in 2005 dollars) failed to move Burroughs Wellcome, a lawsuit was filed in 1991 by consumer groups and generic-drug companies hoping to compel the private drugmaker to share the patent. If the private drug company lost its monopoly, generic copies could be manufactured and distributed far more cheaply. Generic AZT was sold in Canada and in a few other countries to which Burroughs Wellcome's patent did not extend. (Some governments did not believe in patenting essential medicines.) However, in the opening decades of the AIDS pandemic, the U.S. government, under Presidents Reagan, Bush, and Clinton, stood behind the private drug companies.

The plaintiffs alleged that Burroughs Wellcome was not AZT's sole inventor: scientists at the National Cancer Institute (NCI), under the aegis of the National Institutes of Health (NIH), had developed the underlying technologies for HIV drug testing, had provided the only lab at the time willing and able to screen agents for anti-HIV activity, and had documented AZT's efficiency. Indeed, a prominent NCI researcher, Robert Gallo, had been one of the early discoverers of HIV.

NIH supported the plaintiffs' argument that AZT had been developed with reliance on publicly funded research, but the U.S. Justice Department filed briefs siding with Glaxo Wellcome. The federal courts upheld Glaxo Wellcome's exclusive patent. The case traveled through the federal court system for five years. An appeal to the U.S. Supreme Court was denied in 1996; and Glaxo's exclusive ownership of AZT was guaranteed until 2005, preserving its luxury-item price tag.

"Most of the research that showed [AZT]'s effectiveness as an antiretroviral was done by NIH," reported the British medical journal the *Lancet* in 2000. "Nevertheless, Glaxo Wellcome . . . brought the drug onto the market in 1987 as one of the most expensive ever sold. Thirteen years later, the drug remains unaffordable for most people with AIDS. They will have to wait another five years before the patent expires."

In 1991, a second anti-HIV drug was approved in the United States: didanosine [ddl], brought to market by Bristol-Myers Squibb Company, under the brand name Videx.

In 1992, zalcitabine (ddC) was approved by the FDA and was marketed by Roche under the brand name Hivid.

In 1994, d4T was approved, sold by Bristol-Myers Squibb as Zerit.

Roxane Laboratories introduced nevirapine under the brand name Viramune; Abbott Laboratories offered ritonavir under the brand name Norvir; Roche introduced saquinavir, branded as Invirase; Merck marketed indinavir, which they called Crixivan. Glaxo Wellcome introduced 3TC with the brand name Epivir.

It was a roll call of excellence, of brilliance and innovation. The different classes of drugs (there were protease inhibitors and nonnucleoside reverse transcriptase inhibitors) interrupted the virus at different stages as it took over the machinery of the host cells and began to replicate. No cure had been found yet for HIV/AIDS, but the remarkable drugs arrested the progress of HIV, releasing tremendous optimism into the world that lives would be preserved while the search for the cure continued.

In 1995, new drugs (protease inhibitors) were approved by FDA. The combination of a protease inhibitor with two reverse transcriptase inhibitors proved to be even more effective at blocking HIV. Introduced at the eleventh International Conference on AIDS in Vancouver in 1996, the combined therapy—known as highly active antiretroviral therapy [HAART], or the triple-drug cocktail, or triple therapy—revolutionized the treatment of AIDS patients. The three combined drugs (owned by three different drug companies) reduced a patient's viral load to below-detectable levels. AIDS was reduced from a nearly always fatal disease to a chronic but manageable disease.

The American AIDS death rate dropped by 47 percent within two years of the introduction of triple-drug therapy. In 1998, sixteen thousand Americans were still alive who would probably have died the previous year without the new drug therapies. By 2000, AIDS-related mortality in Europe and the U.S. fell by more than 70 percent.

"It returns many who were debilitated and dying to relatively healthy and productive life," stated FDA HIV/AIDS coordinator Richard Klein in the summer of 1999.

With HAART, the recovery of end-stage AIDS patients from the brink of death to active life was so fast and remarkable a turnaround as to be dubbed the Lazarus effect, after the New Testament figure who was raised from the dead.

But the AZT pricing story was the same for nearly all the ARVs, reported the *Lancet*: "often discovered by public laboratories, developed in short time-frames in clinical trials supported by public funds, and then sold at a high price. Public research institutes have heavily funded anti-retroviral development—including that for didanosine, abacavir, stavudine, zalcitabine, and the concept of protease inhibitors . . . but rights to commercialization have been granted to private companies on an exclusive basis.

"Thus, the usual explanation proffered by industry to justify their high prices—that research and development is a long and expensive process—is extremely weak here. Nothing explains why companies charge so much except that [the drugs] were initially put on the market in the USA, a rich country without price controls. Unfortunately for most of the world's 34 million people infected with HIV [in 2000], pharmaceutical companies impose US prices on the rest of the world."

All this was true not only for anti-AIDS medications. The five top-selling drugs in 1995 (Zantac, Zovirax, Capoten, Vasotec, and Prozac) were the products of seventeen scientific papers, and NIH reported that sixteen of those seventeen papers came from outside the pharmaceutical industry. The *Boston Globe* reported that of the best-selling fifty drugs approved from 1992 to 1997, forty-five had received government funding. In 1998, the journal *Health Affairs* reported that only 15 percent of the scientific articles underpinning patent applications for clinical medicines came from pharmaceutical industry research, while 54 percent came from universities, 13 percent from government labs, and the rest from other public and nonprofit institutions. In 2000, *Forbes* magazine estimated that, after plowing $21 billion back into R&D, the ten largest U.S. drugmakers had $100 billion more in sales than manufacturing costs. "There is no question," writes Dr. Marcia Angell, former editor in chief of the *New England Journal of Medicine*, "that publicly funded medical research—not the industry itself—is by far the major source of innovative drugs. That is particularly true of drugs for cancer and HIV/AIDS."

The industry has consistently argued that high drug prices are necessary to repay past investment in research and to fund future innovation, though critics object that research dollars are dwarfed by advertising and promotion dollars. "In 2001, drug companies gave doctors nearly $11 billion worth of 'free samples,'" writes Angell. ". . . The drugs weren't really free, of course. The costs were simply added on to drug prices (these firms are not charities). The same year, drug companies sent some 88,000 sales representatives around to doctors' offices to hand out the free samples, plus lots of personal gifts." In 2001, the drug company Pharmacia spent 44 percent of its revenues on marketing, advertising, and administration versus 16 percent on research and development. Drug companies' budgets are far from transparent, so industry watchers can only guess at where the money is going. "GlaxoSmithKline and its co-marketer Bayer signed a deal with the National Football League to promote their me-too drug Levitra to compete with Viagra for the huge 'erectile dysfuncion' market," writes Angell. "Reportedly the deal cost the companies $20 million. In addition to exclusive league sponsorship, they made individual deals with some of the teams . . . AstaZeneca spent a half billion dollars in 2001 to convince consumers to switch from Prilosec to Nexium . . . These are . . . examples of the pharmaceutical marketing that permeates our existence. No one knows how much of it there really is, because drug companies are even more secretive about their marketing expenditures than they are about their research and development costs. And well they might be. Those expenditures are so immense they simply can't be defended."

The generic and brand names of the HIV/AIDS drugs—Norvir, saquinavir, Invirase, Crixivan, Epivir—are strange compound words, and they describe strange compounds. The words are utilitarian rather than poetic; they sound like vocabulary from the constructed international language of Esperanto. But they became household names across the United States and around the world. They were more than a fountain of youth, they were a fountain of life. The arcane pharmaceutical nomenclature referred to a microscopic world; and the industry built upon those life-preserving molecules became one of the most profitable on earth, surpassing in some years even the oil industry.

"Executive salaries and compensation packages take on formidable proportions within the drug industry," report Alexander Irwin, Joyce Millen, and Dorothy Fallows in *Global AIDS: Myths and Facts*. "The

Panos Institute reports that in 2001 alone, the five highest-paid pharmaceutical company executives received over $183 million in compensation, not including unexercised stock options, 'considerably more than the entire health budget of many impoverished nations.'"

According to the AFL-CIO's annual survey of executive salaries and compensations, twenty chief executives of pharmaceutical companies took home compensations last year in excess of $1 million. Bristol-Myers Squibb's CEO received over $8 million, the chiefs of Eli Lilly and Company and of Abbott Laboratories each more than $11 million, and the head of Pfizer, $16,419,270 in 2005.

HAART, the triple cocktails, did not cure AIDS; they were complicated and had to be taken in strict adherence to instructions; they could generate unpleasant side effects; and they could interact negatively with other medications; but they averted the death decree. They carried the promise of unknown numbers of years of active life. They helped HIV-positive mothers give birth to HIV-negative children, and they helped HIV-positive children grow up indistinguishable from their peers. For those lucky souls—nearly all of them in Western countries—who got their hands on the pills, breath and flesh and muscle and hope returned.

Thus the numbers of AIDS deaths in the United States and Western Europe plummeted just as the numbers of AIDS deaths in Africa were exploding.

With the falloff of mortality in the northern hemisphere, the public engagement with HIV/AIDS diminished.

A 2004 survey of U.S. media coverage of the AIDS epidemic shows that AIDS-related stories peaked in 1987, declined in the early 1990s—other than the 1991 story of Magic Johnson's HIV-positive status—then declined again. The introduction of triple-cocktail therapy also aroused some interest in 1996 and 1997, but overall the stories slid to the newspaper back pages, the obituary notices.

On January 6, 1993, Rudolf Nureyev died. His doctor said that the great Russian ballet dancer "died from a cardiac complication following a cruel illness." In February, tennis champion Arthur Ashe died, less than a year after announcing that he had been infected with the virus. In March 1994, the actor Tom Hanks won an Oscar for playing a gay man with AIDS in the film *Philadelphia*; he dies at the end of the movie. In 1995, author Paul Monette died; he had won the National Book Award for nonfiction for *Becoming A Man*; his 1988 book, *Borrowed Time: An AIDS Memoir*, was about the loss of his partner, Roger Horwitz. In it, he wrote of the early years of AIDS in America, the years when the diagnosis was a death sentence:

"Now, in the seventh year of the calamity, my friends in L.A. can hardly recall what it felt like any longer, the time before the sickness. Yet we all watched the toll mount in New York, then in San Francisco, for years before it ever touched us here. It comes like a slowly dawning horror. At first you are equipped with a hundred different amulets to keep it far away. Then someone you know goes into the hospital, and suddenly you are at high noon in full battle gear. They have neglected to tell you that you will be issued no weapons of any sort. So you cobble together a weapon out of anything that lies at hand, like a prisoner honing a spoon handle into a stiletto. You fight tough, you fight dirty, but you cannot fight dirtier than it."

His words, no longer true in the United States, describe Africa today, not because the medicine hasn't been invented, but in large part because extraordinary patent protection has been invented.

With the creation of the lifesaving drugs, and the pulling of at-risk populations in America and Europe back from the brink, the AIDS story slipped off the obituary pages and fell from popular awareness. The wealthy nations lost interest, reported Barton Gellman for the *Washington Post*, "once they understood they had escaped the worst."

Where is it written that privately owned corporations, and private citizens, should profit by selling products—developed at public expense—back to the tax-paying public?

In the United States, it was written on President Ronald Reagan's watch.

Before 1980, government-financed discoveries were in the public domain, available to any private company that wanted to use them.

"Beginning in 1980," writes Dr. Marcia Angell in her best-selling book, *The Truth About the Drug Companies*, "Congress enacted a series of laws designed to speed the translation of tax-supported basic research into useful new products—a process sometimes referred to as 'technology transfer.'"

The goal was to stimulate the growth of American high-tech businesses at home and in global markets.

The Bayh-Dole Act (after its chief sponsors, Senator Birch Bayh [D-Ind] and Senator Robert Dole [R-Kans]) enabled publicly supported universities and laboratories to transfer their patents to drug companies and to share in the profits. The transfer of NIH discoveries to private industry did indeed stimulate the growth of private industry, as envisioned by the bill.

"These laws mean that drug companies no longer have to rely on their own research for new drugs, and few of the large ones do," writes Angell. "Increasingly, they rely on academia, small bio-tech start-up companies, and the NIH for that . . . Bayh-Dole was clearly a bonanza for big pharma."

Further legislation secured monopoly rights for the private drug companies and extended the life of the patents.

"Exclusivity is the lifeblood of the industry," writes Angell, "because it means that no other company may sell the same drug for a set period. After exclusive marketing rights expire, copies (called generic drugs) enter the market, and the price usually falls to as little as twenty percent of what it was."

But, writes Angell, "Industry lawyers have manipulated some of its provisions to extend patents far longer than the lawmakers intended . . .

"Drug companies now employ small armies of lawyers to milk these laws for all they're worth—and they're worth a lot.

"The result is that the effective patent life of brand-name drugs increased from about eight years in 1980 to about fourteen years in

2000. For a block-buster—usually defined as a drug with sales of over a billion dollars a year (like Lipitor or Celebrex or Zoloft)—those six years of additional exclusivity are golden. They can add billions of dollars to sales."

"The effects of patents on prices can be seen in the price change of a drug when its patent protection expires and generic versions of the medication enter the market," write Irwin, Millen, and Fallows. "Compare the price of CVS or RiteAid generic ibuprofen to the brand drug, Advil. In the US, the average generic medication sells for 48 percent less than the same drug under patent."

Citizenries decimated by HIV/AIDS tended to live in countries too poor to purchase and distribute brand-name HAART drugs. But the patent-extending battles that ensued over the blockbuster AIDS drugs not only added years to their patents, but spread the shadow of the monopolies across nations and continents.

The big drugmakers weren't focused on keeping lifesaving medicines away from the poor; the millions of people dying of AIDS (6.4 million people had died by 1997; and 22 million were HIV-infected) were not of specific interest. What the drug companies wanted to *avoid* was seeing a generic drug—identical to a pricy brand-name drug—sold at rock-bottom prices. There were two big problems with this. The first was that the comparison could prove uncomfortable; if a person in Brazil or India could purchase an exact copy of AZT for $1,000 a year, a customer in Sweden, France, or the United States might question why he was paying $10,000 or $15,000 for the branded version.

The second problem was that if generic-drug companies began churning out knockoffs, the cheap versions of the drugs would surely make their way into the rich markets of the northern hemisphere.

So *global* patent protection was the new frontier.

Most poor countries lacked pharmaceutical industries or had, at best, rudimentary factories unable to produce generic copies of compounds as complex as the ARVs. Importing essential medications was their only lifeline.

"Squarely put," said World Health Organization director Gro

Harlem Brundtland, "the drugs are in the north and the disease is in the south."

The research-based drugmakers (represented by powerful trade associations like the Pharmaceutical Research and Manufacturers of America [PhRMA] and the Geneva-based International Federation of Pharmaceutical Manufacturers Association [IFPMA]) lobbied hard and effectively in the world's power centers to assure that foreign governments—even those in Asia, South America, and Africa ravaged by the AIDS epidemic—would respect their patents.

This campaign resulted in the adoption, in 1995, of strict intellectual property laws by the World Trade Organization (WTO). Intellectual property law protects the economic interests of inventors and owners of original work. WTO's laws are called TRIPS, for Trade-Related Aspects of Intellectual Property Rights. TRIPS required countries to respect pharmaceutical patents for a minimum of twenty years.

All 147 member nations of the WTO were required to sign TRIPS (though their deadlines varied—the poorest nations were given a grace period) or face serious economic consequences.

"Western countries, led by the United States . . . fought strenuously on the international front to protect those patents," writes Daryl Lindsey in *Salon*; "in effect placing a greater value on intellectual property, in the name of spurring innovation and saving more lives in the future, than on saving lives currently at risk."

Although patent protection, with its accompanying high prices, is always cited as the prerequisite for future drug innovations, patients in poor countries were doubly shortchanged. "Even with patents, it is not profitable for companies to produce drugs for diseases that primarily affect the poor," writes Amy Kapczynski in *YaleGlobal*. "Only 13 out of the 1,393 new drugs approved between 1975 and 1999 were for tropical diseases . . . diseases that primarily affect poorer regions of the world. This suggests that the patent system is a raw deal for developing countries, because it gives them monopoly prices without giving them innovation."

The cost of fighting the AIDS pandemic in the 1990s with brand-name drugs was estimated at $3 billion a year. The U.S. government subsidized the cost for some Americans; African governments were too poor, and their AIDS sufferers too numerous, to contemplate doing the same. The *drugs* were not expensive; the *patents* were. The patented drugs cost $15,000 per patient per year, although production costs might have been closer to $200. This led to sticker shock among the world's governments: universal treatment would not be an option for Africans.

With the delivery of essential medications impossibly unaffordable for Africa, a debate ensued at the highest levels of global health planning: prevention versus treatment, with many experts and scholars arguing for prevention as far more cost-effective. Future lives could be saved with attention to public health messages about safe sex and condom use; nothing could be done for those already infected.

A two-tiered global health strategy evolved, with one approach for HIV-positive patients in rich countries (and rich patients in poor countries), and a different approach for the majority of the sick in poor countries. "With powerful defenders among academics, public health experts, and leaders of some of the world's most influential international health and development organizations," write the authors of *Global AIDS: Myths and Facts*, "because of the inadequacy of global AIDS funding . . . people in high-income regions (along with developing-world elites) enjoy access to effective antiretroviral treatment, while public health authorities in low-income countries are advised to concentrate exclusively on prevention, and avoid the technical challenges and expense of treatment programs."

At the end of the twentieth century, there was a discouraging sense that it was too late for the thirty-four million people living with HIV/AIDS: fewer than 2 percent of them had access to the ARVs or even to basic treatment for secondary disease. "Despite years of evidence of AIDS' genocidal toll on poor countries, no one has brought these drugs within reach of ordinary Africans," reported *Time* magazine. "In fact, the people who make the drugs—American- and European-owned multinational pharmaceutical corporations—and their home governments, notably Washington, have worked hard to keep prices up by limiting exports to the Third World and vigorously enforcing patent rights. They argue that drug firms legitimately need the profits to finance research on new wonder drugs. But at what point does the human benefit to desperate, destitute countries outweigh strict adherence to patents and profits?"

"A strategy that emphasizes prevention to the exclusion of treatment offers no hope to . . . tens of millions of human beings," wrote the authors of *Global AIDS: Myths and Facts.* "In fact, it passes a death sentence on them. One international official, speaking anonymously to the *Washington Post,* put it bluntly: 'We may have to sit by and just see these millions of people die.' Such a position may be seen as public health realism. Yet realism of this type contradicts the basic principles of equity and human rights and acquiesces to what has been called a system of 'global medical apartheid.' "

The *Washington Post* quoted a U.S. health official as saying "They're all dead already. They're just still walking around."

The drug companies protested that the high prices of their branded and patented drugs were not the real hurdles to fighting HIV/AIDS in Africa anyway. The real reasons for the health catastrophe in Africa, the industry argued, were government corruption, insufficient medical infrastructure (too few health professionals, labs, clinics, and hospitals), illiteracy in target populations (meaning the patients would not be able to interpret their doctors' orders), and lack of supportive technologies like roads, electricity, and refrigeration.

In 2001, the Bush administration's top foreign aid official, USAID director Andrew Natsios, publicly elaborated on the view that poor populations lacked the sophistication to manage complex medications. Such an argument implied that wealthy populations would be placed at risk by the drug-resistant strains of the virus springing up as a result of poor adherence to drug regimens by illiterate people. The *Boston Globe* reported: "Natsios, who spent a decade in aid work in Africa, said many Africans 'don't know what Western time is.' The USAID director was quoted as saying: 'You have to take these (AIDS) drugs a certain number of hours each day, or they don't work. Many people in Africa have never seen a clock or a watch their entire lives. And if you say, one o'clock in the afternoon, they do not know what you are talking about. They know morning, they know noon, they know evening, they know the darkness at night.' "

Corruption in government was often cited as a major impediment to health care delivery. But the high drug costs condemn HIV-positive patients to death even in the well-organized and committed African democracies that make public health a priority. Forty percent of African states are electoral democracies, so the failure of medical treatment to reach their citizens cannot be attributed entirely to poor leadership by indifferent autocrats. And African nations are far from unique in suffering the spectacle of public corruption, bribery, and misdirection of funds in high office. Would it be argued in any other region of the world that political graft should be punished by the withholding of health care from the citizenry? Meanwhile, organizations like the Global Fund have enacted strict accounting and monitoring policies, so that assistance can be offered confidently and without fear of corruption. "Evidence from Thailand, Uganda, and Brazil shows that countries do not need to wait until systemic corruption has been eliminated before implementing large-scale programs against HIV/AIDS with success," write Irwin, Millen, and Fallows. "Corruption and AIDS can be battled simultaneously."

Inadequate health infrastructure—too few professionals, too few hospitals and clinics and the existing ones inadequate—appears frequently as another explanation for the failure of HAART to reach poor countries. Of course such issues are tremendous and ongoing obstacles, but the description of the difficulty is insufficient justification for denying health care to millions. And such a generality overlooks a hundred exceptions and minor victories. For example, in the fourteen sub-Saharan nations hardest hit by HIV/AIDS, 72 percent of the children are vaccinated against measles. Pilot programs in poor countries—like Dr. Paul Farmer's Partners in Health [PIH] in

Haiti and its partner NGO, Zanmi Lasante [ZL]—have pioneered techniques for delivering complex medical care in resource-poor settings. When the *drugs* are available, resources can be mustered; paraprofessionals can be trained in the absence of educated doctors and nurses; communities coalesce around projects with the potential to save lives. Doctors Without Borders/Médecins Sans Frontières (MSF) launched AIDS treatment programs in Cambodia, Cameroon, Guatemala, Honduras, Kenya, Malawi, South Africa, Thailand, Uganda, and Ukraine in 2001. These organizations practice delivery of sophisticated health care where skeptics said it couldn't be done. They've discovered that individuals report for voluntary testing and counseling in far greater numbers where treatment is available; they've found that other killing and crippling diseases can be addressed, also, in regions where ARV delivery paves the way; and they've found that stigma and secrecy diminish when the disease is scaled back from a terminal to a chronic diagnosis. Drug-resistant strains are an ongoing calamity in this rapidly mutating pandemic, but the poor should not be singled out for blame here. The frontier health programs have established that poor people in poor countries follow their drug regimens with greater adherence than many studied populations in first world countries.

It is sometimes humorously suggested that if only the Coca-Cola company were in charge of getting ARVs to the most remote villages and isolated regions on earth—even those with high illiteracy rates and unreliable refrigeration—it would do so splendidly, accompanied by bright signs and billboards and nationwide advertising. Everyone in the province would know the name of the product, what it did for your life, and where to line up for it.

By the mid-1990s, it was evident that South Africa was the hardest-hit country in the HIV/AIDS pandemic: 4.3 million South Africans were infected with HIV; a quarter of a million South Africans would die of it by 2000; and it was estimated that, by 2010, life expectancy in South Africa would have fallen by more than twenty years.

In 1997, taking advantage of a legal exception in TRIPS, the South African government passed the Medicines and Related Substances Control Amendment Act. Theoretically, under TRIPS, in a public health emergency, a government was permitted to *suspend* the patent protection on a brand-name drug within the country (this was called "compulsory licensing") and was permitted to *shop* for the cheapest versions available of brand-name drugs, rather than buying them directly from their manufacturers (this was called "parallel import- ing"). Less than three months after President Nelson Mandela signed the "Medicines Act" into law, the Pharmaceutical Manufacturers' Association of South Africa, representing thirty-nine pharmaceutical companies, filed suit in South Africa's Constitutional Court, barring the amendment from taking effect. Plaintiffs included Alcon, Bayer, Bristol-Myers Squibb, Boehringer-Ingelheim, Eli Lilly, GlaxoSmith- Kline, Merck, and SmithKline Beecham.

"The pharmaceutical industry and the Clinton administration take the view that compulsory licenses and [parallel importing] pose a threat to the entire system of intellectual property protection," reported the *San Francisco Chronicle.* "Access to AIDS drugs, they say, can be solved without destroying the patent system."

"Patents are the lifeblood of our industry," said David Warr, associate director of tax and trade policy at Bristol-Myers Squibb. "Compulsory licensing and parallel imports expropriate our patent rights."

The *San Francisco Chronicle* continued: "The only beneficiary of an erosion of patent rights, said Warr, is the generic drug industry, which does not subsidize through its sales the costly process of research— research that makes new top-of-the-line therapies available. 'There is a need not to fight the firefighters,' he said. Drug makers stress that even if AIDS medications were magically made cheaper for the African market, the lack of an infrastructure to distribute the drugs and monitor patients means that few would benefit."

Consumer and public health advocates all over the world raised a cry of shock and protest against the big drug companies. MSF, the AIDS

Coalition to Unleash Power (ACT UP), Oxfam, the Health GAP Coalition, and the Washington-based Consumer Project on Technology allied themselves with South Africa's grassroots Treatment Action Campaign (TAC), which had pushed hard for the Medicines Act. In South Africa, Supreme Court Judge Edwin Cameron, a white man who had stood in the forefront of the antiapartheid movement as a human rights attorney, revealed himself to be HIV-positive and compared the struggle to win access to essential medicines to the struggle against apartheid. He described on BBC radio the lifesaving turnabout of his own treatment:

"It was very dramatic. By the end of October 1997, I suddenly became very sick with a lung infection . . . I had lost an enormous amount of weight, my immune system had stopped functioning and the virus was raging throughout my body.

"I knew that I had to contemplate this treatment . . . which was fantastically expensive . . . way out of the reach of most Africans with AIDS or HIV.

"Within ten days of starting antiretroviral medication, I knew that a physiological miracle was happening within me. I knew that the virus had come to a standstill. I felt my health, my energy, my appetite and my joy for life returning."

The moral choices of the 1980s, which galvanized people of conscience to oppose South Africa's apartheid government, are "replicating themselves in a different form in the 2000s," Judge Cameron said, "in the battle for equal access to AIDS treatment." Activists echoed his thoughts with slogans like "Patient Rights Over Patent Rights," and "Stop Medical Apartheid."

"What drug companies are concerned about," James Love, executive director of the Consumer Project on Technology, testified before the U.S. Congress Subcommittee on Criminal Justice, Human Resources and Drug Policy, Committee on Government Reform, "is the embarrassment of seeing a drug like fluconazole selling for $23.50 in Italy but only 95 cents in India. In this sense, it is a public relations issue. But how many millions should literally die of this embarrassment?"

But the U.S. government, under President Bill Clinton and Vice President Al Gore, pressured South Africa to repeal the Medicines Act. Congress temporarily cut off foreign aid to South Africa beginning in October 1998; U.S. Trade Representative Charlene Barshefsky denied South Africa certain tariff breaks and placed the country on a "watch list"; and the Clinton administration tried to defeat a WHO resolution that urged member nations to "ensure that public health interests are paramount in pharmaceutical and health policies" and "to consider, whenever necessary, adapting national legislation in order to use to the full the flexibilities contained in TRIPS."

On February 5, 1999, the office of the U.S. Trade Representative reported to Congress: "All relevant agencies of the U.S. government have been engaged in an assiduous, concerted campaign" to get South Africa to capitulate and abandon the Medicines Act.

On June 16, 1999, Al Gore announced his candidacy for the presidency of the United States, and the public disgust with the big drugmakers suddenly became personal. In Carthage, Tennessee, at the very moment in his speech that the vice president announced his run for the presidency, protests rang out against his bullying of African countries trying to produce essential medicines. At campaign stops across the country, Gore was heckled and questioned; audience members hoisted signs reading AIDS DRUGS FOR AFRICA and GORE'S GREED KILLS; and media reports about his role in keeping lifesaving drugs from dying South Africans began to appear in the mainstream media.

John Judis in the *American Prospect* (7/1/99) outlined Gore's significant ties to the pharmaceutical industry, pointing out that PhRMA contributed heavily to his campaign and that his close advisers included former drug industry lobbyists. Meanwhile CNN showed the vice president handling his detractors with lines like "I believe in the First Amendment, let's give them a hand!" until audience applause drowned out the protesters and they were removed from the scene.

On June 25, 1999, chastened, Gore wrote a letter to Representative

James Clyburn, the chairman of the Congressional Black Caucus, saying, "I want you to know from the start that I support South Africa's efforts to enhance health care for its people including efforts to engage in compulsory licensing and parallel importing of pharmaceuticals—so long as they are done in a way consistent with international agreements."

"On its face, the [vice president's] statement was fine," James Love testified in Congress. "The problem was the longstanding practice of U.S. government trade officials to make up far-fetched and tenuous theories why the South African Act might violate the TRIPS."

On September 9, 1999, drug industry leaders announced they had suspended their suit against South Africa. U.S. Trade Representative Charlene Barshefsky announced that all was now well between the United States and South Africa. President Clinton, his attention diverted by these demonstrations and especially by the scene of twenty-five thousand protestors descending upon the World Trade Ministerial Conference in Seattle in November 1999, reversed course, and no longer stood in the way of the attempts of African governments to acquire essential medicines. His administration's trade representative, Barshevsky, confirmed that "it was the activities of ACT UP and the AIDS activists that galvanized our attention that there was an absolute crisis." Overriding fierce resistance from the Republican Congress, Clinton issued an executive order promising that the United States would not challenge African governments seeking to dispense cheaper AIDS drugs to their citizens.

The big drug companies took a thorough drubbing in the press over their lawsuit against South Africa, which had to be one of the worst public relations missteps of all time. Two years later, still sheepish about the poor judgment, an industry representative addressed a health and human rights conference. He opened with a joke: "People ask me how we could have been so stupid as to sue Nelson Mandela.

"I tell them we had to. Mother Teresa was already dead."

*   *   *

In 2000, an Indian drug manufacturer changed all the rules of the game.

Confident that high drug prices *were* the chief hurdle to universal treatment, and that education, counseling, prevention, lifting of stigma, and development of medical infrastructures would expand upon a foundation of universal access, Yusuf K. Hamied, head of the Indian drug company Cipla (founded in 1935 by his father), announced that his company was prepared to sell anti-AIDS drugs for a fraction of the going rate. There was a delayed-implementation clause in TRIPS for poor countries and India took advantage of the window of opportunity to ignore medical patents legally. The branded drugs then cost $12,000 per patient per year; at a European Commission meeting in Brussels, Hamied announced that Cipla would produce HAART for $800 per patient per year.

The following year, he cut his price again, to $300 per patient per year.

"We are a commercial company," says Hamied. "But I market four hundred products in India. If I don't make money on a half dozen of them, it's no big deal. I do not make any money on the cancer drugs we sell or drugs for thalassemia, a blood disorder that's common in India. We sell these drugs virtually at cost because I don't want to make money off these diseases which cause the whole fabric of society to crumble."

Some believed they heard, in these words, an echo of Dr. Jonas Salk, the inventor of the polio vaccine. He never patented the vaccine and never became a billionaire. When asked why not, he replied: "There is no patent. Could you patent the sun?"

Dr. Mark Rosenberg, of the Atlanta-based Task Force for Child Survival, says, "It is now unquestionably within the reach of the wealthy nations to provide a long-term, low-cost, and high-quality supply of drugs to keep not only the Ethiopian orphans alive, but to keep their parents alive. That is within easy reach. To do this for the rest of Africa would be a little bit of a stretch, and for India and China a little more of a stretch. Stretch, yes. Impossible? Not at all.

"My colleagues compare AIDS in Africa to the Holocaust," he says. "They imagine we will be asked by future generations, 'What did you do to help?'"

Brazil also took advantage of the delayed implementation of TRIPS to scale up a homegrown generic medicine industry. The government of Brazil promised generic ARVs to all citizens in need of them, free of cost, and it has disproved the argument, ever since, that poor countries can't offer access to complex AIDS medications without a mature health infrastructure.

In fact, the generic version of the triple combination was simpler: only the generic drug companies were able to offer the "fixed dose" version of the triple cocktails. Since each of the three elements of the combination therapy was patented and distributed by a different private company, the fixed-dose pill didn't exist in the brand-name world.

Both the Brazilian and the Indian generic companies signaled their willingness to export low-cost generic versions of the drugs to poor countries.

It was their worst nightmare: generic drugs penetrating the marketplace. In response, the multinational drug companies lowered their prices (with great publicity), made donations of specific drugs to specific governments for specific periods of time (accompanied by press releases), allowed generic copies of some brand-name drugs to be produced in specific locations (more press releases), and donated beautiful clinics and buildings with their names on them to a number of poor African countries.

In May 2000, five of the big drugmakers launched the Accelerating Access Initiative (AA), promising to offer steep reductions in brand-name drug prices for poor countries. They reaped PR advantages in advertising their generosity.

But "on-the-ground impact from these moves in Africa is hard to find," reported *Time* the following year. "Each country must negotiate the price of each AIDS-cocktail component with each company, and the tough bargaining has barely begun. While Senegal, for instance, might haggle prices down 75 percent or 80 percent, the therapy is still too costly at $1,200 a year for people who earn $510 a year, Senegal's per capita income."

The philanthropic discounts offered by the drug companies "have systematically come with strings attached," reported ACT UP in 2002, and have enabled the companies to control the supply of ARVs, while staving off competition from generic makers.

"According to the most optimistic of estimates," reported ACT UP Paris, "after two years, Accelerating Access has only resulted in getting an additional 0.1 percent of people with AIDS on treatment . . . Further, many of these treatments are actually dangerous drug regimens—such as single drug therapy, which has been banned from Northern medical practice for the last ten years."

ACT UP Paris also wrote, "Far different from commercial, blanket price reductions, Accelerating Access discounts are philanthropic actions revolving around the signing of an agreement between each company and the health ministry, to set convoluted conditions under which the discounts are actually accessible. Governments are usually required by the companies to keep these agreements entirely secret to the point of leaving all media communication to the company.

"Moreover, AA has completely failed to create significant price discounts for the drugs that lack a generic competitor yet. For example, through Accelerating Access, Swiss drug giant Roche continues to sell its leading protease inhibitor Viracept for an astounding USD $3,139 a year."

AIDS sufferers were saved, if at all, by nongovernmental organizations (NGOs) such as Doctors Without Borders—committed to importing generic medicines—while the patients' own governments got hog-tied by the Accelerating Access Initiative.

History will likely not be kind to Big Pharma and to the politicians and leaders of world organizations who supported it. Some activists long to see drug industry executives—and the political leaders and agency chiefs complicit with them—tried for crimes against humanity.

In 2003, TAC brought manslaughter charges against the health minister and the trade-and-industry minister of South Africa, charging them with the deaths of six hundred people a day who might have been saved with HAART.

At the waning of the twentieth century, the major drugmakers were presented with a historic opportunity. Crisis beckoned to them to recast the industry along ethical as well as profitable lines, to bring their medicines to the front lines of humanity's gravest health emergency.

Instead, they sued South Africa.

In the calculations and spreadsheets of those empowered to alter the fate of Mintesinot's father Eskender—the experts who argued that it was cost-effective to pursue prevention rather than treatment; the private drugmakers and WTO officials who wrapped up the ARVs in twenty-year-long patents; the heads of state of the rich countries who supported the pharmaceutical companies; the heads of state of poor countries who invested in armaments or yachts rather than in public health—Eskender was expendable.

He had not been expendable to Mintesinot.

29

S IX MONTHS AFTER his arrival, Ababu—perhaps three years
old now—was still tiny, still wordless, yet still alive. His eyes
were huge and distressed in his wizened face. His legs were
curved sticks. He did not speak. He whimpered in pain when
Haregewoin lifted him out of his crib and set him on a towel on
the floor to be near people. He crumpled, too weak to keep his back
erect. His head drooped toward his lap, his huge eyes filled slowly with
tears.

Haregewoin squatted near him, cooed to him, opened her arms,
and—with her coaching—he propped himself up on spidery arms and
crept toward her. One day he stood on wobbly legs and took a step
toward her before collapsing, a marionette whose strings were cut.

And Ababu was no longer her only desperately ill child.

A thin-chested little girl was so racked by her coughs she barely
focused on the world around her; she waited, from one minute to the
next, to shake back and forth, rattling like a dried gourd. There was
nothing and nobody left in her world now, other than this cough.

There was a feverish baby with chapped lips whose eyes never
seemed to focus.

There was a boy whose face was so thick with the molluscum
contagiosum unleashed by his damaged immune system that he smiled
sheepishly at newcomers, forgiving them in advance for being
horrified.

A scrawny girl of four clung hard and constantly to her older
brother, a healthy boy of nine; he carried her everywhere in his arms or
on his hip or riding on his back. When she was having an attack of

diarrhea, he apologized to the kids on the playground and ran to the latrine with her. "Our father has died, also our mother," he explained. "Yerusalem has been sick always, since her birth. But she is very nice girl when she is not feeling sick."

Before they came to Haregewoin's, this boy was the one to wash her. He took her to the river, pulled off her soiled clothing, and pounded it on rocks in the water as he saw women do, while Yerus squatted nearby naked.

"It's too much, it's too much," Haregewoin fretted. But there was no one to whom she could say, "It's too much," because everyone agreed with her already; they urged her constantly to divest the house, at the very least, of the sick ones. Old friends and visitors had protested her accepting, in the first place, the children who were likely HIV-positive and the ones suffering from symptoms of full-blown AIDS.

But what choice had there been?

If she groaned, "It's too much," to her friends, nearly all shouted, "Didn't we tell you?!" (Only Zewedu did not shout this.) So she complained only to those too young to understand what she said. "You're too much, you're all too much," she cooed to the babies while changing their diapers, and the babies wriggled and kicked hard in friendly reply.

Haregewoin was gripped by foreboding that she was going to lose a child. There were a few—the feverish baby who didn't focus her eyes, the little girl with the relentless cough, the little sister named Yerusalem—about whom she felt acutely fearful. And then one morning, the baby was too still. Its limbs were thick and cold as if made of clay, its face sunken. She tentatively poked the baby's arm; the indentation stayed. Haregewoin let out a cry and thought she would faint. She turned and bent over, resting her hands on her knees, on the verge of throwing up. Could she ask someone else—anyone else—to gather the body? Perhaps the old guard? Or dare she ask Sara, the ex–college girl? She stood up and turned back. Tenderly she gathered the corners of the dead baby's blanket and swaddled her. The terry-cloth pajamas were a little wet from the diaper . . . change her? Or not? She felt heavier dead than when she was alive. Haregewoin wrapped her up in the blanket, covering the unseeing face; she hurried across the courtyard with her, as if shielding the baby from the elements, from wind or rain, though it was a clear day. She ran with red eyes through the mêlée of children. With the sodden body across her lap, she phoned the *kebele*. She was told which city office to notify and that someone would come later in the day to pick up the body, or perhaps (they were very busy) it would be tomorrow. She shivered in another wave of nausea, deeply suspecting that the baby's body would be dropped into a common grave. And what was she supposed to do all day with the little girl's body?

"I must go to the church," she told the guard. She didn't even change her clothes, not knowing where to place the dead baby while she changed, unable to put her down. She pulled a shawl over her head and let it fall over her arms and cover the baby, and she rode by taxi to the church. She headed to her well-known—almost her beloved— cemetery and arranged for the baby to have an Orthodox burial.

She couldn't remember the last time she'd played with the baby or cooed to her; she couldn't recall the last time the terminally ill baby, with shrunken limbs and bony face, had smiled.

"No, please, it's impossible, please," she cried in dismay when she swung open the steel door and discovered a woman offering a wasted, barefoot, scabby-faced boy of indeterminate age. Wracked with AIDS, he could be four years old, or (she now understood) he could be a dwarfed seven-year-old. "Please, I cannot. You must take him somewhere else. There is no medicine here!"

The young woman released the boy's hand and threw herself violently onto the dirt, scrambling to kiss Haregewoin's feet. She wailed prayerfully, face in the dirt, palms up.

"Please, God, please, God!" cried Haregewoin aloud, joining her shouts to the woman's. "Tell me! What am I to do?"

The peppery-faced old guard hurried to Haregewoin's side, prepared to shoo away the visitor. "Begone!" he would tell her. "Go on your way. You people are killing *Waizero* Haregewoin!"

Haregewoin turned away from the road and covered her face with her shawl. "Take him."

"What?" cried the guard, doubling back.

"Take the child," she said, heading for her house.

"And where will I put this one?" he yelled at Haregewoin's back, for even he had become a critic.

"Let him sleep with you!" she shouted in aggravation.

And he softened instantly.

"Come with me, young fellow," he said, reaching for the hand of the frightened boy. "And what might your name be?"

30

HAREGEWOIN WENT LOOKING for an organization that specialized in housing HIV-positive children.

If she had medicine, it would be a different story! With joy, she would keep all of them, all of her sick ones, and try to heal them and raise them.

But, without drugs for the children, it was a death watch.

All her friends who pretended to find her so extraordinary didn't know how she recoiled in fear and nausea from this: finding that a baby had died alone in the night, being a surrogate mother to terminally ill children.

By the end of 2000, according to UNAIDS, 4.3 million children had died of AIDS since the start of the epidemic, and 1.4 million children were living with AIDS, nearly all of them in Africa.

There were only two houses for HIV-positive orphans in all of Ethiopia, Haregewoin learned, and both were in Addis Ababa. The largest, Mother Teresa's, was overflowing; there was also a small one, not far from her house, run by a husband and wife. She took a taxi there to meet the people and see how the children were treated, secretly planning to ask if she could transfer her sick children to them.

At Enat (Mother's) House for HIV-positive children (later renamed AHOPE for Children), there were happy shouts and hopscotch and random ball-kicking and hair-weaving on an outdoor dirt playground shaded by eucalyptus trees. There was the homey sour smell of *injera* cooking in an outdoor brick kitchen. But some of the children had begun to lose their hair, others were frighteningly thin, others had facial sores. These were the smallest victims of the continent's collision with HIV/AIDS: they had lost their mothers and fathers and brothers and sisters and now they themselves were sick and all but the youngest knew what that meant.

I first visited Enat House in 2001. A young caregiver in a nurse's dress and cotton head scarf called for the children to join her in the dining room. The children—the oldest perhaps seven or eight—ran to seat themselves at tables in the sunny, freshly mopped room. A glass vase of cut flowers sparkled with clean water on the tabletop. The children from rural areas had never seen scissors before, and their fingers wiggled with eagerness when the teacher began to hand out brightly colored plastic scissors. Yes, there were enough, Christ Lutheran Church of Forest Hills, Pennsylvania, had sent plenty in their boxes of donations. Following instructions, the children generated a blizzard of paper scraps in their first venture at making snowflakes (they'd never seen snowflakes before either).

Stocky little Ester was a pint-size Ethel Merman or Ella Fitzgerald with a husky belly laugh and a booming voice. She poked her tongue out of the corner of her mouth as she scissored, in classic kindergarten style. The children held up their lopsided constructions for one another to see, and they hooted in surprise. The teacher praised their work and taped the snowflakes to the cinder-block wall, the only wintry snowscape this city was likely to enjoy.

Later I watched the music class, which consisted of much hands-on-hip swaying and jumping on the dirt yard, under the guidance of a guitar-playing young man. Ester belted out the words of the songs and jerked her fat little tush around. Eyob was a handsome boy with a hopeful raised-eyebrows expression. His baggy brown pants were belted tight at the waist over a tucked-in polo shirt. He danced tilting forward and swinging his arms with the relaxed confidence of an old-fashioned African-American tap dancer. He had a knack for it, somehow slightly stalling his hand claps and foot stomps till the last moment of each beat; he seemed to be independently inventing swing.

But Eyob and Ester could not go to school. None of the HIV-positive children could go to school due to their health status, so the staff of this hole-in-the-wall orphanage—Gizaw and his wife, Tsedie, and their caregivers—taught the children in-house.

Tsedie, a dignified woman with sharp features and a bitter smile, said, "We want the children to enjoy life, to see something of life."

"We have AIDS so we do not go to school," said children too young to understand what that meant.

It was difficult to find staff to work at this orphanage, the directors told Haregewoin on her visit. The children were doubly stigmatized: their parents had died of HIV/AIDS and they themselves were infected.

"People shun me, also my wife, also our staff," said Gizaw, a weary, highly educated man in his fifties. "They say that *we* are positive just because we work with these children. I was at a government office recently and people pointed at me. Two years ago I had a gallbladder problem and I lost very much weight. People said, 'Oh, you see? Look at him now.'"

After I graduate, I want to be a professor of mathematics, wrote, in English, their star student and oldest child, a girl of ten named Amelezud. She had a long, clever face and an ironic smile, which she drew down over long front teeth. She had two younger brothers here and an older brother living on the outside.

In our country there are not many women pilots, so I may want to be a pilot, she wrote. *I want to learn quickly and I want to grow up. In the future, I want to live in my family's house. I want to build my older brother a villa and to plant flowers on the gate to make it beautiful. I want to help children without families, like me. I am going to tell them that I am like them, and help them the way* Mami and Babi [Tsedie and Gizaw] *help me. More than anything, I like to read history books. This makes my life happy.*

But Eyob's hair was coming out in tufts. So was Ester's. And there were no older children at this house: there were no middle-school-aged children, no teenagers. No, Haregewoin was told, they weren't on a field trip; no, they weren't living at a different facility. Their absence made a dreadful silence behind the noisy play of the still-living youngsters. The dearth of older children was like an arctic cold front pushing in behind the warm air of a late autumn day.

Ninety percent of HIV-infected children acquired the virus from their mothers before or during birth, or through breast-feeding. An unknown number were infected by contaminated needles and unscreened blood transfusions, and a small percentage were infected from sexual abuse by HIV-positive adults.

Roughly a quarter of the children born to infected mothers became HIV-positive.

In North America and Europe, it had been discovered that triple-dose combination therapies, beginning twenty-eight weeks into a woman's pregnancy, could reduce transmission of HIV to the baby by 98 percent and save the mother, too. Public health campaigns, counseling, prenatal care, and ARV therapy for HIV-infected pregnant women in the United States reduced childhood infections to below 2 percent of births. In 2002, the number of new cases of pediatric AIDS was ninety-two.

And in 2003, fifty-nine.

But fewer than 10 percent of HIV-positive pregnant women in Africa had access to these drugs.

So, in Ethiopia, the number of new pediatric cases in 2003 was roughly sixty thousand.

And the few HIV-positive pregnant women in Africa who *received* drugs for the prevention of mother-to-child-transmission (PMTCT) did not continue to be treated after giving birth. Those mothers enrolled in PMTCT programs *were* more likely to give birth to uninfected babies, but they were also more likely to sicken and die after delivery when their drug therapies were discontinued.

HIV/AIDS in children generally takes one of two paths. Eighty percent of children infected in infancy will die before they reach the age of two. Such children may never crawl, walk, or talk.

Of the remaining 20 percent, some may reach their eighth birthday, and a tiny minority may live to see their eleventh birthday before dying.

Gizaw knew this. He also knew that pretty Amelezud, who called him *Babi* (Grandpa), who felt she could be happy in life as long as she had history books to read, was already ten.

Gizaw had the bloodshot, haggard look of someone who has been up all night; he had wrestled AIDS for dozens of small lives already, and every single child had been dragged from his arms. "Another beautiful little prince of our country has just left us," he told Haregewoin of an eight-year-old boy who'd died two nights earlier. His first clue that the health of another child had faltered was the child's sudden refusal to enter into the games and exercises he or she had previously enjoyed. A child sitting listlessly on the curb, suddenly uninterested in hair-braiding or dodgeball, shunning the music teacher, was a terrible omen. Most of the children had seen one or both parents die, and many had lost siblings, too. When they began to spot symptoms in themselves—thrush in the mouth and throat, eruptions of molluscum contagiosum around the eyes and lips, and/or diarrhea—even the five-year-olds suspected what was next. It meant they were headed for the back bedroom with the closed door. Then all their visitors other than Gizaw—who would still hug and kiss them and hold their hands and sing to them—would wear surgical masks and rubber gloves.

"A child begins by losing weight," said Gizaw, whose background was in business and government administration, not medicine, but who had been prevailed upon for his experience with start-up NGOs to create this home. "The child develops infections in the mouth and throat—it's hard to swallow. The child stops eating, has diarrhea, pain in joints, pain in ears. It can take five months, three months, two months. The child gets pneumonia, the child starts having seizures. She does not talk about it, but she's kind of depressed. One day she is not playing on the playground, she just wants to sit and to be held." Facial sores, mouth sores, shingles, body rashes, swollen glands, combine to disfigure and hurt the child as her life nears the end.

"We have no antiretrovirals. We know that, in the West, children receive treatment. Our government does not have the hard currency to spend on antiretrovirals. We can fight pneumonia and small infections in the children, but that is all. We are running a hospice program." He grew quiet and stared straight ahead. "It is rather hard to see the children dying."

HIV-positive and AIDS-afflicted orphans lined up politely to greet Haregewoin. The touch of their parents had survived in the children's beautiful and elaborate names. As each lisped his or her name, Haregewoin fleetingly pictured the mother and father, even the poorest of the poor, inclining their heads above a newborn and conspiring to bestow an extravagant and ambitious name on the baby. Most nonbiblical Ethiopian names have meanings; but the names of these HIV-positive orphans seemed exceptionally poignant.

She met *Tidenek* (You Are Amazing), and *Bizunesh* (You Will Become Much), and *Asegdom* (He Who Makes Others Kneel Before Him).

She shook hands with *Mekonnen* (Dignitary) and *Zerabruk* (Descendant of Holiness). *Makeda* (The Beautiful) had been the name of the Queen of Sheba, and here came a little *Solomon*, as well.

Tadelech meant "She Is Lucky" and *Zenash* was "Famous." *Messaye* meant "You Resemble Me"—one couldn't miss the happiness of a mother or father in that one. *Etagegnehu*'s charming "I Have a Sister!" preserved a moment of family happiness, the rejoicing of a baby's older sibling.

Metekie's very common name, on the other hand, signaled the high infant and child mortality rate, for its bittersweet meaning was "Replacement Child."

Tenagne was "My Health," a touchingly hopeful choice given what must have followed (since Tenagne was now an HIV-positive orphan).

Allefnew's name was almost worse: "We Made It Through the Bad Times."

A scrappy little boy was seen by his parents as a future wheeler-dealer: his name was *Million*.

In the era of the pandemic, his name took on a different meaning entirely.

Haregewoin asked Gizaw whether she might transfer her HIV-positive children to Enat.

"I am very sorry, *Waizero* Haregewoin, but we have no room for more children, as you can see," said Gizaw politely.

For every child in this household, sixty more lived and died on nearby streets. Once or twice a week, Gizaw stepped through the gates of the little orphanage with another child in his arms.

When released to the playground, two little girls ran to find Gizaw, to show him the new jump-rope routine they'd mastered. A couple of boys tried to dodge around him with their soccer ball (balled-up plastic bags bound with string), luring him to play. He made a few feints with the ball, making the boys laugh.

When Gizaw jingled the keys to his van and said he needed two helpers to come into town with him on errands, the kids raised their hands high and jumped up and down squealing their desire to be taken. The faces under the bouncing braids of the little girls and the brimmed caps of the small boys were happy and hopeful.

31

S HE HAD THIRTY-TWO children, then thirty-eight children, then forty-two children, then she no longer knew how many children she had.

With these numbers, she had to raise the children as she and her siblings had been raised, as the country children on the dry plateaus were raised: with hard work, occasional rough words or a whipping, and flavorless starches that could be stirred in deep pots and spooned out in great quantities. The older children were obliged to help raise the younger children, as she herself had done for nineteen younger siblings.

"It makes me late to school!" protested Tamrat, age ten, an easygoing, athletic boy. "I am sick of caring for these kids. They can't even feed themselves. I'm late to school *every day.*"

"I fall asleep in class," said Meskerem, now an older child of nine. "The babies are keeping me up at night. She has given me three babies to watch and they wake up every night crying."

"She sends me out late at night to a shop if she runs out of something," Tamrat muttered to others. "I am too young for this. I need my sleep."

They told their complaints to Haregewoin, but she was hurrying past with a baby slung over her left shoulder and a bare-bottomed toddler dangling from her right hand, then running in the opposite direction waving a stick in pursuit of a boy whom she'd found defecating behind a crib in the baby room.

Yonas, Meskerem's eleven-year-old brother, had become Haregewoin's second-in-command in the compound; he was a compassionate boy and did not complain. But the children just below Yonas in rank grew vociferously unhappy. Older children, tapping their feet with impatience, stood on Haregewoin's threshold, hoping to be invited into the living room to complain. They were eager to present their cases and argue for reassignments of duty.

But Haregewoin was too engrossed in high-level strategy and desperate fund-raising sessions, with Zewedu and with her elderly sister-in-law Negede Tchaye Alemayhu, to entertain dissatisfied children. She waved them away with a sharp word and returned to the discussion on the table, where they went round and round on subjects about which they had no expertise:

"Is it better to put the HIV-positive children in bed with each other or with healthy children?"

"Are the HIV-positive children dangerous to the HIV-negative children, or vice versa?"

"Should the child with active TB and the child with hepatitis B sleep together or sleep with healthy children?"

"Will the HIV-positive children make the healthy children sick by eating off the same plates, even if we wash the plates with soap and hot water? Will the healthy children fall sick by using the latrine behind the HIV-positive children?"

Without medical information, they tried to apply common sense to situations that eluded common sense. In fact, the HIV-positive children were at much greater risk *from* the healthy children, not risks *to* them. But that was counterintuitive.

The compound had water sometimes, but not always. It had electricity and phone service most of the time, but not always. There was enough very basic food—such as white rice—for all of the children most of the time, but not always. The children were crammed together, healthy and sick, coughing and wheezing, sometimes hungry, sometimes screaming from nightmares, sometimes soiling the bed-sheets with vomit or diarrhea. It would have taken mathematical and medical geniuses, working with computers and blueprints and spread-sheets, to arrange living quarters and sleeping arrangements that would minimize—rather than optimize—the transfer of infections among the children.

It would have required another order of expert to minimize the contagion of unhappiness and trauma.

Meanwhile school-age children, bringing home good marks from school, shyly waited for the chance to show their papers to Haregewoin. She raced back and forth across the courtyard, yelling and slapping her hands; she herded them in one direction for dinner, in another direction for prayers. "Put that away! It will get dirty!" she'd yell about the schoolwork, so they put it away.

Tariku, age two boy. Mother was working in a house as a maid. Abandoned the child at the house and ran away.

Miret, girl, 8. Addis Ababa. Mother living with AIDS and TB, father died.

Birakadu, 10 year boy, grade 5, mother and father died.

Yimen, girl, one year, fell into fire, brought to city hospital, left at hospital.

Every night, Haregewoin called the children together for bedtime prayers. They sat cross-legged in rows on the floor facing front, within a circle of cots and cribs. She sat on a child-size chair facing them. She picked volunteers to come up and lead prayers and hymns of their choice, some from the Orthodox Church, some from the Protestant. "*Abbatachin-hoy,*" they began, calling out to God. The children's voices were piercing and high. Many had been well reared, she saw; they'd been reared in the church.

Once she had swayed and smiled and clapped and sung along, enjoying their prayers in the happiest moment of her day.

Of late she sat coldly, blankly. Her face went slack. She was hungry and exhausted. When the little ones bustled around for good-night kisses, she sat with a hanging face; they pecked her cheeks anyway before scampering to bed. On she sat, into the darkness and cold air, even after the children had put themselves to bed all around her; she sat and she sat, her mind a blank, her stomach empty.

32

HAREGEWOIN KNEW NOTHING of the epidemiology of HIV/AIDS in Ethiopia. She had no idea that the disease had walked home with soldiers from the front in the Eritrean wars. She didn't know public health experts could map tthe weary treks of soldiers and camp followers across the continent by incidence of HIV/AIDS. She knew nothing of the trends identified by the experts.

The authors of the 2003 book *Global AIDS: Myths and Facts* summarized the hazards of infectious disease in wartime: "Armed conflict often spawns large-scale population displacements, including movements of refugees as well as soldiers. Such displacements have been shown to be a factor in the spread of infectious diseases, including AIDS. During a war, concentrations of military men, often mobile and separated from family and loved ones, combined with high poverty levels among women, create a climate for prostitution and increased risks for HIV transmission. HIV infection rates in African armed forces are among the highest in the world, in some cases exceeding 50 percent."

But Haregewoin didn't read the books. She was just acquainted with a few poor souls in the neighborhood.

There was a humble, hand-wringing fellow named Getachew (Ge-*ta*-chew) Yohaleshet, who began lingering outside Haregewoin's gate. He was in his early fifties. He had a small son, whom he wished for Haregewoin to feed. Sighing, she admitted them one day out of the pouring rain; the boy, Asresahegne (Ahs-re-se-*haygne*) ran to join the other children, hoisting, while he ran, the grubby adult pair of pants with the broken zipper that he wore every day.

Getachew humbly entered the living room. Ingratiatingly twisting his wool cap in both hands, he bowed low to the few people present, showed his yellow teeth in a grimace of a smile, then perched on the edge of a chair, prepared, at the slightest frown from anyone, to evacuate the premises. At a stern word from Haregewoin, Getachew would have hurried out to the mud courtyard, trailing his broken shoelaces, and would have stood in the downpour while looking toward the house with a sad smile of acceptance.

"What's your story, Getachew?" called Zewedu idly across the damp, unlit room. Selamneh and I had stepped in, too, for a coffee break. We all turned toward pathetic Getachew with the combined force of more human respect and kindness than he'd seen in many years. It so unnerved him, he couldn't hold his cup steady and coffee slopped onto his filthy pants leg.

He cleared his throat, looked sadly at the large wet stain on his pants, and hesitantly began to talk, unsure at every moment whether to continue. Getachew was a weaver—he'd learned the art of making heavy-duty wool shawls, sheer delicate scarves, ornate thick curtains, and cream-colored bedsheets and tablecloths from his father and grandfather. He'd been accustomed to sit at his handmade wood loom for ten or twelve hours a day. His work was sold in the Mercato. His family lived in a stone house, set rather high on a hillock of mud, surrounded by collapsing wood shacks. After the death of his father, Getachew's mother, older sister, older brother, and their spouses lived in the family home. Getachew and his beloved wife, Shibarie, and their three children had lived there, too.

"Shibarie and I grew up together," he said. "She was a grade A student and I was a dropping-out student, but I had my skill of a weaver and so she agreed to marry me. It was always a very pleasant time to live with my wife. She was a very sweet wife to me and a very fine mother to our children."

Getachew was drafted into the army under Mengistu for the endless and devastating border war between Ethiopia and Eritrea. Ethiopia forcibly annexed Eritrea in the 1960s, launching Eritrea's thirty-year war for independence, roughly won by Eritrea, but on terms that continued to be disputed by the two governments, pouring their scarce resources into armaments and horrific waste of life. "I fought in Eritrea for thirteen years," said Getachew. "After thirteen years, I was captured by them. I was their prisoner for three years. I worked as a weaver for them in prison. They didn't give us enough food or clothes. They were starving us.

"When the Berlin Wall fell, that's when they freed us. There were ten thousand of us and we had to walk home. We walked for three months and two weeks to reach the Mereb River, the border of Ethiopia. When I came home, I was in bad shape. I returned to my mother's house and I learned that Shibarie had died, leaving our three children. She had been told by the army that I was dead. She was getting her widow's pension at the time she died. I was in grief for a long time. She was not just a wife to me, she was a mother to me, a sister to me. It was a very bad time for me. I did not know I would be making a life without Shibarie."

With a shaky hand, he returned his cup to the tray, bobbing his head in thanks to Sara for the coffee. Afraid to meet anyone's eyes, he looked toward the middle of the floor when speaking.

"After a few years, I married a very nice woman named Ayanechew; she helped my three children to grow up—and also we had that small son."

He was willing to stop there. After a moment he raised his eyes and saw that Haregewoin, Selamneh, Zewedu, and I still looked at him. Was a confession expected or required?

Smiling anxiously, he said, "When I was in military service in Eritrea, after five years the army allowed us to go out one time, to have fun.

"I think that was the time."

He waited, head bowed, for someone to shout or take a stick to him. As no one did, he pushed on, "It was very nice to be married with my second wife, but I was weak, I felt sick. I went to the *kebele* and asked for a letter and fifty birr so that I can go to a clinic for the HIV test. The moment I got my status, I was so shocked I could hardly stand. When I returned home, I told my wife to take the test—she was also having sickness. When she was positive, my family chased her out of the house. She went to live with her family. I joined my wife and I stayed with her until she died, four years ago.

"When I returned with our son to my family's house, they will not admit me. They chase me away. My mother believes that contact with me will make her sick. She pretends not to know me, or my son.

"I went to the *kebele* and told what has happened and the *kebele* forbade my mother to throw me away. So my mother told her servant to build a hovel out of mud and straw behind the family home, and that is where I live now with my youngest son. I am like a squatter, on my own family's land. They would prefer for me to disappear. They feel shame about me. I have nothing. My mother feels nothing for me. 'You are already dead,' she told me. 'We don't need you.' When we pass in the road, she sometimes says hello, but not like a mother. My sister and brother do not speak to me. They do not invite my son into their house. They do not have a welcoming face for him. The children of my brother and sister ridicule my son, who is their cousin. When I use the family latrine, my sister sends her servant out from the house to throw ashes on it."

Everyone sipped the coffee in silence for a while. Suddenly emboldened, seeing as he was the only entertainment, Getachew offered, "I met the Emperor Haile Selassie."

We all looked up in surprise.

"Shibarie and I had a big and wonderful wedding. I was so happy! I wore a new suit and she was in a white wedding dress. It was a grand ceremony in the Orthodox church, plenty of friends and relatives. As we were coming down the church steps, the emperor was riding down the road in his big car, in a line of cars. He loved weddings. He told his car to stop and he got out and he gestured to us. My wife and I ran across the road and we bowed at his feet. He was wearing his special kingly clothes."

Getachew was beaming now with the memory of royal velvets and calfskin leathers, gold epaulets and silver medals, jeweled rings and buckles. The memory of His Majesty radiated from Getachew's worn face into the room. The emperor's guards had held back the crowds, admitting only the bride and groom into the royal presence. Even the palace guards, who sprang out of the cars holding their polished weapons, had nodded benevolently at Getachew.

"He put his hands on our heads and he blessed us and he granted us a happy life." Then Getachew was finished and would say no more. The golden light was slow to fade from his face. Let his lips savor the taste of the words *Haile Selassie* and *the emperor* and *Shibarie* a bit longer before returning to awful realities.

Soon he would go home with his son to their hovel without fuel or electricity, with old newspaper pasted on the walls to buffer the cold; they would lie on a bed that was a raised slab of mud covered with newspapers. But he possessed this one treasure, this memory that sparkled with rubies and emeralds and silks and the long sheen of the black limousine in the long-ago sunlight: he had been in the Divine Presence, the emperor had put out his hand, the emperor had blessed him.

"Is your son positive?" asked Zewedu.

Getachew shook his head no.

And all Haregewoin could think, in her exhaustion, was *I am going to end up with Getachew's son.*

33

ENOK, AGE SIX, was on the lookout for a new mother. In the same way Haregewoin had taken him in, he planned to be taken in again, by someone new.

He had seen unattached women (women without babies slung on their backs) visit Haregewoin; why shouldn't one of them become *his*, his very own new mother, devoted tenderly and exclusively to Henok? Some of the visiting women were a little old (Haregewoin's elderly sister-in-law Negede Tehaye Alemayhu); some were a little young (Sara, the ex–college student); he was on the lookout for one that would be *just right*.

He stood near Haregewoin's front door whenever guests were expected. Enveloped in a girl's pink-and-turquoise windbreaker randomly tossed to him from a stack of clean laundry, he had nonetheless a dignified look, a serious, smooth face, round eyes, full lips. Patiently he rolled up the billowing jacket sleeves to free his hands.

When I disembarked in Haregewoin's compound for the first time, Henok blinked rapidly in my direction with a bit of lively curiosity and friendliness. Somehow his interest quickly faded. I don't know if it was my skin color, my age, or the fact that I had a kid with me in the taxi, but I was not the woman he wanted. He was a young man with criteria.

Having ruled me out, Henok nevertheless greeted me politely every day. I always stopped to find and shake his hand within the drapes of pink-and-turquoise polyester/nylon. Sometimes I won a thin, cool smile from him, but he quickly looked past my shoulder to the metal door, resuming his surveillance. I got out of his way. A more likely mother might come along any minute and it was unkind to block Henok's view.

Around him, on a warm weekday morning, small children cranked up a bit of make-believe. Someone had donated a child's car-seat (though few cars in Ethiopia had seat belts), and it sat on the pavement in front of the house, a staging area for games. Kids took turns sitting in it, as on a throne, and jamming dolls into it headfirst, and storing smooth pebbles (useful in the game of Ethiopian jacks, which does not involve bouncing a ball) deep in its folds. Small children, holding hands, toddled back and forth on obscure missions.

Whenever a car honked outside the gate for entry, the children's play and work flew into disorder. If a strange woman rode inside the car, the children grew agitated. A solo female visitor suggested— unbearably—that there were unclaimed mothers roaming about.

Even children who didn't remember their mothers suddenly felt hollow in their chest or stomach. Their arms flew up in tribute or confusion when visiting women shimmered into view. The little boys who'd happily been shoving the toy truck without wheels back and forth on the gravel began to wrangle over it instead; and small girls began to hurry and then fell down, scraping their knees or palms on the broken concrete, and started to cry. One could almost calculate how long a child had been motherless by its diminished cries: a little girl who has lived a long time, even at age two, without individualized attention, wails silently, mouth open wide, tears flowing, yet voiceless. Such a child has learned that full-tilt wailing—of the type that can only be soothed by a mother—takes her down a long road and drops her there out of breath, and she will have to make her own way back, her clean blouse wet and her toy now in the hands of someone else.

Young teenage girls breezed about the compound with their arms full of dishes or laundry or baby bottles, eager to demonstrate their value. Outside the tin walls, options for orphaned preteen and teenage girls were unspeakable. At the arrival of strangers, the teenage girls picked up extra loads—a baby *plus* a water pitcher; sheets *and* diapers. How useful they were! How helpful to have around! Doe-eyed, skittish, they aimed desperately to please, to be kept. They ducked their heads shyly, all but avoiding eye contact. With the deaths of their fathers and mothers, their futures had gone blank. Their schoolgirl lives had ended. Their best friends, their confidantes in English class and volleyball and choir practice, must have forgotten them by now. Midyear, midterm, these girls had dropped out and disappeared. Landlords or distant male relatives had taken their houses. Their girlfriends, their teachers (the ones who hadn't yet died), wouldn't think to look for them here, walled in at this foster home alongside children in diapers. But they weren't ungrateful! They knelt on the floor of Haregewoin's front room when she entertained; they served cubes of watermelon, bowls of grapes; they poured tea. Beside the front door, despite the tumult produced by visitors, Henok stood still, possessed of his secret strategy. He'd seen it all before: the wet faces lifted up, the chubby arms craning, the older girls seizing brooms and wildly sweeping. At most it won those kids a moment's attention from a female stranger disembarking from a shiny SUV or a battered taxi, a sympathetic word from a kneeling lady, sometimes even a hoist into a perfumed, billowy embrace. But Henok also knew: the children didn't leave with those women.

Once, the love of Haregewoin had been enough for everybody. Babies handed over to visitors protested and reached their arms back to her. She had once shared her love bounteously the way she served out the platters of bread or rice at dinner. She had given and laughed from a seemingly bottomless reserve. Hers was the bosom that consoled, the jiggly arms that lifted up the miserable.

But that was before the numbers of kids grew so large. It felt less like a family now. Henok wasn't certain Haregewoin still knew everyone's name. She called children by diminutives instead: *Mamoosh* for a little boy, *MiMi* for a girl.

At first, Henok had felt pained by all the new arrivals, and even more by Haregewoin's kindness to every one of them. She showered the most pathetic-looking, stinky, no-name kid with the same petting and murmuring she'd once given Henok, when he was new and establishing residence from his own shack down the lane. She took sick, mewling babies into her own bed, wrapped up in her shawl with her.

Henok chalked it up to the strangeness of mothers.

But just when he thought he couldn't bear to share her love with another living soul, she pulled back. Something about Haregewoin was in retreat; she was there in the middle of all of them, a busybody, barking orders, picking up kids by the armpits from one spot and plopping them down in another; but her grandmotherly, crinkly-eyed, welcoming nature seemed diminished.

That was when Henok began to shop for a new mother. So he sighed and he waited, his smooth brow creased a little, a small sentry with an assignment of the utmost seriousness.

And then, one day, she arrived.

She drove the car herself, zipping right up into the driveway and throwing it into park. Not a taxi, her own car. She wore a knit dress and matching short jacket woven of a mix of plain and shiny blue and black threads. She was in her late forties, with a big, open friendly face, wide girth, and brownish hair pulled haphazardly back into a knot. She gave a whoop of laughter in greeting to Haregewoin and yelled the opening words of a conversation before she was all the way out of the car. She talked differently from any woman Henok had heard before; louder, move vivid; he couldn't understand a word she was saying. No matter—he recognized her instantly.

Like a doorman at the finest hotel, he politely approached her and offered his hand. "Well, look at this cutie!" yelled the big woman. She took his hand without a thought. He hurried, skipping a little, to make sure his hand stayed cupped within hers. When she swung a big black handbag over her shoulder, he ducked to avoid being struck. She was his passport into Haregewoin's front room—usually children got a raised eyebrow from Haregewoin, or a single ticking index finger telling no, if they entered when guests were present. He walked double time beside his new mother toward the low sofa. Her hand released his for a second as she smoothed her skirt under her, but he sat down next to her, touching the side of her leg with the side of his, and he slid his hand back into her grasp.

Her words were a babble of nonsense, but he did hear one word clearly: "Ethiopia." It was her name, he thought, falling in love.

She was an American Southern black woman living in Addis Ababa as part of a church mission. Her husband was a minister. The middle-aged couple, awed by the thousands of homeless children milling about on the streets, wanted to help in some way, perhaps through adoption.

"This one's delicious! Who is this?" she asked at one point, and lifted Henok into her lap as if he were a toddler.

"That is Henok," said Haregewoin, laughing with Henok at his good luck and shaking her head at his mischief. He maintained a dignified posture, even while being cuddled.

"Well, tell me all about Henok!" said the new friend.

He would have left with her that instant.

When, after coffee and loud talking and boisterous laughter, the woman whose name was not really Ethiopia stood up, he stood, too. There was one small thing he might run to gather—he had a carved wooden top and string under the pillow of the twin bed he shared with three other boys—but then he thought better of it. Best to remain at Ethiopia's side, so there was no risk of her leaving without him.

He quick-stepped beside her and stood at attention by her side as she opened her car door. He studied her face for a clue.

She hurled her handbag across the front seat, got in, pulled the door shut, and rolled down her window for some parting remarks. Henok looked desperately to Haregewoin.

"What do you think about my friend Henok?" Haregewoin asked.

"He's a doll-baby!" said the woman. "I sure will talk to my husband about him. Okay, little man?" she said, and suddenly took his face in her hand. Understanding nothing, he nodded.

"Okay then!" she yelled.

He backed away into Haregewoin as the woman drove away.

Haregewoin draped her arm over his shoulder and chuckled, "She's going to ask her husband about you."

And he was joyful.

Henok thought he had beaten out all comers, but he hadn't. One of the older girls, a fifteen-year-old orphan, had served the coffee, curtsied nicely, offered sliced oranges. When Haregewoin had asked for a file from her cabinet, the girl had delivered it with a smile and a few words of English. "She speaks English!" said the American woman in surprise.

"Oh, yes, she's an excellent student," Haregewoin said. "She finished eighth grade."

Henok was focused on keeping his hand within the new mother's hand.

The American woman phoned Haregewoin a few days later to talk about the teenage girl. It was arranged for the girl to move to the apartment of the American minister and his wife; if she seemed happy and if it was a comfortable fit for all, they would apply to the Ethiopian courts for permission to adopt her and to the American embassy for a visa for their eventual return to the States.

When the woman he thought of as Ethiopia returned a week later, Henok was so excited he couldn't think where to run first, so he ran to fetch his top and put it in his pocket. He sat beside the American woman, bouncing with happiness, gazing up at her, stroking her hand and studying it. He grinned over at Haregewoin. Haregewoin shook her head at him slightly, but he ignored her warning.

When it was time to go, he was ready! He stood at the rear driver's-side door with his hand just above the handle, waiting for a signal. On the other side of the car, a good deal of hugging and well-wishing was going on, after which the teenage girl got into the front seat. Ethiopia came to the driver's side, flung open the door, threw herself in, and turned the key.

"Mama?" Henok tried.

"Good-bye, all! Wish us luck!" yelled the American woman, and the car backed away.

"She forgot me again!" yelled Henok. He flew to his bed and lay facedown.

"She likes you," Haregewoin said consolingly, sitting beside him and stroking his back as he sobbed. "But they have adopted the girl; I don't think her husband wants a second child."

34

ABABU WAS FAILING.

At three, the child dropped off by his great-grandmother, the wood-bearer, was smaller than the babies with whom he shared a crib. In the mornings, Haregewoin found him crouched in the corner of his crib, soaking wet, looking out with huge, sad eyes while gripping the bars with bony fingers. The weight of his smile, when he saw Haregewoin coming for him, caused his outsize bald head to bob down.

"You're my sweet, aren't you?" she said, extending an arm to him, which he clambered up with sharp nails to his roost on her chest. He leaned his head to rest on her shoulder.

Lately he couldn't climb up her arm. He could barely lift his head.

No! she thought. *Not this one, too. Please, God, don't take Ababu yet.*

She wanted a doctor to look at Ababu but she didn't know a doctor.

It was hard to know a doctor. In 1999, the doctor-to-patient ratio in Ethiopia was one to forty-eight thousand, the worst in the world. In 2003, the ratio of one doctor to thirty-four thousand people was five times worse than the sub-Saharan Africa average. (The doctor-to-patient ratio in the United States is roughly one to 142.)

But Haregewoin wanted a doctor to see Ababu.

The doctor she found would turn out to be one of the remarkable people in her life.

She would discover a person who had disdained every opportunity to build a prosperous life far from a world of suffering and death. Healthy, lured by no particular financial or career incentives, he waded into the disaster areas of the world (Rwanda, Somalia, Albania, Sudan,

Zaire, Tanzania, Lesotho, and Ethiopia), somehow feeling, "This is my fight."

He was a white American doctor. He was widely known, easily spotted. It was said that he would treat anyone who came to him, regardless of ability to pay, regardless of the hour of day or night.

His name was Rick Hodes. He was born in 1953 on Long Island, New York. As far as he knew, he was the only non-Ethiopian observant Jew between Jerusalem and Nairobi. He was the medical director for the American Jewish Joint Distribution Committee (JDC), serving the Ethiopian Jews, the Beta Israel. He treated hundreds of patients pro bono as well, in paupers' hospitals and shantytowns across Addis Ababa. He had lived in Ethiopia for close to twenty years and spoke fluent Amharic.

He was pale, not tall, with the sleek body of a swimmer. He owned a fitness membership to the Sheraton Addis. The hilltop, red-roofed Italianesque palace dominated the city skyline. Every day, Hodes drove up from the slums, removed his dress shirt and slacks and his stainless-steel eyeglasses, dove into the heated outdoor pool into which music was piped underwater, and swam a mile. A replica of an Ethiopian grass hut served as an outdoor bar-and-grill, while a smaller hut dispensed luxurious white towels. In such opulent surroundings, both huts seemed more of a South Seas motif than an Ethiopian one. Blue-and-white-striped umbrellas reflected off the bubbling water, and tuxedo-clad waiters presented iced drinks to guests cocooned in the thick towels.

Rick Hodes, trailing the damp scents of chlorine, sauna, and aftershave, always looked freshly showered and invigorated. His white business shirt had just been shaken free of the pins and tissue paper in which it was delivered from the dry cleaner; his khakis were sharply creased. He seemed rarely to sleep. His friends in the United States received e-mails from Hodes at two A.M., four A.M., six A.M. Addis Ababa time and could picture him perched cross-legged on his unmade double bed, in the middle of a plain bedroom piled high with medical journals and articles in progress, hunched over his laptop.

Hodes's voice was a tenor, but steely, as there was something steely in the friendly gaze behind the metal eyeglasses, and a wiry power in the skinny, white arms. The whiff of thin brown hair lying far back on his head became mussed when the doctor yanked on his stethoscope. His eyes widened during conversation like those of a serious boy presented with a chemistry set.

Hodes lived with his family—five Ethiopian adopted sons and half a dozen or more unofficial foster sons—in a brick ranch house behind high stone walls, on a paved residential street in Addis Ababa. The 1960s-era couches and coffee tables were piled high with books and papers, and the dusty wood-planked floors were littered with sneakers, soccer balls, scooters, and crutches. Boys hobbled around the house in various stages of recuperation from medical procedures. Some were victims of cancer, many of tuberculosis of the spine. TB of the spine, if untreated, is a devastating disease: the spine deteriorates, crippling the child, and he or she ends up permanently bedridden and in chronic pain. Rick had tripped over these kids on the streets, curled up and awaiting death; he found his son Mesfin in the adult ward of a paupers' hospital—a bright-eyed boy popping up between the overcrowded beds, belonging to no one. Between forty and fifty other Ethiopian children and adults had been sent by Hodes to the United States or Israel for medical treatment unavailable in Ethiopia. There was no Mrs. Hodes, despite occasional lobbying from the youths of the household. They knew Hodes went on dates in Israel. He had repeatedly explained to them his failure to return home with a wife: "I always have to tell my date, 'You don't just get nice Dr. Hodes. You get nice Dr. Hodes and a houseful of African boys.'"

On another occasion, he said, "A woman needs to go on several dates with all of you first. If that goes well, *then* I'll meet her."

One of the unofficial foster kids, Temesgen, fourteen, from a distant village, was his mother's only surviving son; she had buried eight children. Hodes had met the Orthodox Christian boy at a paupers' hospital and diagnosed his knee tumor as osteosarcoma (bone cancer). He arranged for Temesgen to see a surgeon at Alert Hospital; the boy's lower right leg was amputated; after which Hodes brought him home to administer six rounds of chemotherapy.

On the same day, in the same hospital, Hodes met eleven-year-old Mohammed, a Muslim boy from Bale. Mohammed had the identical tumor, but on his left knee. Hodes arranged for the same amputation to be performed, brought Mohammed home, and gave him the same six rounds of chemotherapy. The teenagers spent weeks on the porch, sick and needy from the therapy, exhausting Hodes. Then both boys stayed on in the Hodes household as foster sons. They started school, Mohammed for the first time.

"What do you tell kids at school who ask about your leg?" Hodes asked them over dinner one night.

"I tell them I had cancer, but now I'm well," said Mohammed.

"Not me!" said Temesgen, who came from a village so small that the fastest form of transportation anyone had ever seen was the donkey cart. "I tell them I was in an airplane crash."

The two boys wore the same shoe size. One day Hodes took them shoe-shopping together. Temesgen and Mohammed chose the flashiest pair of athletic shoes they could find. Then they shared it.

When Haregewoin reached Hodes on his cell phone, he was with a patient and asked to call her back.

He was responding to an appeal he'd received a few days earlier, when a young man had called to explain, in English, "Doctor, my sister is sick. She cannot up."

Hodes met Kiber (*Kee*-bearr), who was perhaps nineteen, at an intersection in the city's northeast sector. Kiber greeted him as *Abi*, a friendly form of "Father," with which a younger man may honor an older. He shook Hodes's hand vigorously and then took off running down a pebbly road, looking behind occasionally to see if the doctor was keeping up. Kiber veered right and vaulted over a low wire fence into a weedy lot. A green cement house sat back from the road, losing its paint; a footpath led through high weeds to the door. Hodes caught his breath, pushed back his hair, and ducked behind the young man into a single dim room.

Like Haregewoin, Hodes saw the epidemiological data every day, personified. The charts in Geneva, Washington, and Paris showed HIV prevalence in soldiers, babies, prostitutes. Haregewoin Teferra and Rick Hodes knew soldiers, babies, and prostitutes. They looked absolutely nothing like the bar graphs, pie graphs, and line graphs propped on easels in conference rooms in the northern hemisphere.

Green paint was falling off the interior cement walls, too, and the linoleum floor was peeling, but someone had tried to decorate. Ethiopian travel posters had been taped to the walls. The room was dominated by a freestanding wooden bar displaying bottles of local wine and whiskey. It was a *tej* (wine) house and probably something else. Hodes didn't have to peer into the back room to know a bed was there.

Two women hurried forward into the rectangle of light from the front door. Wearing miniskirts, camisoles, and huge teased-out hairstyles, they greeted the patient's brother with kisses to each cheek and shook hands warmly with Hodes. They were young, long-legged, and skinny; they wobbled on high heels; behind the perfume and makeup, their eyes were large and frightened as they directed Hodes to the patient.

The patient lay flat on a threadbare sofa under an Ethiopian Airlines blanket.

World-class Ethiopian Airlines, established in 1946 under Haile Selassie in conjunction with TWA, often had first-time passengers aboard. Some of these people gratefully accepted the blue-and-turquoise-striped, in-flight blanket as a gift, taking it from the stewardess with both hands and a bow of the upper body. Some travelers then disembarked in Cairo, Paris, Stockholm, Newark, or Washington wearing their Ethiopian Air blankets. Men wore them with tribal style and panache, wrapped around the waist and flung over the shoulder. A woman might wrap hers around her head and shoulders like a traditional shawl; I once saw a man who had changed in the airplane bathroom out of whatever clothes he had been wearing and into nothing but his Ethiopian Air blanket, which now hung like a belted shepherd's robe to his knees. Other men tied the lengths of fleece under their chins and strode through foreign airports with the blankets flowing behind them like capes. The Ethiopian people felt a justifiable pride in Ethiopian Airlines; in poor and rural areas, it was a sign of great status to have taken an airplane trip; the striped blanket was a treasured souvenir. It showed that a family knew someone who knew someone who once had *flown*.

The patient lay so thin and flat she was almost invisible. Hodes pulled up a chair beside the sofa and gently drew down the blanket. The sick woman wore a cotton bathrobe. She reeked of urine and an unwashed body. At thirty, she was more than a decade older than the girls in the room.

Hodes had grasped the picture instantly. *This is a prostitute with AIDS. Without ARVs, there will be little I can do for her. Perhaps I will find a different cause, a treatable condition, but I doubt it.*

Still, he would not regret the time he spent there.

In the Jewish tradition, he was thinking, *each visitor is said to take one-sixtieth of the illness away from the ailing person.*

Hodes found her hand and shook it, offering, "*Tena yesteling*" (May God grant you health).

In an unsmiling whisper she replied, "*Tena yesteling.*"

"She was okay until a few months ago," offered one of the teenage girls. "She got weaker and weaker and could not get up from the bed. We carried her out here so she will not be alone. She cannot hold her urine and it has a bad smell."

The sick woman, Gelila, was too far gone for embarrassment. She stared straight at Hodes's face, unblinking. She waited for him to do something.

"We got medicine for her," said the girl, and ran to get an ancient bottle of Bactrim to show him. "The medicine helped her a little, but then she got weak again and now she cannot walk."

Hodes couldn't bear to picture the hope the three must have felt the day the girls came home with medicine for Gelila. He could guess that they'd been driven by loss of parents, poverty, and hunger into the sex trade; they had found unexpected kindness here. This young woman had become a mother to them.

"Where did you get the medicine?"

"At the Mercato [the huge open-air market]. Was it right?"

It was unrefrigerated and expired. "Yes, it's fine."

The girls looked at each other with satisfaction.

"Is one side of your body weaker than the other?" Hodes asked the patient, first in English and then in Amharic.

"You are smart, Doctor!" said the chattier of the two teens. "It is true, Gelila, isn't it?"

Gelila nodded and gestured that her left side was weaker.

"Did this happen gradually, or suddenly?"

"It was sudden," said the teen, "and now it's a little better."

There could be a brain mass or infection, he was thinking; that it is not progressive is a good sign. But she looks horrible. She will not do well.

There is nothing I can do medically, but I will examine her, if only to invoke the magic of the "laying on of hands." I will not deprive her of the hope that an examination can bring.

He asked about fever, cough, mental-status changes.

"Can you help her undress?" he asked the girls. Kiber, the younger brother, stepped outside into the yard. Hodes watched as the woman struggled painfully free of the bathrobe.

Gelila was gaunt, haggard, and wasted. She must have been beautiful a year or two earlier; but her big brown eyes now protruded as her face tightened, dried up, and receded; even her hairline was receding. Hodes helped her to sit up; he tested her reflexes, felt her abdomen, tested her facial nerves, then helped her recline again.

The Talmud says, "The essential feature in the religious duty of visiting the sick is to pay attention to the needs of the invalid, to see what is necessary to be done for his benefit, to give him the pleasure of one's company, and to pray for mercy on his behalf."

"Thank you," he said politely. "I will go now and speak with your brother." Gelila's young friends helped her back into the bathrobe.

In the yard, Kiber sprang forward and shook Hodes's hand vigorously again, fighting down smile after smile. "Yes, Doctor?" he said, full of happy expectation. He had lured a real doctor to his sister! Now her fate would improve.

"Kiber, I cannot say what the problem is without further tests. But she does not look well. Let's think about the problem: She is incontinent, she is weak, she has a problem on the left side. Sometimes liver disease can look like this. She may have a urinary infection. I want to know whether she is anemic and what her blood counts are. I'd like to get some tests of her liver, her kidneys, and her blood. A chest X-ray would be useful."

Kiber continued to nod and to smile.

Here in Ethiopia many things are left unsaid, Hodes knew.

"Of course there is another possibility," Hodes continued, "and that is AIDS. If you would like to test for that, when they are doing the blood tests, ask for an AIDS test as well. Do you have any questions?"

Kiber's smile froze at the mention of AIDS, but he renewed the smile and said, "No, Doctor, thank you."

Hodes wrote out a prescription for the tests.

"I will find the money for the tests, Doctor," Kiber promised. "We have a cousin in America."

"Bring me the results as soon as you have them."

Hodes stepped back into the little house to say good-bye to Gelila.

I am powerless here, he thought. *I would like very much to do something grand. I would like to save her life. In America, we could talk about treatment options. Here there are no "treatment options." In three or four months, she will be dead.*

"Your brother knows what to do," he said to Gelila, shaking her limp hand in farewell.

The Talmud says, "They who visit the sick should speak in such a manner so as neither to encourage him with false hopes nor to depress him by words of despair."

"It was a pleasure to meet you. I'm going to arrange for you to have some medical tests. Then we can talk again. May you be well."

Then Hodes returned Haregewoin's phone call and promised to come as soon as possible to meet a little boy named Ababu.

A week later, Kiber knocked on the door of Hodes's clinic. He had brought the test results. Hodes was impressed that the three young people had followed his instructions carefully and taken Gelila to the hospital promptly. He hoped the tests would reveal a locally treatable cause for her decline, but he knew that was unlikely. He stepped outside to hold up Gelila's X-ray to the sun. It was clear. The urine showed signs of an infection, the blood showed only mild anemia, the kidneys and liver were fine.

"How about the AIDS test, did you do that?" he asked casually.

"No."

"Okay," Hodes said, "fill *this* prescription—throw out the old bottle—and see how she does."

This is only palliative treatment, he thought.

"Kiber," he called, as the young man departed. "I'd love to have an AIDS test, just in case. If it's negative, we can look deeper for a treatable condition. If it's positive . . ." He didn't finish.

"I will try to convince her, Doctor."

"If you get a negative result, call me right away."

"Thank you, *Abi.*" Kiber put his hands together, bowed quickly, and bounded away.

Hodes never heard from Kiber again.

The result must have been positive, he thought.

Probably Kiber did not even share the results with his sister, wanting to spare her the grief of knowing she would soon die.

It is also possible that she has known the truth all along and has been trying to spare Kiber. Perhaps that is why she was reluctant to get tested—not that it would be bad news for her, but that it would reveal the truth to Kiber and the girls and spoil their last weeks together.

The day Rick Hodes drove his van up into Haregewoin's compound, he brought along Dr. Julio Guerra, a pediatrician visiting from New Jersey.

"Oh, no," the doctors said, both kneeling to meet Ababu on the cement floor of Haregewoin's living room. Rick stood, took out his pocket notebook, and jotted first impressions: "emaciated, stunted, dehydrated, looks really terrible."

Julio, standing, jotted in his notebook, "Obvious signs of muscle-wasting on chest and legs, due to chronic malabsorption."

Probably an AIDS baby, Hodes thought. *But you never know in a baby without an AIDS test.*

Guerra thought, *It looks bad, but other conditions like chronic diarrhea and chronic parasitic infection along with poor feeding can give a similar picture.*

"Has he been tested for HIV?" the doctors asked.

He had not.

"What do you feed him?"

Ababu was fed straight cow's milk. "He could have an allergy to cow's milk," mused Guerra. "He may need a soy-based formula. Do you have soy formula in Ethiopia?" he asked Haregewoin.

She'd never heard of it and didn't know.

"We do," said Hodes.

"It looks like he's starving," the doctors agreed.

"Yes, so I think!" said Haregewoin. "The big head is not like AIDS. He came here like that. I get up with him several times every night and still he looks like that."

Children had gathered around the adults and Ababu, eager to share in the attention. Hodes turned to them, compliantly squatted down, pulled out his stethoscope, and began listening to everyone's chest. With great seriousness, Hodes asked a little boy, in Amharic, "How many belly buttons do you have?"

"How many?" said the boy. "I have one."

"Oh, right, right, Ethiopians only have one," Hodes said sadly.

"Ferenge sa? [How about whites?]," asked the boy suspiciously.

"We have a different number every day," said Hodes. "Let's see . . ." He looked inside his shirt. "Oh! Today I have three and a half."

Children began to laugh and others crowded in to see.

"How many *nipples* do you have?" Hodes asked a second boy.

"Two," said the boy. *"Ferenge sa?"*

"We have eight," said Hodes. "Like dogs!" The children screamed with delight.

Before leaving Haregewoin's compound that day, Dr. Guerra pulled $100 from his wallet and gave the money to Haregewoin for soy formula. Rick Hodes told her, "Get him tested."

He returned the following day and gave Ababu a high-dose "vitamin cocktail" and a dose of deworming medicine. "If it's HIV, he's going to die soon," he told Haregewoin, "and I'm not terribly interested in giving him an extra week of lousy life. However, if he's simply in bad shape and it's not HIV, then this combination could be quite helpful. Let's keep him alive long enough to find out what's going on with him."

35

HAREGEWOIN CALLED A taxi and climbed into it with Ababu in her arms, and she invited a six-year-old girl named Kidist to hop in beside her. Kidist's mother had died of AIDS. Though Kidist looked fine to Haregewoin, the two visiting doctors had suggested she get the little girl tested, too.

Kidist was thrilled to have been chosen for the outing. She had taken great care of her clothes all morning and had enlisted someone— evidently someone her own age—to create her hairstyle: fifteen pigtails sticking straight out all over her head. She looked like a child's drawing of the sun.

Kidist knelt on the seat to look out the back window of the taxi. She was full of questions and observations. Where was that bus going? Who gets to drive the buses? Look at those goats!

But a desperately ill child takes no pleasure in a field trip: Ababu did not look out the windows or point at the tall buildings or wonder aloud if there would be ice cream on this trip, like bubbly Kidist. He was in pain and expected more pain; the needle prick at the clinic simply confirmed for him that life was a series of hurtful experiences—he opened his mouth but emitted no sound; he couldn't afford the energy to cry. At the last second, however, he showed a bit of spirit by writhing away from the needle; the nurse lost her grip and drops of Ababu's blood fell on her wrist. She ran for bleach to pour over her skin.

Kidist wailed in huge disappointment at her needle prick. She'd commissioned a new hairstyle for *this*? In the taxi on the way home, Haregewoin called for a detour so that a consoling ice cream bar could be purchased for Kidist.

Later that week, Haregewoin stood in line at the clinic window to sign for the children's blood-test results.

With astonishment she learned that Ababu was HIV-negative.

Haregewoin called Dr. Rick Hodes with Ababu's results.

"All right, it could be a simple milk allergy!" cried Hodes, grateful for the good news. "Go with the soy formula."

That phone call had caught him in the compound of the Missionaries of Charity Home for Sick and Dying Destitutes, where gaunt and unshaved men lay everywhere on the cement courtyard and on cement risers.

Decrepit-looking men were shuffling toward Hodes from all corners, as he spoke by phone to Haregewoin.

These men had shrunk within their faces and within their clothes; they had looped twine around their waists to hold up their pants. They slipped out of their shoes. They came close and craned into Hodes's face while pulling down their cheeks or pulling up their eyelids.

The last time I was here, I had a fresh batch of eye medicine from the States, he remembered. *They think I'm interested in eyes so suddenly everyone has an eye problem.*

Once they had been jaunty fellows, some of them quite good-looking. They'd had their specialty soccer moves; they'd had pretty girlfriends; they'd liked movies and music and the World Cup matches; some had tacked sports posters up on their walls at home; some had owned cassette tapes of their favorite singers. Outside these walls they had mothers and fathers, grandparents and siblings, wives and children. Then AIDS began dismantling them.

Many then learned that they'd infected their wives or girlfriends, too. Others learned that their babies had been born infected. Others had watched their babies die, and some realized they'd brought the sickness home, after pre- or postmarital sexual encounters.

Most still looked dazed by what had happened to them.

Hodes could treat some of the opportunistic infections of AIDS, but without the ARVs, he couldn't save a single life. These men mostly knew that, and those who understood forgave him.

Hodes stepped through an open doorway into a ballroom-sized ward packed with hollow-cheeked, yellow, emaciated men. The patients here had entered more advanced stages of deterioration than those outside. They clung two or three to a cot; others lay on the cement floor. Many men looked comatose, or already dead, but they picked themselves up at the doctor's jocular approach. Living skeletons reached up to slap him high-five or to shake his hand. Their skulls cracked open with toothless grins. He knew scores of them by name. He worked his way hand-over-hand between the beds. He stashed small treatments in every pocket—a lip cream, a muscle relaxant, a cough medicine. When requested, he bent over a man and listened to his chest.

"Hodes," croaked one, in broken Amharic. "My wife sick."

Hodes knew he was a speaker of Oromo, the language of thirty million Oromo people, the majority ethnic group in Ethiopia. "She can phone me, Bekila," Hodes said. "You know my number?"

"No."

"Here," said Hodes, and wrote it on a page of his pocket notebook, which he tore out and handed to the patient.

"*Gelaytoe-minh* [thank you]," the man said in Oromo. "*Negatie* [good-bye]."

"*Ree-behn-senh-nn-fakoni*," replied Hodes in Oromo in respectful farewell, a few of the Oromo words he knew.

Bekila lay back with satisfaction. He'd done something today, a good thing. He had found help for his dying wife.

As Hodes exited through the doorway at the far end of the ward, he called out something in Amharic, which was greeted by hoots and guffaws from one end of the long room to the other.

"Good news for lunch today!" he yelled. "I hear they're serving delicious *assama* and *jib*—pork and hyena meat."

Both were forbidden foods to Muslims and Ethiopian Christians. The ill men chuckled for a long time.

*   *   *

In a world in which the doctor's hands were tied by lack of medicine, the good news about Ababu was welcome indeed.

At Haregewoin's house, sitting in her lap, Ababu latched onto his bottle of soy formula and sucked for dear life. By nightfall, his face looked a little rounder to her, his eyes less sunken. A few mornings later, Haregewoin found him sitting up in his crib waiting for her. On the following day, he greeted her with an enormous smile and bounced up into her arms. By the end of the week, he was walking; by the end of the second week, he was running. By the middle of the third week, he was running while laughing aloud, the memory of his prior life as an invalid forgotten.

Not all the ill children in Ethiopia were dying from AIDS. With far too few clinics, doctors, and nurses, children died every day of common causes like diarrhea and dehydration. Ababu nearly starved to death from a milk allergy. The diagnosis would have been the same as if he'd died of AIDS: the extreme poverty of his family, the poverty of his country, the misallocated resources of his government, the misallocated resources of the world.

In thanks, Haregewoin tucked a photo into an envelope and mailed it to Hodes. In the picture, Ababu was wearing footed pajamas and his arms were full of toys. The photo was blurry because the little boy was running too fast for the camera to capture him.

But not all the news from the clinic that day was good. Kidist, the happy girl, tested positive for HIV/AIDS.

Mother Teresa's Missionaries of Charity Orphanage for Babies and Children had opened a new facility for children with HIV/AIDS. Haregewoin lobbied, made phone calls, begged, and got Kidist admitted. If anyone in the country could find anti-AIDS medicine for children, she thought, it would be the sisters of Mother Teresa.

The new orphanage looked like an exclusive private school, with low sandstone buildings set upon a green lawn. There were bright metal seesaws and an outdoor Ping-Pong table. But, like ENAT, like Haregewoin, the organization had no AIDS medicine and no prospect of any. No one in Ethiopia had access to pediatric anti-AIDS drug therapies. The sisters were able to treat the opportunistic infections of AIDS in the children. After that, their role was to provide for as gentle deaths as was possible for their children.

Kidist blew up her cheeks with surprise upon hearing that she was moving, then she accepted it as another adventure. The day the taxi came for her, she wore a plastic coin purse on a long over-the-shoulder chain. Inside the purse was a tooth she had lost. She swung her feet in the backseat beside Haregewoin, full of high hopes. Once she had been her parents' loved child. She had every expectation that love (and perhaps ice cream) awaited her.

36

CHALTU, GIRL, EIGHT years orphan, a first-grader.
Biniam, age two years boy, mother and father died, kebele sent him.
Hana, girl, age eight years, first-grader.
Tariqua, girl, ten years. Kebele brought her.
Hailegabriel, 14, ninth-grader, mother and father died.

An angular, ebony-skinned boy of thirteen arrived. His small, shaved head and narrow shoulders rode high on his lanky torso and long legs. He'd disembarked from a donkey cart, after riding for an unknown number of days. He politely greeted everyone in words no one understood. He expected to sleep on the floor and was amazed to be offered the opportunity to share a cot with three other boys. He was quick and strong; he could whittle and he could tie good knots. While doing his chores, he chanted something under his breath, a muttered, endless soliloquy. He recited himself to sleep at night, and his lips began to move in recitation before he was fully awake in the morning. Perhaps he was from the Nuer people, near the Sudanese border? He didn't know Amharic, the language of the Amhara people and the official language of Ethiopia, but Ethiopia is a land of eighty-four living languages and five dead ones, including ancient ecclesiastical languages. The boy did not respond to visitors who questioned him in Oromo, Gurage, Somali, Tigrinya, Harari, or Arabic, other than to tilt his head with a polite smile.

Haregewoin took him to the Mercato, positioned him in the middle of a mass of vendors and shoppers, and gestured for him to raise his voice. A passerby caught the gist or the rhythm of it, then concluded, the child was singing the oral history of the generations of his ancestors.

Clearly he'd been tutored to repeat the myths, the legends, the genealogies endlessly, to engrave them on his memory until he himself could relay them to the next generation.

But now the boy was cut off from his parents, elders, tutors, and holy men; from his people. To whom would he pass on the oral traditions? It was the kind of loss not measured by any statistic.

The boy was delighted to be given a ratty maroon sweater and to start school with the other children. One night Haregewoin recognized what he was chanting to himself in bed: it was the *fidele*, the Amharic alphabet. The history and holy tales of his people, so carefully stored in the archive of a bright boy's memory, faded.

Inside the four tin walls of Haregewoin's compound, there was increasing bedlam, confusion, and discontent. At every hour of the day and night, someone was crying.

The adults in the compound slowly went deaf.

One day a year-old baby screamed long and hard from the baby room; she had been parked in an umbrella stroller, dressed and ready for her day, then forgotten.

On another day, shrieks rose from a toddler sitting on the outdoor plastic potty-chair. A stray dog, adopted by the children, was trying to get the child to play; the mutt jumped on the little girl and scratched her bare thighs. She screamed in terror, trapped in the potty-chair at eye level with the bumptious dog, but no one ran to her aid.

Befekadu, 8, brought in by a neighbor.

   Dawit, 10, brought by his mother who was HIV-positive and sick.

   Dagmawit, 4, brought by the kebele *representative from his street.*

   Brothers Daniel, 10, and Yosef, 7, brought by their uncle after both parents died. Uncle too poor to keep them, as he already cares for other orphaned nieces and nephews.

✻　　✻　　✻

Forget honoring the memory of Atetegeb with this foster home in her name. Who could honor? Who could think or feel?

Haregewoin didn't have the blink of an eye to call her own; children were everywhere, everywhere. As teeming with humanity as the streets of Addis Ababa every day and night—that's how her courtyard looked and felt. No fewer than three or four kids were squatting in the dark and awful latrine at any given moment, and her bed was crawling with children, and kids sat two to a chair at mealtime and shared plates and cups; she hated to imagine how many different children claimed a single toothbrush; and clothes were communal, neither boys' nor girls' clothing anymore, and all of it turning yellowish gray from hard use and dust. She no longer knew all the names and ages, nor when they'd arrived, nor where they'd come from.

If she reached for one thing to call her own—like a person rummaging in a drawer in the dark, feeling for the right item—it was still baby Menah, the first abandoned baby brought here by the police. The toddler grew rounder and jollier with every passing day; baby teeth sparkled when she laughed, a curl sprang up on the top of her head. She called Haregewoin *Maye* (*my*-ay), Mommy, and was content with the world.

Sometimes at night, if Menah had fallen asleep in a crowded crib with other babies and toddlers, Haregewoin tiptoed in search of her.

You'd think she'd want solitude in her bed occasionally, a rare moment of peace and quiet if children slept elsewhere for a change.

But solitude was what she still tried to hold at bay, the existential and permanent darkness of Worku's death and Atetegeb's death and her own eventual death.

So she gathered the heavy, warm, sweet baby to her body and went back to bed cradling her.

The kids in the lane still clamored for entry. Ragged, mischievous children knocked at the metal door of her compound day and night, their black eyes laughing, begging to be included.

"Go away! Shoo!" cried Haregewoin with a frown, clapping her hands at them. They flew off in a whirlwind of dust and roosted on a nearby outcrop of rocks and weeds. When she stepped back inside, they swooped down again, tapping at her door. When cars pulled into the compound, the children snuck down and tried to slide in beside the cars, undetected.

She thought she was wise to their tricks, but then she learned that one had fooled her.

One day a small, tidy woman called upon Haregewoin. Speaking in a high, fast voice, she said "*Waizero*, I wonder if you need any help here in your house? I can cook, wash, clean, babysit." She was like a sparrow, hopping in the lane on tiny feet. She had a shiny, pointed, little face. She spoke so fast that it took Haregewoin a moment to take in what she had asked.

"I always need help," she sighed, "but I can't pay anything."

"I'll come to help for as little food as it takes to feed me," said rapid-speaking Tigist. "You already feed my son and I am so grateful!"

"Who is your son?" asked Haregewoin in surprise.

"Henok!"

"Oh? Come in, come in."

"Henok, you never told me," Haregewoin reproached him, while inviting Tigist to be seated in the living room. "Why are you looking for a new mother when you have a very nice mother?"

"Because I am going to help my mother!" said the boy. "If a new family takes me, I will be rich. Then I will have money for my mother for food. Also I will buy her a house!"

Henok's mother nodded wistfully. "I have nothing for him," she said.

"Are you ill?" Haregewoin asked quietly.

"I'm not!" said the peppy woman. "I am divorced, I am healthy."

Henok, the sleek-headed, wise-eyed little boy shopping for a new mother: what a salesman! He alone among the neighborhood raga-muffins had convinced Haregewoin of his need for shelter right away and she had admitted him.

"Henok," Haregewoin said again in amazement. "What were you thinking?"

He continued to defend himself. He had seen what happened to mothers. He had seen the evidence all around him. It was all very well and good to assure him that his mother was fine; all the mothers said that: "I'm fine. Just feeling a little tired." Then they died. Before that happened to him, he would attach himself to a sturdy domestic or foreign new mother, who would enable him to support his current mother. He stood his ground. He made no apologies. It was an excellent plan. He was the man of the family.

Haregewoin was too astonished to rebuke him further.

"Well," she said with a weak laugh to Tigist, "would you like to stay? I could use you in the baby room."

So Tigist moved in, taking as her assignment the sickest of the babies. Half a dozen babies—of low birth weight, malnourished, possibly HIV-positive—rotated in and out of the hospital. Haregewoin had been staying overnight with them at the hospital, for it was unhealthy to leave any family member alone in an Ethiopian hospital. Now Tigist took care of it. When a child was admitted, Tigist spent the night on a mat she spread on the floor beside the hospital crib.

And Henok resumed his watch for a new mother, a backup mother, preferably one with a lifetime warranty.

37

SUDDENLY, ON AN otherwise typical morning, help arrived. A woman from the island of Malta phoned Haregewoin, introduced herself in English, and asked permission to visit. "Of course you are very welcome," Haregewoin replied nicely, so a spry olive-skinned woman in a long skirt, hiking boots, and a graying boy's haircut arrived, sat, and drank coffee. She smiled wrinkly smiles at the children all about her and cooed to them in a foreign tongue. Her fingernails were curled and discolored. She popped a few hard candies out of her skirt pocket and squeezed them into children's hands. Then she unbuckled her sagging briefcase and explained her business. She ran an adoption agency in Malta, she said, and she had a number of waiting couples interested in babies from Ethiopia. Did Haregewoin have orphaned babies here? Would she like to place them abroad? "We'd need to have them tested, of course," said the woman. "We can only place HIV-negative babies."

"How would we do this?" asked Haregewoin. "You don't just walk out of here with a baby . . . ?"

"I work with an orphanage run by a Maltese Franciscan order," said the woman. "The sisters there have permission from your government to assign babies for intercountry adoption. If you would like to give me one of your babies, we would take him to the sisters. We must confirm that the baby is truly an orphan."

The two ladies strolled into Haregewoin's bedroom and viewed babies in the slung-out postures of midmorning naps in circles of sunshine all over Haregewoin's bedspread. The babies stirred in sleep, throwing the weight of their wet, baggy bottoms from one side to another. "They're darling!" whispered the woman, pulling from her briefcase a copy of her license from the Ethiopian government and a small photo album of happy adoptive families.

This is very amazing news, Haregewoin thought. She asked, "The families treat them like their own?"

"Oh, my dear, please! Yes, like their very own children."

"They do not make servants of them?"

"Madame Haregewoin, they give the children their last names. They adopt them in court. These are their children. There are couples who cannot have children, you know? They have 'infertility.'"

"Yes, I know. Some have it here. But why don't they adopt children from their own country?"

"We have too few children! Don't ask me why! Women wait longer to get married, they have careers, they wait until they are thirty-five or forty to start their families, and for some it is too late."

"Here you are a grandmother at forty," said Haregewoin.

"We have somehow a shortage of children. The birthrates are falling all over Europe. School buildings are closing. With birth control and abortion, there are not so many babies born out of wedlock anymore. And then the young women keep their illegitimate babies. Those are the babies I once placed for adoption, but the stigma is much less now."

Standing at the east side of a continent bubbling up with children, Haregewoin found the image of an adult-heavy land alien and cold. She pictured stately streets, pristine shops, trimmed hedges, orderly pedestrians in overcoats and hats. And the emptiness of schoolyards and parks. Why shouldn't women in a barren country, longing for children, reach their arms toward a hot southern continent rolling with babies?

Ethiopia, on the other hand, out of poverty, drought, famine, TB, malaria, HIV/AIDS, autocracy, skirmishes, and war, was running low on adults.

Each side of the equation struck her as poignant: a childless European couple longing for any baby, even an Ethiopian baby;

and an Ethiopian baby compliantly raising its arms toward the adults, even white ones, thinking, *Amaye? Abaye?* eager to start imprinting on its parents like a duckling that will follow the first moving object it sees.

"Yes, please, I would be honored. Please." Haregewoin gestured toward her babies.

It was like picking a flower from a perfumed garden of begonias, gardenias, delphiniums, lilacs. The agile little woman from Malta leaned forward, basking in the sunshine above the curly heads. She hummed close, like a honeybee. It was a bewitching moment as if from a fairy tale, chance and good fortune about to land on one of these luckless orphans. She reached for a fifteen-month-old girl whose face was flushed with sleep. It was Menah. Haregewoin lunged forward, picked up Menah, slung her over her shoulder, and gestured for the woman to consider the others. *Close call!* she thought, feeling the hard, frightened pound of her heart continue even after she'd grabbed her girl.

"Who is this teddy bear?" cooed the woman, tenderly rolling over a snoozing baby boy.

"His name is Abel."

"How old?"

"Five months, six months. I'll get his file."

The woman hoisted the baby, fondled his delicate fingers, turned him over on her palm, and felt his good weight. He woke up blinking and began to twist for escape. His bottom left a wet print on her blouse.

"Shall I take him?"

"You must find him a very good family, he is a very good boy."

"The best, I promise you," said the small woman, putting the boy back down on his back and bending forward to kiss his forehead. His round terry-cloth feet wafted in the air above his tummy. The woman reached over to find Haregewoin's hand with her sharp-curled hand and squeezed, promising. Abel flipped himself over and began his escape, crawling over his bedmates, and the ladies laughed.

The complicated, incriminating story of northern hemisphere

wealth and southern hemisphere desperation boiled down to this: a sunny morning on the Horn of Africa, a hot, untidy bedroom, and two short, graying widows (a little achy, a little too old, a little discombobulated for this) in charge of a quilt squirming with motherless babies.

The Maltese woman with the salt-and-pepper boy's haircut settled Abel in a nest of blankets in the backseat of her car. She called that night to say that the baby had gone to the Franciscan Sisters of the Heart of Jesus; they would care for him and initiate his legal paperwork. She would soon be flying home to Malta and hoped to bring news of a family for Abel when she returned in two months.

Haregewoin then learned that adoption agencies from a dozen or more countries had opened offices in Addis Ababa. Some had opened orphanages and foster homes, as well. They hired locals to be the house mothers and lawyers. As their representatives learned that Haregewoin housed healthy abandoned infants, more and more of them came calling, seeking infants for couples in Spain, Canada, Italy, the Netherlands, Sweden, Norway, New Zealand, Australia, Germany, and the United States.

It is the first recourse of everyone ethically involved with inter-country adoption to place orphans with relatives, with friends, or with families within their home countries; no one imagines or pretends that adoption is a solution to a generation of children orphaned by disease. It is one small and modest option, a case of families in industrialized nations throwing lifelines to individual children even as their governments fail to commit sufficient funds or to free up the medicines to turn back the epidemic.

Healthy babies—especially baby girls! they all wanted baby girls—began to arrive and depart from Haregewoin's compound too quickly for the older kids to get attached to them. Swaddled, freshly washed, curly-haired sleeping babies were handed over from Haregewoin to adoption-agency staff persons; the babies departed in a flurry of many handshakes, kisses, and warm exclamations. Older babies and young toddlers might give a kick and a squeal, reaching in panic for Haregewoin; but she soothed their protests with warm chuckles, knowing it was for the best.

The older children made out that something wonderful awaited the babies out there, beyond the tin walls. To leave on foot? No. Bad idea, they knew. Because if an older child left on foot, he or she could end up homeless, starving, or trading sex for food. But to be escorted out of the gates, riding grandly in a taxi or a car in the company of an Ethiopian or foreign businesswoman, yes! Every child wished to be elevated to such a flamboyant and important leave-taking.

The older children stood back watching. Though none grasped the legal or bureaucratic aspects of international adoption, all had divined the essential truth: there *were* mothers out there, even fathers. Henok was right to watch and wait for one.

As the taxis or vans gave their happy toots and the drivers their merry waves, Haregewoin stood back among the left-behind older children. She draped her arms over their shoulders; she tried to relay that she loved them, that *she* was their mother. But she wasn't their mother: there were too many of them now. Some, looking down, shrugged her arms off their shoulders, dipped and pulled away, and dragged back into their dorm rooms. The compound felt empty and oppressively boring for the remainder of every day on which a lucky baby departed.

But baby Hewan would become Eve; and Hirute, Ruth; and Yoel, Joel; and Mickias, Mickey.

And Bekele might become Joshua; and Dinkenesh, Emily; and Zelalem, Paul; and Temesgen, Alexander.

Her body knew what she was going to do before her mind admitted it. Snuggling with baby Menah at night, kissing the smooth cheeks and closed eyelids, Haregewoin felt her heart knock again, in fear and farewell. She tried to set her pain aside. *You're an old lady*, she told herself, but didn't feel it. *You won't live long enough to raise her. She was never really yours. She was only yours for a little while.*

She sensed it was not her noblest instinct that made her cling to Menah. It was a deep hunger. Never, when all her friends praised her for her selfless mission, her generosity in housing all these lost children, had it felt selfless or generous to her. It had felt as if prayers she hadn't known to ask had been answered. She had lost her daughter. And God sent her these precious children.

But she studied the photos shared by the agency representatives: Ethiopian babies waving from the fancy strollers pushed by North American and European mothers and fathers. Babies in car seats, babies in high chairs, babies in wading pools, babies with puppies, babies looking self-satisfied and content.

Let's see your selflessness now, she scolded herself. *So, go: be generous.*

In a place with no people, be a person.

An Italian-agency staff person phoned one day, inquiring after baby girls.

Like the woman from Malta, the Italian woman stood gazing down at the double bed upon which rosy infants dozed in the sunshine, wet fingers slipping in and out of their mouths. When this woman reached her hands toward Menah, Haregewoin did not lunge forward to stop her.

"Menah? That's a new one for me. What does it mean?"

"It is . . . a name from the Bible."

"Shall I take her?"

"Let me change her. And I will give you her paperwork." She handed Menah's file to the Italian woman, saying, "Just give us a moment to say good-bye.

"Children!" she cried in a choked voice. "Come say good-bye to baby sister."

Menah woke up and sparkled, as always, her chunky legs kicking in happiness, her black eyes dancing.

The woman had a car seat in the back of her car, into which she inserted the girl, who had begun to whimper when taken from Haregewoin's arms. Haregewoin clung to the compound wall as the car drove away, then she hurried back into her bedroom with a dish towel over her face. In her room she sat on the edge of the bed, turned down her mouth, and rocked back and forth in silent grief. As the babies stirred around her, she picked up one, and another, and held them, rocking from side to side in mourning.

Never again! she angrily told herself. *Do not get attached like this again. This is more than a person can bear.*

38

N O CRIB AT Haregewoin's stayed empty for more than a fortnight. The *kebele* referred abandoned babies and toddlers in ever-growing numbers. Police officers brought them. Ill parents and bereft grandparents knocked on the gate at all hours and then limped away in tears without their children. A hospital called Haregewoin to fetch a newborn boy whose mother had just died in childbirth. Older children continued to arrive, too; she was obliged to have the older ones feed, bathe, dress, undress, and sleep beside the younger ones.

If one kid got a runny nose, the next day twelve had runny noses, and the next day twenty-two. If one coughed, then, within days, fifteen would be up in the night, hacking away. Fevers jumped from one to the next as fast as the head lice. And if a small girl started to cry in the night (remembering her mother), the loneliness spread like a plague, like a *pandemic*, until a sorrowful wailing went up from beds and cribs all over the compound and Haregewoin stumbled from one child to the next, petting and murmuring. Her sleep deprivation was so great that she sometimes fell asleep sitting up; sometimes she began dreaming if she simply shut her eyes for more than a second.

And it was still possible—ridiculous given how much of humanity was crammed with her inside the tin walls, but possible—for her to feel alone at night, with a sad cough deep in her chest like that of an orphan.

Atetegeb!

Worku!

Baby Menah!

She understood the children's mournful cries because she felt it, too: the loneliness of all the years you still have to live without the people whom you *need* in order to live.

She understood very well when a girl of about three, Sara, newly orphaned, tugged at her several times a day with an important secret. Haregewoin bent over and Sara stood on tiptoe and loudly whispered into Haregewoin's ear, "I'm ready to go home now."

"Doesn't anyone ever want to adopt an older child?" she asked one day as a Spanish agency rep loaded twin baby boys into his backseat. For these scenes were becoming unbearable, the older children feeling more unwanted with every glorious departure of a baby.

At the beginning, the older children had run to comb their hair and change their shirts when visitors came, hoping that a last-minute excellent impression would make a difference.

"No," said the agency rep. "People want babies. Sometimes toddlers, but mostly babies and, most of all, baby girls."

In the adoption world, Haregewoin learned, even a three-year-old was an "older child," declined by most prospective parents as possibly too damaged or traumatized by early experiences.

"But won't someone adopt the older children?" Haregewoin sighed as a Canadian-agency person prepared to depart with a baby.

"Try the Americans."

"What? Really?"

"The Americans will adopt anyone."

"What does it mean?"

"There was a boy at the Mother Teresa Home who lost both his legs . . ."

"What?"

"I think he was herding his goats over train tracks and the train came and caught the boy. But the Americans are adopting him. They'll adopt school kids. They'll adopt kids with CP. They call them 'special needs.' They'll adopt—"

"Boys?"

"Yes, boys! They adopt boys, they adopt siblings."

"But big boys? School-age boys?"

"Yes, I'm telling you!"

Haregewoin was off like a shot. She sprinted to her house to start making phone calls to find the Americans.

She found Merrily Ripley, director (with her husband, Ted) of Adoption Advocates International (AAI), of Port Angeles, Washington.

AAI ran two orphanages in Addis Ababa: Layla House for school-age children, and WanHa House for babies and toddlers. Under the supervision of the Ministry of Labor and Social Affairs (MOLSA), AAI had placed their first 6 Ethiopian children with adoptive parents in America in 1998, 25 children in 1999, 40 in 2000, 154 in 2004, and they would place 174 in 2005.

Haregewoin reached Merrily by phone during one of her frequent visits to Ethiopia, and she invited Haregewoin to visit her organization.

Haregewoin hired a van, oversaw the courtyard washtub scrubbing and shampooing of twenty of her oldest children, instructed them to choose fresh clothes from the laundry line and from the cardboard boxes piled high in her bedroom, then herded them into the van. "Be good!" she snapped at them from the passenger seat as they got settled, pairs of best friends grabbing seats together. She caught a glimpse of Henok trying to duck down behind a seat back.

"You! Off! Go to your mother!" she barked at him. He dragged his feet, looking at her with reproachful eyes.

"Be smart!" she reminded the others as they drove away. "Use good manners! Use your English!" The children looked at each other and smiled ruefully. They had no idea where they were going. She craned over from the front seat and with a wet forefinger dabbed a smudge off a child's face. She reached into her handbag and pulled out colorful plastic hair-clips and distributed them. A boy stuck one in his own hair and the girls tittered, and Haregewoin frowned and turned to face forward again.

The American orphanage sat in a flat, dry district of dirt roads, vacant lots, and tin and-plywood kiosks. The kiosks displayed soccer balls, wooden jewelry, shrink-wrapped children's clothing made in China, brand-name or pirated CDs, and woven Rastafarian hats. Loudspeakers from competing music-sellers blasted traditional Ethiopian music and American hip-hop.

A pink-faced white woman in her sixties, wearing the thick socks and practical sandals of a Pacific Coast grandmother, Merrily Ripley had expected to meet a local foster mother, not twenty of the local foster mother's foster children. But, as children poured out of the van, Merrily greeted them all with a trilling soprano laugh; her dozens of long, skinny, white-beaded braids ticked back and forth against her shoulders. She and her husband, Ted, had twenty-one children, three by birth and eighteen by adoption from the United States, Korea, Costa Rica, and India; Merrily Ripley was unflappable.

Within the high stone walls of the Layla House compound, dozens of kids milled around the courtyard in a midmorning break from classes. Schoolgirls threw pebbles and waggled their long legs out behind them in *mancha* (Ethiopian hopscotch), or stood and spanked their palms together in timeless singsong hand-clapping games. Others leaned against the cool stone wall of the compound, in the shade of jasmine vines, braiding and rebraiding each other's hair, knitting in colored beads with nimble fingers. The boys loped back and forth with a deflated soccer ball. Teenage girls retreated to their dorm room and flopped across the twin beds and bunk beds like rest time at summer camp. They pulled out stationery and pens to write to friends already adopted to America, or they plucked complicated webs of string in the finger games of cat's cradle, or they got out the deck of Uno cards and settled on the cement floor to play. A few older boys, too hot to keep chasing the soccer ball but lacking the variety of home industries of the girls, leaned into the open window to tease and annoy.

Haregewoin felt instantly that the children living here had adjusted their sights. Somehow, it seemed to her, they acted like Americans already.

They were loud.

Boys and girls who had lived on the streets, who had survived urban squalor or had come from the famine provinces, children who had tried to keep younger siblings alive and either had or had not succeeded, now jostled under a basketball hoop with their PE teacher. He had given them American nicknames like Michaeljordan and Shaq. These few dozen kids—out of millions of their peers across Africa—were being prepared to enter the promised land.

"Everyone is rich in America!" they told each other. And some said, "When you go to America, you turn white."

"When does that happen?" Haregewoin asked a little girl.

The child confidently replied, "As soon as you get off the plane."

Merrily Ripley interviewed children individually or paired with their siblings, and taped their answers on her video camera. Prospective parents who requested babies would be matched by AAI with a baby. But families willing to consider a waiting child were given the opportunity to view the older children first on videotape.

We first saw our future daughter, Helen, in the July 2001, black-and-white AAI monthly newsletter of "waiting children." Then, on an AAI video, we glimpsed her singing among a group of children, and hopping in her excitement. In both photograph and video, she touched her right forefinger to her right front tooth, a gesture of shyness.

I visited Layla House years before Haregewoin did.

In November 2001, sitting in the passenger seat of Selamneh's taxi, I waited outside the steel door of Layla House after he honked for admittance and I prepared to meet five-year-old Helen. Few things on earth are as terrifying as being introduced to a child who has just been instructed to address you as Mama. Selamneh drove me onto the cement playground, and kids scattered in all directions yelling Helen's name. Some big kids found her and towed her in my direction; she was afraid to make eye contact. She stood in front of me and looked down. She was tiny. Her hairdo consisted of heavily beaded cornrows. She touched her front tooth with her finger. I knelt down and hugged her.

She was trembling. I was trembling, too. Photos were snapped of our first meeting, but I was trying hard not to cry and the same was likely true for the child. Sometimes, when orphanage children around the world are told in Amharic or Romanian or Russian or Spanish or Chinese, "Your mother is coming," the children think it is their original mother coming back for them. Helen loved and was loved by her mother, Bogalech, with great tenderness. Now people were saying to her, "Your mother is here." When I released her from my hug that morning, she scampered away across the playground and watched me from a distance.

I'd brought all sorts of goofy things in my backpack: the game of Twister and magnetic darts and Frisbees and whoopee cushions.

"Oh, don't bring *whoopee* cushions," people had warned me. "Ethiopians are very polite people; they will not appreciate whoopee cushions."

I've never met children that polite, I had thought to myself, and I packed half a dozen red rubber whoopee cushions, size large.

On the bright, hot day in November 2001, when I handed them out, the children held the rubber toys limply in their hands and watched me blankly. With enthusiasm, I threw one on the ground and stomped on it. It made its big noise. I looked up expectantly, but the children were frowning. *Americans have to buy something to make that noise?* some were thinking. And others had a look like *Helen's new mother is insane.*

There was a long universal moment of unhappiness. The children didn't like their gifts. They seemed concerned. Selamneh, whom I'd just met for the first time, would have liked to come to my aid, but he couldn't fathom my intention. *I'm going to be a failure in Ethiopia*, I thought miserably. I hated to disappoint the small, dusty girl who, through no fault of her own, was publicly linked to me.

Mortified, trapped, humiliated, I threw a whoopee cushion onto a kitchen chair on the driveway and sat on it. It gave out a tremendous splat, a Bronx cheer. I deliberately jumped up as if startled, as if embarrassed, and a little boy exploded with laughter. He wanted to try it, and did, and two more children laughed. Suddenly they got it—it was something funny, it was nonsense—and the children went wild sitting on the whoopee cushions all over the driveway, outdoing each other in the vulgarity of the noises. Now it was the caregivers' turn to look at me sadly. From across the compound, shy Helen watched me, and—when our eyes met—she smiled behind her tooth and finger.

When asked by Merrily, for her videotapes, "What do you want to be when you grow up?" (the question translated by a teacher if necessary), none of Haregewoin's children replied, "I didn't realize I was *going* to grow up," though many must have thought it.

The children who had lived at Layla House for months had learned to offer snappy, confident replies, in English, such as doctor, teacher, policeman, architect, or chef.

"I want to drive a car," stated a six-year-old girl named Bethlehem, on camera. (Whether professionally or at her leisure, she didn't specify.)

"I will be an actor!" cried a boy named Dagmawi. "An actor like Jackie Chan."

"I want to ride motorcycles!" yelled another boy.

"When I grow up, I want to help the elderly people," offered merry, dimpled Mekdes Zawuda. Like many of the teens, she was keenly aware of being on the receiving end of charity and was eager to be of service to others in the future.

"I want to start an orphanage," said fifteen-year-old Yemisrach.

"In America, I want to learn to preach the word of God," said Robel.

In America, Robel would become a scrappy PlayStation-, Spider-Man-, and baseball-loving little kid; in Ethiopia, he was still the head of household, the surrogate father for his four-year-old sister. "I want to try to teach the peoples who doesn't know the Bible."

A nine-year-old girl named Frehiwot, with thick eyebrows and two thick, shoulder-length braids, surprisingly confessed, "I wish to be a pilot."

"I think America has all things in her hands," handsome Dagmawi told Haregewoin and me. "Everyone is hoping to be chosen by American parents. When the children learn that they have parents, they tell from peoples to peoples their parents' names and their city."

So Haregewoin understood adoption like this: In the epoch of the HIV/AIDS pandemic, a few families from foreign countries were throwing lifelines to individual children. The life-changing opportunity was not without a price, which the Ethiopian government weighed carefully: the adopted children would lose their country, people, faith, language, culture, and history. A child could end up the sole Ethiopian for hundreds of miles; another, the only child of color in his or her school. But the adopted child would gain the one thing on earth arguably worth more than a homeland: family. While most African nations did not turn to intercountry adoption as an option for orphaned children, Ethiopian officials had decided that for the infinitesimal minority of African orphans who could be raised by foreign parents, the trade-off was worthwhile and they would not block their path.

In 2005, Ethiopia had 1,563,000 AIDS orphans, the second-highest concentration of such children in the world; and 4,414,000 orphans from all causes, the second-highest number in Africa. Out of all these children, 1,400 departed for new families abroad that year.

At first doubtful that North American and European families could raise Ethiopian children, Haddush Halefom, head of the Children's Commission, a sociologist by training, made a tour of adoptive households. "I visited France and the Netherlands in 2004," he told me, "also, in America, Vermont and Rhode Island. I saw how they treat the kids, how they give their love to the children, and how the children give their love to the parents. I am even now interested in the possibility of families adopting HIV-positive children, if their governments would be willing; I would like to make that a priority, as it will give life to the children to move them to countries with adequate medication."

Merrily Ripley would ultimately find homes for seventeen of the twenty children of Haregewoin's she met that day. One boy looked sixteen or seventeen, too old to be adopted; and two little girls tested HIV-positive, unacceptable at that time to the American embassy.

That day, all returned home with Haregewoin. But all had been interviewed on camera by Merrily Ripley, who began to circulate their images and basic information to waiting families in the United States. As space opened up in Layla House by the departure of children for America, Haregewoin's children would move over, a few at a time.

When recess was over on the hot November day of the whoopee cushions, the students headed back to their classes: the orphanage offered a two-room school, with a class for advanced students and a class for beginning students, regardless of age. Most of the children were of elementary-school age, though a few perspiring teenagers towered over the rest with the same focused and worried expressions. There were five-year-olds who arrived reading and writing, having been given an early start by educated parents (Helen was one of these); there were nine- or ten- or eleven-year-olds who arrived illiterate, having spent their lives on the dusty plains of goatherding country (our future son, Fisseha, was one of those). In the Ethiopian system, a child begins in first grade, regardless of age.

On this hot, dusty day, it was a relief to enter the cool whitewashed schoolroom. The kids sat on wood benches and chanted lessons in high voices. Under dangling beaded braids and layers of dirt and sweat, their faces were intent and earnest. Sunlight and dust motes streamed onto the cement floor through the square, uncovered windows. Taped to the cinder-block wall was a map of the United States, pierced with dozens of pushpins marking the American cities to which children from this orphanage had relocated.

The teacher, a young man who had never been to America though it was his fondest wish to go, wrote English greetings on the chalkboard.

"How are you?" he tapped out, while pronouncing the words.

"How are you?" the children repeated.

"I am fine," he dabbed in chalk.

"I am fine," they called back in high voices.

"I am very well," he wrote.

"I am very well!" they sang. They rolled their *R*'s, giving a high-tone flourish to *very*.

"I am doing very nicely."

"I am doing very nicely."

There was no preparation for the delivery of bad or mediocre news in their future American conversations. The working premise was that these children were going to be chosen by American families for adoption and their plane fares out of Addis Ababa paid for. Once the paperwork required by both governments was completed, white or black Americans would show up at the gate, shower everyone with handshakes and hugs, take a hundred photos, and sweep off with their new children to live in a hotel or an apartment for a few days before flying to America. From the vantage point of those being left behind, like the teacher, the phenomenal gift of an American future left no room for complaint and thus no need to prepare a vocabulary of grumbling.

"How are you this evening?" he offered.

"How are you this evening?" they repeated.

"I am quite well, thank you."

"I am quite well, thank you."

"Excellent, and yourself?"

"Excellent, and yourself?"

With the next lesson, the teacher offered ways to express "I don't know": "I have no *i*-dea," the young man called over his shoulder, pressing the chalk letters onto the board.

"I have no *i*-dea," sang the sweet, rising voices.

"I shouldn't think so."

"I shouldn't *think* so."

"I don't *expect* so."

"I don't *expect* so."

"Search me."

"Search me."

"I haven't a *clue*."

"I haven't a *clue*."

All the children at Layla House had lost one or both parents; if one parent still lived, then he or she was desperately sick. But none of the kids felt isolated, singled-out, made freakish by tragedy, as the rare orphaned child might experience in the West. Losing one or both parents was the common pattern of their generation.

When the kids were dismissed for lunch, they thanked their teacher politely in English, walked out the door in single file, then broke pell-mell for the dining hall to grab seats near their friends. At long wood tables above a mopped linoleum floor, baskets of orange slices and carved-up bread awaited them. Though the children would have welcomed, at every meal, platters of *injera* and *wat* (a vegetable or meat stew), they were being taught to use American forks and spoons and to maneuver foods like spaghetti and meatballs.

"Please to pass the water," a stout boy boomed. "Thank you very much."

"Excellent, and yourself?" replied his friend who passed the pitcher. "How are you this evening?"

"Search me!" shouted the roly-poly boy. "How are you this evening?"

"I have no *i*-dea. Please, how is your sister?"

"I haven't a *clue*. Please to pass the meatball."

"Thank you very much."

"Thank you very much."

39

IF HAREGEWOIN HAD been able to linger past twilight, rather than rushing home to her own three dozen children who needed her for prayers and bedtime kisses, she would have seen and heard the shenanigans at Layla House die down. As the children undressed and washed for bed, they gathered in a common room for prayers—just like at Haregewoin's house—and the tones grew muffled, even mournful. As a group, the children generated a carefree mood of ruckus and play, dodgeball and *football*, but their secret grief coexisted with their brave frolicking. Bedtime was the worst, when the rabble-rousing of playground and dining hall ceased. At night, ghosts and visions and bad dreams visited the children. Through the open windows, the caregivers heard the children crying into their pillows.

"I come from Shashemene province," twelve-year-old Zerabruk told me in 2001. He had been a doted-upon firstborn son.

"My father was an engineer and my mother was a housewife. We lived in a nice house. I have two small sisters. I went to school and I was very good at English, math, and music. When I was in the second grade, my father had a stomachache. Because of that he died. He was sick a long time. He died at home. I was eight, Mekdes was three, and Samrawit was two.

"After Father died, we moved to a very small house near the bus station. After Father died, we have no money. Then Mother got sick. Mother had a case of kidney. We have nothing to eat. I saw people my age selling sugarcane on the street and I thought, 'Here is something I could do.' I asked them how to do it, and they taught me. One sugarcane costs one birr [nine cents] from a farmer. You cut it with a knife and you sell the pieces, and that way you can make one birr, eighty. I was nine when I started selling the cane. I collected that coin and I gave it to my mother and she bought food.

"Then she was too sick to go out, so I am the one to buy the food and prepare it for my sisters. My father taught me how to cook the food. I can make stew. I buy *injera* from the street.

"Mother is sick for five months, then Mother died at home. When my mother died, I was not there! My younger sisters were screaming and the neighbor people ran to see what was happening. Then they closed the home and prepared my mother for burial.

"After burial, I returned to the house. I didn't find my mother again, only my sisters. I feel so sad. The neighborhood is taking care of my sisters."

He wiped his eyes in frustration.

"When I reach this orphanage the first time, I am crying and I feel sad, but the other children encourage me and acquaint me. My best friend is Behailu. Day by day I am feeling happy and I try to think of bright things. At night I am feeling sad, as I remember my parents. I am very very sorry I was not with my mother the last time. I am afraid I have disappointed my mother."

At AAI, Zerabruk, son of an engineer, asked for work space. He was given a storeroom. In the windowless cinder-block room, he pushed the mountain of used clothing to the back and cleared a work area. Out of paper clips, rubber bands, and sheets of notebook paper, he created an elevator the size of a shoe box. He ran a wire from the wall socket. When he flipped the light switch, the paper elevator ascended, lightly scraping up the wall. His newest project was a medieval trebuchet, a long levering arm that, when released, hurled a projectile. When he placed a bit of trash on the machine and released the arm, the device whipped over and stuffed the trash into a garbage can.

"I remember my father a little bit," round-faced, cheery twelve-year-old Mekdes Zawuda told me. "I remember that he was very sick. The people came and sat beside him. Before she was sick, my mother spun the cotton, prepared the cotton, and sold it. With that profit, she got food for the family. When my mother was seriously sick, my sister worked as an aide and we lived on that money. Some people know my mother is sick and they bring food to us. My mother died by tuberculosis. After that we can no longer live in our home. My sister cannot raise me and so I have come here."

"I live with my parents until age nine," said Yemisrach, a big-boned, innocent-faced fifteen-year-old, smiling briefly at the memory. "We are two girls, two boys. I am the oldest. First Mother died, then Father died of malaria. At nine, I become like a mother to the others."

"My small sister, Gelila, is four," said Robel, age nine, the rambunc-tious kid of the half-baked-schoolwork type. "When Gelila see something in my hand, she cry, so I give her. She does not remember our parents."

"I attended school from first grade to sixth," said Dagmawi, age twelve, a slender boy with a classic Ethiopian triangular look: high wide forehead, big eyes, keen cheekbones, and narrow chin. "Father was a security guard for the United Nations. He earned a fine salary. My mother worked in a clinic. By diseases I lost both my parents. I do not know how Mother died. When my father fell sick, he would always call to me, 'Bring me water!' I helped him. If he wanted something from the shop, I got it for him. In 2001, he got liver case and went to the hospital. After two months, he died. My sister, Kalkidan, is ten years old. We are together here."

Though they tried hard to hold on to their memories, the children sometimes confused their facts. Since it was taboo to speak the word *AIDS*, most children had not been told how their parents had died. "My father drank too much one time and he fell on the gate and he got a stone on his head and he went to the hospital and died. After that, he was buried," said worried-looking Yirgalum, age eight. "My mother and me, we were very sick at that time and she took us to the hospital and both of us were admitted and when I was playing with the hospital staff, at that time she died. My younger brother died before my mother."

Nine-year-old Robel believed the hospital killed his mother. "I was born in Tigray," he said. "Then I went with my parents to Sudan as refugees. My father would get food from the refugee camp and bring it to the house. This is how Mother died in Sudan: she went to the hospital for injections. First injection: good; second injection: she is tired; third injection: she died. Then I hear people crying about our father. They said, 'Your father has died.'"

"My father died when I was four or five," said Fisseha, age ten. "Then my mother was too poor to keep me. There is a rich man in our village who owns goats and cows. My mother gave me to him, to work. I watched his goats; at night he gives me an ear of corn to eat and a place to sleep. In the day, the big boys in the hills show me how to gather wild food like berries to eat and how to catch a fish. There is no chance for school."

Eight-year-old Mekdelawit, from Dire Dawa, remembered the days of her parents' deaths: "My sister Abeltayit is a baby lying on the floor with her feet in the air—like this. Our older sister throw herself in front of the car and scream and yell that she wants to die if our father is dead. Then our mother becomes so ill that she cannot move from her bed. She cannot eat and she has sores all over her body and she loves for us to gently scratch her skin."

Mekdelawit and Abeltayit had eight older siblings who tried to raise them, but the big brothers and sisters were obliged to leave home each day for school and for jobs. The older ones warned the youngest sisters not to leave the house during the day. Afraid that the girls would wander away and be lost in the bush, the oldest brother told them that there were monsters roaming about that would eat little girls. Finally, fearing for the youngest sisters, the older eight conferred and decided to deliver them to the orphanage.

There was a terrible sameness to the stories. They all headed down the same path: the mother's death, then the father's; or *Abaye* died, then *Amaye*, then Small Sister, then funny Baby Brother. Some said, "I *think* my little brother is still alive. I think he is still in the hospital. I'm pretty sure." I always learned later that the little brother or sister also was dead.

Alone, bringing out the words of the family's end, a child's eyes become bloodshot, the chest fills with sobs. No matter that it is *the* common experience of this generation to lose Mother, Father, or both, each child has been uniquely hurt.

"I lived in a very small house with my mother," my daughter Helen tells me.

"My mother was very beautiful. She had long, long, long, shiny hair that fell to her waist. We had two things in our house: we had a shelf and we had a baby bed. The bed is too small for my mother, she has to sleep by pulling up her legs. I don't remember when my mother was not sick. I don't really remember my father; sometimes I think I remember him reading a newspaper. My mother taught me to read when I was four. Amharic when I was four, and English when I was five. When I was five, I was the one taking care of my mother. If she needed something from the store, I go for her. When she needs juice, she gives me the coin and I go to buy the juice for her. One time I saw at the store little sparkly clips shaped like butterflies for your hair. I wanted those clips very much, but I bought the juice for my mother instead. At home I told my mother about the clips, and she said yes! My mother *always* said yes. I ran back and I bought the butterfly clips! But one day a taxi came and I think my mother died in the taxi. People took me away and they didn't let me go into the house to get the butterfly clips and I never saw my house again. But why did my mother have to die?"

One day, about four months after arriving in Atlanta, Helen collapsed in my arms, suddenly stricken with the memory of her late mother. I held her as she writhed, wailing, "Why she had to die?"

A few moments later, she said between sobs, "I know why she died. She was very sick, and we didn't have the medicine."

"I know," I said. "It's true. I'm so sorry."

By then I was well versed in the AIDS orphan crisis, but it floored me that she captured it with such accuracy, brevity, and grief, more powerfully than any of the thousand pages I had read on the subject.

"I wish I had known you then," I told the child in my arms. "I wish I could have sent her the medicine."

"But we didn't have a phone," she wept, "and I couldn't call you."

40

HAREGEWOIN WAS HAPPY for these older children chosen to go to America.

When she visited Layla House, the children who had been matched with new families ran to retrieve the photo albums they'd received from America. The fat little albums brimmed with nearly unbelievable images: grinning adults (white Americans or, in about 20 percent of the cases, black Americans) stood on green front yards or beside tremendous vehicles; laughing children sat on slides and swing sets; children in goggles leapt into swimming pools; children in satin uniforms posed with their teams on green fields; children shook hands with a jumbo Mickey Mouse or wrestled with dogs in front of a fireplace or pulled sleds up a snowy hill.

The orphans turned the plastic pages slowly, trying to make sense of each image. These had to be fairy tales! Yet the owner of each album had been told it was his or her destiny to leap into these scenes.

For lack of evidence to the contrary, the orphanage children chose to believe it, although none of their old friends or roommates had ever returned from America to confirm that it was true.

She was happy for them and yet she felt alone.

It was all for them, for the children, everything Haregewoin did, all the scrounging for money, T-shirts, pants, flip-flops, food, food, food. Her arms and legs moved ceaselessly from dawn to dark as if she were climbing through quicksand; it was all for them.

Once there had seemed something in it for her, too; once she had opened the door with mysterious anticipation.

Now, the moment she reached her bed at night, she blacked out and snored. Love was no longer a possibility. You can't love forty-five children; you can only take care of them in a maternal style. Your hands can stroke, your lips can smile and kiss, your voice can soothe, but your mind veers away.

Children as numerous as stars in the night sky, yet not one of them had become hers.

She understood that her house had become a way station for children, a step up out of suffering and toward unimaginably splendid lives in faraway countries. She was a temporary nurturer, a milepost. Baby Menah was living in Italy now; Meskerem and Selamawit waited at Layla House for families to be chosen for them, as did twins Rahel and Helen; and Ababu had just been introduced to Cheryl Carter-Schotts of Indianapolis, director of a second American adoption agency, Americans for African Adoptions (AFAA).

Adorable children, snaggle-toothed children, brothers and sisters, twins, sibling groups of three, populated Haregewoin's dirt compound, frolicking or bickering, hugging or shoving, screaming and yelling. Half a dozen little ones still piled in around her at bedtime, elbowing each other in their eagerness to be the closest to Haregewoin. And anyone, of any age, who was visited by a nightmare materialized beside her bed in the darkest hours of the night, and she somehow made room for the big boy or girl. But in the night, though she warmed and snuggled them, though she promised to keep them safe from hyenas, she did not know the names of those she snuggled.

Anyway, now that they knew about adoption, they longed for *real* mothers, for mothers of their *own*. They didn't want a group mother, an old, worn-out generic mother like herself. All were acting like Henok now, on the lookout for the best opportunity, the outside chance.

And it seemed to Haregewoin that some went beyond humbly hoping to be loved again; they got specific: they hoped for a *cute* mother; they wanted a *rich* father; they dreamed of a *big* house; they wanted a family with two older brothers, a sports car, and a pony.

(Our small daughter, Helen, arriving at age five with nothing to her name but the travel clothes we'd sent her, was shocked to be expected to share a bedroom with a six-year-old brother. She was further shocked when this brother left action figures, plastic pirates, and his dirty laundry lying about on the floor. Fed up one day with the incorrigible brother, she stomped her little foot and demanded, in English, to know, "If I *wasn't* going to have my own bedroom, *why* did you adopt me?!"

Helen has her own bedroom now.)

When Haregewoin looked around her shabby compound, peopled with adults moving slowly through the dusk of their disease and crammed full of bereft children in dirty clothes, she knew the children were right to fantasize that something grander awaited them. There must be lovelier mothers, prettier houses, more obedient pet dogs, beyond these galvanized-tin walls.

She was a good sport. She resigned herself to this new phase in her life, this minor role as caregiver for children on their way to bigger and better things.

Two little brothers arrived one day, holding the hands of a woman who identified herself as their aunt. "May you take them, *waizero*? My sister has died."

"Can't you care for them? Look at this place, I am completely overwhelmed."

"No, madam," said the woman, lowering her eyes.

The boys stared up at their aunt in astonishment.

"Can you give me anything to help with their upkeep?" She felt short with this woman.

"No, *waizero*," said the woman again, face averted.

The smaller of the two brothers, Teshome (Te-*show*-muh) began to cry.

"They are hungry," the woman whispered.

"Oh, for the love of God," said Haregewoin. "Go," she said to the boys. "The children are having their lunch now."

Heads down, the boys trudged away from their aunt, scuffing the dirt.

"Did you want to tell her good-bye?" asked Haregewoin.

"No!" yelled the older one, Tesfaye (Tes-*fie*-yay), in a strangled voice. He didn't look back.

"Yes!" said the little one, Teshome, and he ran back to bury his face in his aunt's skirts. He began to wail.

"You'll see Auntie again," prompted Haregewoin gently, hoping to inspire the aunt to offer a consoling promise. But, though the aunt's head was bent low, her fingers were scrabbling hard to pry the boy's hands loose from her skirt.

Haregewoin held him back, howling, as the aunt backed out the door, never raising her head.

The boys were inconsolable for a long time.

Teshome stood beside the gate for many weeks, hoping his aunt would return. Every time there was a knock on the door of the compound, a trembling half-smile touched his face; it was soon doused. Tesfaye had a dark, angry look and made no friends and thanked no one for any kindness. He didn't want his picture taken. He shunned Haregewoin's motherly advances. He cared only for Teshome, and for protecting Teshome. He cared nothing for private property, except Teshome's meager handmade playthings, which Tesfaye stood prepared to defend against all other children. He gave no caregiver a cause for complaint; he didn't misbehave; but he was so far withdrawn as to have almost disappeared inside himself. After Teshome adjusted to Haregewoin's compound, the younger boy made friends easily; but his cold, distant brother stood guard. Tesfaye didn't play. He stood at a distance, scowling, lest anyone raise a hand against Teshome.

Haregewoin had no time for this kind of thing anymore. If Tesfaye were her first child, she would have sat with him, held his hands, and compelled him to look into her eyes and talk to her. If he were one of ten children, she still would have found a moment to befriend him. Over a special snack of grapes or an orange, she could have encouraged him, between bites, to reveal his dark secrets. But there were forty or fifty children now and she had no time for this. There was nothing for it but to note in her mind that he was a difficult case and to relay such to AAI or AFAA, if either agency would be willing to take a chance on the brothers.

AAI did and found them a family.

It would be eighteen months before angry Tesfaye would break and tell the truth to his adoptive mother in Oregon, the secret he'd been warned never to speak: the woman who'd left the boys with Haregewoin was not their aunt. She was their mother.

Their father had died, he told his new mom from the backseat of the family van one day. *Amaye* remarried; but the man who, before the wedding, had pretended to like Tesfaye and Teshome, was not nice after all. He didn't care for the boys. He began to beat them and did not want to share his food with them; he was angry all the time with them; so his wife gave them up. *She chose her new husband instead of me and Teshome. I will never forgive her.*

He cried hard in telling this story to his adoptive mom, fearing that it would cause her to abandon them, too.

She assured Tesfaye that he had been right to tell, that none of it had been his fault, and that she would never leave him.

Perhaps, she thinks, *in fifteen years, when he understands economic deprivation, the subservience of women in his country, and the desperation of the very poor, he will soften his heart toward his first mother.*

Perhaps at that moment he will look for her, and forgive her, if she is still alive.

Sweet girls hugged Haregewoin tightly when they departed for AAI or AFAA, thanked her as their tears fell, and promised always to remember her and to help her once they were rich in America. And she squeezed them back, surprised by her own tears, suddenly realizing what a treasure she'd had in this or that child who was now leaving her. Selamawit left with great regret, mortified to leave Haregewoin behind without her; "Go, go, my dear," said Haregewoin, and Selamawit did and flew off to Washington State to the wonderful Murrell family, who named her Carrie.

Others—especially boys—gave a cursory hug and leapt into the AAI or AFAA van, ready to be off.

And Haregewoin was weary all the time with weariness like melancholy.

Until one day, out of the wild tilt and whirl of the galaxy, another little scrap flew her way.

41

S HE DIDN'T RECOGNIZE it at first, as the gift it was.

The police knocked on the gate one sunny morning with another abandoned, nameless baby, this one found outside the gates of a restaurant.

The baby was an aggrieved-looking girl of about two months, with a big, worried face and protruding forehead. She had looked and looked for her mother without success; the confusion and loneliness of abandonment had hardened into a permanent knot behind her forehead.

Haregewoin sighed and took her and signed the paperwork. She avoided eye contact with the baby. The baby avoided it, too.

Haregewoin took her promptly to a hospital's outpatient clinic to be tested. Haregewoin barely flinched at the flash of the needle entering the child's arm. If the infant was negative, she could be referred right away to one of the adoption agencies. A baby girl! Never mind how homely and unloved. A baby girl was what the foreign parents wanted!

Haregewoin rode home in the taxi with the baby in her lap wrapped in a stiff blanket, which covered her face. The baby lay awake but quiet. Haregewoin's mind was on tasks waiting at home. She had no appetite for studying the face of this new baby.

The baby girl tested positive for HIV/AIDS. The adoption agencies wouldn't touch her. Even if a prospective adoptive mother somewhere wanted her, knowing that with the pediatric ARVs in her rich country the baby could grow up and have a normal life, no nation's embassy would issue a visa to an HIV-positive child. The baby was trapped in Africa without medicine, and Haregewoin was stuck with her.

She held the droopy human being at arm's length beside a crib, thinking up a name. She was out of names. She was tired of names. The baby looked down. She hung limply, with no more hope of Mother. Haregewoin called her Nardos, an Orthodox name referring to the holy oil of anointment, and she gave her an impersonal hug to mark the moment. To her surprise, as she lowered the baby into the crib, Nardos clawed at Haregewoin's T-shirt with skinny fingers and held on briefly. When Haregewoin tried to disengage her shirt, the baby instantly let go, looking askance, as if it hadn't happened.

The next morning, Haregewoin plucked Nardos from the bevy of babies having a sunbath on the bedroom quilt and matter-of-factly tied her up on her back with a shawl. It didn't mean anything. She did this sometimes. For the midmorning bottle feedings, she sat down with Nardos and a bottle, though usually the older girls and the young caregivers from the neighborhood handled these feedings. Nardos didn't want to suck until urged to do so by Haregewoin's rubbing the nipple against her gums and tickling her cheek. She sucked dispiritedly, stopping for long moments to look dully at the nothing beside Haregewoin's head.

Slowly, as her tummy filled, as her days became predictable, Nardos seemed to sense that she was being cared for. The same big, warm face swam close whenever she cried. One day, as Haregewoin picked her up from her nap, the side of Nardos's mouth lifted a little in the start of a smile.

"There you are, Nardos!" cried Haregewoin. "You're starting to wake up, aren't you?"

On another day as she inserted the bottle, Haregewoin whispered to her, "You are very, very smart, aren't you, Nardos?" Nardos sucked hard, listening. "I can see it in your eyes. You're like my daughter Atetegeb. You don't miss a thing."

She hadn't consciously been looking to fall in love again, but suddenly, in the mitosis of love, Haregewoin's heart subdivided and a new chamber beat within it, this one labeled *Nardos*.

At five months, the baby had fat, dimpled thighs and delightfully arched, feathery eyebrows. When Haregewoin unsnapped her in the morning for a diaper change, Nardos opened wide her toothless mouth with happiness. The forward-pushing forehead no longer seemed a bruise of sorrow; now it was revealed as a beacon of intelligence.

Haregewoin dressed up Nardos like a new mother with a first baby: she stuffed her into a frilly pink dress and snapped a pink, stretchy headband around her bald head. With pride, certain of the result, she took her back to the HIV/AIDS clinic to be retested. She felt prepared to stand her ground and demand a recount if the news was bad a second time.

She waited in a room full of thin mothers and fathers who sat or stood, all so frightened they could barely move, propping up their pale, huge-eyed waifs, their ghostlike children.

Three quarters of children born to HIV-infected mothers do not carry the virus (hence the orphan crisis), but HIV-negative babies often test HIV-positive due to their mother's antibodies circulating in their system. The change in results from positive to negative (though such a child has been healthy all along) is called seroreversion.

Science aside, when Nardos tested negative this time for HIV/AIDS, Haregewoin believed it was her love that had saved the baby.

"We did it, Nardos! Good girl, good girl!" Haregewoin sang all the way home, and the baby, from her pillows in the backseat, chortled.

At ten months, Nardos was a chunky young lady with a four-tooth grin, cruising the furniture of Haregewoin's front room and patting it affectionately. She alone, out of scores of children, had unrestricted access to Haregewoin at all hours. Haregewoin stopped whatever she was doing, interrupting any phone call or meeting, whenever Nardos shouted, *"Amaye!"*

"Abet?" What?

"*Amaye!*"

"*Abet?*"

Nardos stormed into the front room, parting a crowd of visitors, to pull up into Haregewoin's lap and press her face against Haregewoin's.

Dusty small girls, watching from the doorway or through the window, felt shut out from this sudden flowering of mother love in old Haregewoin. They felt pleased that Haregewoin was relaxed and jolly again, but they couldn't seem to access the joyful love themselves. Some little girls shyly drew near, petting Nardos, letting their fingertips linger on Haregewoin's arm or sleeve at the same time; but she—not unkindly, just obliviously—shooed them back outside.

The visiting adults in the living room made much of Nardos; those wishing to make an excellent impression upon Haregewoin brought a little treat for Nardos when they visited. From an impossibly young age, Nardos pressed her hands together and gave a quick, polite bow of greeting, charming everyone.

Now! thought Haregewoin with satisfaction. *Life is good.*

42

H AREGEWOIN HAD THROWN away her good name. In grief for her daughter, she had discarded her old life as the wife of a high school principal, as an office administrator, as a church caterer in Cairo. She had excommunicated herself and dressed only in black. She grew acquainted with the nation's outcasts—adults ruined by disease, orphaned children—and started a humble new life among them.

It now appeared to some that she had chosen cleverly, even presciently.

Her good name returned.

By 2003, 2004, people of conscience grew increasingly aware that the AIDS pandemic raged ahead in Africa. AIDS was on the front page of every newspaper. The United Nations held a special assembly to discuss AIDS. AIDS billboards went up around Addis Ababa, urging safe sexual practices, urging citizens not to shun the sick. The mayor of Addis Ababa spoke of HIV/AIDS on television and demonstrated how to get a blood test. Everyone knew someone afflicted by AIDS. It was too pervasive to remain hidden any longer.

Haregewoin had been the first of her circle to reach out to AIDS orphans. Suddenly she found herself at the forefront of a popular trend. Her good name rose into high circles. She became a portal through which upper-class women began to extend a helping hand.

A wealthy Ethiopian Muslim woman phoned one day in 2004. The wife of an industrialist, she was among the richest women in the country. It was nearly her daughter's seventh birthday. The little girl and her private-school chums were accustomed to birthday parties with pony rides, swimming, or miniature golf. Their lives included shopping trips by private jet to Dubai or Paris, ski trips to Switzerland. Last year the child's birthday party had been staged at the Sheraton Addis, at the ramparts of the city, at the crest of a long, winding driveway of banners whipping in the air.

The birthday theme this year, the mother explained to Haregewoin, was to be AIDS orphans. It was time for her daughter to begin to learn about helping the less fortunate. Could the party be held at Haregewoin's house?

Ethiopia's orphan crisis had overwhelmed the traditional helping networks of kinship, faith, and village; for wealthy philanthropists to come to the aid of the unrelated poor was unusual, unpracticed.

Most of the city's affluent citizens rode through the dusty streets and nudged through the throngs of beggars with their tinted windows rolled up, their car music systems drowning out the sound of appeals from the streets. No Ethiopian family had ever adopted a child from Haregewoin's compound. There were private elementary schools and secondary schools in Addis Ababa as exclusive as any in North America or Europe; there were handsome, solid, expansive houses filled with artwork, books, and twenty-first-century entertainment and computer systems; there were mansions with green lawns, pools, and badminton nets, which were staffed by Ethiopian gardeners, cooks, and house servants. There was a globe-trotting class of embassy, government, NGO, and aid workers who mingled with the richest Ethiopians.

So if the birthday party was approached awkwardly—if Haregewoin's orphans were offered up a little bit for their instructional value to the rich children—it was due to lack of experience on the part of the wealthy giver and on the part of the poor recipients. The mother meant to relay a lesson to her daughter and friends that there was poverty in the world; and as for Haregewoin's orphans, they were eager to be included in the fun.

*   *   *

At nine A.M. on a Saturday morning, chauffeur-driven SUVs and Mercedes began to park on the pebbly road outside the gate. Haregewoin had awakened the children before dawn and had been frenziedly soaping and moisturizing and combing them ever since. She distributed brand-new clothing, all white, purchased with money given to her in advance by the birthday girl's mother.

Thirty damp, shiny children in white pants and white button-down shirts—the girls' hair in the painfully tight twists of new cornrows—stood in two lines in front of the house waiting to greet the guests. They looked like an Austrian children's choir. Hungry and sleepy, they slumped out of line, but Haregewoin angrily scolded them back into position. They stood at attention for endless minutes or hours, looking with a mixture of impatience and fear toward the compound door.

The birthday girl's schoolmates included the children of foreign diplomats, attachés, and corporate chiefs, so Haregewoin's compound filled up with perky good-natured women from Norway, France, Great Britain, and New Zealand. In short haircuts, khaki slacks, pullover sweaters, and white sneakers, the women stood chatting in the driveway, holding coffee mugs. They looked like Saturday-morning soccer moms anywhere in Europe or America. Their children, in brand-name sports clothing and waterproof wristwatches, lingered near them, at the far side of the courtyard from the rigidly positioned orphans.

The compound door opened again and in swept the birthday girl's mother, draped in a silk lavender robe and a lilac head scarf. If Makeda, Queen of Sheba, were touching her silk slippers to the mud courtyard, Haregewoin's children wouldn't have been more awestruck. The elegant Ethiopian woman glided over to the two rows of scrubbed and terrified orphans, dragging her daughter behind her. She greeted them graciously and obliged her daughter to greet them, too.

"*Salaam,*" the daughter said, shrugging. She looked behind her to her school friends and rolled her eyes.

The exotic lady's lips were outlined in violet; mauve powder shadowed her eyes; there was a scent of cloves and cinnamon.

Haregewoin's children wanted to shake hands with her but were afraid to impose. Her small daughter broke free and ran to join her friends. The fine lady looked around vaguely for a moment, at a loss, until her Swedish nanny ran over to help. The young blond woman ran an electrical cord through Haregewoin's doorway, plugged in a cassette tape recorder, and blasted Ethiopian pop music. Haregewoin's children took it as a signal to scatter.

A wealthy Ethiopian girl ran up to her mother and breathlessly asked, "*May* we play with them?" and the mother nodded.

The nanny clapped her hands and drew all the children—private-school students and orphans, European and Ethiopian—into a hand-holding circle for games. Children danced and batted at balloons on the mud courtyard.

Haregewoin had overseen the preparation of an outdoor stage. Long, fresh-cut grasses were thrown down as a carpet, under a roof of woven branches. She had ordered the oldest boys to drag her upholstered furniture out of the house and up onto the stage, and she had spread leopard-spotted blankets over the sofas and chairs. A throne awaited the birthday girl. The child ascended the stage through a torrent of paper banners and balloons and sat upon a mountain of cushions on the middle chair.

The mother had invited a local TV station to cover the birthday party, to highlight this moment of noblesse oblige in the hopes that others would follow her example. As their bright spotlights beat down on the birthday girl, she was presented with a sheet cake. The entire compound sang the birthday song to her, in Amharic and then (the private-school students) in French and English. She closed her eyes, made her wish, and blew out her candles. Everyone clapped politely; some of the children cheered. Few of Haregewoin's children knew their own birth dates; most could only estimate their ages. From where they stood, it appeared that birthdays—like mothers—were the province of rich children.

Cake was served on paper plates. The Swedish nanny accepted wrapped presents from the private-school students and placed them near the exit in deep shopping bags. A three-year-old girl named Sara stuffed cake into her mouth and staggered about on the mud courtyard moaning, in Amharic, "Oh my God, oh my God, I have gone to heaven, this has got to be the most delicious thing I have ever tasted."

For a tumultuous hour, after the cake and icing hit their bloodstreams, the pampered children and the paupered children played tag and danced and chased balloons, until mud covered them all equally. Then suddenly the party was over, the SUVs revved up outside in the lane, and the birthday girl and her mother distributed small gift bags to every child. Though Haregewoin's children were now completely filthy, they were permitted to shake the queenly lady's hand while expressing their gratitude. With nary a grimace, she delicately shook many eager hands and even bent over to receive a grubby kiss or two on the cheek.

The TV cameramen shouldered their equipment, the private-school children confirmed plans with each other for the rest of the afternoon, and the Swedish nanny staggered out the compound door laden with the wrapped presents.

After the birthday convoy departed, Haregewoin's children fell quiet. Pastel scraps of paper and ribbons had been trampled into the mud; a few limp balloons hung from the compound walls. Haregewoin pulled a kitchen chair to the threshold of the house and ordered the children to come to her, one by one, to strip off the new white clothing. It would be washed, dried, and set aside until the next guests were expected. The older boys were obliged to carry the heavy furniture back into the house.

As if a clock in their fairy tale were striking midnight, the children were restored to their worn-out T-shirts and colorless drawstring shorts. The compound was reduced to strips of broken cement and squares of mud.

Each child went off alone to examine the contents of his or her gift bag. The inexpensive treats—hard candies, bubble gum, peppermints—were counted, lined up, sniffed, examined, and finally nibbled with the very tips of the front teeth. Then they were rewrapped and replaced in the bags and hidden all over the compound. Some of the candies would never be eaten by the children, the joy of ownership trumping the fleeting delight of taste.

Haregewoin was a little depressed when it was over, when the magic exited the courtyard and she was a poor woman again. She'd liked the TV cameras, actually; she'd liked the embassy wives; she'd enjoyed the attention. She'd felt proud to stand with her children, the orphans, yet also proud to be seen as something slightly apart from them. The rich lady had conferred upon her a feeling of equality, as if the two of *them* reached out to the children of the gutter.

If her children felt entitled to daydream of rich fathers and elegant mothers and bicycles and basketballs in America, why couldn't she imagine for a moment that she was a member of her country's elite social circle?

43

AIDS GOT BIGGER. It attracted the concern of musicians and movie stars. It was high on the agenda of the Make Poverty History campaign, demanding justice for the world's poor. In July, Great Britain hosted the G8 (Group of Eight) summit of world leaders in Gleneagles, Scotland. Prime Minister Tony Blair promised that the main themes of the summit would be Africa and climate change. The meeting was preceded by massive Live 8 pop concerts around the world, hosted by rock stars Bono and Sir Bob Geldof and performed on stages erected in Hyde Park, London; the Palais de Versailles, Paris; Circus Maximus, Rome; Museum of Art, Philadelphia; Siegessäule, Berlin; Park Place, Barrie, Canada; Makuhari Messe, Tokyo; Red Square, Moscow; Mary Fitzgerald Square, Newtown, Johannesburg; and Murrayfield Stadium, Edinburgh. Three billion viewers (it has been said) tuned in to watch performances by stars like U2, Paul McCartney, Stevie Wonder, Kanye West, Madonna, and Sting. Images of poor Africans flashed upon screens behind the performers.

The G8 leaders promised to double aid to Africa by 2010, and to cancel the debts of eighteen poor countries, but little or no progress was made in improving trade justice. The leaders did promise to work toward universal access to antiretroviral treatment by 2010.

For those closest to the front lines, the flamboyant displays of caring and self-congratulation didn't necessarily deliver. In 1970, the UN General Assembly had agreed that rich countries should donate 0.7 percent of their gross national products (GNP) to development assistance for poor countries. The underlying principle was not simply moral obligation, but an awareness that northern hemisphere wealth and southern hemisphere poverty were linked; Africa, in particular, had been plundered for hundreds of years by the world's elites, with no thought to the chaos, tragedy, and starvation they left behind. The deadline for reaching the 0.7 percent GNP target was the mid-1970s.

In 1992, rich countries again agreed upon the target of 0.7 percent of GNP for international aid. By 2015 (the year the current UN Millennium Development Goals are hoped to be achieved) the target will be forty-five years old.

Many Americans assume that the U.S. government is doing all it can to alleviate suffering, hunger, and disease in the world (and, indeed, many private individuals, private corporations and NGOs, and public health workers from the United States *are* doing all they can). But there is a widespread misperception that the United States, as a nation, stands in the forefront of the world's biggest donors. Surveys of American opinion consistently reveal significantly more support for cutting foreign aid rather than increasing it (31 percent to 17 percent), while a plurality favors keeping the aid budget at its current level.

In dollar amount, the United States *is* the world's biggest giver; but measured as a percentage of GNP, the American donation is paltry indeed.

Moreover, the so-called aid often is of more benefit to the donor nation than to the recipient nation. "Development assistance is often of dubious quality," stated a Global Policy Forum report in 2005. "In many cases, aid is primarily designed to serve the strategic and economic interests of the donor countries . . . or to benefit powerful domestic interest groups. Aid systems based on the interests of donors instead of the needs of recipients make development assistance inefficient; too little aid reaches countries that most desperately need it; and, all too often, aid is wasted on overpriced goods and services from donor countries . . . Recent increases [in foreign aid] do not tell the whole truth about rich countries' generosity, or the lack of it."

Whatever the quality of the aid, the top givers gave the following dollar amounts between 2002 and 2005: USA ($75,853,000); Japan

($40,138,000); France ($31,051,000); UK ($29,552,000); Germany ($29,502,000); Netherlands ($16,771,000); Italy ($12,221,000); Canada ($10,552,000); Sweden ($9,856,000); Australia ($5,325,000).

Though the United States gave the most in dollar amount, as a percentage of GNP it gave the least: an abysmal 0.1575 percent. Also far behind the stated goals and oft-repeated promises were Japan, at 0.25 percent GNP, Canada and Germany, roughly 0.3 percent, and Italy and Australia, between 0.2 and 0.25 percent.

Compare this to those who gave the most as a percentage of their GNP during the same period (2002 to 2005), all 0.8 percent or better: Norway, 0.91 percent (0.93% in 2005); Denmark, 0.865 percent (.81 percent in 2005); Sweden, 0.785 percent (.92 percent in 2005); Luxembourg, 0.82 percent (.87 percent in 2005); Netherlands, 0.795 percent (.82 percent in 2005).

By April 15, 2006, the U.S. government had spent, according to congressional appropriations, $275 billion on the war in Iraq. According to the National Priorities Project, worldwide AIDS programs could have been completely funded for twenty-seven years with that amount of funding.

"We are in a desperate race against time, and we're losing it," said Stephen Lewis. "It's simply impossible to reduce poverty, hunger, gender inequality, disease, and death significantly at the present pace, and other than the contrapuntal beat of hyperactive rhetoric, the necessary . . . acceleration is nowhere evident. Alas, man and woman cannot live by rhetoric alone."

Foreign epidemiologists and aid workers flew into Addis in increasing numbers. At the Addis Ababa Hilton and the Sheraton Addis, Europeans and North Americans browsed the breakfast buffets: china platters displayed wedges of watermelon, miniature bananas, red grapes bursting with juice. Gelled sugar coated the bitter seeds of the cracked-open pomegranates. Sterling-silver warming trays offered scrambled eggs in thick curds, grilled potatoes and onions, and fried filets of Lake Victoria trout. Outside the bright plate-glass windows, white-collared pigeons and yellow-fronted parrots rode up and down on the windy branches of the eucalyptus trees.

In the hotel lobbies there were airline offices, banks, business centers, jewelry stores, and sports-shoe stores. Swimming pools and fountains sparkled on the landscaped grounds. The Hilton tennis pro, dressed in white, waited for customers while smacking a lone ball against a practice wall. He doubled as the squash pro. A Ping-Pong table and a billiard table stood on a patio near the door of the glass-walled fitness center.

After breakfast, on the circular driveways, beside waist-high flowers, scientists, researchers, representatives of international NGOs, epidemiologists, economists, and export brokers adjusted their fanny packs and hopped up into waiting SUVs. They rode squinting into the bright heartland. Some would do real work here and make meaningful contact with locals; WHO, UNAIDS, Global Fund, and CDC staff, volunteers with medical NGOs like Doctors Without Borders/Médecins Sans Frontières, World Wide Orphans, or the William J. Clinton Foundation would save lives. But too many experts harvested data, to be interpreted through graphs and charts that would be masterworks of colorful and geometric compositions. Presentations would be made in the meeting rooms and ballrooms of Europe's fine hotels; attendees would take notes on their laptops; chandeliers overhead would be dimmed for the slide shows and PowerPoint presentations.

"We're terrific when it comes to studies and documentation," says UN Special Envoy Stephen Lewis. "Reports like the Epidemic Update by UNAIDS . . . are models of statistical compilation, containing pockets of fascinating material. But the report itself acknowledges that real progress against the pandemic is hard to find. We need a superhuman effort from every corner of the international community. We're not getting it. At the present rate, we'll have a cumulative total of one hundred million deaths and infections by the year 2012."

Sometimes it struck the visiting experts that the proud and isolated hilltop kingdom had been cast under a spell, requiring only a magic touch from the West to awaken and turn it toward prosperity. Economic development and political progress sometimes seemed imminent.

Many Ethiopian leaders would have preferred not to approach the West, hand over heart, hand outstretched. Ethiopia had been civilized and self-reliant longer than these flourishing northern hemisphere countries had existed. Ethiopia's symbol and the symbol of the last emperor was the Lion of Judah. The Lion of Judah does not grovel.

But assistance from the rich countries—debt forgiveness, fair trade, and the unshackling of medical miracles from their expensive patents—was indispensable for Ethiopia's struggle out of desperate poverty, so the Lion of Judah was obliged to incline its head. The Lion bent down its eyes.

The Ethiopians were unsure how much their foreign visitors—how much the outside world—understood about local power arrangements and the stage-managed politics of ethnicity and of border disputes with Eritrea.

After the 1991 overthrow of Mengistu's Communist dictatorship, the new government under Meles Zenawi pledged to support democratic freedoms—including freedom of the press and freedom of assembly—and a multiparty political system.

In recent years, the stagnant economy and growing AIDS crisis—added to issues of regional saber-rattling, food insecurity, poor sanitation, lack of clean water, and other public health issues—strengthened popular resolve to unseat the prime minister (who ruled with favoritism to his Tigrayan ethnic group) and his ruling Ethiopian People's Revolutionary Democratic Front (EPRDF).

But would Meles Zenawi really step down if he failed to win reelection in 2005? Many prayed and dreamed that he would. With his democratic pretensions, his liberal talk, and his hobnobbing with world leaders, especially with Britain's Prime Minister Tony Blair, wouldn't he be ashamed to cling to power in defiance of a popular referendum?

In May 2005, Meles Zenawi's reelection was instantly challenged as a stolen election. His refusal to yield power struck what seemed to be a majority of Ethiopians as profoundly antidemocratic. By the end of 2005, the government stood accused of manipulating the election results, jailing journalists and opposition leaders, and attempting to quell protest with live bullets, expulsion of foreign observers, and mass arrests.

The Coalition for Unity and Democracy (CUD) party called for nationwide nonviolent dissent, including a stay-at-home strike and a boycott of ruling-party businesses, to protest the alleged election-rigging. In June 2005 and again in November, antigovernment protesters took to the streets of Addis Ababa and of the smaller towns of Dese, Debre Berhan, Bahir Dar, and Awasa. They were met by armed security forces that opened fire. Forty-six demonstrators and onlookers—men, women, and children—were killed; two hundred were wounded; and four thousand people (including many students) were imprisoned, including such prominent figures as Hailu Shawel, seventy, president of the opposition Coalition for Unity and Democracy (CUD) party; Professor Mesfin Woldemariam, seventy-five, former chair of the Ethiopian Human Rights Council (EHRC); Dr. Yacob Hailemariam, a former UN special envoy and former prosecutor at the International Criminal Tribunal for Rwanda; Ms. Birtukan Mideksa, CUD vice president and a former judge; and Dr. Berhanu Nega, the recently elected mayor of Addis Ababa and university professor of economics. Twenty-five hundred detainees have since been released without charge; it is unclear how many are still being held or where they are. Prime Minister Meles has said the detainees are likely to be charged with treason.

The Coalition for Unity and Democracy gained a third of the legislative seats in the elections but boycotted the new parliament as illegitimately composed.

In November 2005, Amnesty International reported, "Amnesty International fears the detainees may be denied bail and kept in prolonged pre-trial detention in harsh conditions, leading to a lengthy trial with many adjournments, and that they may not receive a fair trial according to international standards."

They were right. In February of 2006, 80 defendants in Ethiopia, 38 in absentia, were called before the Federal Court of Ethiopia to stand trial on charges that included high treason, "outrages against the Constitution," inciting and organizing armed uprising, and "genocide."

Not expecting a fair trial, most refused to plead or to defend themselves. Amnesty International denounced the charges and called for the immediate and unconditional release of opposition leaders, human rights defenders, and activists. "These people are prisoners of conscience, imprisoned solely on account of their nonviolent opinions and activities," said Kolawole Olaniyan, director of Amnesty International's Africa Programme. "Furthermore, the grounds advanced by the prosecution for the charge of 'genocide' do not even remotely match internationally recognized definitions of genocide—or the definition set out in the Ethiopian Criminal Code. This absurd charge should be withdrawn immediately."

I interviewed a shy sixteen-year-old girl, "Yeshi," whose sister and brother-in-law, with whom she lived in Addis, lost track of her in the November unrest.

"I threw one rock," she said, weeping in my hotel room. It was February 2006, three months after the event, yet she still seemed profoundly shaken by it. She wore a plaid skirt and a short-sleeve, white blouse; her hair was prettily braided. "I was on the school grounds and I just threw it over the wall. When the security forces burst in, carrying rifles, they made us all run into the school; people were screaming, crying, and falling. The soldiers were striking them and beating them. Students were crawling around, bloody. Inside, they separated out the Tigrayan students [of Meles's ethnic group] and used them as informers against the rest of us. We had to stand facing the walls, close to the walls, and the soldiers walked through with their informers. Someone pointed to me and said I had thrown a rock, and they grabbed me.

"We had to sit on the floor for hours, waiting for trucks to come get us to take us to jail. We couldn't look up or talk; we couldn't use our cell phones to call home. I couldn't believe it was happening to us, to me. When the trucks came, they screamed at us to get up and they walked beside us, with their rifles. Just before getting on the truck, I was able to look up and see a friend of mine watching; she kind of nodded to let me know she saw me; I knew she would tell my family.

"They put us in a cell all together. Some days they let us outside and our families came to the other side of the fence to see us. My sister came and my brother-in-law law and they brought food to me. I touched my sister's hands through the fence. The worst were the days when we weren't allowed to go out to see our families."

She hung her head and could not stop herself from shaking. She was released after a few weeks, but is changed. She looks haunted. She agreed to talk to me only under conditions of great secrecy and anonymity. She is a high school sophomore whose life was derailed because, in the infectious schoolyard excitement of political protest, she threw a rock over the wall.

"If Meles had accepted the loss and had yielded power, like the democrat he pretended to be, he would have become so popular in the West," an Ethiopian friend, a businessman, told me. "He would have been called a second Mandela. He could have gone on an extended tour of American universities and European capitals, as a lecturer and a consultant. We wouldn't have missed him, believe me! We know who Meles is. But no one would have begrudged him a kind of democratic sainthood in the West, if he had stepped down.

"Instead the ballots have been trashed and we have on our hands another African cliché."

Meanwhile, Westerners came and Westerners flew away. Ethiopian friends saw them off at Bole International Airport. Soon the travelers busied themselves with headphones, ergonomic neck pillows, and in-flight American movies. Even as their planes disappeared from the skies over Ethiopia, new jumbo jets full of outside experts were landing.

Increasingly Haregewoin was seen by outsiders as a gateway to the strange and sad new underworld of HIV/AIDS in Africa. She knew people actually dying of AIDS. She was raising their children.

Some of the foreign visitors called upon Haregewoin to ask how they could help. They sat and thanked her very much for the coffee, for the sliced oranges, for the popcorn. They praised the coffee, the oranges, the popcorn, and the cuteness of the children in the dirt yard. They opened notebooks and calendars on their laps, they tapped on their calculators and hoped to do good work here. They came from Italy, Sweden, and Norway. They asked if they could take photographs of her children, for the boards of their NGOs back home, and they thanked her for allowing them to take the photos.

An article I wrote about Haregewoin for *Good Housekeeping* inspired thousands of readers to send donations to her. Many included notes to express their surprise and sorrow to hear of death and dying in such numbers across Africa. Most wrote, *We didn't know.*

The money donated to the Atetegeb Worku Memorial Orphans Support Association enabled Haregewoin to take a step she'd long worried about. Before anti-AIDS medicines were available for Ethiopian children, it was felt to be risky for the HIV-positive children to be around the HIV-negative children who caught, and easily threw off, childhood complaints such as colds or chicken pox, which could be devastating to an immunocompromised child. The reverse was also felt to be true, that the ill children, plagued by opportunistic infections, could endanger the health of their playmates. Where medications are available, such segregation is not necessary.

With money in the bank, Haregewoin was able to imagine a better life for the children than the increasingly squalid one they shared in the crumbling brick house and mud courtyard. She toured better neighborhoods and resolved to rent two nice houses: one for the HIV-negative children and one for the growing numbers of HIV-positive children.

She took taxis up and down the steep hills of Addis Ababa and peered into every corner of available rental properties. She turned on faucets and felt for water pressure; she sniffed abhorrent smells in outhouses and exited waving her hand back and forth in front of her face; she stood on paved lanes and estimated the distances to schools and hospitals; and she scoffed at attempts by landladies to inflate the value of their properties.

In the past, she had been obliged to conceal her purposes from prospective landlords: that she intended to fill a rental house with AIDS orphans. She'd been obliged to hedge about where the children came from, what had happened to their parents, whether the children were diseased.

But she was becoming person of note, a celebrity. Foreigners called on her; the wealthiest woman in Addis Ababa had asked her to host her daughter's birthday. A local newspaper had translated and reprinted the *Good Housekeeping* story about her. In case anyone had missed it—in English or in Amharic—she kept clippings in her handbag.

So she found and rented two houses, to replace the one with the boxcar and the dirt compound.

An ornate steel door with brass trim opened into the larger compound; the encircling walls were of stone rather than galvanized tin. Three brick houses, with cement porches, faced the courtyard, which was entirely paved.

In the smaller compound around the corner, facing a dirt avenue, a stand of trees scattered cool green light upon the broken cement ground. Here were several old brick buildings and an outdoor kitchen. The HIV-positive children were housed here. Their bedrooms were large and airy, lined with bunk beds.

Then Haregewoin learned that, because of the *Good Housekeeping* article, she'd won an award in America: a $10,000 Heroes in Health award, underwritten by General Electric. The *GH* editors invited her to fly to New York to accept her award. They contacted the American ambassador in Ethiopia to request an expedited visa and it was granted.

Haregewoin took a taxi to an Ethiopian Airlines office and showed them the articles about herself. Ethiopian Airlines presented her with a free round-trip ticket so that she could travel to accept her award. Henok's mother, Tigist, promised to take care of the children in both houses during the two weeks of her absence.

On a Thursday morning in mid-November 2004, the children stood en masse in the courtyard of the larger house to see her off. Big boys shouted and cheered for her and pounded on the hood of the taxi. Nardos had somehow formed the impression that she was going, and when the taxi door slammed with *Maye* on the inside of the car and herself on the outside, she sat down with a thump on the driveway, closed her eyes, opened her mouth, and howled her disappointment. Haregewoin hung her head all the way to the airport, crushed by shame that she was leaving them all, even Nardos, to go strut among strangers. It was *for* them, of course, as she reminded herself; she was raising and collecting money to care for them better. She tried to repress her excitement, but she'd never stepped foot out of Africa before.

PART 3

44

HAREGEWOIN CHANGED PLANES in Frankfurt, disembarked in Washington, D.C., and was steered, by Ethiopian Airlines personnel, through Immigration and Customs, to a commuter flight to Newark, New Jersey.

She landed in Newark on a November night in 2004.

Dressed in her traditional Ethiopian white dress, *shamma* (shawl), and sandals, she was bumped along by the crowd exiting the plane and was swept down the escalators into the baggage-claim area. No one had met Haregewoin's flight because, in her excitement, she had forgotten to tell me on what date and in which airport she was arriving.

In baggage claim, people shoved and grabbed their bags, yelled to others far away, waved their arms, and ran off, wheeling their suitcases behind them. Haregewoin had been traveling for twenty-six hours and suddenly didn't know what to do next. It seemed the airport was emptying out; the squealing wheeled suitcases zigzagged and skated behind their fleeing owners.

She dragged her heavy canvas suitcase (without wheels) across the linoleum, came to a halt before the automatic exit doors through which everyone was evacuating, felt the salty cold wind through the door like a slap, and began to cry.

She made a strange sight on a Thursday night in the Newark airport: a short, round Ethiopian woman in traditional dress and shawl, looking through the glass doors into the dark parking lot, and crying.

Two Ethiopian-American women, hurrying past with their own squeaking wheeled suitcases, slowed down, stopped, and looked at her.

They recognized the clothes, they recognized the physiognomy. In Amharic, they offered, *"Dehna amshee. Indemin allesh?"* (Good evening. How are you?)

"Dehna [I'm fine]," she replied gratefully.

"Can we help you?" they asked in English. They wore tight jeans, high heels, big earrings, and belted black leather jackets. Their hairstyles were composed of thick ringlets.

"Ow, ow [yes yes]," she said. "I don't know where I'm supposed to go," she said in English.

"Was someone supposed to meet you?"

"Yes," she said unfairly.

"Do you want to wait?"

"I don't think anyone is coming for me!" she wailed. "They forgot me!" (That she'd failed to tell me either the date she was arriving or her destination city really can't be held against me any longer.)

"Come with us," said the women. Under their shiny powder and eye shadows, they had Ethiopian faces, but they were bold and cocky. They took long strides, their bootheels rapped confidently across the linoleum. In Ethiopia, girls were raised to be soft and humble, to kneel, to serve, to cast down their eyes. These women tossed their curls, spoke loudly, laughed with long, white teeth, and pushed ahead of others exiting the airport.

Haregewoin followed them, dragging her suitcase on its side behind her. She was shocked by the cold air of the parking lot; it nearly blew off her cotton wraps. Her hands, tugging at the suitcase handle, burned in the cold air. The freezing leather backseat of the car was rigid and she shivered uncontrollably.

"Where are you taking me?" she asked miserably.

"How about an Ethiopian restaurant?! Are you hungry?" one of the young women said. Needing no taxi driver, husband, servant, she got behind the wheel of the car herself, fished money out of her wallet, paid the attendant, and took them speeding into traffic. Haregewoin hung on to her ice-cold door handle with both hands.

It was like blasting into a distant galaxy. She recognized the basic elements of a city landscape at night—here was a highway, and a bridge over a dark river; there were three-story brick apartment houses, and a factory with chimneys; there, on the river, were boats and ships. As they zoomed into Manhattan, she spotted grocery stores, bars, newspaper kiosks, fruit bins. But the dimensions and proportions of everything were outlandish.

"You're both Ethiopian?" she asked the young women uncertainly as they rocketed through the dark streets.

They laughed in reply, as full of easy laughter as Americans.

"Is this . . . Newyorkcity?" she asked.

The city rose within a gray vault of moving clouds or smoke. The sky itself was pushed back in America. There were no stars, just a bright gray, churning canopy. It was as if a dustcover had been tossed over the skyscrapers.

"Is this your first trip to New York?" the young women asked, but they didn't have to ask, as she still clutched her door handle tightly with both hands, staring, breathing through her mouth, exhaling steam into the cold car.

"Yes," she said.

The tall buildings were lit from within. Thousands of glass-covered windows sparkled in the air. Buildings full of the glowing windows marched one after another all the way to the horizon. Each building was like a lantern, radiating firelight through numberless openings.

She understood: America has electricity in abundance. The only thing Ethiopia has in such abundance is dirt.

They parked and hurried through the freezing streets. The two women hoisted Haregewoin's suitcase and ran sideways, holding it between them like a body. They descended cement stairs into the long, warm, noisy room of the Queen of Sheba Restaurant on Tenth Avenue.

"*Selam, indemin allachihu?* [Hello, how are you?]," said the hostess. "Three for dinner?"

Haregewoin dug into the foods set before them: *injera* and *doro wat* (chicken stew), *tibs* (spicy beef), *iab* (a cottage cheese), *sega wat* (lamb stew), and *tej* (honey wine) to wash it down. Almost like home! Well, blander . . . but certainly along the same lines as food at home.

"*Waizero* Haregewoin," said one of her young women, "we have to go now. We're working tomorrow. Where shall we take you? Would you like to come back to my apartment? You are very welcome. And I will call my mother tomorrow to come and keep you company. I promise you her Amharic is better than mine! She scolds me all the time!"

But by then Haregewoin was making friends all over the restaurant. The two young women had explained that they'd found this traditional little lady, in the white, handwoven shawl of the homeland, crying in baggage claim in Newark.

The Ethiopian-American professionals, meeting for drinks and late dinners, were attentive and curious, and Haregewoin was eager to share news of her mission: she was here in America to collect funds to help the orphans. From across the restaurant, many well-dressed people smiled and nodded at her. Encouraged, she dragged her big navy-blue canvas suitcase out into the middle of the room and unzipped it. She extracted three photo albums of the children in her compound and handed them to nearby diners. Then she unrolled twenty handwoven scarves and a dozen heavy traditional shawls, made by people living with HIV/AIDS in her neighborhood, including Getachew. She tried to sell them to the dinner crowd. She would carry the money home to the artisans. A nice young man laughed and pushed back the scarves. "Save your scarves, *Waizero*; sell them elsewhere. Here we are just happy to be able to help you." He emptied out a basket of rolls, passed around the basket, and it came back to him with $460 in it for Haregewoin's children.

All around her, affluent-looking young men and women flipped open their cell phones and dialed information for her. With her help, they reached *my* cell phone. Many of them. A dozen of them.

By the time my flight from Atlanta landed in Newark and I turned on my mobile phone, fifteen voice messages waited for me. In tones of increasing urgency, some in English, some in Amharic, I learned that my round, little Ethiopian friend had wandered off all alone into New York City in the bitterly cold night dragging her suitcase and wearing her sandals. Although many messages were in Amharic, I'm not positive, but I believe—given the tone of voice—that I received numerous angry rebukes. It was now my turn to stand in baggage claim, look through the glass windows into the parking lot, and feel a little tearful myself. I sat there and made arrangements for Haregewoin from afar. I reached a *Good Housekeeping* editor at home, who called a car service, and a limousine pulled up in front of the Queen of Sheba Restaurant with directions to drive Mrs. Teferra to Le Parker Meridien Hotel.

At eleven o'clock that night, Haregewoin exited the Queen of Sheba Restaurant with a purse stuffed with business cards and a great roll of American dollars. Several people accompanied her to the curb, to put her in the limo. Kisses on each cheek, back and forth, back and forth; and a turbaned Sikh limo driver hoisted her heavy suitcase without wheels into the trunk; and off they zoomed to West Fifty-seventh Street in midtown Manhattan.

To this day, I believe she holds me responsible for abandoning her in the Newark airport.

Other than that, she liked America very much.

Haregewoin Teferra stood on a dais above a luncheon audience in a ballroom in Rockefeller Center and read into a microphone (in a low voice, afraid to look up, her legs trembling) a formal statement in English about her work. She stepped off the dais when the lights dimmed. A movie screen descended from the ceiling and a short video of Haregewoin's life amongst the AIDS orphans was shown. Viewers put down their heavy silver knives and forks and wiped tears from their eyes with thick napkins.

After the luncheon, Haregewoin hurried ahead into the polished hallway outside the ballroom and spread, upon a counter, the traditional Ethiopian shawls and scarves made by the HIV-positive artisans. "Show me how to wear it!" begged American women—

editors, reporters, filmmakers, and photographers—in pantsuits, in blazers. Haregewoin stood on tiptoe to fluff and arrange *shama*s over their heads and shoulders. They posed for pictures beside her. It was just before Christmas. The items sold briskly.

Everywhere she turned, she was treated with kindness, with deference.

A woman like herself! A widow, a person consorting with AIDS sufferers and AIDS orphans—it was further confirmation that there were people in the outside world who knew and felt compassion.

Her accommodations were luxurious. The Manhattan hotel room was silver-hued, with textured gray-and-silver wallpaper and dove-gray carpeting; black marble counters gleamed in the bathroom. Sleek gray pillows adorned the king-size bed, and she could have soundlessly touched the remote control device again and again all night long without visiting all the channels. And every morning, when she stepped outside, a car waited for her at the curb, and a white-gloved doorman descended the carpeted cement stairs at her elbow, ready to spring forward if she should stumble.

From New York, she flew to Seattle, Washington, D.C., and Atlanta. She visited the families of children who once lived with her. She slept on guest beds and foldout sofas; in the nights, she received cold-toed invasions by children climbing into bed with her as they'd done long ago in her little house in Addis. In Seattle, beautiful Frehiwot tiptoed to Haregewoin in the night, stood by her bed, bowed, and held out thirty dollars. "Here, *Emama*, I've been saving it for you, to help you."

In Atlanta, Haregewoin watched carefully when my eight-year-old, Helen, flew into the room, jumped onto the sofa, and leapt into my arms. Helen, interrupting our conversation, laughingly shared an anecdote about her school day, leaned back happily, kicked her shoes into the middle of the room, and crunched into an apple. When she flew out again, she barely touched ground, springing from sofa to chair to coffee table, and then hit the floor running. Haregewoin shook her finger at me. "You have ruined her. She is no longer Ethiopian."

Ruined Helen? Top of her class, gifted student, soccer star, winner of footraces, budding pianist, beautiful, funny, working on four languages at once (adding Spanish and Hebrew to the Amharic and English she'd arrived with). Ruined her? I didn't reply, but it hurt my feelings for days, until a friend said, "Melissa, it's true. She's an American girl now." (To my credit, Haregewoin pronounced my then twelve-year-old daughter, Lily, to be *very* polite and gracious. *Just* like a well-mannered Ethiopian child!)

Haregewoin was gratified to see, across the country, the happiness and love her onetime foster children had found with their American parents. She was welcomed by circles of adoptive families of her own children and of Ethiopian orphans she hadn't known. They told charming stories of the children's adjustment to America. While a few had arrived with developmental or psychological challenges based on early loss of parents and disrupted childhoods, the majority had started life in families, breast-fed, loved. They had grown up with grandparents and siblings, they had cared for animals, they had had chores, many had had some schooling, and some had had excellent schooling. ("American school is so much easier than Ethiopian school!" Helen marveled.) Though a round, straw-roofed dwelling in rural Ethiopia might seem an impossibly vast distance from a Chicago condo or a Seattle split-level, it was not. Children who had once known family life were eager to enjoy it again. Abeltayit and Mekdelawit, the little sisters whose eight older siblings had brought them to Layla House, had been adopted by Bob and Chris Little of Port Townsend, Washington. Chris, a petite, blond woman with a Peter Pan haircut, lingered at the door of the girls' bedroom one night and heard Mekdelawit, now called Marta, praying:

"Thank you, God, for my mom. She's a good, good mom. She knows how to be a good mom. Even when I mad, she love me. Even when I sad, she love me. Even when I do bad thing, she love me. My mom, she so cute. My mom, she not ugly. But she ugly, I still love her. Even if she ugly, I love her. Even if she *really, really* ugly, I love her. And she love me, if she ugly. But she not, she cute. Thank you, thank you, God, for good and cute mom."

Some of the children came from the Ethiopian countryside and arrived with tribal markings. Asrat Hehn, age nine, had killed a lion with a flaming torch in defense of his family compound. He proudly wore a ritual scar across one eyebrow, bestowed by his village of Wolayta, which declared him to be a man. Six months after his arrival at Layla House, he was a fifth-grader at Cedar Way Elementary on Puget Sound, Washington. Asrat's brother Amanuel would pluck a leaf from a tree when it rained and shape a handy little drinking cup out of it.

Samuel, a seven-year-old whose parents had died of malaria, missed sleeping on his shelflike bed high under the roof of the family's round hut and listening to the rain scatter when it hit the corrugated metal. Shortly after he was adopted, also by the Little family, he sweetly asked his mother one night if she would like him to butcher a cow for dinner. She thought not.

Ababaw, age seven, missed the *doro wat*—the chicken stew—of his homeland. His American mother, Anna, brought home shrink-wrapped chicken parts from the grocery.

"No, real chicken, you need," he protested.

"This *is* real chicken," she said, but he vigorously shook his head. "Okay, what is 'real chicken'?"

"Ethiopia chicken, the kind you cut head off. Noisy one. Running around. Head off, but running. *That* real chicken."

A little boy named Miseker had been one of Haregewoin's children. He flew to Maryland with his new parents at age seven. "We arrived home on Christmas Eve," said his mother, Cathy Wingate. "That first day, he spent a lot of time going from room to room in the new house, taking it all in. He noticed the manger scene arranged on a table. We thought it was so sweet when he picked up Baby Jesus and kissed him. But the tender moment was short-lived. Next his eyes lit up, he drew in an excited breath as he reached for the small sheep, said, 'Yumm!' and drew a finger like a blade across his own throat."

The Littles' newly adopted son asked at dinner one night, "Why you always talk about 'pass the Milk Police'?"

The children gather in the baby room at night for child-led bedtime prayers. AUTHOR PHOTO

Afterward, kisses goodnight AUTHOR PHOTO

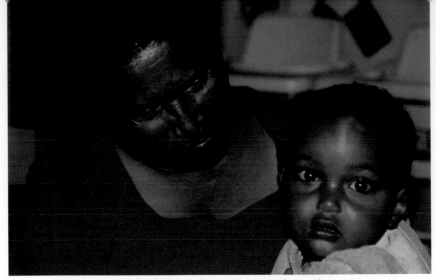

Haregewoin with Nardos AARON ROSENBLUM

Haregewoin
with Nardos
AUTHOR PHOTO

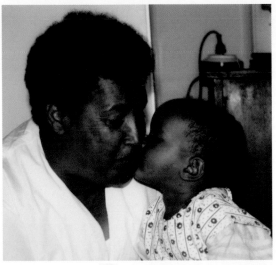

Haregewoin Teferra AARON ROSENBLUM

Haregewoin's boys and girls teams assemble in their hand-decorated uniforms before their first game in WWO's orphanage soccer league, spring 2006. LEE SAMUEL

Children at Haregewoin's front gate in the new compound
AUTHOR PHOTO

In school uniforms, November 2005 AUTHOR PHOTO

Henok (right), ever on the lookout for a new mother, with a friend AUTHOR PHOTO

Dr. Rick Hodes and family in holiday dress COURTESY OF RICK HODES

Ababu, son of Dave Armistead and Susan Bennett-Armistead, in Williamstown, Michigan, in 2006
COURTESY OF BENNETT-ARMISTEAD FAMILY

Amelezewd, the girl who loved history books, died at AHOPE of complications from HIV/AIDS. She holds a picture of herself with her younger brother Tilahun.
PER-ANDERS PETTERSSON/GETTY IMAGES

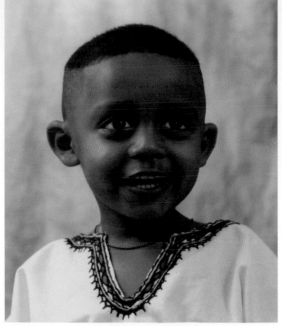

William Mintesinot
Eskender Cheney
of Phoenix, Arizona
COURTESY OF CHENEY FAMILY

Meskerem with her new
parents, Rob Cohen
and Claudia Cooper of
Middlebury, Vermont,
at Haregewoin's before
flying to America in
August 2004
AUTHOR PHOTO

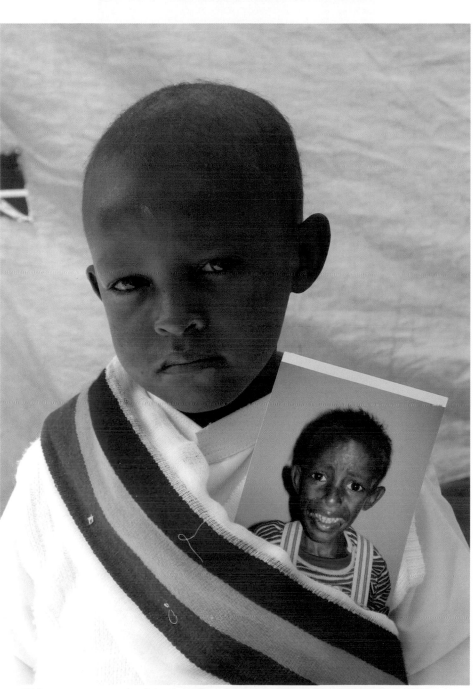

Yohannes was near death in the fall of 2005; he holds in his hands a photo of himself from September of that year. Here, Yohannes celebrates Ethiopian New Year's Day in January 2006. Thanks to WWO's Barlow Clinic, Yohannes has been one of the few HIV-positive African children to enjoy "the Lazarus effect" of anti-AIDS drugs.
DR. RICK HODES

Mikki and Ryan Hollinger meet Mekdes and Yabsira's grandfather and aunt Fasika. COURTESY OF RYAN HOLLINGER

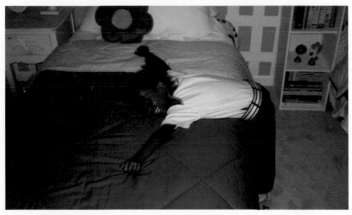

Mekdes discovers her new bedroom in America. RYAN HOLLINGER

The Hollinger family, Snellville, Georgia © ERIKA LARSEN/REDUX

Within days of the arrival of our ten-year-old son, Fisseha, from Ethiopia in May 2004, our kids discovered he could aim and throw a spear *through* a flying plastic Frisbee. "Mom!" screamed the other kids. "You've got to see this!" Fisseha had found a thin, white, metal bicycle flagpole on the driveway and was piercing the flying Frisbee with it. If Lee, fifteen, threw the Frisbee near a tree, Fisseha could spear the disk with the bike flagpole and nail it to the tree. That night at dinner, our non-English-speaking child shook his head to decline the nice cheese lasagna I offered.

"Hmmm, no," observed our oldest son, Seth, then nineteen. "I definitely have the impression he prefers to spear live game."

Later Fisseha would carve his own spears and hurl them, and he would peel bark from the trees and weave it into twine with which he wove slings and bullwhips. He had been a goatherd on the central plains of Ethiopia his whole life before landing in the American orphanage in Addis. One day he came into our kitchen, took a huge knife from a drawer, and hiked into the woods with nine-year-old Jesse. They emerged with two slim, fresh fishing poles over their shoulders. "String, Mom?" barked Fisseha in his loud voice. He accepted thread from my sewing box. He bent two straight-pins into hooks. Then he led Jesse across the street and up the steep sidewalk in search of a good stream. Both boys carried their fishing poles over their shoulders. I watched from the kitchen window and thought, *We've adopted Huckleberry Finn.*

Marta Little, who thanked God for her cute mother, made up a song. She sang it in a sweet, high voice and her mother, Chris, wrote it down:

> My one mommy die, my one mommy die.
> My one daddy die, my one daddy die.
> I sad, I sad.
> Now Mama no die, now Mama no die
> Now Daddy no die, now Daddy no die
> I happy, so happy.

I clothes to wear, I fooding
I good house, thank you Lord.
Ticklish, my daddy,
Good food, my mommy,
Thank you Lord.

Frew, age eight, was adopted to Alaska. The sunny, barefoot little boy of Addis Ababa now appeared in photos in a hooded parka, mittens, and snow boots, grinning broadly between two redheaded sisters. "I heard him praying in English the other night," his mother said. "He said, 'Thank you, family me.'"

Our daughter Helen, who arrived at five in February 2002, made lots of friends quickly in America. But I always heard her ask a child, soon after making her acquaintance or near the start of a play date, "Do you have a mother?" If she was feeling shy, she would whisper to me, "Does she have a mother?" Most children and adults were surprised by the question—"Of course I have a mother!" the children replied. "Of course she has a mother!" said the grown-ups.

Only our African friends were not surprised by the question. Helen had a mother again now, too, as she was eager to tell, but she didn't take it as a given about anyone.

45

AFTER TWO WEEKS in America, Haregewoin was homesick. She worried about the children back home. She deeply missed Nardos and wished she had brought her. (Now *there* was a well-reared Ethiopian child!) She cut her world travels short and flew home to Addis, wearing an I LOVE NEW YORK T-shirt under her robes.

She returned home to two nice new compounds; she returned home to money in the bank.

She rented a third house.

This one stood on the Gojam Road, in the foothills of the mountains. It was three stories tall and immaculate, the bedrooms handsomely paneled in wood, with built-in drawers, the spacious bathrooms tiled. A tiny, bright green yard included potted flowers, a white-pebbled walkway, an outdoor patio, and a television satellite dish. The imposing house rose above its dusty truck-stop and tire-repair-station neighborhood. Herds of goats and cattle rumbled past on the shoulder of the road, and long-distance truckers downshifted all through the night.

It sat empty and still and immaculate all day and all night, and she liked it very much.

"It will be a guesthouse!" she told her friends. As a guesthouse—a bed-and-breakfast—she imagined that it would earn income for the two foster homes. In each room, she arranged a brand-new bassinet. She hoped that families who came to Addis to adopt children from her would stay at the guesthouse and she would stay here with them. She hated the grief and fear of children pulled from her arms by their new families. The guesthouse would make the transitions easier; the children would feel less frightened and the new parents less shaky if she hovered nearby for the first few days. Spanish adoptive parents took advantage of the opportunity immediately.

A new sort of life began.

Haregewoin's days were taken up by foreign visitors, local bureaucrats, adoptive parents, and potential donors. She had less time for individual cries and mutinies; she most often lifted children *out* of her lap now, rather than into it. She was always on the phone, always rushing out. She sometimes entertained potential givers and old friends with a luncheon and coffee ceremony at the guesthouse.

There were eighty children at two houses now: fifty HIV-negative children, babies through young teenagers, and thirty HIV-positive children, most of them small, though there was one twelve-year-old boy. She had a dozen caregivers. She bought a used fifteen-seater van and employed a full-time driver. She hired an accountant to keep track of expenditures coming out of charitable distributions.

She had never been this rich. Not ever. Not even with Worku.

And she'd never been this worried about money.

When she'd had next to nothing, she'd shared it all. She and the children had scraped together whatever fell into their hands, sometimes grain, sometimes collards, sometimes birr. She shared with neighbors, too, when she had food or money, especially with the HIV-positive women and mothers. They feasted or starved together.

It felt different now. There had been this tremendous American windfall. Money had been "gifted" to her. People had called her a "humanitarian." Who knew if she would ever see the likes of this money again?

So she instituted a strict budget. She gave the caregivers and cooks a few birr each week with which to feed and clothe the children. If she didn't carefully count out individual birr for food, the hordes of hungry children would gnaw their way through the entire bank account in a few months.

She had big plans for the money. She wanted to create and open a free neighborhood clinic for HIV-positive people and orphans, where they would not be shunned and insulted.

She wanted to stretch this big money across many years and serve many more children with it.

She saw herself as hosting a sort of intersection, where children from the slums crossed paths with wealthy foreigners with the power to affect their lives. She saw herself as a point of international contact, an ambassador for the Ethiopian street to the European and North American benefactors.

Meanwhile the children she already had wore ragged uniforms and ate rice or pasta at every meal.

The older children were growing restless and bored within the compound. The younger children despaired of getting close enough to Haregewoin to feel mothered; either she was busy and rushing out, or she was tickling and laughing with Nardos. All were tired of eating rice and pasta, they were tired of doing chores, and their ragged uniforms made them look like beggars.

"I don't want to take care of the babies all the time," protested Tamrat.

"Do it," Haregewoin said coldly.

The children had lost the warmth of Haregewoin's undivided attention and affection; she seemed focused on her future plans, her money, her visitors; so they, too, looked beyond the gates. They longed for the day of departure. The older ones prayed to be transferred to an adoption-agency orphanage and to begin the almost unbearably suspenseful wait to be chosen by a distant family in America.

Only Nardos had unlimited access to Haregewoin; only for Nardos did Haregewoin drop everything else. When Nardie stood up and bellowed, *"Amaye?"* Haregewoin called out, *"Abet?"* (Yes?), and Nardie ran to find her.

Whenever she saw Nardos, a smile rose on Haregewoin's face like the moon in the night sky.

At seventeen months, Nardie bowed her head, put her hands together prayerfully, and lisped through a blessing before eating. She picked up Haregewoin's phone and shouted a mix of words and gibberish into it, self-importantly, with her hand on her hip. With only a few baby teeth, she bossed the other children and pointed her finger. She took Haregewoin's shawl and wrapped herself in it. Her short, fat feet were buckled into red leather sandals. She batted the eyelashes of her cinnamon eyes. Her hair popped up in brown tufts.

For Nardie's second birthday, Haregewoin made a party in her living room. Her old friends came, bearing gifts; and Nardie, in a fluffy, lime green dress, danced for them as Haregewoin sang and clapped her hands.

The Ethiopian representative of a Spanish adoption agency visited one afternoon, sipped coffee, opened his briefcase.

It was a sunny school day and only young children and babies were at home. Preschool-age girls sat on the bright cement steps of the main house, hands in their laps, chatting in voices like the peeping of sparrows. Unpredictably, the face of one crumpled, then tears fell; her feelings had been hurt; but orphanage children have learned not only to injure, but to console one another; so her friend scooted over and hugged the sad one around the head and gave her a kiss on the ear, where the hurting words had gone in.

Nardos, the favorite child, hiked up her skirts like a field woman and stomped up the steps to her mother's sitting area.

"*Amaye?*"

"*Abet?*"

Nardos had something to report, a babble of baby syllables about the bickering outside on the steps.

"Come, my love," said Haregewoin, opening her arms.

"Have you thought about finding a real home for this one?" asked the agency rep, as tactfully as possible. He didn't make specific reference to their age difference; but Haregewoin had to be sixty or close to it, while Nardos was two.

Haregewoin shifted Nardos in her lap, picked up her cup of coffee again, and hid behind it, letting the steam rise between her and the man.

I know people think like this, she thought, *but I don't know why they do. I don't appreciate it. We needn't send every single Ethiopian child out of the country. Nardos is happy here with me. Look at her pretty clothes, look at her bright face, see how smart she is. Could anyone be a better mother to Nardos than I am? Let this man send his own child out of the country.*

When she put the cup down, she shooed Nardos back outside to play, and her face was colder.

"Follow me," she said, and stood and led the agency man into the nursery, where half a dozen babies lay in cribs and bassinets, some asleep, some stirring the air with their feet and hands, looking for contact.

But the words of the man representing the Spanish adoption agency followed her and oppressed her.

Every time she remembered them, she got a cramp in her stomach. It felt like homesickness. It felt like Menah. It felt like Atetegeb.

This can't be happening again.

That afternoon, when Haregewoin's old friends dropped by for the coffee ceremony, Nardos pranced about for them as always, knowing she was adored. She wore a ruffled white blouse, orange corduroy overalls, and tiny rubber-toed red sneakers. She didn't have enough hair yet to gather into small braids—her brown hair was like the fluff of a dandelion—so Haregewoin had snapped a frilly, elastic headband around her head. The ladies laughed with surprised delight (they always laughed with surprised delight) when Nardos picked up the phone and shouted baby talk into it, with a tone of impatience. She was a mini-Haregewoin. "She's so smart!" everyone said. "She's just like you!" they said, laughing.

They flatter me, Haregewoin began to think. *They have learned that the shortcut to pleasing me is to praise Nardos. They wonder if I am going to hold on to her forever, even as I release all the other children to fly to new families abroad.*

It hurt her feelings very much to imagine that her old friends criticized her, behind her back, for mothering Nardos.

It seemed they'd grown comfortable with the idea of Haregewoin as a foster mother: one who aided, then shipped off, a few of Ethiopia's orphaned children.

It seemed they found unthinkable, or distasteful, the idea that she would keep one for herself.

Not so long ago, she thought bitterly, *they were indifferent to all the children! They wanted nothing to do with the AIDS orphans. Now they help me, they give money, they are kind; but they also suddenly form opinions about what is the best thing for a child.*

She wished she hadn't let them see how much she loved Nardos. It felt as if her old friends—and even the adoption-agency staff people—begrudged her this one small happiness. She wished they didn't know. She wished no one could identify *her* child out of the dusty rabble of children in the yard. So she began to keep Nardie at bay when visitors called.

Now when Nardie stormed up the steps, shouting, *"Amaye!"* instead of lovingly calling, *"Abet?"* Haregewoin rather coldly set her aside and said, "Not now, Nardos."

Her joy came at night when they were alone together. She was the one to change Nardos into a little sleeping gown; she tickled and hugged her while changing her; it was their special time, on Haregewoin's bed. She read to Nardos and showed her the letters of the *fidel,* the alphabet. Nardos loved to place her hand on Haregewoin's wide chest and to lean her face close and inhale; she loved the traces of Haregewoin's perfume she found there, and she left a whispery kiss in exchange. If Nardos waited in Haregewoin's bed, and Haregewoin continued to sit up by lamplight in the small room she used as an office, going over files and accounts, Nardos went in search of her.

"Nay (come), *Maye,"* she said. "Let us lie down and say, 'Ah ah ah'" (sleeping noises).

So, late at night, when the day's paperwork was finally

finished and the compound was asleep, Haregewoin pocketed her reading glasses, rubbed her eyes, and dragged herself up the cement steps to her bedroom. She tucked herself into bed beside her toddler.

46

S HE AND NARDOS were awakened in the night by hoarse boyish screams. A child was hurt. He yelled, "Oh, oh, oh, ow, stop, help me, somebody, help me!"

"Oh my God," cried Haregewoin. She jumped from bed, stumbled down the steps, across the courtyard, and up the steps into the boys' house. In the main room, bunk beds stood side by side, each with a striped wool blanket.

Wasihun (*wahs*-i-hoon), thirteen, was sitting up on his lower bunk. His face red and drenched with tears, he screamed, "He came into my bed! He came into my bed! He slept with me like a woman!"

He was accusing Sirak (seer-ak), pointing a trembling finger at Sirak. Sirak, twenty-four, came from the foster home's old neighborhood; he worked for Haregewoin in exchange for food and a place to sleep. He stood between the beds wearing a T-shirt and gray sweatpants.

"He held my face, I couldn't breathe!" Wasihun's jaw was swelling.

Haregewoin hurried to his side and tried to put her arms around him, but Wasihun yanked away from her, shoved at her, and screamed, "He hurt me!"

Every boy in the room sat up; all stared, and the younger ones started to cry in fear. In the baby room, back in the main house, wails went up from every crib. Lights went on in the older girls' bedroom, between the nursery and Haregewoin's bedroom. Confused, distracted, Haregewoin ran back across the compound to the babies and ran back into the boys' house with screaming infants in both arms. Sirak stood frozen, his mouth open to protest, his hands wide-open at his sides to demonstrate innocence, but he said nothing.

Other boys scooted over to sit beside Wasihun, who covered his face with his arms and sobbed loudly. Everyone looked at Haregewoin.

A bunch of older girls—barefoot, wild-haired, in their night-gowns—peeked in from the door. A caregiver, Miniya, who slept on a cot in the older girls' bedroom, stood in the courtyard behind them.

At least that was one thing Haregewoin could solve. "All of you! Back to bed! This instant!" she yelled, and they fled.

"You, too," she said sternly to her colleague Miniya, and the woman nodded her head and withdrew.

"Wait!" Haregewoin snapped again. "Take these." She transferred the unhappy infants to the woman. They could hear other babies wailing from the nursery.

"*Ishi, ishi, ishi,* calm down, calm down," she said. "Boys, get back to your beds. It's okay, it's okay, everyone go back to sleep now. I'm here. It was just a bad dream. Everyone go back to sleep now."

"What about *him!*?" screamed Wasihun, raising his swollen, wet face from his arms. "It was not a bad dream! He hurt me!"

"Sirak will sleep outside the house tonight. Let us all go back to sleep. We'll talk in the morning. We'll feel better in the morning. Everyone lie down now. It's over." The small boys lay down. Sirak turned and strode out the door. Haregewoin turned off the light and crossed back to the main house. In the nursery, all the babies were awake, confused and wet and squawking, the older ones standing up in their cribs and rattling the bars. Miniya was among them, trying to lay them down again. "I'll do it," said Haregewoin. "Just bring me some bottles."

"What happened there?" asked Miniya.

"Just a bad dream," said Haregewoin.

It took her a couple of hours to change the babies, feed the babies, and soothe the babies back to sleep. She dozed off erect, in a straight-back chair, with a baby sprawled across her lap.

Then it was dawn.

✳   ✳   ✳

In the morning, she found herself afraid to cross the compound and peek into the boys' bedroom again, afraid Wasihun would still be awake, waiting to glare at her again with hurt, red eyes.

So she stood below the steps of the boys' dorm and called to the children to get ready for school. Wasihun did not emerge from the little house.

With the older children gone, she summoned the adults of the compound to the sitting area in her bedroom. Everyone had heard the commotion in the night, everyone was aware of the accusation. Sirak stepped into her bedroom and stood against the wall, behind the others, as if he, too, were there to hear the day's announcements.

"You," she commanded Sirak.

A year earlier, Sirak's mother, dying of AIDS, sent for Haregewoin, whom she knew slightly from the neighborhood. The former market-woman had been stiff with imminent death. She moved her lips in a face and body in which everything else was still. The eyes stared straight up at the roof of the hut. Haregewoin leaned close to hear.

"Please watch over my son," said the gray lips. "He will be alone now. Please. You will take him. He is a good boy. Please. You will take him."

Haregewoin had picked up the woman's cold hands. "Yes, yes, of course, my dear, I will take him."

She had enjoyed having Sirak. He was a friendly, humble young fellow, with bushy brown hair and the start of a mustache. He had reached only the third grade in school, but he was a hard worker, eager to please. He didn't smoke or chew *chat* (a mild hallucinogen) or drink alcohol. At all hours of the night she heard him clanking around outside with the laundry tubs. He was happy here. He liked the children. At the old compound, he had slept in a bedroll outside. Here, they had more room, so she invited him to take a bunk bed in the boys' room. The boys seemed to like him. She would never have put a man in the girls' bedroom, but it had never crossed her mind that she had put the boys in danger. She had never imagined such an event, she'd barely heard of it, didn't know the vocabulary for it.

"What happened last night?" she asked him.

"Nothing, *Waizero* Haregewoin," he stammered. He wrung his hands. That was all he had to say.

"No, it wasn't nothing. Tell me what happened."

"It wasn't the first time Wasihun did this! He told me, he did it before; where he stayed before, he did it, too."

She was angry. She stood up. "I am not asking you about what Wasihun did. I am asking about what you did."

He twisted his hands, his eyes veered wildly around the room; he tried looking into a few faces, to see if encouragement was to be found among his coworkers; no one would meet his hungry gaze.

"Sirak, you must tell me the truth."

He stood before her with a helpless look on his face, his mouth open.

"If you don't tell me the truth, I will have to call the police."

Still nothing. She sat, then she reached for the phone.

At that moment, he became unhinged. He dropped to his knees, raised his arms to the heavens, and blubbered. Some heard him say, "I did it! I did it!" Others would recall instead his denials and his cry of "Why do you shame me this way?"

He staggered to his feet, tears exploding from his eyes, and fell to his knees again. He prostrated himself before her, stood up, waved his loose arms about, and fell facedown again.

Everyone was shocked, they backed away. He was like a man suffering a seizure. Suddenly Sirak stood up, his hair wilder than usual; he whirled around, lost his bearings, saw the door, and ran out of it. He jumped off the steps, raced across the courtyard, opened the big door, and ran out.

Haregewoin let out a huge sigh of relief. A few people exhaled loudly. "He'll never come back," Haregewoin announced. "If he does, no one let him in. But he won't be back."

"Will you call the police?" asked Miniya, the middle-aged woman who slept in the dorm room with the older girls. She had worked with Haregewoin for four years and had known her years earlier, in Haregewoin's married life. Miniya had long, coarse straight hair, which she wore parted in the middle and pulled back into a bun. She wore a man's wool sports jacket, but had an ample womanly figure under it. She walked about with her hands in the jacket pockets, wore reading glasses on a necklace, and was the least intimidated—of the female staff—by Haregewoin, the only one to feel equal to her.

"Why?" cried Haregewoin. "He's gone! He's gone and that's the main thing."

"But the police should be notified."

Now Haregewoin felt angry. "He's gone and that's the end of it. Why carry these tales into the streets? I'll ask you all not to speak of it outside this room. Who knows if anything really happened?"

"Regardless, Haregewoin," said Miniya, "I believe you must tell the authorities. Let them investigate and discover the truth."

"You want to see me lose my license? The houses closed? The children taken away?" Haregewoin glared at her staff. They shook their heads. They lowered their eyes. Miniya looked her straight in her face.

"All right," Haregewoin snapped. "Then that's the end of it. Finished. End of story. We have more important things to think about than this man. Let us never speak of this again. Go to work."

Miniya put her hands in her pockets and went out with her head bowed in thought.

She understood that Haregewoin wished to pretend nothing had happened. And perhaps she would feel the same way if it were *her* organization at risk of public shame and censure, if it were *her* name around which scandal would stir. Nevertheless, it was clear to her (from the safety of anonymity, the safety of not being chief) that Haregewoin needed to take responsibility for what had happened and report it.

✡   ✡   ✡

Haregewoin had never heard of this.

In a nation in which homosexuality is criminalized and punished with imprisonment, gay life is hidden. The majority of Ethiopians believe as Haregewoin did: *There are no homosexuals in Ethiopia. That is a problem in the West. It is a disease of white people. It does not exist here.*

In reality, what Haregewoin faced within her compound was less the revelation of Ethiopian homosexuality than the crime of child sexual abuse.

If Sirak had raped girls in the compound, she would have been outraged, she would have called the police and had him arrested. But it would have been a normal thing, a typical crime, an unfortunate episode.

But Sirak's crime seemed to be a crime against nature, a crime so monstrous as to be unspeakable. Her house's reputation would be ruined forever if people learned that a homosexual act had occurred here. She believed Sirak would be executed by the state if his crime was revealed. She believed she would be publicly shamed and all her children taken away.

When the staff exited Haregewoin's bedroom that morning, she began to shake all over. She wanted to call someone to come help her, but there was no one to ask. She jiggled so hard she made herself nauseous, as if from motion sickness.

She made her way into the boys' room and, as she feared, found Wasihun's bed occupied.

"No school for you today, Wasihun?" she asked cheerily.

He had the covers pulled up completely over his head. He lay on his side, facing the wall, and did not answer.

"Well, that's all right," she cooed. "A day off for you today is just the right thing. You'll catch up tomorrow."

In the absence of a reply, she realized she was using too jolly a tone.

"Wasihun, my dear," she tried again, more softly. She put her hand on his shoulder. He angrily shook it off.

"Are you hungry?"

He did not reply.

"I'll have cook bring you some rice?"

He didn't answer.

"How . . . well, how do you *feel*?"

In low tones, from under the blanket, he said, "Bad."

"Did Sirak actually touch you?"

"I told you!" came the muffled voice. "I told you what he did."

"Have you washed yourself?"

"No."

"Let me give you some soap and a towel. Go wash up."

So he did.

But he got right back into bed afterward and wouldn't get up. When the kids came in from school and gathered around Wasihun's bed, he wouldn't play or visit. He kept the blankets pulled over his bed. He got up once to use the bathroom in the late afternoon; Haregewoin beamed at him, from a chair on the porch, but he scowled at her.

What does he want from me?

"He wants to see a doctor. He wants you to take him to a doctor," said Miniya.

"He'll feel better in a couple of days," said Haregewoin.

One-sidedly, she adopted a tone with Wasihun as if he'd played hooky from school and she was his indulgent mother. "Oh, here again this morning, Wasihun?" she chirped the next day. "I bet I can find some chores around here that will make a boy wish he were in school."

"If you were my mother, you would take me to the doctor," he said lowly from under the blanket.

She tidied up the room, pretending not to hear him.

He lay still again, his face turned to the wall.

The story got worse.

Two other young teenage boys approached Miniya.

"He did us the same way," said one.

"Sirak?" she whispered.

"Yes," said the fourteen-year-old. "He sleeps with us, like a man with his wife."

"He told us never to tell, or he will hurt us," said the twelve-year-old.

"Haregewoin, there are two more," murmured Miniya in the twilight on the porch one evening.

Oh God, oh God, oh God, how will this end?

"I couldn't have known," hissed Haregewoin. "There is no way I could have known about this. I never heard of this thing."

"Of course you couldn't have known," Miniya said kindly. "I, too, never knew of it."

But Miniya pushed on, "The question is what to do *now?*"

"Now? But there is nothing to do now. The man is gone. He'll never show his face around here again. The boys are safe."

Miniya said nothing more; she pressed her lips closed. She pressed them closed in such a way as to relay to Haregewoin, *You know there is something more. You must report what happened to the police. You must take all three boys to the doctor.*

Haregewoin saw Miniya's tense, unspeaking lips, but she chose not to understand. She stood up and clapped her hands at the kids playing dodgeball on the cement driveway. "Bedtime! Get ready for prayers!"

She knew Miniya watched her, waiting for a signal that she understood what was required. But she gave no signal. Nothing more was required. *It risks everything,* she thought. *We'll lose everything. We'll lose all the children if this news is revealed. I will lose my license and my good name. The children will be taken away. Sirak will be imprisoned. Why generate such chaos and grief?*

On another day, she told herself, *I am the boss here precisely* because *I think about these matters with a long view. She wants me to run about like a headless chicken, run here, run there. But for what? The man is gone. The boys are safe. These are the important things. We need not overturn, for this one episode, everything I have built.*

Miniya was boycotting her. Haregewoin couldn't bear it. They used to stand with their arms crossed and chat and chuckle all day long, as they watched the children.

So Haregewoin blurted out one afternoon, apropos of nothing,

"Don't you think the police will take the children away if I run to them with this tale, which in any case I don't know to be true?" She had a pleading tone in her voice; she tried to find the soft spot again with Miniya, in which Miniya was not an adversary.

"So don't go to the police, go to the doctor," said Miniya. "The boys are asking me every day, 'Why does she not take us to the doctor?' The boys are afraid"—she lowered her voice—"that he has infected them with HIV."

"This is ridiculous!" scolded Haregewoin. "Don't speak of it to me anymore. I'm sick of the whole thing. It's disgusting and horrible and not right for children to think about. It's enough, you hear me? You encourage them and you must stop. Why do they come to you, anyway, and not to me?"

"They say, 'Haregewoin does not help us.'"

"You stir them up. You baby them. Look, the two new ones you tell me about are still going to school, they do not lie about like Wasihun."

"Dereje (*deh*-re-jeh) stayed home today." He was the twelve-year-old.

"He copies Wasihun," cried Haregewoin in aggravation. "It is because we have spoiled Wasihun. You must say to them, 'Be strong. It's over now. Let the past be in the past.' I don't want to hear about it anymore." She hurried up the steps to her bedroom and closed the door. She sat on her bed and shook again.

The oldest boy, the fourteen-year-old, betrayed nothing. He went to school, made good grades, came home, and helped about the house. She liked this cheerful boy very much. "Zelalem," she said one day. "Tell me. Did anyone ever hurt you?"

"No, *Waizero* Haregewoin!" he exclaimed, widening his eyes to emphasize innocence.

"Did Sirak bother you?"

"No, madam."

"He didn't do this bad thing to you?"

"No, *waizero*."

"Do you think . . . do you think it is true, what Wasihun says?"

"Wasihun is a fool."

"Is there anything I can do for you? Is there anything you need from me?"

"No, *waizero*, I am fine."

But Wasihun and Dereje continued to carry on. When they got out of bed, they limped dramatically. They pestered Miniya, "Why she does not take us to the clinic?"

One day, as Haregewoin hurried past with her arms full of laundry, she felt herself watched; Wasihun was lounging bare-chested on the front steps of the boys' dorm.

"You are not my mother," he said lowly.

She heard, but continued on the path between the houses to the laundry lines.

After a few days of this, seeing it resulted only in long, boring days, Dereje got out of bed and went back to school.

Three weeks after the event, Wasihun sullenly got out of bed, threw water onto his face, put on his school sweater, patted his hair into shape, and returned to school, too. But both boys held a grudge against her. Whenever she walked by the two of them, they looked at each other instead of at her. Now it was her turn to widen her eyes when she asked herself, *Me? What did I do wrong?*

47

ACCUSATIONS AGAINST HER multiplied.

She wasn't popular anymore.

As Haregewoin breathed the fine air of higher spheres—greeting visitors from foreign embassies and from global NGOs, whose broad-tired SUVs purred outside her gates—a few old acquaintances suddenly noticed elements of self-promotion in her nature. The good she had tried to do was reconceived as, "She did it for herself." When she stumbled, these people and other onlookers materialized to watch or to accelerate her fall.

First, women in the neighborhood—HIV-positive artisans, with whom Haregewoin shared food, whose work she had offered for sale from her house and from her suitcase—turned against her. They perceived that she'd returned from America a wealthy woman. The owner (they thought) of three houses (they were rentals), and of a van (used), she must be sitting on piles of money.

"She sold our scarves and shawls and did not bring us all the money for them," they told each other. "She is profiting from our work."

"The house on Gojam Road?" said one who had seen it. "A rich woman's house."

Several went to the *kebele* to make reports against Haregewoin: "Many people in America bought our fabrics and gave orders for more, but she did not give us the entire money."

Some, trying to fathom her affluence and importance, wondered if she was selling the children abandoned at her gates. Because it was hard to imagine she'd grown this rich from *scarves*.

Without evidence, suspicions and feelings of betrayal circled unhappily, unable to land. Something must be going on behind the polished steel door with brass trim, behind the handsome stonework of the compound walls. When Haregewoin rode out into the neighborhood, high in the first row of her van, which was driven by an employee, she no longer inspired affection among the poor women of her district. *"She's hiding something,"* they thought.

Then, the confused circumstances of an unwed teenage mother, a girl of the streets I will call Beza, and her baby, generated official interest in Haregewoin and it did not end well. The complicated story took on evil overtones in the minds of those who had begun to disbelieve and distrust Haregewoin Teferra.

Beza was seventeen and homeless when she gave birth to Tarikwa (ta-*reek*-wa). Beza was helped by a local organization dedicated to rehabilitating street youth, and this organization—let us call it Forward Ethiopia—took custody of the baby. But Forward Ethiopia had no facilities for orphan care, so it placed four-week-old Tarikwa at Haregewoin's house on February 4, 2005.

When the visiting Spanish adoption agency representative asked permission to find parents for baby Tarikwa, Haregewoin said, "Thanks, God."

A husband and wife in their late thirties arrived from Spain two weeks later to meet the baby. They stayed with her at the Ghion Hotel. As in all legal adoptions, they were required to appear before an office within the Ministry of Labor and Social Affairs (MOLSA) to be officially approved as the baby's parents.

Forward Ethiopia discovered what was happening and rushed to intervene. Forward Ethiopia believed in family reunification and was opposed to foreign adoption. The organization informed Haregewoin and MOLSA that (in official translation) "the infant's mother is a street girl and, since she has no material capacity to raise her, she said that she wants her daughter to be assisted by local orphanages and that she does not want her to go abroad."

A Forward Ethiopia staff woman attended the MOLSA hearing and objected to the adoption. Speaking on behalf of Tarikwa's *first* foster placement, Forward Ethiopia, she refused to sign off on the adoption.

The Spanish couple left the building in shock, their arms empty, dragging the folded stroller down the steps behind them. The Forward Ethiopia staff person departed in a taxi with Tarikwa.

Haregewoin bowed out of the picture.

But, two days after these events, the young birth-mother, Beza, knocked on Haregewoin's gate. She wore little Tarikwa in a shawl on her back.

"Please, *waizero*, please, you must take her. Look at me. I have nothing. You know how I live. Why have you returned my daughter to me?"

"Forward Ethiopia gave her back to you?" Haregewoin marveled. "I thought they were keeping her."

"They brought her to me and gave me four birr [thirty-six cents] to buy food for her."

The girl was slight, her hair concealed by a tight and soiled scarf. But the baby was full of smiles and quite pretty. "She drinks too much," said Beza. "*Waizero*, please give her back to those parents."

"Well, *I* cannot," said Haregewoin. "I no longer have custody of her. But *you* can give the child."

Haregewoin phoned the Spanish couple at the Ghion Hotel, saying, "You may still find a happy ending."

Beza dictated an official letter to Haregewoin's organization. Dated February 17, 2005, it reads (in government translation):

I the applicant [Beza] . . . was under the assistance of an organization called [Forward Ethiopia] and I declare that I was formerly a street girl and while I was living in the organization I was raped and delivered a child, therefore since I am not able to raise my child it is recalled that the organization [Forward Ethiopia] has requested for another agency [Atetegeb Worku Memorial Orphans Support Association] to take in charge my child and that upon my free will the child has been given to you.

However, since they have handed me over the child for an unknown reason and that I am deprived of any income, remaining under the assistance of the organization [Forward Ethiopia], I have heard that you have given the child to foreign families in adoption. So as I do not want my child to lose that opportunity and to face my fate I request you to give the child back to the foreigners who have handed her over to me.

With regards,

Signed

[Beza] . . .

The following day, all met again at the MOLSA office; the scared teenager placed her baby back in the arms of the Spanish woman. The Spanish woman reached out to hug the girl and they held each other and cried into each other's neck.

Again, the Forward Ethiopia staff woman showed up to halt the adoption.

"The mother is underage, she is only seventeen," said the woman. "She is too young to give permission for the baby to be taken by foreigners."

Again, in shock and grief, the prospective parents melted down the courthouse steps and crawled back to their hotel. They changed their plane tickets, took a taxi to the airport, and flew home to Spain.

Beza, stunned to find her baby in her arms again, abruptly turned at that moment, in the MOLSA office, and gave her to Haregewoin to take home. This was turning into a shell game: under which shell will the pea be found? Tarikwa had, on that day, traveled from Haregewoin's arms to Beza's to the Spanish parents' to Beza's and back to Haregewoin's, all under the disapproving glare of the Forward Ethiopia staff woman.

Haregewoin took baby Tarikwa back home with her.

Two days later, Beza, the birth mother, appeared at Haregewoin's gate again. "May I speak with her alone?" she asked the guard.

In Haregewoin's bedroom sitting room, she whispered, "Look what I have." She pulled from her pocket a false identity card, showing her to be twenty years old.

"Now we can give her to her Spanish mother and father," said the teenager.

"My dear, the poor Spanish people have gone," said Haregewoin. "Tarikwa is fine here. Don't worry about her. Visit whenever you like. Let her be here."

Tarikwa thrived. She woke up in the mornings in the row of white cribs; colorful mobiles hung within high, sheer canopies of mosquito netting. She was clean and well fed. Haregewoin made no further plans to place her for adoption. Beza came occasionally, with Haregewoin's encouragement, to visit her.

Several weeks after the departure of the Spanish couple, Haregewoin received a phone call from the City Social Affairs Bureau, which governed orphan care in Addis Ababa.

Forward Ethiopia had complained to the City Social Affairs Bureau about the haste with which Haregewoin had tried to send Tarikwa out of the country.

"Return Tarikwa," the City Social Affairs Bureau told Haregewoin, "to the organization [Forward Ethiopia]."

"Do you think this is healthy for a child?" Haregewoin cried. "You put it here, you put it there. It makes problems for a child. She is well here; why can't you leave her alone?

"In any case," she said, with aggravation, "I will not give the baby to anyone. The mother placed the baby with me; only the mother can take her from me now."

Haregewoin documented every step, even this refusal to transfer the baby back to Forward Ethiopia. She filed notice with the City Social Affairs Bureau, which read (in official translation):

> Miss [Beza] . . . under the assistance of [Forward Ethiopia] has brought under document the child up to our organization and as she has requested us to take care of the child we have accepted the infant

and the child is still under the care of our organization where her mother visits her once per week.

Formerly we have handed over the child under documents and there is no legal reason to give back the child to [Forward Ethiopia]. Therefore, we hereby declare that we do not hand over the child. However, if the mother claims restitution of the child we declare kindly that we shall hand over the child before the office.

With regards,
Signed and sealed,
Haregewoin Teferra,
Director

But the shell game continued.

In May 2005, Beza visited and said, "Please, *Waizero* Haregewoin, if it is possible, I will take my child now."

"Where will you take her?"

"I have found a place to live now."

"God is good," said Haregewoin. She furnished the mother with bottles, blankets, baby clothes, money, and, finally, Tarikwa. She documented this step as well, asking Beza to sign for the baby.

On May 15, 2005, Beza, now eighteen, signed for her child, before witnesses:

I Miss Beza . . . confirm with my signature that I have taken over my daughter infant Tarikwa that I had given on 2/17/05 to Atetegeb Worku foster home, further to the application that I have filed today to give me back my daughter. Receiver's name: Miss Beza . . .

Haregewoin and four adults in her courtyard that day—including her accountant, her lawyer, her sister-in-law Negede Tehaye Alemayhu, and Miniya—signed as witnesses to the transfer of the baby back to her birth mother.

Forward Ethiopia was entitled to feel vindicated for its tenacity in keeping the baby in the country, and Haregewoin felt proud of the teenage mother for finding the wherewithal to raise her baby.

That should have been the end of that story.

But suspicions against Haregewoin lingered in the Forward Ethiopia office and in the City Social Affairs Bureau.

Several months after baby Tarikwa rode out of Haregewoin's compound for the last time, wrapped upon her mother's back, the City Social Affairs Bureau sent a letter to Haregewoin demanding to know the baby's whereabouts.

Haregewoin wrote back in formal reply that the birth mother had reclaimed her baby.

"Find her," she was told. "Prove it."

And then she could not find Beza and Tarikwa.

The City Social Affairs Bureau leapt on this as evidence of malfeasance, accusing, "You gave her to Spain after all."

"I did no such thing."

"How much money do you make in this way?" they challenged her.

Is it even possible to smuggle a baby out of the country in the way they charge? she wondered. *How would the Spanish people have gotten past security and emigration with an Ethiopian child with no legal adoption decree, no passport?*

It seemed an impossible scenario.

Haregewoin made the first of many trips to the City Social Affairs Bureau to state her case. She presented the document, signed by Beza and by herself and by four unrelated witnesses, asserting that Beza reclaimed Tarikwa from the Atetegeb Worku foster home.

"This is a forgery," a man said, flinging it back at her.

The City Social Affairs Bureau then advised numerous adoption-agency staff persons that, insofar as Haregewoin Teferra was under investigation for "child trafficking," she could no longer sign for adoptions until extensive paperwork was completed on each child, thus none of the cases of her children waiting at adoption-agency orphan-ages, even those already matched with families, could go forward. All the adoptions were placed on hold indefinitely. Waiting families were told that the "orphan status" of Haregewoin's children was suspect and that each had to be researched.

There is long, long life—there is life, and afterlife, and postafterlife—there is an eternal twilit loop of endlessly circulating rumors in the never-never-land of the Internet. If repetition is a fair substitution for fact-checking and accuracy, then Haregewoin was now guilty a hundred times over of baby selling, of child trafficking. "Have you heard?" members of adoption-list servers and chat rooms typed into their computer monitors. "I hate to spread rumors, but . . ." "OMG, there is something really wrong with that . . ." Many families who had completed every step of the complicated and time-consuming adoption paperwork and who waited only to be given a court date and a travel date were told to wait longer, with no hint of when the decree might lift. The anxiety and disappointment of indefinite waiting, and the uncertainty whether their adoptions would ever be finalized, all came under the malodorous fog of "child trafficking."

The Internet gave the accusation long life, eternal life, but the nature of rumor itself sped it along, too. The hide-and-seek narrative of Baby Tarikwa—*Baby, baby, who's got the baby?*—was not easily summarized, nor was it particularly interesting. But the whisper of "child trafficking" came with frissons of fear and outrage and mystery and was far more exciting to share.

Of course it is correct and ethical—it is absolutely necessary—for a government to behave with immaculate precision in adoption matters. It is a crime to sell children. It is unethical to separate children from birth families who want them. The City Social Affairs Bureau was well within its responsibility to research and confirm the orphan status of every child under its umbrella.

But this case—of which a few officials chose to make an example—was flimsy. It dragged on, and on, and on, without resolution. Every once in a while, a few children were allowed out, to join their waiting adoptive families abroad; but most of the children who had once lived at Haregewoin's were held back.

The words *child trafficking* chased after Haregewoin's name in the semi-immortality of cyberspace, and there the words circulate still.

Miniya barely talked to her anymore. Miniya made a point of speaking to her only in clipped sentences on specific subjects: "Is it possible to give the children any meat this week or is it only rice?"

And if Haregewoin tried to use such an overture to start up the old routines of friendliness between them, Miniya did not respond with a smile; Miniya turned away. *She sides with the boys against me. I couldn't have stopped any of this from happening. She is wrong to blame me.*

It was too late to call the police now about Sirak. Sirak had disappeared and the events of that night were nine months past. But Wasihun's hostility had hardened against her. If she reached out to stroke his head, he dramatically ducked and swerved away.

It has all gone wrong, she thought one night. *But why?*

Miniya could have told her. Miniya would have said, "Because you put yourself above the children. What was once beautiful about you was your ability to love each child. Now you don't know who they are. And there is a hurt child, Wasihun, whom you will not take to a doctor. You are putting yourself and your organization above the needs of this boy. You ask me, 'But should I lose everything for this case? Should I sacrifice everything I have built for this one boy?'

"If you have to ask me that, I am no longer interested in what you have built."

Then Miniya quit, citing issues of back pay. Haregewoin asked the accountant to pay out whatever amount Miniya felt entitled to, but nothing would alleviate Miniya's disappointment in Haregewoin.

Meanwhile, accusations surrounding Baby Tarikwa heated up. The City Social Affairs Bureau was practically pounding down her door, demanding to know what she'd done with the baby, to whom she had sold it.

Haregewoin felt shut out from the world. Her own children— eighty of them now (fifty in the large house, thirty in the small)— hugged and loved their caregivers, but no longer loved her. Some moped after Miniya's departure. The caregivers grumbled that Haregewoin gave them too little money for food and clothes for the children, and that their salaries were too small. The HIV-positive children looked awful—covered with sores, going bald, some nearly skeletal. She'd had such great luck with HIV-positive babies—many had become HIV-negative (technically, they'd seroreverted) under her care; it didn't work that way with older children, she was belatedly learning. This was no place for magical thinking.

In the first few weeks of owning the used van she had purchased with the American donations, she had felt proud of it. She sat high in the passenger seat, with fine posture, arranging her shawl about her shoulders, enjoying the cooling wind on her face and through her hair. But lately, as she rode out through her gates, she felt the neighborhood women watching her through half-lowered eyelids, thinking, *Where is our money?*

"Haregewoin does not help us," a pair of neighborhood women told me. They were HIV-positive and destitute. One was strikingly beautiful. "She is supposed to help us and she does not help us."

"I am hungry all the time," said a narrow-faced one. "And my mother is dying."

I thought, but did not say, *She is not "supposed" to help you. She is still only a volunteer. No one helps her to help you. She has raised her money privately; it is not government money. She does all she can for you, but her resources are not limitless. She cannot raise you up out of poverty.*

They knew about the fine three-story house on Gojam Road; they did not know it was supposed to be an income generator (though the income from it, with her adoptions frozen by the City Social Affairs Bureau, dropped to nothing). They suspected she lived there part of the time in a secret rich life. *Let her sell that house!* they thought in the agony of daily hunger, in the face of their children's hunger.

I asked Haregewoin again about the house on Gojam Road.

"It is rented with the help of some of the European adoption agencies," she told me. "No charitable donations for the children helps me with that rent; it is a separate account. Also I have shown it to government people—I invited them; I wanted to show them how I try to make income for the foster homes, and they said it is a good project."

I asked Haregewoin about these particular women who stood near her gates complaining about her and inviting others to join in their complaints.

"I send them *teff* several times a year," she said. "I invite them here whenever we have a holiday. At different times, I have taken in their children. Last month, that one brought me her bill from the pharmacy and I gave her the money to pay it." She then showed me the receipt.

No one helps the poor women. No one. There is no state or federal or regional office to which they can say, "I'm hungry." Millions of people in this country cannot find enough to eat and to feed to their children. I understood: Haregewoin was the only person who had *ever* opened her gates to them, who had *ever* said, "Let me see if I can help you. Let me feed your children for you for a while. Let me see if I can sell your fabrics. Spend Christmas here with us."

But they were still poor, still sick, and still hungry. So it must be Haregewoin's fault.

They do not stand at the end of the long winding driveways of the rich people—Ethiopian and foreign—because there would be no point. The rich people's guards would disperse them. They stand here and wail against Haregewoin because she hears them.

These same ladies like me very much because I help them whenever I visit. "You are my mother!" each cries to me, kissing my hands even as I murmur that she need not kiss my hands and, oh, oh no, *please* don't fall to the ground and kiss my feet. "Mama!" they call me (even women my age call me this); it is their word of greatest respect and gratitude, and it is also a word intended to generate a long-term sense of obligation in me.

But I came to understand that if I lived year-round in Addis Ababa, angry, bitter, hungry, and sick women would gather outside my gate, too, saying, with pinched lips, "She doesn't help us. She is supposed to help us and she does not. Let her sell her suitcases, then; let her sell her American clothes and her camera and her sunglasses if she really wants to help us." I am exempt—unlike Haregewoin—only because I get to fly away.

48

Wasihun had a new friend.

In June 2005, an American volunteer, on his first trip to Africa, dropped off donations in Haregewoin's compound and there he saw Wasihun.

A psychologist in his forties from the Pacific Northwest specializing in childhood sexual trauma, the American volunteer recognized that the boy was troubled. He made a point of spending time with Wasihun every day that week, whenever he returned to Haregewoin's compound. He asked Haregewoin's permission to take Wasihun out of the compound on outings around the city and even outside the city. He said he felt interested in adopting Wasihun.

On his extended visits with Wasihun, the American psychologist extracted or intuited scenes of Wasihun's abuse. He would later say that Wasihun did not tell *him* about it first, but *did* tell his fellow volunteer.

Children speaking about sexual abuse make notoriously unreliable witnesses. It is well established in legal and psychiatric literature that a child who has never been touched by an adult may—with encouragement—invent or confirm fictions involving not only sexual abuse but witchcraft, torture, forcible abortion, and/or animal sacrifice; day-care providers in the United States have gone to prison on evidence like this.

Another child who *was* abused may, in shame, swear it never happened.

The American psychologist had experience in this field and was adept in earning an abused child's trust. Being far from home base, however, there were cultural markers that he might have missed.

He might have reacted with greater caution to the picture of an Ethiopian boy eagerly talking about homosexual abuse, rather than burying it or denying it as might be expected in a land where homosexuality is widely regarded as "an abomination." It doesn't mean it didn't happen; it means tremendous care had to have been taken to interpret and to understand, before sharing the news.

The psychologist was far outside his element. On a humanitarian mission, he had stumbled across a boy in distress like one of his own patients back home. He had none of his usual resources to summon to the boy's aid, and was compelled to invent a rescue strategy on the spot.

In the summer and early fall of 2005, the American psychologist came to believe that Sirak's alleged rape of Wasihun was part of an ongoing pattern of abuse in Haregewoin's compound, that she was allowing men to come in on a regular basis to sexually abuse children.

Wasihun revised that story and reported that she took money from one man only, a relative of hers, and was allowing *him* to rape the children.

Wasihun told the psychologist that this unnamed relative raped many boys over many months; then that the male relative raped five boys each on two successive nights; and then that he raped five boys on one night; and then three boys on two nights; and finally Wasihun settled on three boys on one night a year ago.

The American formed the impression that children were beaten and starved in Haregewoin's compound. He suspected they lived in fear of her. "I know trauma when I see it and those children are traumatized," he said. He believed Haregewoin lived like an heiress outside of town in a "half-million-dollar house, with a hot tub, a Jacuzzi, and servants" and that she used the orphanage as a cover. "The joke is that we're all idiots that we don't know the mansion is her home, while the children live in squalor."

So alarmed was he on Wasihun's behalf, he grew anxious about the well-being of all Haregewoin's children. "The children are so afraid of her, they're afraid to eat," he said. "Even with the food in front of them, they look toward her to see if they are allowed to start. And while they're eating, they constantly look at her as if to ask, 'Are we eating too much?'"

"There's a little child there whom she's trained to beg like a dog," he said. "She summons the child, who trots in, folds its hands, and begs. Only then will she feed the toddler."

"She doesn't allow the children to go to school," he reported.

"She doesn't seek medication for the children when they're sick."

The story snaked around, shedding its skin and growing new skin every day.

The psychologist was persuaded that Haregewoin was planning to flee the country at any moment.

He came to believe that Haregewoin was plotting to have a child assassinated: "She put out a hit on a child, to be killed, by her nephew."

The story was hard to pin down, veering from the terrifying to the ridiculous.

Before visitors came, he noticed, she gave the children new clothes to put on. This may have been good manners, or it may have been deception about the level of care.

The American said, "My friend and I donated two goats for the New Year's feast on September 11. When we visited the compound, we saw that only one goat was being eaten."

When asked what had become of the other goat, he said, "I'm sure she sold it, for her own profit. Just like she sold all the used toys, books, and clothing we donated to her."

When he was asked, "You went to her compound, saw seventy children enjoying a holiday meal of goat stew, and you could tell the meal was made up of only one goat?" he replied, "Yes, my Ethiopian friend could tell."

(*First baby trafficking and now this!* I thought, when I heard of it. *Goat trafficking! Is the goat is on its way to Spanish parents?*)

As Wasihun's tale fattened and twisted during the time he spent with the American psychologist, the American did everything he could to alert the authorities to the possible pervasive maltreatment of Haregowoin's chlildren. He spoke of beatings, starvation, and sexual abuse to whoever would listen. He said he would publish the true story, the real story.

He found, in the City Social Affairs Bureau, willing listeners.

He took Wasihun to a pediatrician and the boy was given a blood test. Wasihun tested negative for HIV. No evidence remained of the alleged rape because to much time had elapsed since the event. He did not, however, take Wasihun to the hospital clinic for follow-up, despite the pediatrician's recommendation.

The American visitor was well-intentioned and outraged. He had stumbled upon the heart of darkness in Africa, it seemed, and he wanted to set it right. "I am a clinical psychologist who works with abused kids, and *she* has infuriated me," he said.

His suspicions surfaced online, where they began their infinite orbits, permanent satellites in deep cyberspace.

But it happened that the psychologist from the Pacific Northwest was not the only visitor to Haregewoin's compound in the summer and fall of 2005. There were many visitors, and some filed reports, and one made a handheld video.

These visitors (who typically made surprise visits to decrease the possibility of seeing prearranged situations) were running reconnaissance for several international NGOs. As part of due diligence and fact-finding, prior to the commencement of funding, it was necessary to appraise and document the treatment and condition of the children at the Atetegeb Worku foster homes.

The spontaneous video, made on September 5, 2005, by a middle-aged Ethiopian-American woman on a rare visit to Addis, shows a clean and friendly operation. She did not find Haregewoin home, but Henok's mother, Tigist, greeted her and invited her to make herself at home. The young children (the older ones were at school) bunch around their visitor, eager to make friends and to stick their faces close to her camera lens and shout *Allo!* The children look clean and well nourished. The older children, in school uniforms, come in for lunch, causing a hoopla; some eat quickly and then play soccer in the courtyard. The beds are made in every room; clean clothes are stacked on the shelves, and children's art is taped to the walls. In the baby room, one baby is being bottle-fed in the arms of a caregiver, though another has had his bottle propped against a pillow. After the lunch dishes are cleared away by caregivers, the dining hall serves as a study hall.

Also in September 2005, two American medical students working under the aegis of the New York–based World Wide Orphans Foundation (WWO) made surprise visits to Haregewoin's, scouting out the possibility of working with her. They filed a long, detailed report with Dr. Jane Aronson, director of WWO. Dated September 23, 2005, it reads, in part:

Haregewoin is a dynamic and engaging woman. Her English was excellent and expressive. She moved with energy and spoke with passion about her beliefs. She openly expressed that being orphaned is a sad state, and that her orphans are often sad, and that she cannot give the attention to 80 children that their own families could. This struck us as honest and not a description of any failing on her part.

After talking with Haregewoin in her office, we toured her first compound. This one houses 50 children of unknown HIV status, ranging in age from newborn to fourteen years of age. The compound was a little thin on children, as all the ones from seven years old and up were in school, leaving a dozen preschoolers and six or eight babies in residence. The living room was well-stocked with books and toys. The bunk rooms had eight to twelve bunks apiece, and over the bunks hung posters and art work by the children. The children we did see were nicely dressed, appropriately shy around us, and had small toys to play with. Their bedrooms were clean.

Next we saw the infant room. It had two or three nannies for the six or eight babies. This room had no windows or natural sunlight and was rather dark. It did smell of urine or diaper pail, but frankly no worse than I have smelled at other orphanages. Two of the babies I picked up did not appear well (a little floppy, eyes not tracking); the others looked fine.

Final impression: lovely facility, children of school-age all at school, younger children well tended with appropriate cleanliness and nice supply of playthings. Some infants looked unwell, but probably because they are sick from "the current disease." Would want more air, light, and circulation in the infant room, but that seems a minor quibble.

The second orphanage was housed in a very nice compound with garden space, trees, and birds. This compound houses 30 children, ages four months to 14 years. These children are all HIV-positive. These children do not go to school, but are taught in the compound. There is a nurse on duty. She has a VERY NICE dispensary/clinic, with a separate handwashing station, ample space to see and examine children, and a phenomenally well-stocked OTC medicine cabinet. I did NOT see the widespread tinea capitis/ alopecia/fungal skin infections I have come to take almost for granted among HIV-positive orphans . . .

The older children (18 of them) were eating lunch when we arrived, bowls of pasta. All of them giggled and smiled when we came in, and it was easy to elicit smiles when I took their pictures. They appeared clean and well-dressed. The room they were in had a shelf of books and toys, and bright posters of alphabet letters on the walls. Again I complimented Haregewoin on how nice and well-supplied the facility was . . .

In early October 2005, a European official with an international child welfare organization made two surprise visits to each of Haregewoin's two compounds. Alerted that suspicions had started to accrue to her name, he pulled children aside for one-on-one conversations and invited them to reveal their feelings through artwork. His report also was positive. Dated October 7, 2005, it concludes:

Children's drawings and poems as well as one-to-one discussions
with eight randomly-selected children reveal no trace of abuse or
corporal punishment perpetrated within the orphanage or by
orphanage's members/staff/volunteers . . . To me what sum-
marizes the children's experience is this phrase: "She (referring
to the orphanage director) is taking care of us according to her
capacity. Here is not perfect but she's giving us all what she can."

But other potential givers were alerted by the American psychologist
and the City Social Affairs Bureau that all was not right in the house of
Haregewoin Teferra, and several potential donors—including an
Italian organization that had promised to sponsor three of the
HIV-positive children—backed away and declined further contact
with Haregewoin. The Italian organization did send one last letter
specifying that if the HIV-positive children they had chosen were
promptly moved to a different facility, they would renew their
commitment of support through that facility, once that facility
contacted them.

Haregewoin read the letter, sighed, and stuck it in her files. "There
is no other 'facility' for these children," she said. "Who do the Italians
think will take them?"

Meanwhile, Wasihun was escorted—by the Ethiopian friend of the
American psychologist—to the Ministry of Labor and Social Affairs
(MOLSA) to enter a complaint against Haregewoin Teferra. The City
Social Affairs Bureau now gathered evidence against her on two
cases—the alleged child-trafficking of Baby Tarikwa, and the sexual
abuse of children in her houses. A few adoptions were approved, but
most of her children were held up. E-mails came from across the
United States asking her discreetly—or not so discreetly—about the
child-trafficking charges. Families unable to proceed with their
adoptions lamented their plight online, and adoption agency directors
vowed to avoid taking children from Haregewoin in the future. And
poor women outside her gate accused her of not helping them.

Haregewoin, under siege on all sides, by unknown sources, baffled and lonely, prayed, "God, I know I must have done wrong, but I cannot find how to undo it."

Finally, one night, letting herself into the sheets in which her precious toddler slept, she lay down and faced Nardos and whispered, "I have to let you go."

49

THE ETHIOPIAN REPRESENTATIVE for the Spanish adoption agency returned to Haregewoin's compound with three adoptive mothers. They were nervous and giddy. They wore jeans, backpacks, soft leather slip-on shoes.

Two had been promised infant boys.

The third . . . the third had come for Nardos. Haregewoin had phoned the Ethiopian man who headed the local office of the Italian adoption agency and had said, "You can find a family for Nardos now."

A beautiful family, she had tried to say, but began to cry and quickly hung up the phone.

One of the Spanish women pulled out a complicated harness with cotton straps and buckles; she hung it around her neck and inserted her new son. He hung there spread-eagled, looking a bit bewildered, while she kissed him on the top of his head. Another mother sat on the steps of the main house, taking her new son into her lap, unwrapping his baby blanket to admire his little toes and fingers.

A black-haired woman in her late thirties stood back, waiting to be introduced to Nardos. Her hair framed her face in a shag haircut; she wore stylishly narrow plastic eyeglasses and a V-necked, sleeveless blouse; she had an expectant look on her face, the eyebrows higher than the glass frames.

But this is not what I wanted! Haregewoin thought in a panic. *They have just told me she is not married. She is holding a cigarette—it means she is not religious! I wanted a young religious family for Nardos. In any case, not this woman.*

Exhausted by the scandal of Sirak, fearful that word of it had leaked beyond her gates, she was living day to day with the apprehension that the authorities would arrive and denounce her. *Though to all appearances a decent Orthodox woman*, the newspapers would say, *she allowed perversity to prey upon orphans.* Why should innocent Nardos be trapped here with her, a foolish old lady?

So now here was this woman, Nardos's new mother.

The Spanish woman had brought new clothes for Nardos. In Haregewoin's bedroom, Nardos consented to let the woman unbutton her frock and help her step into new clothes. Nardie looked frequently over the woman's shoulder at Haregewoin, who sat dejectedly on her bed; the child willed Haregewoin to stay nearby during this unusual transaction.

But those are not the right clothes for a little girl! thought Haregewoin, adding to her instant dislike of the woman from Spain. *Brown, cuffed sweatpants? A green quilted jacket? All so thick and heavy? These are boy's clothes!*

Nardos, who didn't know there was anything wrong with the new clothes, pulled away from the woman and trotted out to the porch. As always, voices rose to praise her; today the voices were in Amharic and Spanish.

Haregewoin called Nardie to come back inside, squatted down on the floor of the bedroom, and helped Nardos step out of her new clothes. She pulled, from a special box under her bed, Nardos's most beautiful outfit: a traditional white Ethiopian dress and shawl with lace trim, wrapped in tissue paper. Haregewoin, on her knees, plucked and picked and arranged the dress perfectly around Nardos, until Nardos stood like a tiny bride, a pearl.

She led Nardos to the porch now, to a finer ovation of praise than had greeted the Spanish woman's outfit. She held the child's hand and led the two-year-old gracefully down the cement steps and out into the middle of the courtyard. Nardos flew about like a white butterfly.

The afternoon is young, is it not? Haregewoin urgently felt. She called for the coffee to be prepared, she called for popcorn to be served, she called for chairs to be carried out for everyone; even though the

Spanish group demurred every offering. She knew they wanted to get away; she pretended they declined her hospitality from shyness, or from lack of traditional manners.

She called for the caregivers and even the accountant—a graying businessman—to step outside and behold adorable Nardos. She saw the Spanish women look at their watches; she saw the worried looks they cast at the Ethiopian agency person.

She sat on the steps of her house, acting her jolliest, posting her biggest smiles and emitting her biggest laughs. She helped Nardos sing a song; she sang along loudly and clapped while Nardos sang in her baby voice. She looked around eagerly to make sure everyone enjoyed Nardos's song. *We're having so much fun together! Let us relax and visit and not rush away. It is only two o'clock.* When she thought no one was watching her, she batted away the tears starting in her eyes.

It is only three fifteen.

It is not quite four thirty.

She couldn't keep her hands off Nardos. Nardie was radiant; Nardie was an angelic presence, with wings of gauze and lace, who had momentarily touched down in these humble surroundings and would soon fly away. Haregewoin followed humbly behind Nardos; she stooped to arrange Nardie's white cotton skirt and shawl; she pressed her face into the warm neck and pink cheek. In the small circles she tripped behind Nardos in the courtyard, as the minutes ticked toward the end of their life together, she aged ten years.

The Spanish woman captured Nardos for a moment and removed the elegant Ethiopian clothes. Nardos was sturdily dressed like a Spanish boy again, ready for travel.

The Ethiopian driver from the Spanish agency stepped outside the gate and turned on his van, as if it had to warm up. The two ladies adopting the baby boys took gentle leave of everyone and got into the van.

"Come! Come, everyone! Come tell Nardos good-bye!" cried Haregewoin, frantic to delay the departure.

The accountant stepped back outside in his long leather shoes, and the caregivers flowed back into the courtyard. Nardos was passed from person to person, smothered with farewell kisses, until it began to wear on her and she whimpered and reached for Haregewoin.

Haregewoin wrapped her arms around her again, buried her face in Nardos, inhaled Nardos; the accountant wrangled her out of Haregewoin's arms and Nardos began to cry, which was perhaps what Haregewoin needed: for Nardos to *realize* and to *understand*. For there to be a partner in her grief.

Suddenly Nardos was back in Haregewoin's arms again and Haregewoin's face collapsed in pain.

Through all this, the Spanish mother stood back politely. She was not trying to deprive Haregewoin of her farewell moments; only, one felt, it was enough. It was time.

The accountant pulled Nardos out of Haregewoin's arms again and Haregewoin began to cry openly. When Nardos saw her mother's tears, she began to wail in solidarity; the accountant gently hoisted her over his shoulder—because someone had to do it—and walked out the gate with her. Haregewoin stood at the doorway, watching, as a crying Nardos was buckled into a car seat. Then the van was gone. When Haregewoin turned around, she saw Nardos's little, white outfit draped on the porch steps, as if the child in it had evaporated.

Haregewoin raced up the short steps into her bedroom before anyone could look at her.

She sat on her bed and stared.

Alone.

50

When, in mid-december 2005, the police came to arrest Haregewoin Teferra, she had no spirit left with which to protest.

"Please may we do this quietly, so as not to upset the children?" she asked.

They allowed her to gather her pocketbook, cell phone, and shawl. "Take over," she said to Tigist, Henok's mother, and she walked with dignity out her gate with one officer ahead of her and one behind. They opened the back door of the police car and she got in, while bystanders watched. She was driven through the steel doors of a dusty police compound. The main brick building was a converted house, and she was escorted to one of the bedrooms, where several women sat on cots, leaning against the whitewashed walls. Haregewoin's purse and cell phone were not taken away, and the door was left unlocked.

No one told her why she was there, but she could guess.

Later it was confirmed that the arrest was made on the basis of the complaint lodged by Wasihun in September.

Feeling she had fallen out of favor with God, she accepted the arrest as her due. In jail she prayed, "God, I do not know what I did, but I know I have done something and you want to punish me. I humbly accept my punishment."

In December 2005, jails and prisons were full to overflowing with political protesters, opposition leaders, journalists, street demonstrators, and bystanders caught up in the mass arrests. The prisons were full of students, many as young as fifteen or sixteen. Families claimed that even younger children had been caught.

Tigist phoned Haregewoin's friends and they reached Suzie.

Suzie flew in from Cairo to try to help her mother, while old friends rushed to the *kebele* to protest the absurdity of arresting Haregewoin. Those with connections lobbied the highest-placed officials they could reach, for information and for help.

They learned that Haregewoin was being held as a witness—not unusual in Ethiopian law—until Sirak could be located and brought in.

The caregivers at the foster home rushed to her aid now, shocked at what had happened to her, and fearful of what imprisonment might mean (at her age!) to her health. It seemed their pay issues had been sorted out by now. The female caregivers and the oldest girls sat around in Haregewoin's front room, on the leopard-print sofas and chairs, wringing their hands and crying. The accountant, and an older lawyer who helped Haregewoin with paperwork, and a young male house-manager for the HIV-positive children, all took to the streets in search of Sirak. They easily found him staying in his old neighborhood and they reported his location to the police. Sirak was arrested. Back at the main compound, Suzie, Henok's mother Tigist, the lawyer, the accountant, the caregivers, the oldest children, all waited for the moment of Haregewoin's release, prepared to rejoice. She should no longer be held as a sort of hostage, now that Sirak was found.

But she was not released.

There were weeks of uncertainty; who in Ethiopia did *not* have a loved one in jail this month? Well, for most it was not a *grandmother*, but many families were running nonstop from jail to police headquarters to prison, seeking release and pardon.

Haregewoin, in her cell, waited to be sentenced for her failure to report the alleged rape of Wasihun.

The most influential of her old friends finally reached a contact high in the Ministry of Justice. "Who put this woman in jail?" cried Haregewoin's friend. "Is there justice in Ethiopia?"

She learned more details: Haregewoin was being investigated for child trafficking.

"Mother, are you all right?" cried Suzie, when permitted into the police compound to visit her mother and to hand a covered plate of food through the wire fence.

"Everyone is very kind to me," said Haregewoin. "I didn't want them to tell you, I didn't want you to worry. The policemen here are fine, they are good men. They let us walk about the house during the day—the room is not even locked! There are no bars on the window. And there is a girl in my room who has a very beautiful voice and she sings for us at night. But there are so many young people here! Here, I've written down these names—could you phone their families to tell them they're here and they're all right?"

Haregewoin was sleeping deeply at night and in the afternoons, too; she hadn't slept truly and profoundly for many years; it was like visiting a sky-blue lake and spring-green landscape from her childhood. The colors of her dreams were vivid; and multitudes of beloved faces, past and present, pushed close. She was resting; she was sitting on her cot and looking through her window at the trees at the far edge of the dusty compound and she was thinking. She was in repose. She heard young people crying at night but she was not crying. There were magazines and a few books and papers lying about, but she was not reading or writing. She ate just a little of the food they offered and drank the water. She declined the tea and the coffee. She was slowing down, coming down, coming to a halt. She was sitting still; she watched the sun cross the dusty compound; she watched the skinny pine-tree branches move stiffly in the wind. Being short, she sat against the wall with her bare feet sticking straight off her cot, not touching the cement floor. If the ladies in her room wanted to talk, she talked a little; sometimes she just sighed and shrugged and smiled mildly in reply. At night, she craned her head from her mattress to see the night sky through the window and to watch the constellations rotate in slow motion above the dusty compound. Haregewoin was viewing her whole life from afar, from behind a barbed-wire fence, pine trees, and guard towers.

She was seeing this: she had recoiled instinctively from Sirak's attack on Wasihun but had fled in haste down the wrong road.

She should have raced to comfort him; she should have phoned the police, phoned a doctor. Maybe a rape (*penetration* as she now knew it was called) had happened; maybe it hadn't; but she should have moved to protect the hurt and frightened child.

Instead, her instincts had told her to secure herself, her organization, her good name, and her money.

Wasihun had been right to accuse her: "You are not my mother."

Now, locked away from the *children*—children who were turning to others for love and protection—she saw them again as she had seen them at the very beginning, when Selamawit and Meskerem were given to her by the Catholic charity MMM. The children were life itself. They didn't generate income; they weren't the foundation of a life lived importantly; they neither enhanced her reputation nor pulled it down; they weren't placed on her driveway to waylay her on her self-important outings beyond the gate every day; they had no idea they were *recipients* of the good performed by her *charitable organization*, nor that they partook of a valued *grassroots initiative*. They had no clue that their little names, translated into numbers, appeared on the spreadsheets of several international organizations. Once they had needed a mother, and she had been their mother, and that had been enough.

Shedding tears, she felt she didn't care if she never saw the elegant house on Gojam Road again; while she would hurry, barefoot, down the dirt road, under the stars, if the police set her free, she would scurry back to her two little foster homes. The children in them were life, the thick of life, the very middle and sweetness and silliness of life. Without the children in her two compounds, she had no life. She wanted no other life besides the one she lived with them in noise and sloppy kisses and broken windows and the kicking of little feet in her bed at night.

Meanwhile, that life was almost surely coming to an end.

Suzie learned that the City Social Affairs Bureau was preparing to shut Haregewoin down. They were making plans to transfer all her children permanently. At both houses, while Haregewoin was in prison, caregivers were told to start preparing the children to move out; at ENAT (now called AHOPE) the director was told to make room for thirty HIV-positive children. ("Do you know how few orphanages in the entire country take in HIV-positive children!" cried an Ethiopian board member of AHOPE. "And you're going to close down one of them? What *sense* does that make? And God knows we have no room for them here.") Other orphanages were put on notice that Haregewoin's healthy children would be transferred to them.

Many people, American and Ethiopian alike, felt confused about who Haregewoin was at this moment: goodness of heart mixed with haphazardness; excellence of intent dragged down by exhaustion, age, and perhaps a touch of pride.

There was also the fact that a few organizations—WWO's pediatric AIDS clinic, AAI's Layla House, AHOPE, Wide Horizons for Children's orphanage—were raising the standard for orphan care. Orphaned children could be healthy and joyful, engaged with the outside world through school and art and sports. Haregewoin was heroic in orphan rescue. In a country deep in crisis, she hauled children to safety within her gates. Like few others, she reached out to the hopeless cases. Perhaps she was frozen at this stage of triage: capable of saving lives, but a little confused about how to move with huge numbers of children up the ladder of institutional excellence. What was always true, however, remained true: she had no life apart from the children. She lived there, among them, twenty-four hours a day, seven days a week.

"I accept it, God, I accept your decree, I know I deserve it," cried Haregewoin into her mattress in the jail, writhing in grief. "Please, God, can you leave me a few? I know I disappointed your trust, but please."

PART 4

51

I T MAY BE possible to chart a greater arc on a world map than the trip from the wood-framed villages of central Vermont with their antique shops, wilderness stores, ice cream parlors, and aging all-white populations, to the mud roads and tin-roofed shantytowns of populous, sprawling Addis Ababa, but it's hard to imagine what that trip would look like.

In the in-flight magazines of British Air, KLM, Ethiopian Air, or Lufthansa, you fold out the world map and trace the route across three pages and staples. You fly from New York to London, Frankfurt, or Amsterdam, then land to refuel in Cairo or Khartoum, the names increasingly exotic, the purplish whorl of compass-drawn blue and red route-lines thinning out, until there is only a single thread tying a destination to a tangled hub, and you follow the thread to a city with a name as mysterious and alluring as Timbuktu or Mombasa or Dakar or Kinshasa: Addis Ababa.

It's a pretty wild project to fly to the ends of the earth to collect a new family member, a child whose bedroom awaits her under the slanting eaves of the home farmhouse: a bright quilt on her bed; new dolls and stuffed animals stiffly arranged on the dresser; new jeans and sweaters hanging in the closet, though they may not be the right size.

On the all-night transatlantic flight, Rob Cohen, Middlebury College professor of English and American literatures, novelist, writer-in-residence, author of the critically acclaimed novel *Inspired Sleep*, age forty-seven, lanky and bushy-haired, sat hunched in his airline seat. He faced—in the cold oval window—his own reflection: the steep, curly-bearded, classic face of Jewish melancholy. Beside him slept his wife, Claudia Cooper, director of Teacher Education and visiting assistant professor of English and American literatures at Middlebury, blond and pale, also forty-seven, mother of two sons (Nick Rogerson, nineteen, and Eli Cohen, fourteen).

The jet rumbled through thunderclouds over the North Atlantic. In the cabin, the reading lights clicked off. Below there was vast, churning darkness, the realm of naval vessels, surface currents, submarines, deepwater ravines, fish.

Rob did not mind being borne away with such force, at such speed; the whole adoption had felt something like this, an acceleration of powers beyond his control, a veering away and apart, an almost heart-stoppingly sudden ascent.

Claudia had visited Ethiopia first. In November 2003, she traveled with a small medical mission in the hopes of sharing her expertise in education, teacher training, and literacy.

On *her* first flight beyond the rim of North America and then Europe, she had bent over her journal and written at great length. Were they descending toward mayhem? Would they encounter un-washed hordes of desperate, damaged children? Could she make meaningful contact with any?

At dusk from the air, it is lovely to glide low over Africa: the silver-white deserts of Egypt and Sudan are the colors of moonscape. How do human beings find footholds here? How do their long-lipped camels find even the odd thistle to masticate? Then you veer again, or you turn back to your shiny map pages, and you see that the continent wears a veil of greenery from which the ashen-faced north peeks out; greenery swings like a grass skirt below the Sahara Desert and the Sahel. It is pinned to Senegal in the west, drapes Nigeria and the Central African Republic around the middle, falls to calf-length and gives out in the Kalahari Desert, and tacks up in the east in Ethiopia.

Then you come down out of the sky far sooner than you expect, landing at the modern steel-and-glass airport of a city propped high in the mountains, a kind of mezzanine between desert and sky.

*   *   *

Claudia was wonderfully welcomed by the glorious children she met in Addis Ababa: smart children jostled around her everywhere, eager to shake her hand, to practice their English. "Hellohowareyou?" yelled children on the streets, flinging their words the moment they saw sunshine reflect off her long yellow hair.

"I am fine. How are *you?*" she enunciated in smiling reply, thrilling the children, who covered their mouths in happiness and ran off to tell friends and family of their successful encounter with a pure-born exotic.

At AAI's Layla House, she was surrounded by giggling little girls attracted to the yellow silk of her hair. They led her to a kitchen chair in the courtyard and got to work, combing and braiding the fine threads. Those with families ran to get their photo albums to show her and to inquire, "You know my mom?" or "You know my Seattle?" Older boys and girls conversed with her in English on a high plane. Her opinion on President Bush was solicited, also on the war in Iraq, also why Americans were often poor soccer players in World Cup matches. When she stood and walked across the courtyard, two or three children hung on each of her hands; others sprinted ahead into the dining hall to save a seat for her.

Then Claudia flew back home to her nineteenth-century, wood-planked farmhouse in Vermont's central Champlain Valley. Skis leaned against the wall of the mudroom; books and magazines were stacked everywhere. On the long winter nights, she or Rob lit a fire in the hearth; they drank tea from clay mugs; music of Dylan or The Band or Bob Marley or the blues great Robert Johnson played in the background. Spruce, birch, and maple trees shaded the house; a meadow and hay farm lay across the road; an occasional moose lumbered past in the night, leaving deep prints in the snow.

Claudia was absorbed by thoughts of flying back to Addis Ababa and returning home to Middlebury with a child, and Rob thought about it with her. They filled out AAI's applications, filed orphan-adoption immigration papers, got blood tests, inoculations, and fingerprints, were interviewed, and were matched with a ten-year-

old girl named Meskerem (Haregewoin's Meskerem), with a triangular, intelligent face and thick and beautiful eyebrows.

Their colleagues and fellow parents and children's coaches and
neighbors were blindsided and amazed: a *ten-year-old*? From *Africa*?
Some said they just hadn't realized the couple was so desperate for
more children. Rob and Claudia couldn't describe exactly what had
happened to them. They loved their sons more than life; obviously they
were both *teachers*, adults who treasured children; and then they'd
discovered a country full of orphans. Both halves of an equation were
suddenly obvious to them, even if it sounded slightly crazy to their
friends.

Naturally, like all prospective adoptive parents—especially prospective parents of older children—they wondered if they were doing
the right thing for their family, and if they were the right family for this
child. They wondered if Vermont was the right spot in which to raise
an Ethiopian. They wondered how she'd manage at school, given her
past, compared to the sons and daughters of professors and businesspeople. At risk was everything precious to them: the happiness of Eli
and Nick, the family happiness.

Deep in the mind of nearly every waiting adoptive parent of an older
child lurks the unspoken prayer *Please don't let me bring home a child unable to
bond*. Meanwhile, expressions of total shock and astonishment, of jolly
congratulations and lavish praise, came at them from every direction. If
the couple had announced that Claudia was pregnant with quadruplets,
the reactions might have been roughly the same.

And yet, although strange, the decision didn't strike them as
mistaken, so they filed the legal papers, they crammed orphanage
supplies into duffel bags, and in August 2004 they buckled their seat
belts and rose and rounded the globe.

It didn't *exactly* feel—as they took to the air—like the night they
drove to the hospital when Claudia was in labor with Eli; but it felt a
little bit like that.

Airborne, they relaxed; they were talked out. The time of discussion
and reconsideration and explanation was over. Claudia slept. Rob

closed his eyes but did not sleep right away, in order to savor for another moment the sensation of being lifted and propelled across the dark water.

On a morning of dazzling heat and brightness—denim sky sparkling with sunlight; dirt roads teeming with people, donkeys, goats, and sheep; flags snapping in the wind; hundreds of tin shops and wooden kiosks displaying their wares—they rode by taxi to Layla House and honked outside the steel door. A guard pulled it open.

Kids spied them in the taxi's backseat and scattered, sprinting in every direction and yelling Meskerem's name.

Claudia hadn't met Meskerem on her first visit to Layla House. Now she shakily got out of the taxi and tried to acknowledge greetings from children who remembered her. Rob stood beside her in an agony of thrilling overstimulation, trepidation, and excitement. It was all about to happen. It began.

Meskerem came out the doorway of a far building and turned in their direction. They both registered instantly, "She's as beautiful as her pictures." Thick, curly hair gathered back into a ponytail, tall, slender child, elegant face, the thick, arched eyebrows and shy smile. She walked toward them sweetly, alternately looking at them and looking down at the ground; she carried herself gracefully all the way across the compound straight to them (they were paralyzed); she put her arms (she was nearly as tall as Claudia) around Claudia's neck and delivered the great hug of Claudia's lifetime: an unrelentingly hard, grateful, and loving hug, a hug that went on so long that Rob (towering over both of them) bent to be included. They held on to each other for a long time. The white sun edged an inch across the sky, changing the angles of silver light bending from car bumpers and wristwatches and window hardware around the compound; they hugged as classes changed and children danced around them and skipped away; they hugged for so long that, by the time they let go, they'd leapt across the oceans and continents, they'd reassured one another, they'd found one another.

Meskerem didn't speak above a whisper for her first twenty-four hours with them; but, when the taxi driver invited her in Amharic to come away with them, she flashed a bright smile and assented; she slipped into the backseat next to Claudia and held Claudia's hand and shyly, smilingly, returned Claudia's gaze as they rode. She checked into the Ethiopian-owned Ghion Hotel with the Cooper-Cohens as if a hotel stay were part of her everyday experience; only the slight give in her knees, when the old elevator gave a jerk, exposed the truth that this was her very first elevator ride.

By nod and gesture, she asked and understood which bed was hers. At bedtime, Rob uncertainly presented her with a toothbrush and toothpaste. *Does she know what this is? How would we even begin to explain it? It seems impossible to approach with no language in common. It's just a tiny thing, but it symbolizes the huge cultural divide here . . .* But she accepted both with a smile, gave her teeth a thorough brushing, and returned the damp items to Rob with a twinkle in her eye that seemed to say, "I know what a toothbrush is. It's not like I just stepped out of the African *bush*." Claudia had brought pajamas from home, and Meskerem emerged from the bathroom looking absolutely adorable and sweet, and the parents were again smitten by her loveliness.

They had given her a backpack full of new belongings: clothes, swimsuit, art supplies, and a disposable camera. Before getting into bed, she extracted each item and examined it; she laid everything out on her bedspread; then (oblivious that her new parents watched her in amazement) she carefully repacked the backpack, largest items in first on the bottom, middle-size items halfway up, building a careful pyramid to the very top, upon which she laid a pair of earrings. Rob and Claudia were touched by her pride of ownership, and they were moved to acknowledge a remarkable and marvelous new element that Meskerem would bring to the family: she was a *girl*.

She went to sleep between the crisp hotel sheets, cradling the teddy bear they'd brought her, her long, curly hair spread across the pillow like a shawl.

✻   ✻   ✻

At breakfast the next morning, hard-hit by jet lag, not yet realizing that he was really getting sick, Rob chafed at the sight of couples like themselves—many from Spain, a few from Australia—chasing after their Ethiopian children, all being served by Ethiopian waiters and waitresses. *All us chirpy, cheery white folk having breakfast with our African children*, he thought. *Is there an imperialist angle to this? Is adoption, on some level, another form of consumerism? What is the meaning of white parents flying in from a rich country to adopt the children of a poor black country? Is this some kind of twenty-first-century plunder?*

But by then he felt too sick with a stomach bug to think it through, and he set aside the misgiving for a later date.

Dr. Rick Hodes was an alumnus of Middlebury and knew them slightly from Claudia's visit to Addis and his own visits back to Middlebury. He welcomed Rob and Claudia like old friends.

Leading a delegation of visiting *ferange* down the sidewalk, Hodes bounced ahead in leather boots, a flak jacket, and his Yankees cap. He ducked into the unpromising doorway of a smoky, hole-in-the-wall, traditional restaurant known only to locals and assured his foreign visitors that the spicy lentil stew here was the best in East Africa. He led the outsiders across the low-ceilinged room to the corner *mesob*, an hourglass-shaped basket-table encircled by low, fur-covered stools. He ordered off the menu, speaking loudly and clearly in Amharic. For himself, the *tsom* (fasting menu), no meat, as the meat here would not be kosher. His high syllables rang out like a knife tapped against glassware; he happily registered the surprise of Ethiopians within earshot, the Ethiopians who didn't already know him.

Back at the Hodes house, Rob faded, sick, deep into the sofa, but dimly grasped that he was witnessing a grand thing: how a family was knit together from such disparate strands, how there was fantastic closeness and warmth here.

They returned on Friday night for a Shabbat dinner and enjoyed the sight of the many Hodes sons dressed up, wearing yarmulkes, and singing Hebrew blessings and English songs at the top of their voices.

Those raised Ethiopian Orthodox stayed Orthodox; and those raised Muslim stayed Muslim; but those who landed in the Hodes house without religion took on their dad's Judaism.

Dejene at fourteen was an Americanized hip-hop kid, accustomed to visiting New York, Connecticut, and California. His American accent was perfect; his headphones and baggy jeans and oversize jacket and unlaced boots were perfect. But he made his adoptive father happy by chanting the traditional Hebrew kiddush over the Sabbath wine.

One long-term Hodes family houseguest was an Ethiopian Orthodox priest from the Simien Mountains. Hodes had found the man on a cot in a paupers' hospital, with a cantaloupe-sized tumor on his elbow. The gray-bearded, sun-darkened priest, *Kes* (Father) Mulat, looked sixty, but was only forty-three.

"Mind if I take a look at that?" Hodes had asked in Amharic. He contacted an orthopedist volunteering at Mother Teresa's, and the surgeon removed the tumor and amputated the arm below the elbow. Hodes brought the long-faced father to his house to recuperate and ordered a prosthesis for him. When *Kes* was strong enough to travel, Hodes gave him bus fare and travel money, drove him to the station, and put him on the bus for home, provoking widespread surprise and joy; the people thought their priest had died in Addis. *Kes* Mulat then returned to Hodes's house and took up residence on a daybed on the porch while continuing his medical treatment.

The somber, six-foot-tall, weathered priest joined the family and their guests at the Friday-night table. The priest nodded approvingly as the candles were lit and the Hebrew prayers chanted. He did his best to hold hands and to hum along to the welcoming hymn "Shalom Aleichem," and to the American folk song "If I Had a Hammer," which Hodes had installed as part of the family service.

Ethiopian Airlines offered direct flights from Tel Aviv for the growing numbers of Israeli tourists, backpackers, and businesspeople. Before Passover every spring, Hodes dispatched two of his sons to the airport to meet incoming Israel flights. Outside baggage claim, the boys held up a sign that read, in English and Hebrew, "*Rotse Seder*

Pesakh Kasher? Daber Itanu. Looking for a kosher Passover seder? Talk to us."

They always came home with guests.

Hodes told Claudia and Rob that he recently had called a family meeting. The boys had flopped over sofas and chairs in the living room and looked at him.

"Are we a real family?" he began.

"Yeah, Hodes, we're a real family," said Addisu Hodes, fifteen. Addisu wore his long hair in cornrows and favored satin soccer jerseys since he was a soccer star at high school.

"Are we a happy family?" asked Hodes.

"Yeah, yeah, we're a happy family," said Mohammed.

"Do we have any family problems?" asked Hodes.

"Well, all right, yeah, there are some problems," the boys agreed.

"Okay," said Hodes. "What's our worst problem?"

The boys conferred briefly among themselves, after which Dejene removed his music earphones and announced, "Farts."

"How are you?" Claudia asked with concern later that night as Rob shakingly put himself to bed.

"Impressed as hell," said Rob.

Meskerem's behavior for the first few days was so ladylike and perfect that her new parents put on excellent manners, too, just to keep up. Claudia and Rob became paragons of tidiness and careful planning, and of pronouncing every word and syllable crisply, to help Meskerem understand. "After you," and "No, after you" and "Thank you very much" and "Won't you have some more?" and "Let me just tidy up the bedroom before we go out" and "Well, it's good night then!" They sounded like hearty characters in a British film of World War II vintage, keeping up a jolly good front.

On the fifth day, as they were about to give out from all the excellent behavior, Meskerem showed herself a little more. She pointed to Rob's hair—unruly, dark ringlets—and then to her own unruly, dark ringlets, and she laughed a real laugh, peals of bright laughter. "I look like you," she was relaying, and it struck her as funny; her laughter was infectious, it *was* funny, they *did* look alike—the bushy hair, the long faces, the dark eyebrows, the tall, slender builds. The laughter went on—in the Ghion restaurant, as the dinner dishes were cleared away—just like the first hug, a deliriously long time, and when it was over, it seemed they had again reached new ground.

Rob now realized he could tease his new daughter, that she had a sense of humor. He could push the wrong elevator button and see if she noticed; he could pull out a chair for her at dinner and then leap into it himself; he could race her down the hotel steps to the taxi and grab the front seat, yelling, "Shotgun!" She swiped and hid his things in the hotel room; pretended to take his place in the bed next to Claudia; put on his jacket in the morning and acted as if she didn't realize.

Nothing else they did—the sightseeing day-trip outside the capital, the visits to museums and historic sites—held as much meaning as the silly, teasing, ticklish stuff in the idle minutes. Claudia properly rolled her eyes at them, as Meskerem and Rob discovered they not only looked *just* alike, but they both had the souls of comedians.

A week later, they boarded the plane together. As the jet accelerated and tilted up into the air, Meskerem panicked. Rather than cry from fright, she grew still and seemed to enter a trancelike state. She said little and moved little on the journey; she declined food. Rob and Claudia leaned back their heads in exhaustion, counting the hours until they would land and drive to pick up Eli from his summer camp and introduce him to his sister.

Sometimes dozing, sometimes just sitting, sometimes feeling separate, sometimes holding hands, Claudia, Rob, and Meskerem had begun to sketch their own colorful arcs and lines on the world map. They would describe loops and twirls, spirals and doodles, of a sort no airline flight-planner or geographer ever imagined.

52

B ACKSTAGE, A SIX-YEAR-OLD girl shivers inside her pink-
and-turquoise leotard. She is fifth in the line of eight beginning
tap students at the Carol Walker Dance Academy in suburban
Atlanta, and this is her first recital. Her hands are clammy, she can
barely swallow, and her ballerina bun is drawn back so tightly it seems
to pull her to her toes. She hears the applause of the crowd in the
Gwinnett Cultural Arts Center as the previous act finishes; then those
girls, with flushed cheeks, thunder past on their way backstage. For
eight months she has prepared for this moment.

She clackety-claps across the polished stage in her tap shoes and faces
a darkened auditorium rustling with cellophane-wrapped bouquets.
Somewhere out there are her parents, her younger brother, one of
her two doting grandmothers, and half a dozen family friends. In the last
moment before the music starts, Mekdes Hollinger, age six, who once
threw herself at a steel door and then groveled grief-stricken in the dirt
of Haregewoin's yard, lifts her hand to her lips and blows a kiss to her
mother. Malaika "Mikki" Hollinger, a woman of African-American and
New Orleans Creole descent, promised she would catch Mekdes's kiss.

Music booms from the loudspeakers: the "Digga Tunnah Dance"
from *The Lion King*. African singers chant lyrics warning the animals to
dig a tunnel and hide before the hyena comes. The tap dancers
pantomime scanning the horizon for hyenas, digging a hole, then
hopping inside to hide.

As in all recitals, a few children watch the teacher coaching from
backstage and never look at the audience; a few dancers turn left
instead of right and slam into the ones doing it correctly; one girl's

sequined headpiece falls off and she's afraid to pick it up, though she looks at it yearningly every time she leaps past it. The audience laughs and cries with enjoyment—with the exception of Mekdes's four-year-old brother, Yabsira. At the first warning of hyenas, he yelps, "I don't like this show." When the dancers mime the approach of the hyenas, Yabsira dives under his seat and stays there for the rest of the performance.

Too quickly it is over, and the children stampede offstage to the ovations and whistles of the crowd. Mekdes shyly emerges from the dressing room into the hail of her father's flash photography. She accepts bouquets and kisses from a circle of her admirers. She consents to be treated to lunch at a nearby restaurant and exits the crowded lobby of the arts center hand in hand with her father.

In Snellville, Georgia, twenty-five miles east of downtown Atlanta, earthmovers smoothed out the corrugated farmland and replaced it with subdivisions. A few cows still graze along the state route, but their acreage is disappearing. At night, the horizon blazes with lights from new shopping centers and cineplexes. A handful of the old stars dangle overhead, but they look dusty and outmoded, like oil lamps, the kind of thing that gave light around here a hundred years ago.

The Hollingers' new brick house is decorated with gold-framed wedding portraits, and their china and glassware chime with the cleanliness of freshly unwrapped wedding gifts. Ryan, thirty-six, grew up in rural Ohio and still looks like a farmboy football player. His mother was a nurse, his father a factory worker, his stepfather an accountant. Ryan Hollinger is white, blond, fit, and blue-eyed, his hair short and moussed. He wears a gold stud earring. He works in computer software sales and graphic design.

Malaika Jones Hollinger, thirty-four, still acts the part of high school salutatorian. She wears bangs and a pert expression and moves with the precise and erect posture of a ballerina. Her mother was a kindergarten teacher, her father a New Orleans chef. She works in public health.

Ryan is this Ohio-bred white man of French, German, and Irish descent, she wrote in her journal, when she met him in Houston, where she was in graduate school. *I am a pecan-colored woman of African and French descent. Go up Momma's family tree and you meet the French-speaking café-au-lait Catholic Creoles.*

Ryan likes land, because the family had so much of it. He was raised in a big house on a farm. I like water, because I saw so much of it. The Louisiana swamp sat outside my house, full of cypress trees and Spanish moss and egrets.

Later Mikki would ask "When did you know I was the one?" and Ryan would say, "Instantly."

On March 18, 2000, in New Orleans, under a black sky churning with tornadoes, they married. There were three hundred guests at the wedding.

Ryan is a gentleman, a romantic, an artist, a superb cook. We have candlelit gourmet dinners at least once a week. Among our friends, the Hollinger dinner parties are legendary. He is the most thoughtful man alive. He and Momma talk on the phone every night. They talk more than Momma and I do.

I rarely remember that we have what is called an "inter-racial marriage." Society has been kind to us. I never even think of Ryan as <u>white</u>.

Well, no, that's not true. When he puts Metallica on the stereo, I am compelled to remember.

Bright future, two cars, three-bedroom house. This friend was pregnant, that friend was pregnant; at the dinner parties, a few wives sipped goblets of milk instead of French wine. When expectant friends yelled, "Hey, what about you two?" Mikki and Ryan looked at each other, smiled, and shrugged. She wasn't getting pregnant. Medical tests revealed no reason why she shouldn't, but it wasn't happening.

They decided to look overseas for a baby. Or maybe a baby and an older sibling? "All right, two, as long as one of them is out of diapers," they agreed.

In late summer 2003, they signed up with AAI and began to get monthly newsletters and occasional videos of children living in orphanages in Thailand and Ethiopia.

On December 24, 2003, an AAI videotape arrived by mail. Mikki's parents were visiting from New Orleans, so Mikki stashed the videotape in her night table and said nothing. At four thirty A.M. Christmas morning, Ryan shook her awake and whispered, "Let's watch it!" The two of them crept past the guest bedroom to the living room and inserted the tape into the VCR. The first children to appear were Mekdes and Yabsira Asnake: a wistful girl in a ripped blue dress, a jolly boy in a girl's pink sweatshirt.

They rewound the tape and studied the pair again. It was the third video they'd received from AAI; they'd been charmed by dozens of children's images; but none had hit them like this. They rewound and watched again, inching closer. They rewound and watched and inched and rewound and watched and inched until the images of the children grew large and pixilated and expanded into the brilliant future. Mikki and Ryan tiptoed back to bed and talked all night. She got up once to turn on the computer and send an e-mail to AAI: "We want to adopt Mekdes and Yabsira Asnake."

They said nothing to the future grandparents, but spent Christmas Day glowing with the sense of having become, overnight, expectant parents.

On December 26, Mikki jogged down the block with her cell phone and called AAI. She was put on hold while the children's file was located. "I'm so sorry," said a staff person. "Mekdes and Yabsira have been matched with a family already."

"What?" cried Mikki. "It's not possible!"

"Did you see anyone else on the tape you liked?"

"We didn't watch anyone else," Mikki sobbed in reply.

She understood instantly that they'd been fools to fall in love with children on a videotape; nonetheless, they had.

On January 7, 2004, AAI called back. "Are you still interested in Mekdes and Yabsira? The other family decided to adopt just one child and we don't want to separate the siblings."

In August 2004, Mekdes, who was waiting for it, saw the taxi pulling into the orphanage compound in Addis Ababa and she broke into a run. She leapt into Mikki's arms. Yabsira strolled over to Ryan, looked the big man up and down, and raised his arms to be lifted up. From the height of his new dad's shoulder, he benevolently smiled down upon the other children. Later in America, after Mekdes spoke English, she would recall, "First day? Mommy look like Ethiopian mommy. Daddy not look like Ethiopian daddy."

The Hollingers gave Mekdes a doll and Yabsira the Hokey-Pokey Hamster, a battery-powered, eight-inch-tall furry toy that sneered, in a feverish digital pitch, "You do the hokey-pokey and you turn yourself around, that's what it's all about," while waving its arms and wobbling backward and forward.

It was the most ridiculous thing ever to enter the gates of the orphanage. From every corner of the compound, children came running to see, to point, and to scream at the Hokey-Pokey Hamster. It would be the only aspect of the adoption that Mikki and Ryan would regret: by the end of two weeks of living in a small apartment in Addis with Mekdes, Yabsira, and the a cappella Hokey-Pokey Hamster, the adults thought they would lose their minds.

And Yabsira was not to be tricked: one of his first English words, when the Hokey-Pokey Hamster fell silent, was the command "Batteries."

Hokey-Pokey Hamster serenaded them in the night. Finally, before dawn one morning, Ryan removed the batteries and barely restrained himself from hurling them off the balcony into the street below. "Hokey-Pokey needs to *sleep* now, Yabsira," he said through clenched teeth. Yab may not have understood the English, but he got the gist.

On their first night as a family, Mikki bathed the children, smoothed lavender lotion on their skin, and dressed them in soft, enormous pajamas. They bypassed their own twin beds and hopped onto the parents' double bed, where Ryan was stretched out, exhausted. Mikki collapsed, too. The children moved back and forth, petting and kissing them, playing with their hair and tickling their arms, until they fell asleep between them.

Earlier that evening, Mikki had presented Mekdes with a child's suitcase of new clothing. There were pastel cotton sweat suits, jumpers, blouses, pajamas, socks, underwear. It couldn't all be for her? All for *her*? When Mekdes realized these were hers, she stripped out of her gray orphanage wear in an instant and stood before Mikki. "Naked as a jaybird," Mikki told Ryan later, "with a thousand-kilowatt smile." Everything was huge on Mekdes, but she loved it all. She flopped around all week in a pair of sneakers three sizes too long.

On the day of the departure to America, Mikki and Ryan woke up Mekdes first. It was three o'clock in the morning.

"Go America, Mommy?" she asked in excitement, stepping into another new outfit. Then she panicked. "Yabsira, Mommy? Yabsira!? No Yabsira America, no Mekdes America. Yabsira America!"

"Of course Yabsira is coming," said Mikki.

They flew for a nightmarish twenty hours—Ryan was sick and Yabsira was a wild man: he pushed all the buttons on his seat so relentlessly that a stewardess arrived and virtually ripped the controls out of their sockets. He sang and yelled and kicked the seat in front of him and banged on the tray and ran to the bathroom where there were more buttons to push. Fortunately, at three A.M. that morning, Ryan Hollinger had had the presence of mind to stuff Hokey-Pokey Hamster into a sock and bury him deep in a suitcase that traveled in the cargo bay.

They reached Atlanta the following afternoon and drove the last forty-five minutes to the ranch house in Snellville. Mikki led the children to Yabsira's bedroom.

"Yabsira's room!" she announced, stepping back to let the children take in the sunshine-yellow walls with a soccer ball border, twin bedspreads and switch plates and lamps all decorated with soccer balls, baseballs, and footballs.

Mekdes touched one of the twin beds and said, "Yabsira!" Then she touched the other and said, "Mekdes!"

"No," said Mikki, patting first one and then the other bed, "Yabsira, Yabsira."

Alarmed, Mekdes tried again: "Yabsira, *Mekdes?*"

"Come," said Mikki, and drew Mekdes into the other bedroom, the one in which Ryan had created a garden: spring-green walls with a real white picket fence attached, hand-painted butterflies fluttering among huge flowers. "Mekdes's room!" said Mikki.

Mekdes screamed. She threw herself across the nearest bed, hugging the puffy flower bedspread. She raised her head and asked "America?"

Mikki opened her mouth to explain, then simply said "Yes."

"*America*," sighed Mekdes happily, and laid her head down.

It turns out not to be very difficult for children to adapt to electricity and plumbing, a clean water supply, modern medicine, cars, groceries, paved streets, playgrounds, school, shoes, bikes, dance lessons, and loving parents. What is hard—even impossible—is for children to survive the death of their parents without loving substitutes.

For Mekdes, the transition to her new life was smooth, despite normal setbacks of confusion and mourning. Ethiopian-American friends Tarik and Saba took the family to dinner at a local Ethiopian restaurant soon after the children's arrival. Atlanta has an Ethiopian community of thirty thousand, with a lively subculture of churches, markets, restaurants, soccer teams, student and professional organizations, and festivals. At the restaurant, with the foods and people and artwork and music and smells of Ethiopia enveloping them, Yabsira dug into his traditional dinner with both hands. Mekdes, stunned by the scene, withdrew and could not eat.

At home that night, she threw a fit; she wailed and howled and stomped. "It's not a temper tantrum," Ryan observed to Mikki.

"It's grief," said Mikki.

"Mekkie, Mekkie, can you calm down? Mekkie, can you tell Mommy what's wrong?"

Gasping for breath, drenched with tears, she shook her head, unable to answer.

"Mekdes, is it Ethiopia?" asked Mikki.

Mekdes recoiled as if she'd been punched, then looked with tearful eyes into Mikki's eyes and deeply nodded yes.

That night, Mekdes mourned for her lost country and family, and her parents were sad. But Tarik and Saba became constants in Mekdes's life. One day they took her and her brother to a feast in honor of a new baby in the community. Mekdes's criticism was withering. "These are *not* the right foods to eat for a feast for a new baby," she told them, appalled. "They're not playing the right music. They're not wearing the right clothes."

Finally, out of patience, she said in Amharic to Tarik on the drive home, "Mommy wants me to do Ethiopian things with you and Auntie Saba, so if you are going to come and get us, you need to bring us around some *real* Ethiopians."

Yabsira, meanwhile, lost his ability to speak Amharic.

"I try to speak Ethiopia," he said. "But when I open my mouth, America comes out."

There was a birthday party for Mekdes two months after she'd landed in Atlanta. From then on, whenever someone asked, "How do you like America, Mekdes?" she proudly answered in English, "Mekdes like America. America make Mekdes *six*."

At dinner one night, Ryan said, "Mekdes stopped me on my way out to work this morning. She said, 'Oh, Daddy, you do so much for us. I have something for you. Here, take this. It's for you.'

"She handed me a dollar."

Stella Jones, Mikki's mother, cried, "She did me the same way. A few days ago, she came in my room, said, 'Here, Granny. Get yourself something.' She gave me fifty cents."

Yabsira was not as easy: he threw tantrums constantly. Several times a day, when opposed to the way things were going—obliged to get dressed when he didn't want to get dressed, obliged to brush his teeth when he didn't want to brush his teeth—he fell to the ground in a rage, took off his shoes and socks, and threw them. While Yabsira screamed, Mekdes ran back and forth in a panic. In

Amharic, she begged Yabsira to behave; in English, she asked Mikki and Ryan, "No yell Yabsira."

"I know people wonder, 'How could this orphan from a poverty-stricken country be *spoiled*?'" Ryan said to Mikki. "This kid is *spoiled.*"

When Yabsira wanted to hurt Mekdes, he came and kicked the wall of her beautiful room, and she wept. But she didn't want him punished.

"She has her hands full," Mikki said to Ryan one night. "I told them to clean their rooms today. She got to work, Yabsira dawdled. I yelled, 'Yabbie, get to work!' and then I hear him yell, 'Mekdes!' And Mekdes ran over and cleaned his room for him."

Finally, about two months after the children's arrival, Mikki and Ryan heard a new type of exchange. Yabsira had gone into Mekdes's room to grab something of hers; she ordered him out; he refused to leave.

"No, Yabsira," she yelled. "This is mine and you get out of my room!" followed by the slam of her door.

"I *think*," said Ryan, "that she just got finished being his mother."

Still, Mekdes got up in the night for Yabsira. He required her to stand guard against the hyenas while he went to the bathroom. Hyenas don't live in Addis Ababa, but they roam the Ethiopian countryside and are a source of fear in song and folklore for children. Every night, Mekdes stood yawning and rubbing her eyes in the dark hall outside the bathroom, keeping her brother safe from the Snellville hyenas.

Mikki found her there one night and offered to be the lookout instead. When Mekdes said yes and went back to bed, it struck Mikki that Mekdes had come to trust her new parents to keep Yabsira safe.

The little boy began to behave, and he began to believe what everyone was telling him: that there are no hyenas in America. Then Mekdes's dance recital delivered a bit of bad news. The song warned, "Dig a tunnel before the hyena comes." Before the tap dancers could execute a kick-ball change, Yabsira was gone.

Mekdes keeps alive the memory of her first parents and drills her brother on the family history.

"Who was our mother?" she demands.

"Mulu!" she yells if he hesitates.

"What was our father's name?"

"Asnake," says Yabsira.

"Good," says Mekdes.

While still in the apartment in Addis Ababa, Mekdes drew six stick figures and labeled them: Mekdes, Yabsira, Mommy, Daddy, Mulu, Asnake. She asked her parents to tape them to the bedroom wall.

"Mommy, did Granny get you out of her stomach or out of Ethiopia?" she asked one day.

On another day, she began a story and stopped: "When I was with my mo—I mean Mulu."

"Baby, you can say Momma," Mikki said.

"Do *you* like Mulu, Mommy?"

"I love Mulu!" said Mikki, and Mekdes embraced her.

Mekdes soon told her mother about the day her aunts took her to Haregewoin's house. "Yabsira cry a little. I am scream."

"Why did you cry, baby?" asked Mikki.

"I don't know *this* Ethiopia. I want *my* Ethiopia with *Goshay* [Grandfather] and Fasika. I don't want new Ethiopia."

"You were sad," said Mikki.

"No hope, Mommy. I have *no hope*."

"Oh, honey . . ."

"Because no one told me, Mommy."

"Told you what?"

"That you are here in America. I will not feel so sad if I know you are here."

"Yeah, I was here getting ready, getting your rooms ready. I was here, me and your daddy, waiting and getting ready."

"I am cry because I don't know you will coming."

Of course, for most of Africa's ten million, fifteen million, twenty million orphans, no one is getting a room ready. No one will come.

53

INSIDE A WEATHER-BEATEN 1880s farmhouse in rural Michigan, a little boy is bouncing in his socks on a tired sofa. He has an enormous toothless grin (his top front teeth were rotten and had to be removed). The boy is the size of a three-year-old, and he looks and acts like a three-year-old, and everyone outside his family believes him to be about three. He may be five, or even older. But the question of his age is the furthest thing from his mind.

Outside the grimy storm windows, the midwinter fields are nearly colorless: the bright summer greens and golds of hay, corn, and soybeans have faded to lusterless straw, and the sloughs of old snow in the gullies beside the state route are spattered with gravel, road salt, and muddy water. This is the sloppiest type of Northern winter day— the diamond ice on the ponds and streams has gotten mushy and opaque; the gutters and rooftops are dripping. Bare tree branches knock about in the damp wind with a hollow sound.

But inside the peeling old farmhouse, the jumping boy has plenty to feel excited about: Mommy has said it's nearly time for his afternoon cartoon, *SpongeBob*, which he will watch with his five-year-old sister, Violet (who was adopted from China as a baby, though the boy doesn't know that); Mommy is making them a snack of juice, cheddar cheese, and crackers; he and Violet will sit together at the child-size wooden table and chairs and watch the show. His mother reminds him that the crackers are *ovals*, that the juice cup is *yellow*, that his paper napkin is a *square*. His two big brothers, Dawson, twelve, and Tim, fifteen (who are the biological sons of his parents, though the boy doesn't know that either), have promised to take him later this afternoon to play basketball in their friend's driveway. One of the big brothers might swing him by the arms as they cross the fields, since the little boy's snow boots tend to get stuck in the cold mud. His brothers will let him roll and bounce the basketball on the driveway, and they will lift him so high in the air he will feel as if he is flying under the tattered gray sky; the huge black metal hoop will loom in front of him; using all his strength, he'll raise and tip the fat ball up and over and through the net, and the big boys will cheer and give him "high fives."

Ababu, once starving due to lactose intolerance, loves the high fives. Ababu likes the high fives almost as much as he likes gripping the giant ball and flying in Tim's hands toward the hoop.

And best of all, greatest of all, the daily miracle will occur that will send the boy into paroxysms of screams and gymnastics and make the goofy, toothless grin so huge it will push his eyes into little slits: Daddy will come home from work! Daddy comes home from work every day (Dave Armistead, who wears a light brown beard and a single silver hoop earring, a button-down shirt and khaki slacks, teaches history and social studies at the high school in Williamston). The moment Ababu hears the truck in the driveway, the ice-and-salt-encrusted crunch of leather field boots on the back deck, he shoots into the kitchen even if *SpongeBob* is still on TV and he dances a square dance, a fox-trot, a tap dance, he grabs his crotch and dances and leaps his joy that Daddy—*yes, Daddy!*—Daddy has come home again.

From the moment Dave ducks into the chilly wooden rooms—the target of a screeching human missile—until Ababu's neck-lock is unlaced at bedtime, Ababu is on him, mashing his face into Dave's neck, kissing him, patting his beard. If not on him, then beside him, with a little hand somewhere on Dave's sleeve or shoulder or pants leg, or trotting beside him with his arms up, requesting, "Carry you? Carry you?"

Ababu loves his new mother and siblings; he's comfortable with his day-care teacher and his preschool teacher; he's fond of *SpongeBob* and his cheese and crackers and the bedroom he shares with Violet (the twin mattresses are thick with wool blankets and populated by ancient wobbly-necked stuffed animals, while barefoot Barbie dolls in ball gowns mill around near the closet, on their tiptoes). But Dave Armistead is the love of his life. When Dave comes home, there should be the smash of cymbals, the shout of trumpets, Mendelssohn's "Wedding March" or Beethoven's "Ode to Joy." There is no happier boy on earth than Ababu Armistead when Daddy comes home from work.

Dave loves him, too, now, and has no regrets; but, in the early months, Dave ruefully said to his wife, "This is less like an adoption and more like I've invited a stalker into my life."

On January 1, 2003, HIV-negative Ababu was transferred from Haregewoin's compound to the foster home run by Americans for African Adoptions (AFAA), with a home office in Indianapolis, Indiana. "I put him on the floor to see if he paid attention to his new surroundings," AFAA director Cheryl Carter-Schotts noted in his file. "I put a toy in his hands and he seemed to marvel at it, turning it around again and again. I wanted to see what type of strength he had, so I tried to take the toy away from him and he held on to it very strongly. I feel confident that he will make it."

A few weeks later, she wrote in his file, "Ababu is doing beautifully. He runs around, plays in the yard, rides the little riding toys, climbs out of his crib, and is a delightful little boy."

Susan Bennett-Armistead (a big woman, solid and strong, with a short crop of prematurely gray hair) is the program supervisor for Michigan State University's Child Development labs and has nearly completed her doctorate on literacy in young children; she is frank-talking, well-read, and widely published. Dave Armistead, in addition to teaching high school, is midway through his doctorate in education. Both forty-two, they grew up nearby; they were high school sweet-hearts who married in 1985. A few years ago, though stretched thin and having no biological success, they wanted a third child. In 1999, they applied to adopt a baby girl from China. Their old farmhouse didn't have the airy foyers and kitchens, the bathrooms with skylights, the wraparound decks of the mini-mansions closer to town in which many of their students lived; but every kind of puzzle and learning toy was stored in plastic containers, and all of children's classic literature stood in the old bookcases. It was a cozy home for children—Tim and Dawson were bright and treasured—and the couple were approved by a social worker for adoption.

To raise the needed money, Dave Armistead moonlighted as a pizza deliveryman. A big order was called in from his own high school one night. Twenty or thirty of his students had gathered in the gym. They cheered when Mr. Armistead stepped in with their pizzas and they presented him with a $700 tip—money they'd raised to help with his adoption.

Violet was a dainty child, a delicate presence in the majority-male household. From the typical orphanage delays, Violet caught up to her age level developmentally and cognitively, then surpassed it, under the doting supervision of the child development expert who happened to be her mother.

The Bennett-Armisteads felt they had one more child in them. Again they raised money; this time they applied to the Indianapolis home office of Americans for African Adoptions which ran a foster home in Addis Ababa. Then, they waited.

They waited most of a year for a referral. They'd requested a child under the age of two, which hadn't seemed such a tall order at the time.

"Twelve million orphans?" Dave ranted one night in the kitchen. "And they can't find one child for us under the age of two?" (Dave, an easygoing and soft-spoken man, rants like a soft-spoken man trying to raise his voice.)

In June 2004, they learned by e-mail from Cheryl Carter-Schotts that a boy of two and a half had become available for adoption. She frankly told them that Ababu had been offered to another couple, but that the first couple had declined him after studying his profile and medical report: they were concerned about the long-term implications of malnutrition.

"Where did they think he was coming from? *Connecticut?*" asked Dave.

But there *are* long-term, devastating consequences of malnutrition. Children can be irreversibly damaged by malnutrition in infancy and early childhood, their cognitive and physical growth arrested. The World Bank recently reported that malnutrition is stunting the development of more than one hundred million poor children around the world. Susan Bennett-Armistead knew better than most prospective parents the kind of issues malnutrition could present.

But she had hated the part of adoption in which a prospective parent is asked to choose which medical challenges are acceptable in a child and which are not. Every time she checked no on the questionnaire, she thought fondly of one of her own students. When she checked no for Down syndrome, a particular well-loved little face of one of her students came to mind. Besides, those checklists lacked all nuance. She knew that "cleft lip, cleft palate" were relatively easily addressed medical issues in America; she also knew that many cultures shun children born with such features, putting those children at risk for developmental delay and psychological damage, which would require more complex solutions than plastic surgery.

"Let's not go crazy trying to overthink this," Dave said. "There are plenty of unknowns when you give birth to a child, too."

And Susan agreed, with the codicil: "We'd better plan on the fact that there's been some cognitive impairment."

The couple said yes to AFAA's referral of Ababu, without ever seeing a photograph of him.

Ababu was stiff with terror, and silent, when he was carried off the plane, by an AFAA escort, into Washington Dulles airport on March 14, 2005. The Bennett-Armistead family had made a jolly car-singing, nine-hour, 572-mile trip to Washington, D.C., to pick him up, eager for the enlarged family fun to begin.

"He looks like a little owl," said Dave, "with those huge, round eyes."

To the children he looked like E.T., with an enormous head and spindly body. He walked like E.T., too, tilting and swaying deeply on underdeveloped legs on the airport carpeting.

On the long drive home, everyone noticed that tiny, mute Ababu, strapped into a car seat, was looking out his window and weeping. There was no sound, but tears poured from his sad eyes. If someone offered him a toy or a snack, it startled him, and his lips turned down, and the profuse, silent crying increased. They rode beside him through all the strange cities and landscapes, knowing that he must feel completely alone in the world. The jocular road trip turned melancholy.

More than one of the family members began to wonder, on the long highways across Pennsylvania and Ohio, "What have we done?"

Which question could be subdivided into "What have we done to him?" and "What have we done to our family?"

"He acts like an eighteen-month-old," Dave said to Susan a few days later. "Okay, so he's a two and a half, acting like eighteen months, that's not so bad, right? That's not unbridgeable. We'll close that gap easily."

She, pondering, withheld comment.

Dave had arranged to take a six-week parental leave from school when Ababu arrived; he would return to work for the last six weeks of the semester, then stay home with the children the rest of the summer. From that first Monday morning, his life altered dramatically, from popular history teacher to stay-at-home dad. He'd imagined that, in this leisure period (because how hard could it be to watch one small boy compared to the hours he spent in classrooms with thirty teenagers?), he'd catch up on his own academic work, devise new lesson plans, *read*. But the disturbed, bald, frantic boy consumed him.

By the end of his first week in America, Ababu recognized—out of the extraplanetary landscape of fields, paved streets, huge brilliantly lit stores, and weirdly white and strange-talking people—only Dave. Dave was his link to food, to water, to warmth, to dry clothes, to the outdoors, to the indoors. In Dave's arm, he drank his cup of milk (he was no longer lactose-intolerant), he was carried from one room to another and laid on a towel for a diaper change, he was bathed in warm water and given time to splash with bathtub toys. His existential fall through space and time, across the Atlantic Ocean, across time zones and continents and the diversity of human races, came to a halt with solid Dave Armistead, and Ababu was not going to let go.

Among his first sounds he emitted was a name for Dave: *Abada*, a word of his own coinage, a halfway point between the Amharic *abat* and the American *daddy*. (He'd never had an *abat* of his own, had barely known adult males in Ethiopia.)

He began each morning by reaching out his arms for Dave and only reluctantly let go, with grumbled, unhappy noises, twelve hours later when Dave tried to extricate himself for Ababu's bedtime. Then Ababu wanted Dave to stay nearby as he fell asleep.

"He's more infant than child," Dave told Susan at night. "When I try to put him down, his reactions are *extreme*."

"I'm completely exhausted," said Dave in his second week home. "I don't know if I can do this. He weighs thirty pounds. He's on me the *entire day*."

"He is *strong*, and wiry, he is *not* fragile," said Dave on another night. "He was throwing a tantrum in the dining room this afternoon and I tried to lift him and he held on to the heavy wooden chair and carried it out of the room with him."

Their growing suspicion that the needy and tiny boy, who'd lost whatever toilet training he'd had, was not two years old but five, or five and a half, the same age as ladylike and precocious Violet, was alarming.

"Ababu is isolating words for meaning," said Susan one day. He was now saying things like "C'mere" and "Up" and "Watch me."

"That's good, right?" asked Dave.

"It's good, but . . . it's not a two-year-old skill. It's the skill of an older child learning a second language. He doesn't mistake 'Ababu-doyouwantaglassofmilk?' for either a stream of nonsense syllables or for a single word. He quickly turns it around to say, 'Want milk.' He's got the concept of words, that things have names, that a string of sound coming from someone's mouth has a specific meaning."

"What does that tell us?" asked Dave.

"It tells us that this is not his first language. It tells us that he mastered enough of a first language to grasp the fundamentals of speech. It tells us that he's not a two-year-old trying to learn language for the first time."

The family drove one night, that first month, to a children's band concert in Ann Arbor.

"Look at Ababu," Susan whispered to Dave. Ababu sat between them.

"He's enjoying the music!" said Dave. Ababu was swaying with the music and clapping.

"Look how he's clapping."

"What?"

Ababu was clapping on the off beat. "He's syncopating," said Susan. Syncopation picks out the weaker beats, the almost unheard beats in a musical measure.

"That's nice," said Dave.

"A two-year-old cannot do that. You have to be five to do that."

Together they watched him. "I'm thinking," said Susan, "this is *not* what two-and-a-half looks like."

Although spring in Michigan usually signals the *end* of cabin fever, Dave's was just starting. He felt himself a prisoner in his own house, a prisoner of the demanding, fit-throwing, clinging boy.

He tried to follow Susan's advice to "just wait and see," but—in the endless hours of every day, walking the endless small circles inside the cramped house with Ababu in his arms or riding on his back—he couldn't help but wonder. "How bad is his cognitive impairment? Is there mental illness, too? Is this autism? Have we adopted a child with autism spectrum disorder?"

One day, Dave left him for a few hours at Violet's old day-care provider, but Ababu roared his outrage; he went berserk with panic and grief; he would not be held or comforted; diarrhea poured into his diaper, but he let no one near him to change him. He screamed himself hoarse for most of three hours, occasionally rolling on the floor, stinking up the colorful little room with all the bright nursery-rhyme murals on the yellow walls, until Dave returned. Ababu flew across the room into Dave's arms, and through his down jacket, Dave could feel Ababu's pounding heart. It took Ababu a few hours to calm down, to catch his breath. It was a setback in their relationship, after which Ababu couldn't sit at the dining room table if Dave stepped into the kitchen to toss a bowl of noodles into the microwave; Ababu had to go with him. For days, Ababu looked at Dave with reproachful eyes.

"How delayed *is* he?" Dave asked Susan, his own eyes reproachful now.

"It's so hard to judge since we don't know how old he is. The birth certificate they gave us says May thirtieth, 2002, but it's just not possible. And I need language to do most of the cognitive testing and he doesn't have language. Did he even speak Amharic?"

"You know, he stands around all day sticking his hands into his diapers, into his *poopy* diapers," Dave reported one night. "The smell will knock you back, and he gets it all over him, all over his hands and his clothes. I had to bathe him three times today."

On another night he said, "There is something *seriously* wrong with him."

"We don't know that yet," said Susan.

But Dave was reeling into a depression. By whose slip of a pen on what paperwork, by what strange spin of the globe, had this orphan of Addis Ababa landed in Dave Armistead's kitchen? "I love teaching," he was thinking, as he staggered around the house or the backyard with Ababu's stranglehold on him. "I love history; I love teaching high school history. I traded *that* for *this*?"

Dave toppled facedown on his bed at night. The family went into a kind of lockdown. They kept friends and family members at bay—

Ababu was too unpredictable and too overwhelmed to risk piling on more stimuli. Susan kept up a jolly patter in the evening, as if everything were normal, but nothing felt normal. They were in survival mode.

Dave's extended family seemed content to remain aloof. An African adoption had not struck them as a rational plan. Some of Dave's relatives complained they couldn't even pronounce *Ababu*.

On the phone one night, Susan heard Dave, exasperated, say to his mother, "Can you pronounce *banana*? It's like that. Where's the problem?"

A popular metaphor in adoption literature compares a family system to a mobile. The tying-on of an additional element to a delicate, hanging work of art requires an adjustment of all the parts. To add even a newborn baby (by birth or adoption) to a family throws off the balance. To add an older child from a distant country, who may have suffered loss and trauma, has a dramatic effect on the metaphorical wires and strings. It can be a long time before the family mobile finds its lightness and balance again.

While everything is still tangled and awry, it can feel as if the adoption were a mistake, as if the family won't recover. Susan and Dave privately wondered, "What were we *thinking*?" but neither went so far as to say aloud to the other, "This was a mistake." Susan forbade herself to perform a negative professional assessment of Ababu; at this moment, she needed to be a mother and wife, not a child development expert. And Dave was relieved by Susan's refusal to pronounce the big words, the grim prediction of a difficult journey for the rest of their lives.

"The medical perspective is interested in determining the child's chronological age; of course we can make an educated guess by studying his teeth and bones; but I'm more interested in looking at the kid in front of me," she thought. "I'm not prepared to make a prognosis. Some cognitive impairment can result in long-term disability; I'm not ready to say that yet for Ababu."

To Dave she said, "I am not at the place where I am worried. I can provide him with the help he needs without sticking him with a label."

Susan took Ababu for the last six weeks of Dave's semester, but Dave knew what awaited him at home every day and what awaited him in the long summer lying ahead, and what awaited him in the *years* ahead, and he was not sure he had the strength for it.

Susan pointed out the progress *she* was already seeing, the changes in Ababu. For example, Tim and Dawson had been afraid to play with Ababu at first; he looked too unsteady and fragile and his swaying walk scared them. But then neighbors donated their old trampoline to the family and Ababu—first scared to climb up—soon understood the fun of it and spent hours jumping every day. His legs grew strong; his walk became normal; and tumbling play with his big brothers became a possibility. Soon there was almost nothing he liked better (other than sitting on Dave) than rolling on the floor or beds or trampoline in wrestling play with Tim and Dawson.

He learned to take turns with Violet, rather than grabbing her toys. He learned to be seated and stay seated for a meal, rather than grabbing food and running with it. His vocabulary increased.

One day he said to Dave, "I mad," and he scowled to illustrate his point. It startled Dave and touched him: Ababu had just expressed his feelings in words rather than pitching a yowling, flailing fit. Dave realized he hadn't seen a tantrum for a week. There was a real person inside there, he suddenly felt; there was a little mind starting to wake up.

Every day, little by little, Ababu matured. He grew into the family. He grasped its rhythms, and what was funny, and what was allowed, and what was forbidden. He got the timing of breakfast, and day care; of dinner, and bedtime. In the car, you climb into your car seat and wait for someone to buckle it. In the grocery, you sit in the cart and you keep your hands to yourself. In the parking lot, you hold Mommy's or Daddy's hand. Nobody enjoys seeing you throw a tantrum and you won't get your way, so you might as well cut it short. You're not allowed to go into Tim and Dawson's room and push the buttons on their electronic stuff unless they invite you. Violet does not appreciate your popping the heads off her Barbie dolls. Daddy would prefer you not to investigate your diaper status manually.

Susan's mother, Janice Bennett, had hesitated to visit. She gave the family a few weeks to begin to bond without outside interference; but she also feared she'd feel no warmth for the little stranger, that she would not find the love for him she felt for Tim, Dawson, Violet, and her other grandchildren. She had tried tactfully, but in vain, to caution her *extremely* well-educated and *obviously* expert-in-these-matters daughter. "You're going to bring an African child into this lily-white world? Do you think people will accept him?"

Now Susan invited her mother to meet her newest grandson. Janice Bennett crept down the hall anxiously, holding aloft a new play outfit she'd bought, half as a peace offering and half to ward off whatever was coming her way. She timidly opened the door into Violet and Ababu's bedroom. Ababu jumped to his feet and ran to her with his arms wide-open, smiling his huge toothless smile. He ran all the way into her arms. She was enchanted.

A few days later, Janice Bennett rode in the car with Susan to take Ababu to a doctor's appointment. Ababu called, "Ghee!" from his car seat. He was calling his grandmother. When she turned around, their eyes met.

"You know, we connected," she told her son-in-law that night, marveling. "We really connected."

Now when Janice Bennett visits, *she* steps in with arms wide-open and a huge smile, calling, "Where's my boy?"

"If Ababu acted like an eighteen-month-old when he arrived, I'd say he's acting more like a three-year-old now, wouldn't you?" asked Dave one night. "In just six months. Isn't that pretty amazing progress?"

Susan had to agree that it was.

"He's changing and maturing so fast, it's like you can *watch* it happening," said Dave.

"He's got one hundred expressive words now," says Susan. "Maybe a thousand receptive words."

Sometimes, they noticed, Ababu grew very still and looked off into the middle distance, as if remembering.

Was he trying to match the two unmatchable halves of his life, to figure out how he got from *there* (motherless, wet, and hungry) to *here* (in flannel pajamas and fuzzy socks, getting tucked into bed in preparation for a bedtime story)?

He's a beautiful child now, with soft curls and thick eyelashes, bright, happy eyes and gigantic smile. In his blue-jean overalls, yellow boots, red parka, and blue cap with fuzzy earflaps, there's no cuter boy in all of Michigan.

"He may *not* have 'special needs,'" said Dave one night. "Let's just say, he has 'unique needs.'"

Ababu *is* unique. Not many children get to travel the journey from starving African orphan on the brink of death, to the well-fed, well-loved child of a pair of teacher parents who ask, in high voices, "Do you want your apple juice in the *pink* cup or the *green* cup, Ababu?" How could there be a prognosis when few have walked this road before?

Recently Dave told Susan, "I don't really worry anymore. If it's true you pick up twenty IQ points from a good home, and he's got at least eighty, we'll do fine. I really think all his cylinders are clicking."

Whatever physical and cognitive challenges lie ahead for Ababu Armistead, one thing is clear: what he has in abundance is the capacity to love. Love was the only thing his first mother and great-grand-mother could afford to give him; he learned more about love from Haregewoin; and he loves Dave, Susan, Tim, Dawson, and Violet with all his heart.

"Are you going to change his name?" many people ask them.

"No," Susan tells them. "He wasn't a baby, like Violet, when he arrived—he knew his name. His birth mother gave him that name and we respect that. His name is the only thing he brought with him. Besides, it's him; it's who he is: he's Ababu."

54

E VEN AFTER DARK in Phoenix, Arizona, midsummer heat roasts the yellow stubble in the yards, the pebbled walkways, and the dangerous prongs of the yucca bushes. Desert heat shoulders up against the double-paned windows and closed garage doors. Anything left outside in the subdivision—a coiled hose, a bicycle, a soccer ball—is too hot to touch. Someone must have ordered this heat, by the cubic mile, from the *sun*, and it has been delivered, and now here it sits. It is a third presence, apart from sky and land. From behind shutters and curtains, from air-conditioned rooms, the citizens look out their windows and see it, in its invisible monstrosity, shimmering. Nine o'clock at night, 108 degrees. Outside of town, in the Sonoran Desert, 122 degrees.

Behind a red-roofed house on a little cul-de-sac, there is a small, round swimming pool. Plumes of light rise through the water from underground lamps. A mother sits in a folding chair at the edge of the wet patio, holding a dry towel in her lap. In the tepid water, a barrel-chested, middle-aged father stands waist-deep. From the edge of the pool, a little boy in tropical-print swim trunks catapults into the air, lands a messy cannonball, and sinks like a rock.

In her beach chair, the mother straightens her spine and leans forward slightly, watching closely.

The father—a high school wrestling coach—plunges both hands under the bubbly surface like King Midas digging into a pile of gold and produces the slippery boy.

"I did it! I did it! Daddy, did you see me? Mommy, did you see me?"

"I saw you!" calls the mother. She wears a white, sleeveless top, capri slacks, and gold sandals and has a cascade of long blond curls. Her face and arms are pink and sun-freckled year-round. She is thinking, *Of course I saw you. I can't take my eyes* off *you. I haven't looked at anything other than you since the moment you arrived.*

"Again?" yells the boy, and before the mother can mention bedtime and the father can say, "Enough," he somersaults, disappears into an explosion of bubbles, and is hauled out of the depths again. Both father and son bark in waterlogged laughter. They cling to each other, their hair slicked back, shiny as seals. The mother relaxes.

The two white Americans, Karen and Bill Cheney, found each other after failed first marriages, divorces, and long solitudes. She is a nurse and he is a training coordinator for blood-bank services and a wrestling coach. They met at a Phoenix hospital. She was ebullient and pretty and full of laughter; he was good-hearted and steady. They married in 1994 when she was thirty and he was thirty-three. Bill's son from his first marriage grew to be a fine young man; he now attends the Naval Academy. Karen and Bill lived together quietly until this unlikely marvelous Ethiopian boy cannonballed into their life.

The man piggybacks the three-year-old up the pool steps and hands him off; the mother wraps him like an infant in the fluffy towel and runs with him upstairs for a quick bath. She will give his hair a good rubdown; she will spread baby oil on his solid chest and round arms and behind his little sticking-out ears; she will button him into short-sleeved pajamas; and she will sit beside him as he falls asleep.

The boy's name is William Mintesinot Eskender Cheney. Minty was the first boy I saw fetched from the street by Haregewoin.

In 2003, Karen was called to the pediatric intensive care unit and assigned the worst case of her life: Samuail, a fourteen-month-old boy, had been dipped into boiling water by a deranged, angry mother. It was punishment, she later explained, for his gorging food and then throwing up on her new carpet. He was the youngest of her seven children.

His legs look like boiled chicken, Karen saw. In addition to the third-degree burns on his feet and legs, there were human bite marks, multiple bruises, handprints, and slap marks. *Even worse than the marks of physical abuse is the fact that he has completely given up. He has decided not to live. He responds to nothing.*

The toddler reacted only when his mother visited, prior to her arrest: he vibrated, in fear of her.

Karen stayed after hours to sit with Samuail; she spoon-fed him; she introduced Bill to him. The child timidly began to open toward her, though he panicked every time his mother was allowed into the hospital room. Finally, the woman was arrested. Karen testified at the criminal trial. She came home one night and bitterly reported, "She was sentenced to nine months, with time off to allow her to continue giving piano lessons."

Bill and Karen Cheney asked to be considered foster parents for the toddler when he was released from the hospital. They wanted to adopt him, following termination of parental rights, and the boy's social worker encouraged their application.

The judge, in the name of "family unification," delivered Samuail back to his family. The maternal aunt was awarded custody.

The Cheneys felt frightened for the boy and personally devastated.

When they came in from court after losing Samuail, Bill said, "No more. Don't ever ask me to do that again."

I had thought God was leading me to adopt this boy, Karen thought. *I can't trust God again.*

In time she thought, *I got something wrong, I misunderstood.*

After more time, she tried to be informed by the story of Moses, who said to God, *You don't want me.*

And God said, *I do.*

"I think maybe there's another child out there for us," she said cautiously to Bill.

He said, "No way."

She looked into international adoption anyway. She found Americans for African Adoptions (AFAA), based in Indianapolis, which arranged adoptions from Ethiopia. Again she broached the subject with Bill.

He said, "I can't go through that again."

"It would be different this time," she said. "The child would be ours. No one could take him away from us. Please, just think about it."

He shook his head.

Privately he brooded about his age: *Become a father again at forty-four? It's not going to happen.*

At church, he began to notice adopted children. He asked fellow congregants how old they'd been when adopting their children, and some said, "In my forties."

"Here's the thing," Bill said to Karen one morning. "I think I'm changing my mind."

They applied to AFAA to adopt a toddler boy. Like Samuail.

A few months later, Cheryl Carter-Schotts, AFAA director, phoned the Cheneys and said, "We have a little boy, but he's older than what you're looking for. He's three or four." He was an orphan, his parents had died of AIDS, his physical history was good, he could scribble with a crayon.

They said yes.

They barely had time to rejoice, to study the photos, to tell their friends and family ("A black boy?" a few asked in concern), and to begin to prepare a child's bedroom, when they got weird news: Mintesinot's father, Eskender, was still alive. He was living on the streets, dying of AIDS.

Suddenly the Cheneys weren't sure that this boy would be theirs, either. He wasn't an orphan. *Was I wrong again?*

It took them one night to decide. They understood their decision could result in their son being restored to his father, instead of being given to them. They knew that assuming lifelong treatment for a man living with HIV/AIDS would drain from them the resources required to complete an adoption. But it felt like the right thing to do.

The Cheneys e-mailed AFAA: "We would like to pay for the medical care and monthly HIV drugs for Mintesinot's father."

Another phone call came from Cheryl Carter-Schotts: it was too late. Eskender was dead.

✳   ✳   ✳

In March 2005, accompanied by an AFAA escort, Mintesinot boarded the long flights from Addis to Cairo to Frankfurt to Los Angeles. He had been given photographs of his new parents and he recognized the Cheneys the moment he saw them in the L.A. airport: Mommy. Daddy. At his new house in Phoenix, there was so much to examine: the hose in the front yard, and how you could turn a knob and make water come out of it. That was a grand thing. Just as grand, but in a different way, was the hairdryer plugged into the upstairs bathroom wall. With the slide of a button, hot air blew out the nozzle and warmed his face. He laughed hard at this. (*In this climate?* he should have wondered. *They need an electronic device to produce hot air in Phoenix?*) With the push of a button on a giant TV, a cartoon of Pocahontas sprang into action. If his dad picked him up high, he could push a button to make the big garage door rumble and ascend.

He gathered his new clothes in his arms and kissed them. Ditto his new shoes; each shoe got a kiss. When dressed in a new outfit—a bright-striped T-shirt and short jean overalls—he ran to the full-length mirror in his parents' bedroom and kissed his image. There was a downstairs closet full of toys—a wagon of wooden blocks, magnetic ABCs, Mickey Mouse puzzles—and he was allowed to open the door of the toy closet whenever he liked, except for bedtime. Which was when he wanted to open it the most.

He thought toilet paper was a funny idea.

He loved wristwatches. "Minty's!"

"No, Minty, that's Mommy's watch."

"Minty's!"

"Take that back up to Mommy's room."

"No!" he cried. "Minty's." But he stomped upstairs to return the watch.

He returned with a fancier one. "Minty's?"

His parents bought him a miniature wheeled suitcase for his first trip to Disney World. He carried it on his head through the airport, African-style.

One night, six weeks after Mintesinot's arrival, Karen said to Bill, "I did so much preparing for the worst possible transition. I read up on attachment disorders, post-traumatic stress disorder, grief in children. I forgot to think about a normal kid. What am I supposed to do now?"

"He could still bust out," said Bill. Bill spent his afternoons in the high school gym with every kind of teenage boy.

Karen nevertheless checked out library books on how to discipline a normal middle-class American child. She learned about counting to three after giving an instruction and moving to install a gentle consequence, such as time-out, if the child failed to comply by the count of three.

"I almost never get past two," she complained to Bill at bedtime.

"Just wait. Give him time. We haven't seen the worst of it."

Three months after arrival, Minty's behavior was improving rather than disintegrating.

"Well?" she asked one night.

"That's it," said Bill. "This is just who he is."

"He's a wonderful little boy!" she cried.

"He's amazing."

"He's left-handed!" she marveled.

"He's incredibly athletic. He can kick a ball, throw a ball . . ."

"He's going to be a wrestler!" she said.

"Big-time. Have you seen those shoulders?"

At night in the den, Minty did crunches and sit-ups and learned wrestling moves from his father.

"Bill? Minty took down two little girls at church this morning," said Karen one Sunday afternoon.

"I know!" said Bill. "Did you see his technique?"

"Bill!"

"Okay, I'll talk to him about it . . . But did you see his technique?"

They drove Minty to a petting zoo one day, and the sight of goats excited him. "Look!" he yelled. "Remember in Ethiopia? We go Ethiopia?"

"Yes, we'll go one day, when you're a little bigger," they promised.

"Go and come right back?"

"Yes, we'll go and come right back."

On another day, he told Karen, "My mom carries me on her back."

"How did you use the bathroom?" she asked. "Did you go in the street?"

"No, Mommy," he chided her.

"Well?"

As if it ought to be obvious, he replied, "In mine pants."

Karen reclined on the sofa one afternoon and Minty bounded over to ask, "Mommy, lay down you?"

"Sure!"

He climbed on top of her and laid his head on her chest.

"Is this how you lay with *Abi* and *Enat*?" asked Karen.

With a wistful smile, he said yes.

"On your mother or on your dad?"

Still smiling, he said, *"Enat."*

"Were you there when *Enat* died?" Karen asked the three-year-old.

He grew somber; he nodded.

"What did *Enat* say?"

"Enat ouch, hurt, cry," said Minty.

The Cheneys built a fire in the backyard one winter afternoon and Minty was thrilled. "Did you have fires in Ethiopia, Minty?" they asked.

"Yes," he said with a faraway look, growing still. "My dad made fires."

"Did he make fires to keep you and your Ethiopian mommy warm?"

Minty said yes again, with the same distant smile.

Later that night, Bill took Minty by the hand and they headed down the dark street and along the canal in search of a lost baseball. Minty ran ahead and Bill called him back, to hold hands.

"We need to hold hands so no one will take us, Daddy?" asked Minty, running back.

"My heart fell," Bill told Karen later. "I wondered if he was thinking about his last day with Eskender."

He told the boy, "No one will ever take us, Minty, but it's still a good idea to hold hands."

Before their son's arrival, the Cheneys had received a photograph of Eskender and Mintesinot standing together near their small sidewalk pen of tin and rags. Karen framed the picture and placed it on the shelf beside Minty's bed, awaiting the boy's arrival.

Mintesinot lived in America with his new parents for two months—hopping past the photograph every night and every morning—before he saw it. Suddenly, one night, his mouth opened wide in surprise and happiness. "*Abi!* My dad!" he cried in a high voice. He picked up the photograph, studied the image of the man closely, then kissed it.

55

I N HAREGEWOIN'S ROOM on a fine Monday morning in February 2006, she sat on her bed with her important papers spread around her, her sandaled feet flat and apart on the cement floor. The house phone stood on a kitchen chair beside her; the cell phone trilled from the pocket of her housedress.

"Allo? Abet?" She listened closely, then her eyes crinkled in laughter; she leaned back helplessly chuckling.

On the floor at her feet sat three preschool-age girls, too little to stampede through the gates every morning with all the schoolchildren in their V-necked, maroon sweaters. The threesome sat quietly on the sunny floor and watched her. They watched like children watching a morning educational-television show like *Mister Rogers' Neighborhood* or *Sesame Street.* They watched her adoringly. They watched the phone slip out of her pocket and flip open; they watched it snap shut and return to the pocket; they watched her jot with a pencil in a notebook. With their legs crossed, they watched, and they scooted closer. Each felt happy to have a mother again, or—as Haregewoin suggested they call her—a grandmother, *Emama.* Her thick, short hair had grown out gray now and she left it alone. Occasionally she looked at the children over the sheet of paper in her hands, over the top of her reading glasses; a mere look from her caused them to giggle and inch closer.

The papers she read through were letters of support, of clearance, of exoneration, of permission to continue with her work.

The first glimmer of hope had arrived in a letter postmarked January 2, 2006, from the Ministry of Justice.

It read (in official translation):

It is to be recalled that on the basis of information received on your organization, a committee that has been formed by our organization is engaged in undertaking investigations into the operational, organizational, child care, and related problems reportedly associated to your organization. As indicated by the preliminary reports of the investigation, we understand that your organization has some problems but we found that these problems are not serious enough to cause closure of your organization.

Thus you are hereby advised to take note that it has been determined for you to keep operating under provisional terms, subject to your responsibility to avoid unnecessary inconveniences on the orphaned children under your custody, pending the completion of the investigation underway and issuance of a decision to remedy the case.

In other words, we are not closing you down yet, pending further investigation.

Other promising news trickled in: she heard that when Wasihun (who had moved out) was called into court to testify about the rape, he said, "Nothing really happened. Someone told me to say it."

That may or may not have been the truth, as she now understood; even Wasihun might not recall the literal truth anymore of what happened to him one night sixteen months ago.

Dereje and Zezalem had been adopted to other countries and all reports were positive: both seemed untroubled by past trauma. Their new parents had been advised that they might have been sexually assaulted, but ten months after the adoptions, no one detected evidence of it.

Haregewoin learned that the City Social Affairs Bureau had claimed to be caring for children who were, in fact, Haregewoin's children, for whose upkeep she never received help from the city.

Because of this and other suspicions of possible slip-ups by the City Social Affairs Bureau, the Ministry of Justice intervened in Haregewoin's case. On March 13, 2006, it issued a final decision about her organization. It reads (officially translated):

To The Ministry of Labor and Social Affairs

From The Ministry of Justice, Federal Democratic Republic of Ethiopia

Subject: It concerns the Atetegeb Worku Metasebia Welage Aleba Histanet Merj Mahber [The Atetegeb Worku Memorial Orphans Support Association]

The aforementioned organization has obtained an operational permit from the Ministry of Justice and it is currently operating in Addis Ababa, within the country, and in some regions. The operations carried out in Addis Ababa City are monitored by the Addis Ababa City Social and Civil Affairs Bureau.

However from June 2005 it is transferred to the Ministry of Justice.

Moreover the Ministry of Justice is empowered to register and monitor NGOs operating in Addis Ababa and Dire Dawa Cities, in limited or nonlimited regions, under Article 23/8 of the Proclamation Number 471/98.

Therefore it has taken over the responsibility and it is currently managing the task. Accordingly, we hereby declare that your office can monitor the cases related to the organization in cooperation with the Ministry of Justice.

With regards,

Signed & sealed,

Minister of Justice

Cc:

Senior Minister of Legal & Administrative Affairs

Senior Minister of the Controversial Affairs

Atetegeb Worku now operated directly under the aegis of the Ministry of Justice (MOJ). With the MOJ's permission, Haregewoin continued with her work and had the authority to sign for children's adoptions. The cases of children who were already matched with adoptive parents, who lingered in agency orphanages, began to move forward again through the courts.

In the most unexpected piece of good news, Haregewoin's former son-in-law, Ashiber, with whom Suzie had stayed in touch, finally yielded to Suzie's longtime pleas to let his son, now seven years old, meet Haregewoin.

"If she dies without seeing him, someday when he is grown, he will reproach me," Ashiber said, relenting.

He had raised the boy to believe that an aunt, Ashiber's sister, was his mother. No corrections were made at this time; on the day Suzie was permitted to collect the boy—beautifully dressed in a khaki cargo-pants-and-vest-and-cap set—and drive him to Haregewoin's compound, he did not know that the huge framed photograph of the mother and child was a picture of his late mother and of himself as an infant. But he *was* told that Haregewoin was his grandmother.

He was a shy boy, sweet and withdrawn and silent. Haregewoin drew him close gently and kissed him with enormous love on each cheek, then again, then again, and lifted him up onto the bed beside her so she could beam at him from close by. "Just like his mother," she pronounced. "The image. The image of his mother."

He had lived the life of a coddled and protected only child, raised by servants. He was frightened of the boisterous shenanigans in the paved courtyard and the anarchic soccer and dodgeball. When Haregewoin lured him outside, he sat on the porch step close beside her. If she ran back in to pick up the phone, when she turned around again, he was there in the house.

"He is a *very* smart boy, very smart," she said. "Just like his mother."

She and I and her grandson, and my eighteen-year-old son, Lee, and her oldest foster son, Hailegabriel, went out for pizza one Sunday afternoon. We sat on a patio, under a canvas canopy. Though the grandson was silent, speaking only in whispers, he had opinions. He wanted a Coke. He did want pizza. And he wanted to ride on the chipped plaster horse that sat beside the building. For a coin, it would lurch back and forth to the noise of a churning motor. He was a little old and a little large for such a toy, but he'd never seen one before. He stood facing it for a long time, with his hands in his khaki pockets, until Haregewoin called to him from the patio to ask if he wanted to ride. He nodded. She fished out a coin and he ran to get it. With nervous fingers, the boy inserted the coin and climbed on. He sat on the horse and was jolted back and forth roughly. He didn't smile. He didn't yell. He tugged his cap low on his forehead to keep from losing it and could barely get a grip again. He hung on with grim determination. But when Haregewoin called, "You like it?" he suddenly looked up with his somber brown eyes and lit up and cried, "Yes!"

"He is such a good boy," she said.

"Just like this mother?" I asked, and she laughed.

If she could have bought him a cowboy hat and a cowboy belt and cowboy boots, she would have; if she could have given him a real white stallion and a green pasture in which to gallop, she would have done all that and more.

Every Saturday now, Ashiber's driver drops the boy off at Haregewoin's compound, so he can have a visit with his grandmother.

There was much to be thankful for.

A turning point for the world's poor came with the introduction, by UNAIDS and by the World Health Organization (WHO) under Dr. Lee Jong-wook, of the "3 by 5 Initiative": the goal of having *three* million people in poor and middle-income countries gain access to the lifesaving anti-AIDS drug therapies by *2005*.

The existence of such a target (impossible to think about before generic ARVs became available) galvanized every government and inspired enormous hope. At the highest levels of global health, certain conversations—about whether it was cost-effective to seek treatment for the sick, or better to abandon the sick and focus on prevention instead—were tabled forever. The notion of *universal access* eclipsed all other discussions.

Public health workers in every country reported that, by offering *treatment* now, rather than just bad news, they found that patients' interest in testing, counseling, and prevention grew, while social stigma against them decreased. New strategies evolved for delivering sophisticated ARV treatment in "resource-poor settings," including the training of non–health professionals to deliver certain procedures.

The returns on these experiments were great: people in Africa, it turned out, *could* tell time; people in Africa could tell the blue pills from the pink ones.

The number of people suffering full-blown AIDS with access to combination ARV therapy went from 400,000 in December 2003 to 1.3 million in December 2005. The WHO estimated that expanded access to treatment had saved between 250,000 and 350,000 lives during 2005.

The Global Fund to Fight AIDS, Tuberculosis and Malaria is the single greatest hope for the world's poor. Inaugurated in 2001 by UN Secretary-General Kofi Annan, it channels contributions from the world's affluent governments, companies, and citizens to organizations fighting AIDS, TB, and malaria. In 2002, the Global Fund endorsed the use of generic drugs. But the Global Fund faces a resource shortfall of approximately $1.1 billion for 2006, and $2.6 billion dollars for 2007.

By late 2005, it was clear that the World Health Organization's 3 by 5 plan would fail to achieve its goal of three million people on treatment in resource-poor countries by the end of the year. Dr. Jim Yong Kim, head of the WHO's HIV/AIDS Department, said, "All we can do is apologize. I think we just have to admit we've not done enough and we started way too late." But he said the initiative should not be deemed a failure: "Before 3 by 5, there was not an emphasis on saving lives . . . Many leaders in the world were saying we just have to forget about this generation of people who are infected, we're really thinking about the next generation . . . So something has happened that's extraordinary."

"If 3 by 5 fails," said Stephen Lewis, "as it surely will without the dollars, then there are no excuses left, no rationalizations to hide behind, no murky slanders to justify indifference. There will only be the mass graves of the betrayed."

In 2005, GlaxoSmithKline (formerly Burroughs Wellcome) saw the expiration of its patent on zidovudine (AZT). Generic drugmakers in China, India, and Africa applied to the U.S. Food and Drug Administration with requests to manufacture generic versions and four American generic drugmakers applied, as well. GSK's Retrovir costs $3,893.64 for a year's supply; between 1987 and 2005, Retrovir generated $4 billion in sales. The generic versions cost $105 for a year's supply.

Free ARVs have begun to be administered by the Ethiopian government, with the support of the U.S. President's Emergency Plan for AIDS Relief (PEPFAR); the Global Fund to Combat AIDS, Tuberculosis and Malaria; UNICEF; the World Bank; the Gates Foundation; the William J. Clinton Foundation; the Rockefeller Foundation; and some nongovernmental organizations. Generic ARVs are imported from the Indian company Cipla, and generic manufacturers in Brazil and South Africa are willing to make drugs available, as well. Several Ethiopian pharmaceutical companies have been identified to produce generic antiretrovirals, but most await further investment before they can scale up and begin.

In 2005, former U.S. president Bill Clinton brokered a deal enabling four generic companies, including Cipla, to supply HAART to millions of people in developing countries for roughly $140 per patient a year. Last year Cipla won the approval of the WHO to market its ARVs wherever local governments allowed their sale. Roughly sixty countries now supply Cipla generic drugs to their citizens. And Dr. Hamied of Cipla has offered to share ARV-manufacturing technology free "to state-owned companies in all third world countries."

The greatest stumbling blocks ahead fall again within the realm of the multinational drug companies. Over years of treatment, patients often develop resistance to the "first-line" ARVs, the ones now available as generics. The drug companies have fought hard to preserve their exclusive patents for the "second-line" ARVs, and most of these are currently unaffordable for the poor countries.

By February 2006, according to UNICEF, more than five million children had died in the HIV/AIDS epidemic and 2.3 million children were living with HIV/AIDS.

Eighty-five percent of those children lived and died in sub-Saharan Africa.

Until recently, Ethiopia was without pediatric AIDS drugs, the special triple-cocktail combinations effective in children.

Last year, WWO's Barlow Clinic medical director Dr. Sofia Mengistu Abayneh began treating HIV-positive children under the aegis of World Wide Orphans Foundation (WWO). Dr. Jane Aronson, founder of WWO, opened the Barlow Clinic in 2003 specifically to treat HIV-positive children, most of them orphans. It was an enormous step from a little doctor's office in Manhattan to the streets of Addis Ababa because of the lifelong commitment implied to the children. You can't start a child on a lifesaving regimen in January and then apologize in May, or two years later, because you've run out of funds. If you start a child on ARVs, you better plan for that funding to be in place for a long, long time. By last year, WWO felt confident it could provide medicine and support services for about fifty children for as long as would be required until the Ethiopian government or the outside world shouldered the commitment.

Aronson was thinking, *In future years, the cost of treatments will surely fall even more; someday a cure for AIDS will be invented. Meanwhile, let's save some lives.* With help from the Ethiopian government and from UNICEF, generic pediatric ARVs were imported. The forty children Dr. Sofia began to treat in September 2005 were among the first in the country to receive pediatric triple therapy, out of perhaps a quarter of a million HIV-infected children.

The Ministry of Health and PEPFAR hope to have 5,250 children on pediatric HAART by March 2007. According to Dr. Tadesse Wuhib of CDC-Ethiopia, "Despite these efforts, pediatric interventions continue to lag far behind that of adults."

At AHOPE, Eyob—the little tap-dancing boy, and Ester, swinging her little tush at exercise time—both died before WWO or the Ethiopian government got to them. Amelezud, the lovely girl who loved history books, died just as Barlow Clinic was opening its doors. Happy Kidist is gone; and the father and daughter—Theodros and Betti—I have not been able to find for over a year.

Haregewoin's old friend and ally Zewedu Getachew also died last year of untreated AIDS.

Last fall, Haregewoin took a boy named Yohannes to the Barlow Clinic, fearing it was too late for him. Gaunt and pockmarked, weak and balding, he was five years old and looked like a grim old man; his skull had taken on the death's-head grin of receding, tightening skin. Under his shirt, he was a skeleton. Dr. Sofia started him on ARV treatment and suddenly—almost overnight—he was a round little boy again. At Ethiopian Christmas, January 7, 2006, Yohannes wore traditional white robes and looked strong and rosy-cheeked and handsome. Haregewoin shared with her holiday guests a photo taken of Yohannes three months earlier, when he was near death; they refused to believe it was the same child; they refused to believe such a turnabout was medically possible.

Dr. Rick Hodes, visiting the compound that day, knew it was possible. He hadn't seen it before in Ethiopia, but the miracle had finally arrived.

Recently Yohannes remarked to Haregewoin, "*Emama*, I do not really like it when you go out and I cannot talk to you. Yesterday I needed to call you. Wouldn't you like to get me a little mobile phone of my own, so I can call you if I need you to stop and pick up something for me?"

At AHOPE, dozens of children now take their medicine. Surafel, a twelve-year-old boy, had suffered acutely from stomach cramps, diarrhea, and an itchy rash covering his body. Finally he balked at going to school and wouldn't get up in the morning.

"What's the use?" he asked bitterly.

He knew.

Last September, Surafel was one of the first children in the country to be offered WWO's pediatric HAART, and now he feels fine. He looks handsome, he's a terrific athlete, and he's happy. "My favorite movies are action movies," he told me, "and that's why I want to become a motorcycle rider when I grow up."

Eyob, age eleven (a different Eyob) came reluctantly inside to talk to me at AHOPE, hating to miss the dodgeball game in the yard. Dr. Sofia told me he'd come to AHOPE with severe scalp lesions and severe conjunctivitis and he was alarmingly thin. Like all the children there, he not only suffered horribly from disease, but he suffered alone, his parents long dead. Since September, when she'd begun treating him, Eyob's eyes had cleared up, his scalp had cleared up, and he'd gained weight. "I'm ranked twenty-first in my grade of sixty-five children," he told me. "But I'm going to make top ten."

Adoption is newly possible for HIV-positive Ethiopian children. A few U.S. couples braved the bureaucratic obstacles last year and brought home children they had been sponsoring at a time when adoption was out of the question. Half a dozen AHOPE children have prospective adoptive American families currently pursuing the paper chase for them.

Our eighteen-year-old son, Lee Samuel, volunteered with these children for several months in the spring of 2006. Since most had felt too sick and depressed to play for most of their childhoods, WWO had dispatched Lee to Addis Ababa to *play* with them.

He arrived as the sickest children at AHOPE and in Haregewoin's compound for HIV-positive children reached the fifth month of ARV treatment through the Barlow Clinic. He got confused, at first, about who were the ill children and who were the healthy ones, as all the kids mobbed him with glee, enlisted him in games, and ran him into the dirt. "I worried about the wrong thing," he told me a week into his stay.

"I was afraid I would get attached to children who would be really sick and were going to die. I forgot to worry, 'What if the kids are better athletes than I am?'"

Lee tried to interest Haregewoin's big boys, such as Hailegabriel, Zemedikun, and Daniel, in American baseball; he showed them baseball movies like *Sandlot* on his laptop and pulled out a plastic bat and Wiffle balls. "The point of all this is for the kids to learn a sport in which I can beat them handily," he e-mailed the family. "My already bottomed-out self-esteem can't take any more soccer game debacles. Unfortunately they didn't really take to the baseball movies. When I asked them if they wanted to learn baseball now, all they wanted to know was, 'Why they no play *football?*' and, 'Lee, why baseball players have to rest after running so short?'"

He organized an orphanage soccer league for WWO. Uncertain if the AHOPE boys and girls had the strength to compete against Haregewoin's healthy children and healthy children from other orphanages, he broached the subject with them of dividing the AHOPE players into other teams. "No!" they protested. "We will represent our house!"

They designed uniforms reminiscent of Britain's Arsenal team.

"They're seriously going to win some games," Lee said. "They have the most incredible goalkeeper I've ever seen."

Children continue to arrive at Haregewoin's compound.

From the countryside, a limp and pale child of about three was handed over. Sara has a lovely face and light ringlets, but she is blind and deaf and developmentally delayed. No one knows what to do for her. The caregivers prop her in a plastic infant-seat. She rolls her head back and forth and aimlessly cries and flails; sometimes she falls quiet; sometimes she gives a random smile. A caregiver feeds her like a baby. Haregewoin has called every orphanage and adoption agency in the city to see if anyone is interested in taking the child, if anyone knows how to work with such a child, if a parent may be found somewhere in a foreign country for such a child, but no one wants her. On pretty days, she brings the girl into the courtyard and puts her on a blanket in the sunshine so she can move her limbs. Both her smiles and her whimpers seem unrelated to anything happening around her. She recognizes no one. Still, Haregewoin and the caregivers call her by her name; they bring her outside when the other children come in from school and play in the courtyard, in case some distant impression of joy may reach her.

Zemedikun, 10 years boy, parents died. Kebele *brought him.*
   Betelehem, girl, three years, mother and father died.
   Two sisters, they speak Guragge.
   Tsegaye, boy, four years, from Harar.
   Abele, six and a half years boy. Orphan. Kebele *assigned him.*

In the fall of 2005, as accusations multiplied against Haregewoin, a destitute woman from the neighborhood banged on her gates on a night of wild wind and rainstorms. "Help me, please!" she cried to the guard. "Emergency!"

He admitted her. She ran up the cement steps to the porch of Haregewoin's house; Haregewoin came to her bedroom door.

"I took in a pregnant girl from the streets," said the poor woman. The woman was black-skinned and gaunt, wild-haired, in dripping rags and mud-covered flip-flops. She was shaking in the cold gusts of wind.

"The girl worked as a servant in a big house, but was thrown out when they saw that she is expecting a child. I have nothing, madam, please understand. I have five young children, my husband is dead, we live in mud and my children are always hungry. But I took her in, for her sake and the sake of the child in her belly. She gave birth to a boy two weeks ago. Now that she is getting stronger, all she talks about is killing him. She is HIV-positive and she believes he has the sickness, too. She believes they will both die horrible deaths and that she will die before him. Just now, she got up in the storm and woke me up to tell me she is putting the baby in the gutter, so he will be washed away in the storm. She asked me to help bail the water onto him, to wash him away faster. Instead I took the baby from her. She didn't want to let him go, but I told her I knew of a deep sewer."

"Where is the baby?"

"He is here," said the poor woman. She parted the filthy rags on her chest and a lovely boy peeked out, his mouth an O and his dark eyes concerned.

"Oh my God," said Haregewoin.

"But you can't leave him here," said Haregewoin. "I wouldn't be allowed. The City Social Affairs Bureau has forbidden me . . . We don't have the proper paperwork . . . There is an ongoing investigation . . ."

The woman raised her voice in near hysteria.

"She will kill the boy *tonight*. Do you understand? This boy will die *tonight*."

But Haregewoin was already opening her arms for him.

"God will bless you," said the gaunt woman. She turned to flee back into the night, before the young girl discovered that she had absconded with the baby instead of drowning him.

"Wait, what is his name?" called Haregewoin.

"Name?" shrieked the woman from the compound. "He has no name. She is planning to *kill* him. She gave him no name."

At a friend's suggestion, Haregewoin named the beautiful boy Leuel. "Prince."

He lives with her still, an erect and handsome baby. He is HIV-negative. When Haregewoin plops him down on her bed and sings to him, he jiggles his shoulders in dance and she laughs with delight and fondness until she nearly cries.

Recently, someone parked a rosy-cheeked little girl, of about two years old, outside the gates and ran away. The girl was just sitting there on a brick beside the door, in a mild and matter-of-fact way, seemingly confident that whoever had left her there would be coming back for her. But nobody came back. She was warm and clean and had been snugly dressed in many layers of ragged clothing, all tucked in tightly. Haregewoin looked up and down the lane for a long time, searching for a clue, and asked the guard to stand outside the gate, in case someone came back to check on the child.

"*Semesh man no?* [What's your name?]," she asked the pretty child, who smelled of soap and fragrant oil.

The girl smiled a secret smile and said, "Mimi."

But *mimi* was not a name; *mimi* was a diminutive; *mimi* was "sweetie pie."

But Mimi was the only name the little girl recalled, so she became Mimi, her given name lost.

Mimi withdrew with great sorrow for a week, sitting on the floor and screaming if anyone came near her. This was her grieving. Then she latched onto Haregewoin with great devotion and became the latest in a series of little girls to sleep in Haregewoin's bed. She liked to sit on Haregewoin's floor in the morning with the other preschoolers and admire the mother figure. Like breast-fed children all over the world, she enjoyed sticking her cold little hand possessively right down the front of her mother's dress, laying her fingers across a soft expanse of skin, and grabbing hold.

Recently Haregewoin entertained a few Norwegian guests, male and female, in the sitting area of her bedroom; they were considering whether to direct some small funding to her from their church organization; the coffee ceremony was being prepared, long grasses thrown down onto the floor by Henok's mother. Mimi walked in, climbed onto Haregewoin's lap, and, without warning, jammed her cold and grubby hand deep inside Haregewoin's brassiere.

On a recent hot night, after a long hot day, Haregewoin faced hours of paperwork ahead. She had been schooled in the rigors of record-keeping required by overseas charitable foundations. An accountant helped her, but she liked to go over the day's receipts herself; and she liked to review nice letters that sometimes came in along with small donations, words of encouragement and friendliness from overseas. There was a small alcove, off the dining hall/study hall, which she called "the office and library." Donated children's books, in English, stood on a couple of shelves, while a lower shelf held construction paper and crayons. She had an old wooden desk there, and a desk lamp, which warmed even now the papers waiting for her. At night, the only person awake in the quiet compound, she touched the outside world from that office, sensed the shifting currents of concern and of funds and of help in the world. Sometimes she got a scrap of a note from a former child of hers, now living abroad, enclosed in a letter with photos from the child's parents. Two hundred and fifty children had passed through her house to new families in foreign countries. There were fifty-three children in the neighborhood for whom she was paying school fees. (No in-country Ethiopian family had yet adopted a child from her.)

But Mimi was having trouble falling asleep tonight. Haregewoin sat hunched over beside her. The drowsy child was sucking her thumb and had her other fat little hand jammed down Haregewoin's dress-front. Haregewoin rested her head on her hand, elbow on knee, fighting to stay awake. Finally the little hand patting her chest fell still. Mimi was asleep. Gently, Haregewoin extricated herself and stood up; quietly and slowly she tiptoed out her bedroom door and down the cement porch steps. Halfway across the courtyard, she froze at the sound of Mimi's wail of disappointment and protest—Haregewoin's disappearance had woken her up.

Would she fall back asleep? Haregewoin waited, head bowed.

With silence, she took another step toward her office.

No, the wail built toward a bigger cry of grief and abandonment and the start of fear. Ahead of Haregewoin, the lamplight gleamed through the dusty window; the stack of papers awaited her attention. She humbly turned and plodded back to her bedroom. She sat down again on the bed beside the child, murmured consoling syllables, and leaned across her. Mimi sleepily reached out with one hand, which landed on Haregewoin's upper arm, and fell back to sleep with the good, warm feel of a mother in her fist.

56

BEFORE DEPARTING WITH Mekdes and Yabsira from Ethiopia in August 2004, Mikki and Ryan Hollinger decided to search for the grandfather whose name appeared in the adoption paperwork. They had debated this at great length, before leaving Snellville.

"It could be an emotional disaster," Mikki had said. "I can see it now: the kids will be screaming to stay with their grandfather, we'll be surrounded by mourning relatives, hostile villagers will gather, and I'll want to die."

"It may be our only shot," Ryan had said. "It's not like we can change our minds later. We're talking about our children's *grandfather.*"

In a cold, gray downpour, the family of four and I rode out of town in Selamneh Techane's taxi. We stopped first at the compound of Haj Mohammed Jemal Abdulsebur, who had led Aunt Fasika and Aunt Zewdenesh to Haregewoin's house the previous year (the nice man to whom I'd given a single balloon).

Haj, a tall, gangly, enthusiastic old fellow, greeted us exuberantly and insisted we come inside his compound for some refreshment before commencing the search. We filed into a compound protected by high walls of narrow, pointed wooden spikes, like the walls of a medieval fort. Several rows of attached cabins—like a low-budget American rural motel—stood in the backyard; he'd had them built to house scores of the village's orphans. In a break between cloudbursts, we balanced on kitchen chairs unevenly perched atop long, dark green weeds. Haj's two shy elderly wives served bottles of Coca-Cola and Fanta.

Haj then took the passenger seat, the rest of us stuffed ourselves into the back, the windows fogged up, and the taxi lurched from one muddy, poverty-stricken landscape to another. Mikki had woken up that morning with a sore throat and it worsened as the day wore on.

Half an hour from Haj's compound, we turned onto a long, narrow, descending dirt road, with a row of mud-and-tin constructions on one side and a row of scrappy trees on the other side. At this inauspicious spot, following Haj's directions, Selamneh turned off the taxi, jumped out, and jogged down the road. Haj exited the car and also disappeared. The Hollingers and I weren't sure what to do, so we sat crammed together in the backseat. Mikki, feeling sick, fearing it was strep throat, leaned her head back on the seat; the Hokey-Pokey Hamster put his right hand in and his right hand out. Mekdes gazed out the window. A fine drizzle started again.

Selamneh reappeared, asked for photos of the children with which to comb the neighborhood for someone who had known them, and jogged away again. Mekdes continued to gaze dreamily at the gray sky and wet streets. A boy of about six, strolling by with his mother, glanced over at the taxi and called, "*Selam*, Mekdes!"

"*Selam*, Birhanu," she called back with a friendly wave. The child and his mother continued on their way.

"What just happened?" cried Ryan. "Can someone please tell me what just happened? Mekdes, you know him? You know him?" (Mekdes didn't speak English yet.)

"Wait, wait!" Ryan rapidly disengaged himself from muddy-shoed Yabsira, feverish Mikki, myself, and the Hokey-Pokey Hamster. He grabbed Mekdes and jumped out of the parked car with her. "Wait!" he called to the people disappearing down the long road. (They didn't speak English either.) "Hello? Hello? Do you know her?"

They turned around. They hurried back. Suddenly women and children poured out of all the tin huts lining the road and surrounded the taxi. They called, "Mekdes! Baby!"

Without waiting for permission, ladies lifted Mekdes out of Ryan's arms and leaned forward to look into the taxi window for "Baby."

Yabsira climbed out through the open window and was swept off by the crowd, too.

The children traveled from embrace to embrace through a growing sea of excited men, women, and children. An attractive young woman at the fringe of the crowd pushed forward, took Yabsira, slung him onto her back, and wrapped him up in her shawl.

"Who is that? What's happening?" asked Mikki feebly from the backseat. Selamneh reappeared and took charge. He dove into a windstorm of excited, high-pitched chatter. A woman with a narrow face and a head scarf had a lot to say. Selamneh listened, then translated for Ryan and Mikki: "She was the best friend of their mother. She has photographs of the children at home, if you would be pleased to accept them."

Then he drew the young woman—who was wearing Yabsira on her back—through the crowd to the taxi.

"This is Aunt Fasika," he said.

She was in her twenties, the younger sister of the children's late father, Asnake.

The friend returned with photos from a child's birthday party attended by Mekdes and Yabsira at her house two years earlier. I pulled out my notebook and passed it around, asking everyone who knew the family to write down their names and addresses against a future day when Mekdes and Yabsira would return from America and visit their old neighborhood.

Fasika joined the four Hollingers, the battery-powered hamster, and myself in the muddy and slippery backseat of this small, elderly taxi, Haj got back in front, and we drove off to look for the grandfather. Meanwhile, young men from the neighborhood fanned out, calling for Addisu, the children's grandfather.

Directed by Fasika, Selamneh steered onto a paved street alongside a sodden open-air market. We drove slowly past it, while Fasika looked through the window for her father.

In a steady rainfall, Selamneh began to accelerate out of the market area. Suddenly, young men jumped out from behind a striped tent and ambushed the car. They ran alongside it, forcing it to slow down, pounding on the hood and roof, shouting. This alarmed the Americans crammed in the backseat.

"They have found Grandfather," said Selamneh.

"Look."

He yanked the car onto the shoulder of the road. Through the rain, Addisu came painfully jogging. He was a slight man with a drooping mustache; he wore a triangular, beige woolen shawl over one shoulder. He searched the faces of the adults as they got out of the car, and then, crying, he touched his long fingers to Mekdes's face, then Yabsira's. He lifted both children into his arms at once, beaming and crying. His mustache and his hair were curly and coal black. He *was* a grandfather; he moved gingerly and humbly, hovering on the edge of an uncertain invitation; he was, for his country, an elder. But the man was maybe fifty.

After some moments of hugging and reacquaintance with his grandchildren, Addisu asked the Hollingers, through Selamneh, whether they would like to visit the graves of the children's parents. He then added his length and smoky, damp wool scents to our backseat, where people now lay like pieces of firewood atop one another, Yabsira bouncing on top. The car revved its motor hard and crept up a long, sloping road to a church and graveyard. Selamneh parked and we got out.

In the distance, coming by foot from different directions, were dozens of people from the old neighborhood and from the open-air market. The reappearance of Mekdes and Yabsira with American parents had become a major village event.

Addisu led the way through the graveyard, carrying Mekdes; Fasika followed, once again wearing Yabsira on her back. Ryan escorted Mikki, who felt sicker by the minute. I fell into step alongside teenage boys, eager to practice "Hellohowareyouwhatisyourname?" The Ethiopian Orthodox priest emerged from the cathedral and joined the procession as it wound first up, then down a grassy and muddy hillside full of fresh graves.

We reached the markers for Mulu Azeze and Asnake Addisu. Rocks had been laid atop the dirt mounds in a rough mosaic. The names of the children's mother and father had been handwritten in black paint, in Amharic, on thin squares of tin. Each small sheet of tin had been nailed to a wood stake and pushed into the dirt.

The priest waited until the most distant stragglers had arrived, then he addressed the crowd of thirty or forty people in Amharic. It was like a spontaneous second funeral. He spoke of his warm memories of the deceased young couple and he blessed the gathering and he blessed the children and their new parents from America.

When he finished, there was an uncertain lull. Mikki nudged Ryan, then elbowed him. "*Say* something."

"*I* don't know what to say," he whispered.

"Ryan," I whispered from the other side. "You have to."

"I'm not a great public speaker," he whispered back.

"Go to Selamneh," I said. "Just tell him something and let him translate it."

Sheepishly, with the eyes of everyone on him, Ryan shuffled over to Selamneh.

There were whispers in the crowd, in Amharic, piecing together who Ryan was exactly.

Selamneh bowed his head to catch what Ryan mumbled to him in English, then loudly called out the translation to the assembled mourners.

"This is what Ryan Hollinger says: 'We feel sad for your family's terrible loss.'"

More mumbled words; then Selamneh, in Amharic: "Your tragedy has turned into an incredible gift for our family."

People in the crowd grew still.

Whispering, then: "We feel deeply honored to be able to adopt these children."

A few people started to cry.

"We will love them and take care of them forever . . . We will always stay in touch with you."

Men and women cried openly. Ryan finished and stood back with his arms crossed and his head bowed as Selamneh translated the last bit: "We will raise the children to know Ethiopia and to love their first family. We are all one family now."

There is a sound Ethiopian women make when they are touched: a drawn-out *tzz-tzz* sound of the tongue coming unstuck from the roof of the mouth. As Ryan spoke and Selamneh translated, *tzz-tzz*es began to buzz up and down the bleak graveyard hillside until it rattled like a meadow full of crickets in summer.

NOTES

4 **in Ethiopia's listless economy** With a gross domestic product (GDP) of approximately $8 billion, a per capita annual income of $116, and 50 percent of its population living below the poverty line in 2004, Ethiopia is one of the world's poorest countries. U.S. Department of State, Bureau of African Affairs, "Background Note: Ethiopia," http://www.state.gov/r/pa/ei/bgn/2859.htm (accessed April 16, 2006); and Central Intelligence Agency, "The World Factbook Ethiopia," http://www.cia.gov/cia/publications/factbook/geos/et.html (accessed April 15, 2006).

8 **TB was one of the typical opportunistic infection** Human immunodeficiency virus (HIV) causes AIDS. A person whose blood tests positive for HIV has been infected but does not necessarily have AIDS. Without treatment, nearly every infected person will develop AIDS and die. Acquired immune deficiency syndrome (AIDS) is the medical designation for the set of symptoms, opportunistic infections, and laboratory markers indicating that a patient's HIV infection is advanced and that his or her immune system has stopped functioning. Opportunistic infections vary by region of the world; TB is a common OI of AIDS (OIA) in Africa.

For more information on HIV, the case definition of AIDS, and OIAS, see Tony Barnett and Alan Whiteside, *AIDS in the Twenty-First Century: Disease and Globalization* (Houndmills, Basingstoke, Hampshire: Palgrave Macmillan, 2003), 28–46; Theresa McGovern and Raymond A. Smith, "AIDS, Case Definition of," in ed. Raymond A. Smith, *Encyclopedia of AIDS: A Social, Political, Cultural, and Scientific Record of the HIV Epidemic*, rev. ed. (New York: Penguin Books, 2001), 32–36; Harry W. Kestler with Ronald Medley and Tim Horn, "HIV, Description of," in *Encyclopedia of AIDS*, 327–29; Tim Horn, "AIDS, Pathogenesis of," in *Encyclopedia of AIDS*, 37–40; Antonio Mastroianni, "Tuberculosis," in *Encyclopedia of AIDS*, 673; Avert, "The Different Stages of HIV Infection," http://www.avert.org/hivstages.htm (accessed April 4, 2006); Avert, "HIV-Related Opportunistic Infections: Prevention and Treatment," http://www.avert.org/aidscare.htm (accessed April 4, 2006); and Avert, "AIDS, HIV & Tuberculosis (TB)," http://www.avert.org/tuberc.htm (accessed April 4, 2006).

According to the World Health Organization, TB is the primary cause of death among people living with HIV. The majority of people coinfected with TB and HIV worldwide live in sub-Saharan Africa. World Health Organization, "Tuberculosis," http://www.who.int/mediacentre/factsheets/fs104/en/index.html (accessed April 4, 2006).

10 **Standing like a mountain fortress** Sources for Ethiopian and African history in this and subsequent chapters include Harold G. Marcus, *A History of Ethiopia*, updated ed. (Berkeley and Los Angeles: University of California Press, 2002); Richard Pankhurst, *The Ethiopians: A History* (Oxford: Blackwell, 2003); Bahru Zewde, *History of Modern Ethiopia: 1885–1991*, 4th ed. (Athens: Ohio University Press; Oxford: James Curry Publishers; Addis Ababa: Addis Ababa University Press, 2001); Martin Meredith, *The Fate of Africa: A History of 50 Years of Independence* (New York: Public Affairs, 2005), 4–5, 206–17; and BBC, "Timeline: Ethiopia," http://news.bbc.co.uk/1/hi/world/africa/1072219.stm (accessed October 2, 2005).

10 **Sacred literature in both Israel and Ethiopia** See I Kings, 10:1–13.

10 **"The Queen of Sheba heard"** *Tanakh: The Holy Scriptures* (Philadelphia/Jerusalem: The Jewish Publication Society, 1985), I Kings, chap. 10, p. 537.

11 **"This Queen of the South"** *A Modern Translation of the* Kebra Nagast *(The Glory of Kings): The True Ark of the Covenant*, trans. and ed. Miguel F. Brooks (Lawrenceville, NJ: Red Sea Press, 1998), 19. E. A. Wallis Budge's 1932 English translation of the *Kebra Nagast* is available online at http://www.sacred-texts.com/chr/kn/ (accessed April 17, 2000).

11 **Nearly two thirds of school-age children** United Nations Development Programme, *Human Development Report 2005: International Cooperation at a Crossroads; Aid, Trade and Security in an Unequal World*, Table 1, Human Development Index, http://hdr.undp.org/reports/global/2005/pdf/HDR05_complete.pdf (accessed April 14, 2006).

12 **The urban unemployment rate here** Berhanu Denu, Abraham Tekeste, and Hannah van der Deijl, "Characteristics and Determinants of Youth Employment, Underemployment and Inadequate Employment in Ethiopia," employment strategy paper 2005/07 (International Labor Office, 2005), iv, http://www.ilo.org/public/english/employment/strat/download/esp2005-7.pdf (accessed April 11, 2006). A 1999 survey conducted by the Central Statistical Authority on the Ethiopian labor force recorded an urban unemployment rate of 38.1 percent and a national unemployment rate of 8.1 percent. These figures—which do not cover certain areas of Somali and Afar Regional States—are unanimously dismissed as misleadingly optimistic. The country's rampant poverty and the biological impulse to survive force most individuals to seek some type of job, even if no decent work is available, and many of those Ethiopians considered "employed" are actually underemployed. In 1997, the poverty rate among working Ethiopians was over 35 percent. Central Statistical Authority, *Statistical Report on the 1999 Labor Force Survey* (Federal Democratic Republic of Ethiopia, 1999); Denu, Tekeste, and van der Deijl, "Characteristics and Determinants of Youth Employment," 5, 13, 22–25; Pieter Serneels, "The Nature of Unemployment in Urban Ethiopia," Working Paper 201 (The Centre for the Study of African Economies, 2004), 1, http://www.bepress.com/cgi/viewcontent.cgi?article=1201&context=csae (accessed April 14, 2006); Graeme J. Buckley, "Decent Work in a Least Developed Country: A Critical Assessment of the Ethiopia PRSP," Working Paper 42 (International Labor Office, 2004), 11, http://www.ilo.org/public/english/bureau/integration/download/publicat/4_3_234_wp-42.pdf (accessed April 14, 2005); and United Nations Economic Commission for Africa, *Economic Report on Africa 2005: Meeting the Challenges of Unemployment and Poverty in Africa*, fig. 2.4, http://www.uneca.org/era2005/full.pdf (accessed April 11, 2006).

Despite a GDP growth of 11.6 percent in 2004 (Ethiopia is one of only six countries that attained the 7 percent growth in 2004 required to achieve Millennium Development Goal 1 to halve poverty by 2015), the Ethiopian job market cannot catch up with its rapidly expanding labor force. While the unemployment rate in Ethiopia is higher among the uneducated, a recent survey revealed a rapid increase in unemployment rates among high school and college graduates. United Nations Economic Commission for Africa, *Economic Report on Africa 2005*, 4; Denu, Tekeste, and van der Deijl, "Characteristics and Determinants of Youth Employment," 15, 27; and Yodit Abera, "Unemployed Graduates," *Ethiopian Reporter*, December 10, 2005, http://www.ethiopianreporter.com/modules.php?name=News&file=article&sid=1512 (accessed April 11, 2006). For more information on the Millennium Development Goals, see United Nations, "UN Development Goals," http://www.un.org/millenniumgoals/index.html (accessed April 14, 2001). For more information on the Millennium Development Goals in Ethiopia, see the Earth Institute at Columbia University Center for National Health Development in Ethiopia, "Millennium Development Goals in Ethiopia," http://cnhde.ei.columbia.edu/ethmdg/newindex2.html (accessed April 14, 2001); and Jeffrey D. Sachs, *The End of Poverty: Economic Possibilities for Our Time* (New York: Penguin Press, 2005), 210–25.

12 **live on less than a dollar a day** United Nations Development Programme, *Human Development Report 2005*, Table 3, Human and Income Poverty: Developing Countries, 229.

13 **"In a country where good governance"** Abdullahi Mohamed, "Ethiopian Private Sector Blames Meles," *Geeska Afrika*, April 1, 2005, http://www.geeskaafrika.com/ethiopia_ 1apr05.htm (accessed April 16, 2006).

13 **"After fourteen years or so"** Ibid.

13 **the escalation into war in 1998** Library of Congress Federal Research Division, "Country Profile: Ethiopia, April 2005" (Washington: GPO for the Library of Congress, 2005), 19, http://1cweb2.loc.gov/frd/cs/profiles/Ethiopia.pdf (accessed March 30, 2006).

13 **Even across sub-Saharan Africa, health spending** Ibid., 8; and World Health Organization, *World Health Report 2005: Make Every Mother and Child Count* (Geneva: World Health Organization, 2005), 201, http://www.who.int/whr/2005/whr2005_en.pdf (accessed March 30, 2006).

20 **the hardest hit were the men and women** By causing massive deaths in adults who would otherwise have the lowest mortality rates, AIDS has changed and will continue to change the demographic and household structure of African societies, effectively "cutting out the middle generation" in a way never seen before. Barnett and Whiteside, *AIDS in the Twenty-First Century*, 159–81, 196–221.

20 **"a continent of orphans"** David Fox, "AIDS Making Africa a Continent of Orphans," Reuters NewMedia, June 27, 1997, 12:50, http://ww4.aegis.org/news/re/1997/ Re970614.html (accessed April 17, 2006).

20 **had killed more than twenty-one million** By the end of the year, AIDS had killed 17.5 million adults and 4.3 million children, and 5.3 million people had become newly infected with HIV. UNAIDS and World Health Organization, "AIDS Epidemic Update, December 2000," 3, http://www.aegis.com/files/unaids/WADDecember2000_epidemic_report.pdf (accessed March 16, 2006).

Twenty million of these children will have lost one or both parents to HIV/AIDS. UNAIDS, UNICEF, and USAID, *Children on the Brink, 2004: A Joint Report on New Orphan Estimates and a Framework for Action* (Washington: USAID, 2004), Table 2, http://www .unicef.org/publications/files/cob_layout6-013.pdf (accessed April 16, 2006). See also UNICEF, *Africa's Orphaned Generations* (New York: UNICEF, 2003), http://www .unicef.org/media/files/orphans.pdf (accessed April 17, 2006).

20 **In Ethiopia, 11 percent of all** UNAIDS, *Report on the Global HIV/AIDS Epidemic, June 2000* (Geneva: UNAIDS, 2000), 6, http://data.unaids.org/Global-Reports/Durban/Durban _Epi_report_en.pdf (accessed April 16, 2000); and UNAIDS, UNICEF, and USAID, *Children on the Brink, 2004*, Table 2, Table 3. See also UNICEF, *Africa's Orphaned Generations*, 11.

20 **a disease of which few Westerners died** UNAIDS, "New UNAIDS report warns AIDS epidemic still in early phase and not leveling off in worst-affected countries," press release, July 2, 2002.

20 **By 2010, between twenty-five million and fifty million** 20 million of these children will have lost one both parents to HIV/AIDS. UNAIDS, UNICEF, and USAID, *Children on the Brink, 2004*, Table 2. See also UNICEF, *Africa's Orphaned Generations*.

21 **In a dozen countries, up to a quarter** UNICEF, *Africa's Orphaned Generations*, 11.

23 **a generation of parents, teachers** AIDS has decimated Africa's teacher population. Avert, "The Impact of HIV & AIDS on Africa," http://www.avert.org/aidsimpact.htm (accessed April 4, 2006); BBC, "AIDS Ravages Teachers," May 8, 2002, http://news.bbc.co.uk/2/ hi/africa/1974111.stm (accessed April 17, 2006); and Diana Jean Schemo, "Education Suffers in Africa as AIDS Ravages Teachers," *New York Times*, May 8, 2002, http:// query.nytimes.com/gst/fullpage.html?sec=health&res=9A03E0D91530F93BA35756C0A 9649C8B63 (accessed April 17, 2006).

AIDS has decimated health care workers. According to Avert, "Malawi and Zambia are experiencing a 5 to 6 fold increase in health worker illness and death rates," http:// www.avert.org/aidsimpact.htm.

USAID reports:

- African health care systems may lose one fifth of their employees to HIV/AIDS.
- The mortality rates among female nurses in Zambia jumped from 2 percent in 1981–85 to 26 percent in 1989–91 due to HIV.
- 25 percent of nurses are HIV-positive in some countries in southern Africa.
- Deaths among nurses rose three times from 1995 to 1999 in Mozambique.
- HIV prevalence among nurses in Lusaka was 34 percent in 1991 and 44 percent in 1992.
- Mortality among female nurses in sub-Saharan Africa rose thirteen times between 1981 and 1991.
- Deaths among Malawi health care workers increased sixfold between 1985 and 1997.

Source: USAID, "The Impact of HIV/AIDS on Health Systems and the Health Workforce in Sub-Saharan Africa," June 2003, 5–8.

See also http://www.iht.com/articles/2005/07/07/news/edntaba.php and http://bmj.bmjjournals.com/cgi/content/full/329/7466/584.

Peter Piot said, in a *NewsHour* interview, "People who have to deliver the goods—[the] nurses, the doctors, the teachers—they're dying from AIDS as well; they also don't have access to treatment in many countries. And what you are seeing is a phenomenon that I saw in Malawi, a small country in Central Africa, where—in the main hospital that should be the reference for treatment for HIV . . . only one out of three slots for nurses are filled because the nurses have emigrated to South Africa or to Great Britain or the U.S. because their salary conditions are so lousy . . . and one-third have died from AIDS." http://www.pbs.org/newshour/bb/health/july-dec04/aids_12-01.html (accessed April 23, 2006).

25 **in Zimbabwe, a child dies of AIDS** "Zimbabwe: AIDS Kills One Child Every 20 Minutes, Says UN Children's Agency," U.S. Centers for Disease Control and Prevention, International News, April 13, 2006, http://www.thebody.com/cdc/news_updates_archive/2006/aprl3_06/children_aids.html.

25 **$20 billion per year by 2007** http://www.data.org/whyafrica/issueaids.php.

26 **the disease bringing down governments** Mark Shoofs, "A New Kind of Crisis: The Security Council Declares AIDS in Africa a Threat to World Stability," *Village Voice*, January 12–18, 2000; Karen DeYoung, "U.N. Pledges Support in Fight Against AIDS," *Washington Post*, June 28, 2001; and Elizabeth Bumiller, "Bush Chooses U.S. Executive for AIDS Job," *New York Times*, July 3, 2003, http://query.nytimes.com/gst/fullpage.html?sec=health&res=9B05E3D7103AF930A35754C0A9659C8B63 (accessed April 16, 2003).

35 **More than eight hundred species of birds** African Bird Club, "Ethiopia," http://www.africanbirdclub.org/countries/Ethiopia/species.html (accessed April 17, 2006).

35 **Forty-five different tribal groups** For more information on Ethiopia's tribal groups, see Donald N. Levine, *Greater Ethiopia: The Evolution of a Multiethnic Society*, 2nd ed. (Chicago: University of Chicago Press, 2000).

36 **"Gondwanaland stands once again exposed"** Graham Hancock and Richard Pankhurst, with photography by Duncan Willetts, *Under Ethiopian Skies* (Nairobi: Camerapix Publishers, 1997), 8.

38 **"His army was remarkable not only"** Zewde, *History of Modern Ethiopia*, 77.

38 **"News of his march had preceded him"** Ibid.

38 **"The root of Italian disaster lay"** Ibid., 79.

39 **"The battle at Adowa [sic] was . . . the greatest defeat"** Greg Blake, "Ethiopia's Decisive Victory at Adowa," *Military History Magazine*, October 1997, 63. See also Alistair Boddy-Evans, "Battle of Adowa Timeline: Significant Events of the Battle," http://africanhistory.about.com/library/timelines/bl-Timeline-BattleOfAdowa.htm (accessed April 17, 2006); and History World, Ltd., "History of Ethiopia: 19th to 20th Century," http://www.historyworld.net/wrldhis/PlainTextHistories.asp?groupid=2114&HistoryID=ab92 (accessed April 17, 2006).

39 **the first written language in Africa** The ancient Aixumites—whose kingdom encompassed lands south of the Roman Empire and whose influence reached its zenith in the fourth and fifth centuries AD—developed Africa's "only indigenous written script, Ge'ez, from which

the written form of the languages spoken in modern Ethiopia has evolved; they traded with Egypt, the eastern Mediterranean and Arabia, and financed their operations with gold, silver, and copper coinage—the first and only coinage known in sub-Saharan Africa until the tenth century, when Arabian coins were used along the East African coast." John Reader, *Africa: A Biography of the Continent* (New York: Vintage Books, 1999), 208.

42 **Emperor Haile Selassie, "the Lion of Judah"** Sources on Haile Selassie for this and subsequent chapters include Aberra Jembere, *Agony in the Grand Palace: 1974–1982*, trans. Dr. Hailu Arraya (Addis Ababa: Shama Books, 2002); BBC, "Timeline: Ethiopia," http:// news.bbc.co.uk/2/hi/africa/1072219.stm (accessed April 17, 2006); Ryszard Kapuscinski, *The Emperor*, trans. William R. Brand and Katarzyna Mroczkowska-Brand (New York: Vintage International, 1989); Ryszard Kapuscinski, *The Shadow of the Sun*, trans. Klara Glowczewska (New York: Vintage, 2002); Samuel Kasule, *The History Atlas of Africa* (New York: Macmillan, 1998); Marcus, *History of Ethiopia*; Harold G. Marcus, *Haile Selassie I: The Formative Years 1892–1936* (Lawrenceville, NJ: The Red Sea Press, 1995); Colin McEvedy, *The Penguin Atlas of African History* (London: Penguin Books, 1995); Martin Meredith, *The Fate of Africa: A History of 50 Years of Independence* (New York: Public Affairs, 2005); Nega Mezlekia, *Notes from the Hyena's Belly* (New York: Picador, 2002); Alan Moorehead, *The Blue Nile* (New York: Harper & Row, 1962); Pankhurst, *The Ethiopians*; Richard Pankhurst and Denis Gerard, *Ethiopia Photographed: Historic Photographs of the Country and Its People Taken Between 1867 and 1935* (London and New York: Kegan Paul International, 1996).

43 **"Scramble for Africa"** At the end of the nineteenth century, European powers—including Great Britain, France, Germany, Belgium, and Portugal—made use of technological advances in medicine (the use of quinine against malaria), transportation (including steamships), and weaponry (muskets and cannons) to invade and claim African lands. With scarce knowledge of the territories that lay beyond the coastlines, statesmen met in European capitals, bargained and traded with one another, and imposed colonial borders by drawing straight lines on maps. For more information, see Davidson, *Africa in History*; Howard W. French, *A Continent for the Taking: The Tragedy and Hope of Africa* (New York: Alfred A. Knopf, 2004); Philip Gourevitch, *We Wish to Inform You That Tomorrow We Will Be Killed with Our Families: Stories from Rwanda* (New York: Picador, 1998); Adam Hochschild, *King Leopold's Ghost* (New York: Mariner Books, 1999); John G. Jackson, *Introduction to African Civilizations* (Secaucus, NJ: The Citadel Press, 1974); Kasule, *The History Atlas*; David Lamb, *The Africans* (New York: Vintage, 1984); McEvedy, *Penguin Atlas*; Meredith, *Fate of Africa*; and Reader, *Africa*.

43 **unequal struggle between a government commanding** Haile Selassie, "Speech to the League of Nations" (League of Nations, Geneva, June 20, 1936), posted online by the Harvard Rhetorical Society, http://hcs.harvard.edu/rhetoric/selassie.htm (accessed April 16, 2006). A recording of this speech can be downloaded from HistoryChannel.com, http:// www.historychannel.com/broadband/home/ (accessed April 16, 2006).

43 **"all small peoples who are threatened"** Ibid.

45 **"On the ground, in the filth"** Kapuscinski, *Shadow*, 133.

45 **"The government could, of course"** Ibid., 134.

46 *The Unknown Famine* *The Unknown Famine*, directed by Ian Stuttard for Thames Television's *This Week*, premiered on ITV on September 18, 1973. By Christmas, the thirty-minute documentary had raised an estimated £1.5 million in aid. Paul Harrison and Robert Palmer, *News out of Africa: Biafra to Band Aid* (London: Hilary Shipman, 1986), 44–62; and Jonathan Dimbleby, "Ethiopia Proves There Can Be Life After Death," *Observer*, July 28, 2002, http://observer.guardian.co.uk/worldview/story/0,11581,764433,00.html (accessed April 17, 2006).

46 **One of the leaders of the revolution** Sources on Mengistu Haile Mariam and the Derg for this and subsequent chapters include James Fenton, "Ethiopia: Victors and Victims," *New York Review of Books*, November 7, 1985, http://www.newyorkreviewofbooks.com/; Marcus,

History of Ethiopia; Paulos Milkias, "Mengistu Haile Mariam: The Profile of a Dictator," *Ethiopian Review*, February 1994, http://ethiopianreview.homestead.com/Article_PaulosMilkias_Feb1994.html (accessed April 17, 2006); Bernard Weinraub, "Ethiopia, an Unknown, Violent Country," *New York Times*, May 30, 1976; and Paul B. Henze, *Layers of Time: A History of Ethiopia* (New York: Palgrave, 2000).

48 **Between the mid-1970s and 1980** Sources on the discovery and spread of the AIDS virus used in this and subsequent chapters include AIDS Education Global Information System, "So Little Time: An AIDS History," http://www.aegis.com/topics/timeline/default.asp; Avert, "History of AIDS: Pictures and Posters," http://www.avert.org/historyi.htm (accessed April 17, 2006); CNN, "AIDS: 20 Years of an Epidemic," http://edition.cnn.com/SPECIALS/2001/aids/interactive/timeline/frameset.exclude.html (accessed July 5, 2005); Catherine Campbell, *Letting Them Die: Why HIV/AIDS Prevention Programmes Fail* (Oxford: The International African Institute, 2003); Jon Cohen, *Shots in the Dark: The Wayward Search for an AIDS Vaccine* (New York: W. W. Norton, 2001); John Crewdson, *Science Fictions: A Scientific Mystery, a Massive Cover-up, and the Dark Legacy of Robert Gallo* (Boston: Little, Brown and Company, 2002); Laurie Garrett, *The Coming Plague* (New York: Penguin Books, 1994); Jonathan Mann, a Daniel Tarantola, and Thomas Netter, eds., *AIDS in the World 1992* (Cambridge: Harvard University Press, 1992); Jonathan Mann and Daniel Tarantola, *AIDS in the World II* (Oxford: Oxford University Press, 1996); and Randy Shilts, *And the Band Played On* (New York: St. Martin's, 2000).

48 **And it was a lentivirus** References on the pathogenesis of HIV and AIDS include Avert, "Different Stages of HIV Infection"; McGovern and Smith, "AIDS, Case Definition of," 32–36; Kestler with Medley and Horn, "HIV, Description of," 327–29; Horn, "AIDS, Pathogenesis of," 37–40; and Darrell E. Ward, "The Medical Science of HIV/AIDS," in *The Amfar AIDS Handbook: The Complete Guide to Understanding HIV and AIDS* (New York: W. W. Norton, 1999), 279–836.

49 **"Slim disease" was the early name** Susan Hunter, *Black Death: AIDS in Africa* (Houndmills, Basingstoke, Hampshire: Palgrave Macmillan, 2003), 227n3.

49 **Its first appearances were these** Thomas C. Quinn, Jonathan Mann, James W. Curran, and Peter Piot, "AIDS in Africa: An Epidemiologic Paradigm," *Science* 234 (1986): 955–63.

49 **"The dominant feature of this"** Jonathan Mann, "AIDS: A Worldwide Pandemic," in *Current Topics in AIDS*, vol. 2, ed. Michael S. Gottlieb, Donald J. Jeffries, Donna Mildvan, Anthony J. Pinching, Thomas C. Quinn (John Wiley and Sons, 1989), quoted in Avert, "History of AIDS, 1981–1986," http://www.avert.org/his81_86.htm (accessed March 30, 2006).

49 **By 1990, sixty-one thousand children** UNAIDS, UNICEF, and USAID, *Children on the Brink 2002: A Joint Report on Orphan Estimates and Program Strategies* (Washington: USAID, 2002), 16, Table: 1990—Africa: Orphan Estimates, by Year, Country, Type, and Cause, http://www.unicef.org/publications/files/pub_children_on_the_brink_en.pdf (accessed April 17, 2006).

56 **health stations were decrepit** Ministry of Health, *Health and Health Related Indicators, 1994 E.C./2001/2002 G.C.* (Addis Ababa: Ministry of Health, 2002). Available for download at http://www.etharc.org/ (accessed April 17, 2006); Fran von Massow, "Access to Health and Education Services in Ethiopia: Supply, Demand and Government Policy," working paper (Oxfam, 2001), http://www.oxfam.org.uk/what_we_do/resources/wp_healthedu_ethiopia.htm (accessed April 17, 2006); and Library of Congress, "Country Profile: Ethiopia," 8.

57 **"A million people died in Ethiopia"** Kapuscinski, *Shadow*, 134.

57 **there has never been a famine** Amartya Sen, "Global Doubts" (Commencement Day Address, June 8, 2000), http://www.commencement.harvard.edu/2000/sen.html (accessed April 16, 2006). "A well-functioning market economy does not obviate the need for democracy and civil and political rights. The latter not only give people more freedom to live the way they would like (without being bossed around), they also allow people to have more voice to demand that their interests not be ignored. The fact that no famine has ever

occurred in a democratic country with a free press and regular elections is only one rudimentary illustration of this connection."

58 **Clouds faded from the sky** *Unheard Voices: Drought, Famine and God in Ethiopian Oral Poetry*, comp. Fekade Azeze (Addis Ababa: Addis Ababa University Press, 1998).

59 **AIDS orphans had reached 294,000** UNAIDS, UNICEF, and USAID, *Children on the Brink, 2002*, 19, Table: 1995—Africa: Orphan Estimates, by Year, Country, Type, and Cause.

59 **"Terminology like 'developing countries'"** Mark Heywood, "Drug Access, Patents and Global Health: 'Chaffed and Waxed Sufficient,'" *Third World Quarterly* 23, no. 2 (2002): 218.

60 **When, in 2005, the UN appraised** United Nations Development Programme, *Human Development Report 2005*, 222, Table 1: Human Development Index; 302, Table 25: Gender-Related Development Index; 229, Table 3: Human and Income Poverty: Developing Countries.

74 **"In some cases, zoonotic diseases"** Samuel D. Uretsky, "Zoonosis," *Encyclopedia of Medicine*, ed. Jacqueiline L. Long (Thomson Gale, 2002). Available online at http://www.healthatoz .com/healthatoz/Atoz/ency/zoonosis.jsp (accessed April 17, 2006).

75 **"All of the primates that carry these SIVs"** Preston Marx, Phillip G. Alcabes, and Ernest Drucker, "Serial Human Passage of Simian Immunodeficiency Virus by Unsterile Injections and the Emergence of the Epidemic Human Immunodeficiency Virus in Africa," *Philosophical Transactions of the Royal Society of London Series B—Biological Sciences* 356 (2001): 911.

75 **"[One] is trying to explain why"** Ernest Drucker, interview by Norman Swan, *The Health Report*, Australian Broadcasting Company Radio National, November 27, 2000. Transcript available online at http://abc.net.au/rn/talks/8.30/helthrpt/stories/s217997.htm (accessed April 17, 2000).

76 **"Under that hypothesis . . . the epidemic emerged"** William Carlsen, "Quest for the Origin of AIDS," *San Francisco Chronicle*, January 14, 2001, A1, A14–A15, <http://www.sfgate .com/cgi-bin/article.cgi?file=/chronicle/archive/2001/01/14/MN140641.DTL>.

76 **"Gentlemen and ladies, people of the town"** Edward Hooper, "The Story of a Man-Made Disease," *Suppression of Dissent*, April 22, 2003; Brian Martin, University of Wollongong, Australia, April 1, 2006, http://www.uow.edu.au/arts/sts/bmartin/dissent/documents/ AIDS/Hooper03/Hooper03story.html>; and *London Review of Books* 25, no. 7 (April 3, 2003), http://www.lrb.co.uk/v25/n07/hoop01_.html (accessed April 1, 2006).

79 **Production increased a hundredfold** Ernest Drucker, "Over One Million Die Every Year World Wide by Injections," *eHealthy News You Can Use*, December 26, 2001, Dr. Joseph Mercola, *The Best Natural Health Information and Newsletter*, April 9, 2006, <http://www.mercola.com/2001/dec/26/injection_deaths.htm>.

79 **"enthusiasm for dealing with disease"** UNICEF, "The 1950's: Era of the Mass Disease Campaign," *Fifty Years for Children: The State of the World's Children, 1996*, December 11, 1995, *United Nations International Children's Emergency Fund 16th Annual Report of the State of the World's Children, 50th Anniversary Edition*, April 12, 2006, <http://www.unicef.org/sowc96/ 1950s.htm>.

79 **As the 1940s gave way to the 1950s** Ibid.

80 **By the 1990s, injections were being administered** Ibid.

80 **"The process had already been witnessed"** Carlsen, "Quest for the Origin."

80 **"If you take a weakly pathogenic virus"** Drucker, interview by Swan.

81 **"Based on findings demonstrating the simian ancestry"** Preston A. Marx, Cristian Apetrei, and Ernest Drucker, "AIDS as a zoonosis? Confusion over the origin of the virus and the origin of the epidemics," *Journal of Medical Primatology* 33, no. 5–6 (October 2004): 220–26. Abstract.

82 **"It's striking that the first cases"** Drucker, interview by Swan.

83 **"We hypothesize . . . that the massive increase"** Businesswire News, "UNIVEC Heralds Work of Scientists Pointing to Unsterile Injections as Source of Worldwide AIDS and

Hepatitis Cases," *Aegis Today's News*, September 13, 2000, http://www.aegis.com/news/bw/2000/BW000903.html (accessed April 20, 2006).

83 **"The norm . . . was to simply"** Drucker, interview by Swan.

84 **WHO estimates that unsafe injections** Ernest Drucker, Philip G. Alcabes, and Preston A. Marx, "The injection century: Massive unsterile injections and the emergence of human pathogens," *Lancet* (London, England): 358, no. 9297 (December 8, 2001): 1989–92.

84 **As recently as 1998, WHO recommended** Drucker in Mercola, 2001.

84 **"These respected experts confirm"** Businesswire News, "UNIVEC Heralds Work of Scientists."

85 **"Since the late 1980s, the dominant hypothesis"** Conversations with author, Atlanta, 2005.

86 **"We know the source"** Preston Marx in radio interview with Brian Lemberg, "Tulane University Health Sciences Center, the Tulane Center for Gene Therapy and the Tulane National Primate Research Center—Dr. Darwin Prockop, Dr. Preston Marx, Dr. Paul Whelton," *Biotech Today*. Originally broadcast March 10, 2003, World Talk Radio, Science and Technology. Access archived version at <http://www.worldtalkradio.com/archive.asp?aid=1288.

95 **MMM, the Catholic charity** Medical Missionaries of Mary (MMM) was founded in Nigeria in 1937 by Dublin-born Mother Mary Martin; the sisters came to Ethiopia in 1960. Today, in nineteen countries, MMM cares for the destitute, among them people living with HIV/AIDS, and offers a variety of services, including medical care and training of health professionals. For more information, see the Web site of the Ethiopian Catholic Church: http://www.ecs.org.

98 **"Orphaned girls are at the absolute margins"** Sharon Lafraniere, "AIDS, Pregnancy and Poverty Trap Ever More African Girls," *New York Times*, June 3, 2005, http://query.nytimes.com/gst/fullpage.html?res=9D04EFD81738F930A35755C0A9639C8B63&sec=health (accessed April 17, 2006).

98 **A survey by French epidemiologists** Michel Garenne, Romain Micol, and Arnaud Fontanet, letter to the editor in response to "Unsafe Healthcare Drives Spread of African HIV," *International Journal of STD & AIDS* 15, no. 1 (January 2004): 65–67.

108 **"AIDS is God's punishment"** Greg Behrman, *The Invisible People: How the United States Has Slept Through the Global AIDS Pandemic, the Greatest Humanitarian Catastrophe of Our Time* (New York: Free Press, 2004), 27.

108 **"The poor homosexuals"** Ibid.

109 **"What I see is a commitment"** Ibid.

109 **"Up until then it was entirely a gay epidemic"** Daniel McGinn, "MSNBC: AIDS at 20: Anatomy of a Plague; an Oral History," *Newsweek*, http://www.msnbc.com/.

110 **"strong indication of heterosexual transmission"** Peter Piot, Thomas Quinn, Helena Taelman et al., "Acquired Immunodeficiency Syndrome in a heterosexual population in Zaire," *Lancet* 2 (1984): 65–69, quoted in Avert, "History of AIDS, 1981–1986."

110 **"African patients with KS"** Robert Downing, Roger Eglin, and Anne C. Bayley, "African Kaposi's sarcoma and AIDS," *Lancet* 1 (1984): 478–80. See also Lawrence K. Altman, "New Form of Cancer Seen in African AIDS Patients," *New York Times*, December 9, 2005, http://query.nytimes.com/gst/fullpage.html?sec=health&res=9D02E6DD173BF93AA357 51C1A963948260 (accessed April 18, 2006).

110 **In November 1983, the World Health Organization** World Health Organization, "Acquired Immune Deficiency Syndrome Emergencies" (Meeting Report, World Health Organization, Geneva, November 22–25, 1983), quoted in Avert, "History of AIDS, 1981–1986."

111 **By the end of that year, twenty thousand cases** Avert, "History of AIDS, 1981–1986."

111 **President Ronald Reagan did not officially address** According to Greg Behrman, Reagan's first public acknowledgment of AIDS was in a speech at the "Meeting on the Potomac" gala thrown by Elizabeth Taylor in the summer of 1985 (see *Invisible People*, 27), and he delivered

speeches on AIDS and compulsory testing early in 1987. According to Aegis, he first mentioned the word *AIDS* in public in response to reporters' questions in 1985. He mentioned AIDS in a message to Congress in February 1986. Not until April 1987 did he deliver his first "major speech" on AIDS (to the College of Physicians in Philadelphia).

111 **"It was often remarked acidly"** Paul Monette, *Borrowed Time: An AIDS Memoir* (New York: Harcourt Brace, 1988), 110.

112 **"slim disease cannot be distinguished"** Thomas Kamradt, Dieter Niese, and Frederick Vogel, "Slim disease (AIDS)," *Lancet* 2 (1985): 1425, quoted in Avert, "History of AIDS, 1981–1986."

112 **it was not impossible that ten million** Nancy Krieger and Rose Appleman, *The Politics of AIDS* (Frontline Pamphlets, the Institute for Social and Economic Studies, 1986), quoted in Avert, "History of AIDS, 1981–1986."

112 **"'Brother,' Castro told Museveni"** Arthur Allen, "Sex Change: Uganda v. Condoms," *New Republic*, May 27, 2002, 14.

113 **"At least 30 million Africans"** Alex Duval Smith, "Focus AIDS: A Continent Left to Die," *Independent*, September 5, 1999.

113 **"It exploded at the end"** Conversation with the author, Toronto, August 2005.

115 **Ethiopian patients were first diagnosed** Lisa Garbus, "HIV/AIDS in Ethiopia" (AIDS Policy Research Center, University of California, April 2003), 6.

117 **Of every eleven people in the world** Clare Bishop-Sambrook, "The Challenge of the HIV/AIDS Epidemic in Rural Ethiopia: Averting the Crisis in Low AIDS-Impacted Communities" (Food and Agriculture Organization Sustainable Development Department, Rome, March 2004), 2, http://www.fao.org/sd/dim_pe3/pe3_040402_en.htm (accessed April 17, 2006).

123 **In 2000, there were no anti-AIDS drugs** David Shinn, "The Silence Is Broken, the Stigma Is Not," *Africa Notes* (Center for Strategic and International Studies, Washington, DC, July 2001), 5, http://www.csis.org/media/csis/pubs/anotes_0107.pdf (accessed April 15, 2006).

164 **UNICEF noted that the "survival strategy"** UNICEF, "Africa's Orphan Crisis: Worst Is Yet to Come," Johannesburg/Geneva, press release, November 26, 2003, http://www.unicef.org/media/media_16287.html (accessed October 1, 2005).

184 **they were two of twenty-six million** UNAIDS and WHO, "AIDS Epidemic Update, 2004," 3, http://www.clintonfoundation.org/pdf/epiupdate04_en.pdf (accessed April 19, 2006).

184 **perhaps 4 percent of them had access** IRIN, "The Treatment Era: ART in Africa," *PlusNews*, December 2004, http://www.plusnews.org/webspecials/ARV/ARV-PlusNews.pdf (accessed April 19, 2006).

184 **It was zidovudine, commonly known as AZT** For more information on AZT and AIDS drugs and treatment, see George Manos, Leonardo Negron, and Tim Horn, "Antiviral Drugs," in *Encyclopedia of AIDS*, 51–53; Darrell E. Ward, "Treatment of HIV Disease," in *Amfar AIDS Handbook*, 68–103; Ian V. D. Weller and I. G. Williams, "ABC of AIDS: Antiretroviral Drugs," *British Medical Journal* 332 (2001): 1410–12, http://bmj.bmjjournals.com/cgi/reprint/322/7299/1410 (accessed April 20, 2006); U.S. Department of Health and Human Services, "AIDSinfo Drug Database," http://www.aidsinfo.nih.gov/DrugsNew/Default.aspx?Menu Item=Drugs (accessed April 19, 2006); Body Health Resources Corporation, "FDA-Approved Antiretrovirals," http://www.thebodypro.com/antiretroviral_link.html (accessed April 19, 2006); and Avert, "Introduction to HIV/AIDS Treatment," http://www.avert.org/introtrt.htm (accessed April 19, 2006).

186 **"Most of the research that showed"** P. Chirac, T. von Schoen-Angerer, T. Kaspter, and N. Ford, "AIDS: Patent Rights versus Patient's Rights," *Lancet* 356, no. 9228 (August 5, 2000): 502.

187 **The American AIDS death rate** John Henkel, "Attacking AIDS with 'Cocktail' Therapy:

Drug Combo Sends Death Plummeting," *FDA Consumer Magazine*, July-August 1999, http://www.fda.gov/fdac/features/1999/499_aids.html (accessed April 19, 2006).

187 **"It returns many who were debilitated"** Ibid.

187 **"often discovered by public laboratories"** Chirac, von Schoen-Angerer, Kaspter, and Ford, "AIDS," 502.

188 **of the best-selling fifty drugs approved** Alice Dembner, "Public Handouts Enrich Drug Makers, Scientists," *Boston Globe*, April 5, 1998, http://www.bostonglobe.com/ (accessed April 19, 2000), reported in Angell, *Truth About Drug Companies*, 65.

188 **In 1998, the journal *Health Affairs*** Darren E. Zinner, "Medical R & D at the Turn of the Millenium," *Health Affairs*, September-October 2001, 202, quoted in Angell, *Truth About Drug Companies*, 64.

188 **In 2000, *Forbes* magazine estimated** Reported in Barton Gellman, "A Turning Point That Left Millions Behind: Drug Discounts Benefit Few While Protecting Pharmaceutical Companies' Profits," Death Watch: AIDS, Drugs, and Africa, *Washington Post*, December 28, 2000.

188 **"There is no question . . . that publicly funded"** Angell, *Truth About Drug Companies*, 65.

188 **"In 2001, drug companies gave doctors"** Ibid., 115–16.

189 **Pharmacia spent 44 percent of its revenues on marketing** Alexander Irwin, Joyce Millen, and Dorothy Fallows, *Global AIDS: Myths and Facts* (Cambridge, MA: South End, 2003), 118.
   According to a recent *New York Times* report, "a rebellion is under way by some doctors" against "overzealous sales practices among the nation's estimated 90,000 drug company representatives." Particularly objectionable to many physicians is the availability of computerized dossiers showing who has prescribed which drugs, and making doctors subject to specific pressure by drugmakers to prescribe more of their branded products. See Stephanie Saul, "Doctors Object to Gathering of Drug Data," *New York Times*, May 4, 2006, http://www.nytimes.com/2006/05/04/business/04prescribe.html (accessed May 6, 2006). New Hampshire is the first state to pass a bill barring data-mining companies, pharmacies, and others from selling the information. See Katie Zezima, "National Briefing: New Hampshire: Bill on Drug Data is Approved," *New York Times*, May 5, 2006, http://www.nytimes.com/2006/05/05/us/05brfs.html (accessed May 6, 2006).

189 **"GlaxoSmithKline and its co-marketer"** Angell, *Truth About Drug Companies*, 118.

189 **"Executive salaries and compensation packages"** Irwin, Millen, and Fallows, *Global AIDS*, 118.

190 **Bristol-Myers Squibb's CEO received** AFL-CIO, "Executive Paywatch: Health Care," http://www.aflcio.org/corporatewatch/paywatch/db_console_r.cfm?f=0&ind=Health+Care (accessed April 20, 2006).

190 **the numbers of AIDS deaths in the United States and Western Europe** According to the CDC and the Centre for the Epidemiological Monitoring of AIDS, respectively, 17,849 people died of AIDS in the United States and 3,454 in Western Europe in 2003—compared to UNAIDS estimate of 2 million to 2.5 million in sub-Saharan Africa. Centers for Disease Control, "HIV/AIDS Surveillance Report: Cases of HIV Infection and AIDS in the United States, 2004," 16, Table 7: Estimated Numbers of Deaths of Person with AIDS, by Year of Death and Selected Characteristics, 2000–2004, http://www.cdc.gov/hiv/stats/2004SurveillanceReport.pdf (accessed April 20, 2006); EuroHIV, "HIV/AIDS Surveillance in Europe, Year-End Report 2004," 42, Table 24: Deaths Among AIDS Cases by Country and Year of Death; 193, Table 2: AIDS Deaths, http://www.eurohiv.org/reports/report_71/pdf/report_eurohiv_71.pdf (accessed April 20, 2006); and UNAIDS, *2004 Report on the Global AIDS Epidemic* (Geneva: UNAIDS, 2004).

190 **Rudolf Nureyev died** Avert, "The History of AIDS, 1993–1997," http://www.avert.org/his93_97.htm (accessed April 19, 2000).

191 **"Now, in the seventh year"** Monette, *Borrowed Time*, 2.

191 **"once they understood they had escaped"** Barton Gellman, "World Shunned Signs of Coming Plague," Death Watch: AIDS, Drugs, and Africa, *Washington Post*, July 5, 2000.

192 "Beginning in 1980 . . . Congress enacted" Angell, *Truth About Drug Companies*, 7.

192 "These laws mean that drug companies" Ibid., 8.

192 "Exclusivity is the lifeblood" Ibid., 9.

192 "Industry lawyers have manipulated" Ibid., 9–10.

193 "The effects of patents on prices" Irwin, Millen, and Fallows, *Global AIDS*, 119.

193 6.4 million people had died Avert, "History of AIDS, 1993–1997."

193 "Squarely put . . . the drugs are in the north" Gellman, "Turning Point."

194 WTO's laws are called TRIPS For more information on TRIPS and intellectual property rights, see Avert, "TRIPS, AIDS, and Generic Drugs," http://www.avert.org/generic.htm (accessed April 19, 2000); Avert, "Providing Drug Treatment for Millions," http://www.avert.org/drugtreatment.htm.

194 All 147 member nations There are now 148 member nations.

194 "Western countries, led by the United States" Daryl Lindsey, "The AIDS-Drug Warrior," *Salon*, June 1, 2001, http://archive.salon.com/news/feature/2001/06/18/love/index.html (accessed April 20, 2006).

194 "Even with patents, it is not profitable" Amy Kapczynski, "Strict International Patent Laws Hurt Developing Countries," December, 16, 2002, http://yaleglobal.yale.edu/display.article?id=562 (accessed April 12, 2006).

195 "With powerful defenders among academics" Irwin, Millen, and Fallows, *Global AIDS*, 68.

195 "Despite years of evidence of AIDS' genocidal toll" Johanna McGeary, "Paying for AIDS Cocktails: Who Should Pick Up the Tab for the Third World?" *Time*, February 12, 2001, http://www.time.com/time/2001/aidsinafrica/drugs.html (accessed April 20, 2006).

196 "A strategy that emphasizes prevention" Irwin, Millen, and Fallows, *Global AIDS*, 61.

196 "'We may have to sit by'" Ibid.

196 "They're all dead already" Gellman, "World Shunned."

196 "Natsios, who spent a decade" John Donnelly, "Prevention Urged in AIDS Fight: Natsios Says Fund Should Spend Less on HIV Treatment," *Boston Globe*, June 7, 2001. See also Brenda Wilson, "Treating AIDS in Africa Undermined by Lack of Funds," *All Things Considered*, National Public Radio, November 28, 2003, http://www.npr.org/templates/story/story.php?storyId=1524909.

197 organizations like the Global Fund Global Fund to Fight AIDS, Tuberculosis and Malaria, "A Partnership to Prevent and Treat AIDS, Tuberculosis and Malaria," http://www.theglobalfund.org/en/files/publications/qaen.pdf (accessed April 20, 2006).

197 "Evidence from Thailand, Uganda, and Brazil" Irwin, Millen, and Fallows, *Global AIDS*, 43.

197 sub-Saharan nations hardest hit Senate Committee on Foreign Relations, *Halting the Spread of HIV/AIDS: Future Efforts in the U.S. Bilateral and Multilateral Response: Hearing Before the Committee on Foreign Relations*, 107 Cong., 2nd sess., February 13–14, 2002, http://frwebgate.access.gpo.gov/cgi-bin/getdoc.cgi?dbname=107_senate_hearings&docid=f:77846.pdf.

198 Doctors Without Borders . . . launched AIDS treatment Toby Kasper, David Coetzee, Francoise Louis, Andrew Boulle, and Katherine Hilderbrand, "Demystifying Antiretroviral Therapy in Resource-Poor Settings," *Essential Drugs Monitor* 32 (2003): 20–21, http://mednet2.who.int/edmonitor/32/edm32_en.pdf (accessed April 20, 2006); and WHO, "Scaling Up HIV/AIDS Care." For more information on Doctors Without Borders/Médicins Sans Frontières and its Treatment Access Campaign (inaugurated in 1999 to campaign for greater access to essential medicines), see http://www.accessmed-msf.org/ (accessed April 20, 2006).

198 poor people in poor countries Donald G. McNeil Jr., "Africans Outdo U.S. Patients in Following AIDS Therapy," *New York Times*, September 3, 2003.

198 if only the Coca-Cola company In fact, the Coca-Cola Africa Foundation has pledged to spend $30 million by the end of the decade fighting HIV/AIDS in Africa and is aware of its company's unparalleled deployment capacity. "The use of our core competencies—logistics to deliver condoms using our trucks, and marketing skills to communicate HIV/AIDS

information—presents an area of great potential and these need to be exploited for maximum gain." The foundation has invested in clinics, child centers, orphanages, and workplace projects. Coca-Cola Africa Foundation, "Our 2004–2005 HIV/AIDS Initiatives in Africa, Manzini, Swaziland," http://www2.coca-cola.com/citizenship/TCCAF_HIVAIDS_report.pdf (accessed April 25, 2006).

198 **South Africa was the hardest-hit country** UNAIDS, *Report on the Global HIV/AIDS Epidemic, June 2000*, 124, Table of Country-Specific AIDS Estimates and Data, End 1999; and United Nations Development Programme South Africa, "HIV/AIDS and Human Development: South Africa, 1998," http://www.undp.org.za/docs/pubs/hdr.overview.htm (accessed April 20, 2006).

199 **Plaintiffs included Alcon, Bayer** L. J. Davis, "A Deadly Dearth of Drugs," *Mother Jones*, January–February 2000, http://www.motherjones.com/commentary/power_plays/2000/01/AIDS_drugs.html (accessed April 20, 2006); Alex Duval Smith, "Focus AIDS: A Continent Left to Die," *Independent*, September 5, 1999; "A War Over Drugs and Patents," *Economist*, March 8, 2001, http://www.economist.com/displaystory.cfm?story_id=529284 (accessed April 20, 2001); Chris McGreal, "South Africa's Sick Wait for Judgment Day," *Guardian*, March 5, 2001, http://www.guardian.co.uk/Archive/Article/0,4273,4146083,00.html (accessed April 20, 2001); and Avert, "TRIPS, AIDS, and Generic Drugs."

199 **"The pharmaceutical industry and the Clinton administration"** Russell Sabin, "New Crusade to Lower AIDS Drug Costs: Africa's Need at Odds with Firms' Profit Motive," *San Francisco Chronicle*, May 24, 1999, http://sfgate.com/cgi-bin/article.cgi?file=/chronicle/archive/1999/05/24/MN104738.DTL (accessed March 30, 2006).

199 **"Patents are the lifeblood"** Ibid.

199 **"The only beneficiary of an erosion"** Ibid.

200 **"It was very dramatic"** Edwin Cameron, interview by Carrie Grace, August 22, 2005, http://news.bbc.co.uk/2/hi/africa/4166848.stm (accessed April 20, 2006).

200 **"What drug companies are concerned about"** Subcommittee on Criminal Justice, Drug Policy, and Human Resources, House Committee on Government Reform, *What Is the United States Role in Combating the Global HIV/AIDS Epidemic?: Hearing Before the Subcommittee on Criminal Justice, Drug Policy, and Human Resources, House Committee on Government Reform*, 106th Cong., 1st sess., July 19, 1999, http://frwebgate.access.gpo.gov/cgi-bin/getdoc.cgi?dbname=106_house_hearings&docid=f:65308.pdf (accessed April 22, 2006).

201 **"ensure that public health interests are paramount"** Evelyn Hong, "Globalisation and the Impact on Health, a Third World View—the Agreement on Trade Related Aspects of Intellectual Property (TRIPs)" (Section, "U.S. Threatens South Africa"), *The Agreement on Trade Related Aspects of Intellectual Property (TRIPs)—Globalisation and the Impact on Health—a Third World View—Issue Papers*, August 2000 (last updated March 2005), People's Health Movement, April 14, 2006, http://www.phmovement.org/pubs/issuepapers/hong15.html; and World Health Organization, *Resolution on Intellectual Property Rights, Innovation and Public Health* (56th World Health Assembly, May 28, 2003), http://www.who.int/gb/ebwha/pdf_files/WHA56/ea56r27.pdf (accessed April 22, 2006).

201 **"All relevant agencies of the U.S. government"** U.S. Department of State, "Report on U.S. government efforts to negotiate the repeal, termination or withdrawal of Article 15(c) of the South African Medicines and Related Substances Act of 1965," February 5, 1999.

201 **Gore's significant ties to the pharmaceutical industry** John B. Judis, "K Street Gore," *American Prospect*, July/August 1999, http://www.prospect.org/print/V10/45/judis-j.html (accessed April 21, 2006), reported in Janine Jackson, "Media Blow the First Issue of the Campaign," *Extra: The Magazine of Fair, the Media Watch Group*, September/October 1999, http://www.fair.org/extra/9909/gore-aids.html (accessed April 21, 2006).

201 **"I believe in the First Amendment"** Jackson, "Media Blow."

202 **"I support South Africa's efforts"** Al Gore to James E. Clyburn, June 25, 1999, http://www.cptech.org/ip/health/sa/vp-feb-25-99.html (accessed March 5, 2006).

202 **"On its face, the [vice president's] statement"** Subcommittee on Criminal Justice, Drug Policy and Human Resources, *What Is the United States Role?*

202 **"it was the activities of ACT UP"** Irwin, Millen, and Fallows, *Global AIDS*, 124.

202 **"Mother Teresa was already dead"** Kapczynski, "Strict International Patent Laws."

203 **Hamied announced that Cipla would produce** Soutik Biswas, "Indian Drugs Boss Hails Aids Deal," October 29, 2003, http://news.bbc.co.uk/2/hi/south_asia/3220619.stm (accessed April 21, 2001).

203 **"We are a commercial company"** Lindsey, "AIDS-Drug Warrior."

203 **"There is no patent"** Ibid.

203 **"It is now unquestionably within the reach"** Mark Rosenberg, Task Force for Child Survival, in discussion with author, September 2001.

204 **They reaped PR advantages** The Accelerating Access Initiative was started as a joint initiative between the UN (the UNAIDS Secretariat, UNICEF, UNFPA, WHO, the World Bank) and the five companies (Boehringer Ingelheim, Bristol-Myers Squibb, GlaxoSmithKline, Merck & Co., and Hoffmann–La Roche. For more information on Accelerating Access, see WHO/UNAIDS, "'Accelerating Access' Initiative Moving Forward; 72 Countries Worldwide Express Interest," press release, December 11, 2001, http://www.whoint/inf-pr-2001/en/pr2001-54.html (accessed April 21, 2001); ACT UP Paris, "'Access' Serves Pharmaceutical Companies While Corrupting Health Organizations," press release, May 15, 2002, http://www.actupparis.org/pdf/nord_sud/02_05_15_Accele _Acc_ENG.pdf.

204 **But "on-the-ground impact"** McGeary, "Paying for AIDS Cocktails."

205 **"have systematically come with strings attached"** ACT UP Paris, "'Access' serves Pharmaceutical Companies."

205 **"According to the most optimistic"** Ibid.

205 **"Far different from commercial"** Ibid.

268 **In 2005, Ethiopia had 1,563,000 Aids orphans** Indrias Getachew, "Ethiopia: Steady increase in street children orphaned by AIDS," UNICEF, http://www.unicef.org/ infobycountry/ethiopia_30783.html).

295 **Surveys of American opinion** Pew Research Center, "Bush's Base Backs Him to the Hilt," April 26, 2001, http://people-press.org/reports/display.php3?ReportID=14 (accessed April 24, 2006).

295 **"Development assistance is often of dubious quality"** Pekka Hirvoenen, "Stingy Samaritans: Why Recent Increases in Development Aid Fail to Help the Poor," *Global Policy Forum*, August 2005, http://www.globalpolicy.org/socecon/develop/oda/2005/ 08stingysamaritans.htm (accessed April 24, 2006).

296 **Though the United States gave the most in dollar amount** Anup Sha, "The U.S. and Foreign AID Assistance," http://www.globalissues.org/TradeRelated/Debt/USAid.asp (accessed April 24, 2006). Country-specific statistics from Organization for Economic Co-operation and Development, "Aid Statistics, Donor Aid Charts," http://www.oec- d.org/countrylist/0,2578,en_2649_34447_1783495_1_1_1_1,00.html (accessed April 24, 2003).

296 **"We are in a desperate race"** Lewis, *Race Against Time*, 145.

297 **"We're terrific when it comes to studies"** Stephen Lewis, "Statement by Stephen Lewis, Special Envoy for HIV/AIDS in Africa, on World AIDS Day, December 1, 2005," http:// www.pih.org/inthenews/WorldAIDSDay2005-StephenLewis.pdf (accessed April 16, 2006).

299 **In May 2005, Meles Zenawi's reelection** For more information on the months following Meles Zenawi's reelection, see Befekir Kebebe, "Historical Timeline: Politics; Ethiopia's Election and Its Aftermath," http://www.ethiopianmillennium.com/timeline_politics.html (accessed April 21, 2006).

300 **In February of 2006, 80 defendants** Amnesty International, "Ethiopia: Prisoners

of Conscience Prepare to Face 'Trial,'" press release, February 22, 2006, http://www.am-nestyusa.org/countries/ethiopia/document.do?id=ENGAFR250052006 (April 21, 2006).

300 "These people are prisoners of conscience" Ibid.

301 "Instead the ballots have been trashed" Interview with friend, Addis Ababa, November 2005. I have withheld the interviewee's name by mutual consent.

On March 9, 2006, the Committee to Protect Journalists (CPJ) reported, "The CPJ delegation was allowed rare access today to Kality Prison, on the outskirts of the capital, Addis Ababa, where dozens of opposition leaders and at least 14 journalists have been held following post-electoral riots in November . . . Fourteen Ethiopian journalists are currently on trial on treason and 'genocide' charges. They have been in jail since November, when Ethiopian authorities launched a massive and ongoing crackdown on the private press. Police have blocked most private newspapers from publishing; driven dozens of journalists into hiding and exile; raided newspaper offices, confiscating computers, documents, and other materials; expelled two foreign journalists; and issued a 'wanted list' of editors, writers, and dissidents." Committee to Protect Journalists, "Ethiopia: Court drops charges against five Voice of America journalists," March 22, 2006, http://www.cpj.org/news/2006/africa/ethiopia22mar06na.html (April 25, 2006).

On March 22, Ethiopia's Federal High Court dropped charges of treason and genocide against eighteen people, including five Washington-based journalists for the Voice of America. The five, Negussie Mengesha, Addisu Abebe, Tizita Belachew, Adanech Fessehaye, and Solomon Kifle, never were in police custody in Ethiopia.

Also in March 2006, 395 prisoners were freed without prosecution, months after illegal roundups and detentions in sometimes remote and overcrowded prison camps. The freeing of these political prisoners brings to around 11,600 the number freed since the two outbreaks of deadly violence last year. The exact number of political prisoners is not known, but it is suspected that several thousand government opponents are still detained without charge. http://www.ethiopianmillenium.com/news.html# (accessed April 25, 2006).

See also Amnesty International, "Ethiopia: Prisoners of Conscience"; Amnesty International, "Ethiopia: Fear of torture/possible prisoners of conscience," press release, March 31, 2006, http://web.amnesty.org/library/Index/ENGAFR250082006?open&of=ENG-ETH (accessed April 25, 2006); Amnesty International, "Ethiopia: Further information on possible prisoners of conscience/fear of torture or ill-treatment/health concern: New names," January 19, 2006 (accessed April 25, 2006); and Amnesty International, "Ethiopia: Disappearance/excessive use of force/impunity/detention without charge or trial," January 30, 2006.

362 "Do you know how few orphanages" Interview with AHOPE Ethiopia board member, Addis Ababa, December 15, 2005. I have withheld the interviewee's name by mutual consent.

411 The WHO estimated that expanded access "Progress on Global Access to HIV Anti-retroviral Therapy: A Report on '3 by 5' and Beyond," WHO Publications, March 2006, World Health Organization and United Nations Programme on HIV/AIDS (UNAIDS), March 30, 2006, http://www.who.int/hiv/fullreport_en_highres.pdf. For more information on "3 by 5," see Avert, "AIDS Treatment Targets and Results."

411 But the Global Fund faces a resource shortfall Global Fund to Fight AIDS, Tuberculosis and Malaria, "Global Fund Closes Funding Gap: Round Five Grants Approved by Global Fund Board; Round Six Planned for 2006," press release, December 16, 2005, http://www.theglobalfund.org/en/media_center/press/pr_051216.asp (accessed April 22, 2006). At the time of writing, the Global Fund has no money to fund a new round of grants (Round 6). For more information on the fund, see Avert, "The Global Fund to Fight AIDS, Tuberculosis and Malaria," http://www.avert.org/global-fund.htm (accessed April 21, 2006); Avert, "Funding the Fight Against AIDS," http://www.avert.org/aidsmoney.htm (accessed April 21, 2006); and Bernard Rivers, "Stalled Growth: The

Global Fund in Year Four," *Global Fund Observer Newsletter*, November 7, 2005, http://www.aidspan.org/gfo/archives/newsletter/GFO-Issue-52.pdf (accessed April 22, 2006).

411 **"All we can do is apologize"** Madeleine Morris, "Apology Over Missed AIDS Target," November 25, 2005, http://news.bbc.co.uk/2/hi/health/4476978.stm (accessed April 17, 2006). See also International Treatment Preparedness Coalition, "Missing the Target: A Report on HIV/AIDS Treatment Access from the Frontlines," November 25, 2005, http://www.aidstreatmentaccess.org/itpcfinal.pdf (accessed April 22, 2006); and WHO, "Progress on Global Access."

412 **"If 3 by 5 fails . . . as it surely will"** Stephen Lewis, UN Special Envoy for HIV/AIDS in Africa, press release, March 3, 2004, http://www.aegis.com/news/unaids/2004/UN040301.html (accessed April 21, 2006).

412 **between 1987 and 2005, Retrovir generated** Sabine Vollmer, "Cheaper AZT on the Way," *Raleigh News and Observer*, September 20, 2005, http://www.natap.org/2005/HIV/092005_02.htm (accessed April 21, 2006).

412 **Several Ethiopian pharmaceutical companies have** Gilbert Kombe (Senior Associate for HIV/AIDS, Abt Associates, Inc.), e-mail message to research assistant, February 24, 2006; and Yordanos Tadesse (CEO, Bethlehem Pharmaceuticals, PLC, Addis Ababa), e-mail to research assistant, March 13, 2006.

413 **"to state-owned companies in all third world countries"** Biswas Soutik, "Indian Drugs Boss Hails AIDS Deal," April 17, 2006, http://news.bbc.co.uk/2/hi/south_asia/3220619.stm (accessed April 22, 2006).

413 **By February 2006, according to UNICEF** UNICEF, "UNICEF/Baylor Agreement Signals Brighter Outlook for Pediatric AIDS Treatment in Africa," press release, February 27, 2006, http://www.unicef.org/uniteforchildren/press/press_31343.htm (accessed April 22, 2006).

413 **Eighty-five percent of those children lived** UNAIDS and UNICEF, "A Call to Action: Children; the Missing Face of AIDS," October 2005, 4, http://www.unicef.org/publications/files/AIDS_Launch_final_14Oct.pdf (accessed April 22, 2006).

413 **The forty children Dr. Sofia began to treat** By April 2006, WWO had 120 children enrolled in their Barlow Clinic free pediatric AIDS program, with the hope of including 80 more by the end of the year. With government support and encouragement, WWO has begun outreach to orphanages across the capital and in other towns. Also in April 2006, Dr. Jane Aronson (founder and executive director of World Wide Orphans) launched a theater project with the help of volunteers from the American film and theater worlds; HIV-positive children at AHOPE were assisted in the creation of a dramatic production—complete with scenery, costumes, and makeup. The staging of a show by these children ought to enlighten many people who are oblivious to the potential for creativity, fun, and joy within the African orphan population, even within the HIV-positive orphan population. WWO plans a state-of-the-art community center for adults and children living with AIDS, which will include a clinic, classrooms, a theater, and a soccer complex.

414 **"Despite these efforts, pediatric interventions"** Tadesse Wuhib, "Speech on the Opening of National Pediatric Conference" (National Conference on Expanding Access to Pediatric HIV/AIDS Care and Treatment: Challenges and Prospects, Addis Ababa, January 25, 2006), http://www.columbia-icap.org/ethiopia/pdf/intro_2.pdf (accessed April 16, 2006).

SELECTED BIBLIOGRAPHY

Books

Angell, Marcia. *The Truth About Drug Companies: How They Deceive Us and What to Do About It.* New York: Random House, 2004.

Arno, Peter, and Karyn L. Feiden. *Against the Odds: The Story of AIDS Drugs Development, Politics and Profits.* New York: HarperCollins, 1992.

Azeze, Fekade, comp. *Unheard Voices: Drought, Famine and God in Ethiopian Oral Poetry.* Addis Ababa: Addis Ababa University Press, 1998.

Barnett, Tony, and Alan Whiteside. *AIDS in the Twenty-First Century: Disease and Globalization.* Houndmills, Basingstoke, Hampshire: Palgrave Macmillan, 2003.

Bayer, Ronald, and Gerald M. Oppenheimer. *AIDS Doctors: Voices from the Epidemic: An Oral History.* Oxford: Oxford University Press, 2000.

Behrman, Greg. *The Invisible People: How the U.S. Has Slept Through the Global AIDS Pandemic, the Greatest Humanitarian Catastrophe of Our Time.* New York: Free Press, 2004.

Bernstein, William J. *The Birth of Plenty: How the Prosperity of the Modern World Was Created.* New York: McGraw-Hill, 2004.

Brooks, Miguel F., trans. and ed. *A Modern Translation of the* Kebra Nagast *(The Glory of Kings).* Lawrenceville, NJ: Red Sea Press, 1998.

Bryson, Bill. *African Diary.* New York: Broadway Books, 2002.

Campbell, Catherine. *Letting Them Die: Why HIV/AIDS Prevention Programmes Fail.* Oxford: International African Institute, 2003.

Cohen, Jon. *Shots in the Dark: The Wayward Search for an AIDS Vaccine.* New York: W. W. Norton, 2001.

Crewdson, John. *Science Fictions: A Scientific Mystery, a Massive Cover-up, and the Dark Legacy of Robert Gallo.* Boston: Little, Brown, 2002.

Davidson, Basil. *Africa in History.* New York: Collier Books, 1974.

Diamond, Jared. *Guns, Germs, and Steel.* New York: W. W. Norton, 1997.

Easterly, William. *The Elusive Quest for Growth: Economists' Adventures and Misadventures in the Tropics.* Boston: MIT Press, 2002.

———. *The White Man's Burden: Why the West's Efforts to Aid the Rest Have Done So Much Ill and So Little Good.* New York: Penguin, 2006.

Eaton, Jenny, and Kate Etue, eds. *The aWAKE Project: Uniting Against the African AIDS Crisis.* Nashville: W. Publishing Group, 2002.

Farmer, Paul. *Pathologies of Power: Health, Human Rights, and the New War on the Poor.* Berkeley and Los Angeles: University of California Press, 2003.

Foster, Geoff, Carole Levine, and John Williamson, eds. *The Global Impact of HIV/AIDS on Orphans and Vulnerable Children.* New York: Cambridge University Press, 2005.

French, Howard W. *A Continent for the Taking: The Tragedy and Hope of Africa.* New York: Alfred A. Knopf, 2004.

Garrett, Laurie. *The Coming Plague*. New York: Penguin Books, 1994.

Goozner, Merrill. *The $800 Million Pill: The Truth Behind the Cost of New Drugs*. Berkeley and Los Angeles: University of California Press, 2004.

Gordon, Frances Linzee. *Lonely Planet Ethiopia and Eritrea*. 2nd ed. Victoria, Australia: Lonely Planet, 2003.

Gottleib, Michael S., Donald J. Jeffries, Donna Mildvan, Anthony J. Pinching, and Thomas C. Quinn. *Current Topics in AIDS*. Vol 2. Somerset, NJ: John Wiley and Sons, 1989.

Goudsmit, Jaap. *Viral Sex: The Nature of AIDS*. Oxford: Oxford University Press, 1998.

Gourevitch, Philip. *We Wish to Inform You That Tomorrow We Will Be Killed with Our Families: Stories from Rwanda*. New York: Picador, 1998.

Guest, Emma. *Children of AIDS*. Pietermaritzburg: University of Natal Press, 2003.

Guest, Robert. *The Shackled Continent: Power, Corruption, and African Lives*. Washington, DC: Smithsonian Books, 2004.

Hancock, Graham. *Lords of Poverty*. Nairobi: Camerapix, 2004.

Hancock, Graham, Richard Pankhurst, and Duncan Willetts. *Under Ethiopian Skies*. Nairobi: Camerapix, 1997.

Harden, Blaine. *Africa: Dispatches from a Fragile Continent*. New York: HarperCollins, 1993.

Harrison, Paul, and Robert Palmer. *News out of Africa: Biafra to Band Aid*. London: Hilary Shipman, 1986.

Henze, Paul B. *Layers of Time: A History of Ethiopia*. New York: Palgrave, 2000.

Hertz, Noreena. *The Debt Threat: How Debt Is Destroying the Developing World and Threatening Us All*. New York: HarperCollins, 2004.

Hilts, Philip J. *Protecting America's Health: The FDA, Business, and One Hundred Years of Regulation*. New York: Alfred A. Knopf, 2003.

Hochschild, Adam. *King Leopold's Ghost*. New York: Mariner Books, 1999.

Hooper, Edward. *The River: A Journey to the Source of HIV and AIDS*. Boston: Little, Brown, 2000.

Howe, Marie, and Michael Klein. *In the Company of My Solitude: American Writing from the AIDS Pandemic*. New York: Persea Books, 1995.

Hunter, Susan. *Black Death: AIDS in Africa*. Houndmills, Basingstoke, Hampshire: Palgrave Macmillan, 2003.

Irwin, Alexander, Joyce Millen, and Dorothy Fallows. *Global AIDS: Myths and Facts*. Cambridge, MA: South End, 2003.

Jackson, John G. *Introduction to African Civilizations*. Secaucus, NJ: Citadel, 1974.

Jembere, Aberra. *Agony in the Grand Palace: 1974–1982*. Trans. Dr. Hailu Araaya. Addis Ababa: Shama Books, 2002.

Kaplan, Robert D. *Surrender or Starve: Travels in Ethiopia, Sudan, Somalia, and Eritrea*. New York: Vintage, 2003.

Kapuscinski, Ryszard. *The Emperor*. Trans. William R. Brand and Katarzyna Mroczkowska-Brand. New York: Vintage International, 1989.

———. *The Shadow of the Sun*. Trans. Klara Glowczewska. New York: Vintage, 2002.

Kasule, Samuel. *The History Atlas of Africa*. New York: Macmillan, 1998.

Kidder, Tracy. *Mountains Beyond Mountains*. New York: Random House, 2003.

Lamb, David. *The Africans*. New York: Vintage, 1984.

Levine, Donald N. *Greater Ethiopia: The Evolution of a Multiethnic Society*. 2nd ed. Chicago: University of Chicago Press, 2000.

Lewis, Stephen. *Race Against Time*. CBC Massey Lectures Series. Toronto: House of Anansi Press, 2005.

Long, Jacqueiline, ed. *Encyclopedia of Medicine*. Thomson Gale, 2002. Searchable online at Health A to Z: Your Family Health Site, http://www.healthatoz.com/healthatoz/Atoz/ency/zoonosis.jsp (accessed April 17, 2006).

Mann, Jonathan, and Daniel Tarantola, eds. *AIDS in the World II*. Oxford: Oxford University Press, 1996.

Mann, Jonathan, Daniel Tarantola, and Thomas Netter, eds. *AIDS in the World 1992.* Cambridge: Harvard University Press, 1992.

Marcus, Harold G. *A History of Ethiopia.* Updated ed. Berkeley and Los Angeles: University of California Press, 2002.

McEvedy, Colin. *The Penguin Atlas of African History.* London: Penguin Books, 1995.

Meredith, Martin. *The Fate of Africa: A History of 50 Years of Independence.* New York: Public Affairs, 2005.

Mezlekia, Nega. *Notes from the Hyena's Belly.* New York: Picador, 2002.

Monette, Paul. *Borrowed Time: An AIDS Memoir.* New York: Harcourt Brace, 1988.

Moorehead, Alan. *The Blue Nile.* New York: Harper & Row, 1962.

Naim, Asher. *Saving the Lost Tribe: The Rescue and Redemption of the Ethiopian Jews.* New York: Ballantine Books, 2003.

Nattrass, Nicoli. *The Moral Economy of AIDS in South Africa.* Cambridge: Cambridge University Press, 2004.

Pankhurst, Richard. *The Ethiopians.* Oxford: Blackwell, 2003.

Pankhurst, Richard, and Denis Gerard. *Ethiopia Photographed: Historic Photographs of the Country and Its People Taken Between 1867 and 1935.* London and New York: Kegan Paul International, 1996.

Reader, John. *Africa: A Biography of the Continent.* New York: Vintage, 1999.

Sachs, Jeffrey D. *The End of Poverty.* Foreword by Bono. New York: Penguin, 2005.

Schwab, Peter. *Africa: A Continent Self-Destructs.* New York: Palgrave, 2001.

Sen, Amartya. *Development as Freedom.* New York: Anchor, 2000.

Shelemay, Kay Kaufman. *A Song of Longing: An Ethiopian Journey.* Chicago: University of Illinois Press, 1994.

Shilts, Randy. *And the Band Played On.* New York: St. Martin's, 2000.

Smith, Dan, with Ane Braein. *The Penguin State of the World Atlas.* 7th ed. London: Penguin Books, 2003.

Smith, Raymond A., ed. *Encyclopedia of AIDS: A Social, Political, Cultural, and Scientific Record of the HIV Epidemic.* Rev. ed., with forewords by James W. Curran and Peter Piot. New York: Penguin Books, 2001.

Treichler, Paula A. *How to Have Theory in an Epidemic: Cultural Chronicles of AIDS.* Durham, NC: Duke University Press, 1999.

Ward, Darrell E. *The Amfar AIDS Handbook: The Complete Guide to Understanding HIV and AIDS.* New York: W. W. Norton, 1999.

Wooten, Jim. *We Are All the Same.* New York: Penguin, 2004.

Wrong, Michela. *"I Didn't Do It for You": How the World Betrayed a Small African Nation.* New York: HarperCollins, 2005.

Zewde, Bahru. *A History of Modern Ethiopia: 1855–1991.* 4th ed. Athens: Ohio University Press; Oxford: James Curry Publishers; Addis Ababa: Addis Ababa University Press, 2001.

Articles, Book Chapters, Working Papers, Press Releases, Speeches, Radio Documentaries, Etc.

Abdullahi, Mohamed. "Ethiopian Private Sector Blames Meles." *Geeska Afrika*, April 1, 2005, http://www.geeskaafrika.com/ethiopia_1apr05.htm (accessed April 16, 2006).

Abera, Yodit. "Unemployed Graduates." *Ethiopian Reporter*, December 10, 2005, http://www.ethiopianreporter.com/modules.php?name=News&file=article&sid=1512 (accessed April 11, 2006).

Aberra, Rakeb Messele. "Human Rights Report of Ethiopia." *Selamta*, http://www.selamta.net/politic.htm (accessed August 23, 2005).

ACT UP Paris. "'Access' Serves Pharmaceutical Companies While Corrupting Health Organizations." Press release, May 15, 2002, http://www.actupparis.org/pdf/nord_sud/02_05_15_Accele_Acc_ENG.pdf (accessed April 20, 2006).

African Bird Club. "Ethiopia." http://www.africanbirdclub.org/countries/Ethiopia/species.html (accessed April 17, 2006).

AIDS Project Los Angeles. "Timeline of the Epidemic." http://www.apla.org/facts/timeline.html (accessed April 19, 2001).

Allen, Arthur. "Sex Change: Uganda v. Condoms." *New Republic*, May 27, 2002.

Altman, Lawrence K. "In Africa, a Deadly Silence About AIDS Is Lifting." *New York Times*, July 13, 1999, http://query.nytimes.com/gst/fullpage.html?sec=health&res=9C0DE6DE113CF930A25754C0A96F958260 (accessed April 23, 2006).

———. "New Form of Cancer Seen in African AIDS Patients." *New York Times*, December 9, 2005, http://query.nytimes.com/gst/fullpage.html?sec=health&res=9D02E6DD173BF93AA35751CIA963948260 (accessed April 18, 2006).

Amnesty International. "Ethiopia: Prisoners of Conscience Prepare to Face 'Trial.'" Press release, February 22, 2006, http://www.amnestyusa.org/countries/ethiopia/document.do?id=ENGAFR250052006 (accessed April 21, 2006).

———. "Ethiopia: Recent Arrests of Opposition Leaders and Police Killings of 46 Demonstrators." Press release, November 11, 2005, http://web.amnesty.org/library/Index/ENGAFR250192005?open&of=ENG-2F4 (accessed April 21, 2006).

Baleta, Adele. "S. Africa's AIDS Activists Accuse Government of Murder." *Lancet* 361 (March 2003): 1105.

BBC. "AIDS Ravages Teachers." May 8, 2002, http://news.bbc.co.uk/2/hi/africa/1974111.stm (accessed April 17, 2006).

———. "Timeline: Ethiopia." http://news.bbc.co.uk/2/hi/africa/1072219.stm (accessed April 17, 2006).

Beaubien, Jason. "AIDS Ravages Swaziland." *Morning Edition*, National Public Radio, September 24, 2003, http://www.npr.org/templates/story/story.php?storyId=1444263.

———."South Africa Forms Plan for AIDS Drugs." *Morning Edition*, National Public Radio, October 7, 2003, http://www.npr.org/templates/story/story.php?storyId=1457235.

Beaumont, Peter. "Deaths spiral out of control in AIDS crisis." *Observer*, February 20, 2005.

Bishop-Sambrook, Clare. "The Challenge of the HIV/AIDS Epidemic in Rural Ethiopia: Averting the Crisis in Low AIDS-Impacted Communities." Food and Agriculture Organization Sustainable Development Department, Rome, March 2004, http://www.fao.org/sd/dim_pe3/pe3_040402_en.htm (accessed April 17, 2006).

Biswas, Soutik. "Indian Drugs Boss Hails AIDS Deal." BBC.co.uk, April 17, 2006, http://news.bbc.co.uk/2/hi/south_asia/3220619.stm (accessed April 22, 2006).

Blake, Greg. "Ethiopia's Decisive Victory at Adowa." *Military History Magazine*, October 1997.

Buckley, Graeme J. "Decent Work in a Least Developed Country: A Critical Assessment of the Ethiopia PRSP." Working Paper 42, International Labor Office, 2004, http://www.ilo.org/public/english/bureau/integration/download/publicat/4_3_234_wp-42.pdf (accessed April 14, 2005).

Bumiller, Elizabeth. "Bush Chooses U.S. Executive for AIDS Job." *New York Times*, July 3, 2003, http://query.nytimes.com/gst/fullpage.html?sec=health&res=9B05E3D7103AF930A35754C0A9659C8B63 (accessed April 16, 2003).

Cameron, Edwin. Interview by Carrie Grace. BBC.co.uk, August 22, 2005, http://news.bbc.co.uk/2/hi/africa/4166848.stm (accessed April 20, 2006).

Carlsen, William. "Did Modern Medicine Spread an Epidemic?" *San Francisco Chronicle*, January 15, 2001.

———. "Quest for the Origin of AIDS." *San Francisco Chronicle*, January 14, 2001.

Chirac, P., T. von Schoen-Angerer, T. Kaspter, and N. Ford. "AIDS: Patent Rights versus Patient's Rights." *Lancet* 356, no. 9228 (August 5, 2000): 1611–12.

CNN. "AIDS: 20 Years of an Epidemic." http://edition.cnn.com/SPECIALS/2001/aids/interactive/timeline/frameset.exclude.html (accessed July 5, 2005).

Cooke, Jennifer G., principal author. "Battling HIV/AIDS in Ethiopia. A Report of the CSIS HIV/AIDS Delegation to Ethiopia, May 23–28, 2004." Washington, DC: Center for Strategic and International Studies, November 2004.

———. "The Second Wave of the HIV/AIDS Pandemic: China, India, Russia, Ethiopia, Nigeria. A Conference Report of the CSIS Task Force on HIV/AIDS." Washington, DC: Center for Strategic and International Studies, December 2002.

Davis, L. J. "A Deadly Dearth of Drugs." *Mother Jones*, January-February 2000, http://www.motherjones.com/commentary/power_plays/2000/01/AIDS_drugs.html (accessed April 20, 2006).

Dembner, Alice. "Public Handouts Enrich Drug Makers, Scientists." *Boston Globe*, April 5, 1998, http://www.bostonglobe.com/ (accessed April 19, 2000).

Denu, Berhanu, Abraham Tekeste, and Hannah van der Deijl. "Characteristics and Determinants of Youth Employment, Underemployment and Inadequate Employment in Ethiopia." Employment Strategy Paper 2005/07, International Labor Office, 2005, http://www.ilo.org/public/english/employment/strat/download/esp2005-7.pdf (accessed April 11, 2006).

DeYoung, Karen. "U.N. Pledges Support in Fight Against AIDS." *Washington Post*, June 28, 2001.

Dimbleby, Jonathan. "Ethiopia Proves There Can Be Life After Death." *Observer*, July 28, 2002, http://observer.guardian.co.uk/worldview/story/0,11581,764433,00.html (accessed April 17, 2006).

Donnelly, John. "Prevention Urged in AIDS Fight: Natsios Says Fund Should Spend Less on HIV Treatment." *Boston Globe*, June 7, 2001.

Downing, Robert, Roger Eglin, and Anne C. Bayley, "African Kaposi's sarcoma and AIDS." *Lancet* I (1984): 478–80.

Drucker, Ernest. Interview by Norman Swan. *The Health Report*, Australian Broadcasting Company Radio National, November 27, 2000, http://abc.net.au/rn/talks/8.30/healthrpt/stories/s217997.htm (accessed April 17, 2000).

The Economist. "AIDS in the Third World: A Global Disaster." January, 2, 1999, http://www.economist.com/ (accessed April 20, 2006).

———. "Leaders: Too Much Morality, Too Little Sense." July 30, 2005, http://www.economist.com/ (accessed April 20, 2006).

———. "A War Over Drugs and Patents." March 8, 2001, http://www.economist.com/displaystory.cfm?story_id=529284 (accessed April 20, 2006).

Ellman, Tom, Heather Culbert, and Victorio Torres-Feced. "Treatment of AIDS in conflict-affected settings: A failure of imagination." *Lancet* 365 (January 22, 2005).

Endailalu, Shimelis, Hailu Tadeg, and Negussu Mekonnen. "ARV Procurement: The Ethiopian Experience." Presentation, National Conference on Expanding Access to Pediatric HIV/AIDS Care and Treatment: Challenges and Prospects, Addis Ababa, January 25–27, 2006, http://www.columbia-icap.org/ethiopia/pdf/panel5_23.pdf (accessed April 23, 2006).

Epstein, Helen. "AIDS in South Africa: The Invisible Cure." *New York Review of Books*, July 17, 2003, http://www.nybooks.com/ (accessed April 22, 2006).

———. "AIDS: The Lesson of Uganda." *New York Review of Books*, July 5, 2001, http://www.nybooks.com/ (accessed April 22, 2006).

———. "God and the Fight Against AIDS." *New York Review of Books*, April 28, 2005, http://www.nybooks.com/articles/17963 (accessed April 22, 2006).

———. "The Hidden Cause of AIDS." *New York Review of Books*, May 9, 2002, http://www.nybooks.com/articles/15371 (accessed April 22, 2006).

———. "The Lost Children of AIDS." *New York Review of Books*, November 3, 2005, http://www.nybooks.com/articles/18399 (accessed April 22, 2006).

———. "The Mystery of AIDS in South Africa." *New York Review of Books*, July 20, 2000, http://www.nybooks.com/articles/9 (accessed April 23, 2006).

——. "Something Happened." Review of *The River: A Journey to the Source of HIV and AIDS*, by Edward Hooper. *New York Review of Books*, December 2, 1999, http://www.nybooks.com/ (accessed April 23, 2006).

——. "Time of Indifference." *New York Review of Books*, April 12, 2001.

Epstein, Helen, and Lincoln Chen. "Can AIDS Be Stopped?" *New York Review of Books*, March 14, 2002, http://www.nybooks.com/articles/15188 (accessed April 23, 2006).

Fenton, James. "Ethiopia: Victors and Victims." *New York Review of Books*, November 7, 1985, http://www.newyorkreviewofbooks.com/ (accessed April 19, 2006).

Garbus, Lisa. "HIV/AIDS in Ethiopia." Country AIDS Policy Analysis Project, AIDS Policy Research Center, University of California, April 2003, http://hivinsite.ucsf.edu/pdf/ countries/ari-et.pdf (accessed April 20, 2006).

Garenne, Michel, Romain Micol, and Arnaud Fontanet. Letter to the editor in response to "Unsafe Healthcare Drives Spread of African HIV." *International Journal of STD & AIDS* 15, no. 1 (January 2004): 65–67.

Gellman, Barton. "A Turning Point That Left Millions Behind: Drug Discounts Benefit Few While Protecting Pharmaceutical Companies' Profits." Death Watch series, *Washington Post*, December 28, 2000.

——. "An Unequal Calculus of Life and Death: As Millions Perished in Pandemic, Firms Debated Access to Drugs." Death Watch series, *Washington Post*, December 27, 2000.

——. "World Shunned Signs of Coming Plague." Death Watch series, *Washington Post*, July 5, 2000.

Gibbs, Nancy. "Saving One Life at a Time: A special report on the world's most dangerous diseases—and the heroes fighting them." *Time*, November 7, 2005.

Global Fund to Fight AIDS, Tuberculosis and Malaria. "Global Fund Closes Funding Gap: Round Five Grants Approved by Global Fund Board; Round Six Planned for 2006." Press release, December 16, 2005, http://www.theglobalfund.org/en/media_center/press/ pr_051216.asp (accessed April 22, 2006).

Goldberg, Robert. "Bountiful Bogeymen: The drug companies—so easy to defend." *National Review* 18, September 25, 2000.

Goldyn, Lawrence. "Africa Can't Just Take a Pill for AIDS." *New York Times*, July 6, 2000.

Gottlieb, Scott. "UN says up to half the teenagers in Africa will die of AIDS." *British Medical Journal* 321 (2000): 67.

Haile Selassie. "Speech to the League of Nations." League of Nations, Geneva, June 20, 1936. Posted online by the Harvard Rhetorical Society, http://hcs.harvard.edu/~rhetoric/ selassie.htm (accessed April 16, 2006). A recording of this speech can be downloaded from http://www.historychannel.com/broadband/home/ (accessed April 16, 2006).

Hargreaves, James R., and Judith R. Glynn. "Educational attainment and HIV-2 infection in developing countries: A systematic review." *Tropical Medicine & International Health* 7 (June 2002): 489–98.

Henkel, John. "Attacking AIDS with 'Cocktail' Therapy: Drug Combo Sends Death Plummeting." *FDA Consumer Magazine*, July–August 1999, http://www.fda.gov/fdac/features/1999/ 499_aids.html (accessed April 19, 2006).

Heywood, Mark. "Drug Access, Patents and Global Health: 'Chaffed and Waxed Sufficient.'" *Third World Quarterly* 23, no. 2 (2002): 217–31.

Hogle, Janice A., ed.; Edward Green, Vinand Nantulya, Rand Stoneburner, and John Stover. "What Happened in Uganda? Declining HIV Prevalence, Behavior Change, and the National Response." *Project Lessons Learned Case Study*, U.S. Agency for International Development, September 2002.

Hooper, Edward. "The Story of a Man-Made Disease." *Suppression of Dissent*, April, 22, 2003.

IRIN. "South Africa: Caring for Abandoned HIV-Positive Babies." March 25, 2005, http:// allafrica.com/stories/printable/200503290641.html (accessed April 17, 2005).

——. "The Treatment Era: ART in Africa." December 2004, http://www.plusnews.org/ webspecials/ARV/ARV-PlusNews.pdf (accessed April 19, 2006).

Jackson, Janine. "Media Blow the First Issue of the Campaign." *Extra: The Magazine of Fair, the Media Watch Group*, September/October 1999, http://www.fair.org/extra/9909/gore-aids.html (accessed April 21, 2006).

James, John S. "(ATN) Convergent Combination Therapy." *AIDS Treatment News*, March 5, 1993, http://www.aegis.com/pubs/atn/1993/ATN17001.html (accessed April 23, 2006).

Kamradt, Thomas, Dieter Niese, and Frederick Vogel. "Slim disease (AIDS)." *Lancet* 2 (1985).

Kapczynski, Amy. "Strict International Patent Laws Hurt Developing Countries." December, 16, 2002, http://yaleglobal.yale.edu/display.article?id=562 (accessed April 12, 2006).

Kasper, Toby, David Coetzee, Francoise Louis, Andrew Boulle, and Katherine Hilderbrand. "Demystifying Antiretroviral Therapy in Resource-Poor Settings." *Essential Drugs Monitor* 32 (2003): 20–21, http://mednet2.who.int/edmonitor/32/edm32_en.pdf (accessed April 20, 2006).

Kebebe, Befekir. "Historical Timeline: Politics; Ethiopia's Election and Its Aftermath." http://www.ethiopianmillennium.com/timeline_politics.html (accessed April 21, 2006).

Lafraniere, Sharon. "AIDS, Pregnancy and Poverty Trap Ever More African Girls." *New York Times*, June 3, 2005, http://query.nytimes.com/gst/fullpage.html?res=9D04EFD81738F930A35755C0A9639C8B63&sec=health (accessed April 17, 2006).

Lewis, Stephen, UN Special Envoy for HIV/AIDS in Africa. Press release, March 3, 2004, http://www.aegis.com/news/unaids/2004/UN040301.html (accessed April 21, 2006).

———. "Statement by Stephen Lewis, Special Envoy for HIV/AIDS in Africa, on World AIDS Day, December 1, 2005." http://www.pih.org/inthenews/WorldAIDSDay2005-StephenLewis.pdf (accessed April 16, 2006).

Library of Congress Federal Research Division. "Country Profile: Ethiopia, April 2005." Washington, DC: GPO for the Library of Congress, 2005, http://lcweb2.loc.gov/frd/cs/profiles/Ethiopia.pdf (accessed March 30, 2006).

Lindsey, Daryl. "The AIDS-Drug Warrior." *Salon*, June 1, 2001, http://www.archive.com/news/feature/2001/06/18/love/index.html (accessed April 20, 2006).

Marx, Preston A., Phillip G. Alcabes, and Ernest Drucker, "Serial Human Passage of Simian Immunodeficiency Virus by Unsterile Injections and the Emergence of the Epidemic Human Immunodeficiency Virus in Africa." *Philosophical Transactions of the Royal Society of London Series B – Biological Sciences* 356 (2001): 911–20.

Massow, Fran von. "Access to Health and Education Services in Ethiopia: Supply, Demand and Government Policy." Working paper, Oxfam, 2001, http://www.oxfam.org.uk/what_we_do/resources/wp_healthedu_ethiopia.htm (accessed April 17, 2006).

Matshalaga, Neddy Rita, and Greg Powell. "Mass Orphanhood in the Era of HIV/AIDS." *British Medical Journal* 324 (January 2002): 185–86.

McGeary, Johanna. "Paying for AIDS Cocktails: Who Should Pick Up the Tab for the Third World?" *Time*, February 12, 2001, http://www.time.com/time/2001/aidsinafrica/drugs.html (accessed April 20, 2006).

McGreal, Chris. "South Africa's Sick Wait for Judgment Day." *Guardian*, March 5, 2001, http://www.guardian.co.uk/Archive/Article/0,4273,4146083,00.html (accessed April 20, 2001).

McNeil, Donald G., Jr. "Africans Outdo U.S. Patients in Following AIDS Therapy." *New York Times*, September 3, 2003, http://query.nytimes.com/gst/fullpage.html?sec=health&res=9805E3DD1338F930A3575AC0A9659C8B63 (accessed April 20, 2006).

———. "Plan to Battle AIDS Worldwide Is Falling Short." *New York Times*, March 28, 2004, http://query.nytimes.com/gst/fullpage.html?sec=health&res=9F00E5D91130F93BA15750C0A9629C8B63 (accessed April 17, 2006).

McVeigh, Tracy. "How we failed to lift Ethiopia's curse." *Observer*, June 12, 2005.

Mehret, Mengistu, Lev Khodakvich, Bekele Shanko, and Fikirte Belete. "Sexual Behaviors and Some Social Features of Female Sex Workers in the City of Addis Ababa." *Ethiopian Journal of Health Development*, Special Issue on HIV Infection and AIDS in Ethiopia 4, no. 2 (1990): 133–37.

Milkias, Paulos. "Mengistu Haile Mariam: The Profile of a Dictator." *Ethiopian Review*, February

1994, http://ethiopianreview.homestead.com/Article_PaulosMilkias_Feb1994.html (accessed April 17, 2006).

Morris, Madeleine. "Apology Over Missed AIDS Target." November 25, 2005, http://news.bbc.co.uk/2/hi/health/4476978.stm (April 17, 2006).

NAM. "Use of Generic Antiretrovirals." http://www.aidsmap.com/en/docs/A3270CE3-9940-4F28-AE36-84F81640IE5F.asp (accessed April 23, 2006).

Ncayiyana, Dan J. "Doctors and Nurses with HIV and AIDS in Sub-Saharan Africa." *British Medical Journal* 329 (September 2004): 584–85.

Nevin, Tom. "Industry backlash over cheaper drugs." *African Business* 306 (February 2005).

Ntaba, Hetherwick. "AIDS: Africa's Doctors." *International Herald Tribune*, July 8, 2005, http://www.iht.com/articles/2005/07/07/news/edntaba.php (accessed April 23, 2004).

Okubagzhi, Gebreselassie, and Surjit Singh. "Establishing an HIV/AIDS Programme in Developing Countries: The Ethiopian Experience." *AIDS: Official Journal of the International AIDS Society* 16, no. 2 (August 2002): 1575–86.

Peeters, Martine, Coumba Toure-Kane, John N. Nkengasong. "Genetic diversity of HIV in Africa: Impact on diagnosis, treatment, vaccine development and trials." *AIDS: Official Journal of the International AIDS Society* 17, no. 18. (December 5, 2003): 2547–60.

Piot, Peter. "Global AIDS Epidemic: Time to Turn the Tide." *Science* 288 (June 23, 2000).

———."Women and AIDS." Interview by Susan Dentzer. *Online NewsHour with Jim Lehrer*, December 1, 2004, http://www.pbs.org/newshour/bb/health/july-dec04/aids_12–01.html (accessed April 22, 2006).

Piot, Peter, Michael Bartos, Peter D. Ghys, Neff Walker, and Berhhard Schwartlander. "The global impact of HIV/AIDS." *Nature* 410 (April 19, 2001): 968–73.

Piot, Peter, Thomas Quinn, Helena Taelman et al. "Acquired Immunodeficiency Syndrome in a heterosexual population in Zaire." *Lancet* 2 (1984): 65–69.

Quinn, Thomas C., Jonathan Mann, James W. Curran, and Peter Piot. "AIDS in Africa: An Epidemiologic Paradigm." *Science* 234 (1986): 955–63.

Reyn, C. Fordham von, and Jonathan Mann. "Global Epidemiology." *Western Journal of Medicine*, Special Issue on AIDS—a Global Perspective 147 (December 1987): 694–701.

Richman, Joe, and Sue Johnson. "On the Front Lines of the AIDS Epidemic in Soweto, South Africa: Just Another Day at the World's Biggest Hospital." *All Things Considered*, National Public Radio, December 1, 2003, http://www.npr.org/templates/story/story.php?storyId=1525600.

Rivers, Bernard. "Stalled Growth: The Global Fund in Year Four." *Global Fund Observer Newsletter*, November 7, 2005, http://www.aidspan.org/gfo/archives/newsletter/GFO-Issue-52.pdf (accessed April 22, 2006).

Rosen, Sydney, Ian Sanne, Alizanne Collier, and Jonathan Simon. "Hard Choices: Rationing antiretroviral therapy for HIV/AIDS in Africa." *Lancet* 365 (January 22, 2005).

Sabin, Russell. "New Crusade to Lower AIDS Drug Costs: Africa's Need at Odds with Firms' Profit Motive." *San Francisco Chronicle*, May 24, 1999, http://sfgate.com/cgi-bin/article.cgi?file=/chronicle/archive/1999/05/24/MN104738.DTL (accessed March 30, 2006).

Schemo, Diana Jean. "Education Suffers in Africa as AIDS Ravages Teachers." *New York Times*, May 8, 2002, http://query.nytimes.com/gst/fullpage.html?sec=health&res=9A03E0D91530F93BA35756C0A9649C8B63 (accessed April 17, 2006).

Schneider, Mark, and Michael Moodie. "The Destablizing Impacts of HIV/AIDS: First Wave Hits Eastern and Southern Africa; Second Wave Threatens India, China, Russia, Ethiopia, Nigeria." Washington, DC: Center for Strategic and International Studies, 2002.

Schoofs, Mark. "AIDS: The Agony of Africa: An Eight-Part Series. Part I: The Virus Creates a Generation of Orphans." *Village Voice*, November 9, 1999.

———."A New Kind of Crisis: The Security Council Declares AIDS in Africa a Threat to World Stability." *Village Voice*, January 12–18, 2000.

Sealey, Geraldine. "An Epidemic Failure." *Salon*, June 2, 2005, http://dir.salon.com/story/news/feature/2005/06/02/aids/index.html (accessed April 22, 2006).

Serneels, Pieter. "The Nature of Unemployment in Urban Ethiopia." Working Paper 201, Centre for the Study of African Economies, 2004, http://www.bepress.com/cgi/viewcontent.cgi?article=1201&context=csae (accessed April 14, 2006).

Shinn, David. "The Silence Is Broken, the Stigma Is Not." *Africa Notes*. Washington, DC: Center for Strategic and International Studies, July 2001, http://www.csis.org/media/csis/pubs/anotes_0107.pdf (accessed April 15, 2006).

Smith, Alex Duval. "Focus AIDS: A Continent Left to Die." *Independent*, September 5, 1999.

Steinbrook, Robert. "The AIDS Epidemic in 2004." *New England Journal of Medicine* 351, no. 2 (July 2004): 115.

t'Hoen, Ellen. "Industry and Institutions Failing AIDS Victims." *Financial Times*, July 21, 2000.

Urestsky, Samuel D. "Zoonosis." *Encyclopedia of Medicine*. Ed. Jacqueline L. Long. Thomson Gale, 2002. Available online at Health A to Z: Your Family Health Site, http://www.healthatoz.com/healthatoz/Atoz/ency/zoonois.jsp (accessed April 17, 2006).

U.S. Department of State, Bureau of African Affairs. "Background Note: Ethiopia." http://www.state.gov/r/pa/ei/bgn/2859.htm (accessed April 16, 2006).

Vollmer, Sabine. "Cheaper AZT on the Way." *Raleigh News and Observer*, September 20, 2005, http://www.natap.org/2005/HIV/092005_02.htm (April 21, 2006).

Weiss, Robin A. "Gulliver's Travels in HIVland." *Nature* 410 (April 19, 2001): 963–67.

Weller, Ian V. D., and I. G. Williams. "ABC of AIDS: Antiretroviral Drugs." *British Medical Journal* 322 (June 2001): 1410–12.

Wilson, Brenda. "Treating AIDS in Africa Undermined by Lack of Funds." *All Things Considered*, National Public Radio, November 28, 2003, http://www.npr.org/templates/story/story.php?storyId=1524909.

Workalemahu, Muluaeta, Debrework Zewdie, Seyoum Ayehunie, and Tigist Kebede. "Laboratory Network for HIV Infection in Ethiopia." *Ethiopian Journal of Health Development*, Special Issue on HIV Infection and AIDS in Ethiopia 4, no. 2 (1990): 115–21.

Wright, Joe. "Commentary: South African AIDS Crisis Sparks Activism." *All Things Considered*, National Public Radio, November 20, 2003, http://www.npr.org/templates/story/story.php?storyId=1514950.

Wuhib, Tadesse. "Speech on the Opening of National Pediatric Conference." National Conference on Expanding Access to Pediatric HIV/AIDS Care and Treatment: Challenges and Prospects, Addis Ababa, January 25–27, 2006, http://www.columbia-icap.org/ethiopia/pdf/intro_2.pdf (accessed April 16, 2006).

Web Sites

AIDS Education Global Information System http://www.aegis.com/

AIDSinfo: A Service of the U.S. Department of Health and Human Services http://www.aidsinfo.nih.gov/

AIDS Resource Center (Ethiopia) http://www.etharc.org/

AVERT (AVERTing HIV and AIDS Worldwide) http://www.avert.org/

TheBodyPro: The HIV/AIDS Resource for Healthcare Professionals http://www.thebodypro.com/

Doctors Without Borders Campaign for Access to Essential Medicines http://www.accessmed-msf.org/

Global AIDS Alliance http://www.globalaidsalliance.org/

HIV InSite (Center for HIV Information, University of California) http://www.hivinsite.com

In Their Own Words: NIH Researchers Recall the Early Years of AIDS http://aidshistory.nih.gov/

Medilinks Africa: The Gateway to Africa Health Information http://www.medilinkz.org/

PEPFAR Watch: Promoting Accountability of U.S. Global HIV/AIDS Programs Through Information and Advocacy http://www.pepfarwatch.org/

Documents and Reports

Centers for Disease Control. "HIV/AIDS Surveillance Report: Cases of HIV Infection and AIDS in the United States, 2004." http://www.cdc.gov/hiv/stats/2004Surveillance Report.pdf (accessed April 20, 2006).

Central Intelligence Agency. "The World Factbook Ethiopia." http://www.cia.gov/cia/publications/factbook/geos/et.html (accessed April 15, 2006).

Central Statistical Authority. *Statistical Report on the 1999 Labor Force Survey.* The Federal Democratic Republic of Ethiopia, 1999.

Earth Institute at Columbia University Center for National Health Development in Ethiopia. "Millennium Development Goals in Ethiopia." http://cnhde.ci.columbia.edu/ethmdg/newindex2.html (accessed April 14, 2001).

EuroHIV. "HIV/AIDS Surveillance in Europe, Year-End Report 2004." http://www.eurohiv.org/reports/report_71/pdf/report_eurohiv_71.pdf (accessed April 20, 2006).

Global Fund to Fight AIDS, Tuberculosis and Malaria. "A Partnership to Prevent and Treat AIDS, Tuberculosis and Malaria." http://www.theglobalfund.org/en/files/publications/qaen.pdf (accessed April 20, 2006).

International Center for Research on Women. *Disentangling HIV and AIDS Stigma in Ethiopia, Tanzania and Zambia.* 2003.

International Treatment Preparedness Coalition. "Missing the Target: A Report on HIV/AIDS Treatment Access from the Front Lines." November 28, 2005, http://www.aidstreatmentaccess.org/itpcfinal.pdf (accessed April 22, 2006).

Ministry of Health. *AIDS in Ethiopia.* 4th ed. Addis Ababa: Ministry of Health, 2002. http://www.policyproject.com/pubs/countryreports/ETH_AIM_2002.pdf (accessed April 20, 2006).

Ministry of Health. *Guideline for Implementation of Antiretroviral Therapy in Ethiopia.* Addis Ababa: Ministry of Health, January 2005.

Ministry of Health. *Health and Health Related Indicators, 1994 E.C./2001/2002 G.C.* Addis Ababa: Ministry of Health, 2002. Available for download at http://www.etharc.org/ (accessed April 17, 2006).

Ministry of Health and Columbia University International Center for AIDS Care & Treatment Programs. "Pediatric HIV/AIDS Care and Treatment in Ethiopia: Results of a Situational Analysis." http://www.columbia-icap.org/ethiopia/pdf/psar.pdf (accessed April 23, 2006).

Office of the U.S. Global AIDS Coordinator, U.S. Department of State. "Focusing on our Future: Prevention, Diagnosis, and Treatment of Pediatric HIV/AIDS." *The President's Emergency Plan for AIDS Relief,* September 2005.

UNAIDS. "Fact Sheet: Sub-Saharan Africa." http://data.unaids.org/Publications/Fact-Sheets04/FS_SubSaharanAfrica_Nov05_en.pdf (accessed April 22, 2006).

UNAIDS. "New UNAIDS report warns AIDS epidemic still in early phase and not leveling off in worst-affected countries." Press release, July 2, 2002.

UNAIDS. *Report on the Global HIV/AIDS Epidemic, June 2000.* Geneva: UNAIDS, 2000. http://data.unaids.org/Global-Reports/Durban/Durban_Epi_report_en.pdf (accessed April 16, 2000).

UNAIDS. "2004 Report on the global AIDS epidemic." Executive summary, June 2004.

UNAIDS. *2004 Report on the Global AIDS Epidemic.* Geneva: UNAIDS, 2004. http://www.unaids.org/bangkok2004/GAR2004_html/GAR2004_00_en.htm (accessed April 23, 2006).

UNAIDS and UNICEF. "A Call to Action: Children; the Missing Face of AIDS." October 2005, http://www.unicef.org/publications/files/AIDS_Launch_final_14Oct.pdf (accessed April 22, 2006).

UNAIDS, UNICEF, and USAID. *Children on the Brink, 2002: A Joint Report on Orphan Estimates and Program Strategies.* Washington, DC: USAID, 2002. http://www.unicef.org/publications/files/pub_children_on_the_brink_en.pdf (accessed April 17, 2006).

UNAIDS, UNICEF, and USAID. *Children on the Brink, 2004: A Joint Report on New Orphan Estimates and a Framework for Action.* Washington, DC: USAID, 2004. http://www.unicef.org/publications/files/cob_layout6-013.pdf (accessed April 16, 2006).

UNAIDS and WHO. "AIDS Epidemic Update, December 1998." http://www.aegis.com/files/unaids/WADDec1998_epidemic_report.pdf (accessed April 23, 2006).

UNAIDS and WHO. "AIDS Epidemic Update, December 1999." http://www.paho.org/English/HCP/HCA/aidsunai99.pdf (accessed April 19, 2006).

UNAIDS and WHO. "AIDS Epidemic Update, December 2000." http://www.aegis.com/files/unaids/WADDecember2000_epidemic_report.pdf (accessed March 16, 2006).

UNAIDS and WHO. "AIDS Epidemic Update, December 2003." http://www.who.int/hiv/pub/epidemiology/epi2003/en/index.html (accessed April 23, 2006).

UNAIDS and WHO. "AIDS Epidemic Update, December 2004." http://www.clintonfoundation.org/pdf/epiupdate04_en.pdf (accessed April 19, 2006).

UNAIDS and WHO. "AIDS Epidemic Update, December 2005." http://www.unaids.org/epi/2005/doc/EPIupdate2005_pdf_en/epi-update2005_en.pdf (accessed April 20, 2006).

UNICEF. *Africa's Orphaned Generations.* http://www.unicef.org/publications/files/africas_orphans.pdf (accessed April 23, 2006).

UNICEF. "Orphans and Other Children Affected by AIDS." http://www.unicef.org/publications/files/Orphans_and_Other_Children_Affected_by_HIV_AIDS.pdf (accessed April 19, 2006).

UNICEF. *The State of the World's Children 2000.* Geneva: UNICEF, 2000. http://www.unicef.org/publications/files/pub_sowc00_en.pdf (accessed April 23, 2002).

UNICEF. *The State of the World's Children 2001.* Geneva: UNICEF, 2001. http://www.unicef.org/publications/files/pub_sowc01_en.pdf (accessed April 23, 2002).

UNICEF. *The State of the World's Children 2002.* Geneva: UNICEF, 2002. http://www.unicef.org/publications/files/pub_sowc02_en.pdf (accessed April 29, 2006).

UNICEF. *The State of the World's Children 2003.* Geneva: UNICEF, 2003. http://www.unicef.org/publications/files/pub_sowc03_en.pdf (accessed April 29, 2006).

UNICEF. *The State of the World's Children 2004.* Geneva: UNICEF, 2004. http://www.unicef.org/publications/files/Eng_text.pdf (accessed April 29, 2006).

UNICEF. *The State of the World's Children 2005.* Geneva: UNICEF, 2005. http://www.unicef.org/sowc05/english/sowc05.pdf (accessed April 29, 2006).

UNICEF. *The State of the World's Children 2006.* Geneva: UNICEF, 2006. http://www.unicef.org/sowc06/pdfs/sowc06_fullreport.pdf (accessed April 29, 2006).

UNICEF. "UNICEF/Baylor Agreement Signals Brighter Outlook for Pediatric AIDS Treatment in Africa." Press release, February 27, 2006, http://www.unicef.org/uniteforchildren/press/press_31343.htm (accessed April 22, 2006).

UNICEF and UNAIDS. *Children Orphaned by AIDS: Front-Line Responses from Eastern and Southern Africa.* New York: UNICEF, 1999. http://wmc.who.int/images/uploaded/Children_orphaned_by_aids.pdf (accessed April 22, 2006).

United Nations. "UN Development Goals." http://www.un.org/millenniumgoals/index.html (accessed April 14, 2006).

United Nations Development Programme. *Human Development Report 2004: Cultural Liberty in Today's Diverse World.* http://hdr.undp.org/reports/global/2004/pdf/hdr04_complete.pdf (accessed April 17, 2006).

United Nations Development Programme. *Human Development Report 2005: International Cooperation at a Crossroads; Aid, Trade and Security in an Unequal World.* http://hdr.undp.org/reports/global/2005/pdf/HDR05_complete.pdf (accessed April 14, 2006).

United Nations Development Programme South Africa. "HIV/AIDS and Human Development: South Africa, 1998." http://www.undp.org.za/docs/pubs/hdr.overview.htm (accessed April 20, 2006).

United Nations Economic Commission for Africa. *Economic Report on Africa 2005: Meeting the*

Challenges of Unemployment and Poverty in Africa. http://www.uneca.org/era2005/full.pdf (accessed April 11, 2006).

USAID. *Children on the Brink, 2000*. Washington, DC: USAID, 2000. http://www.usaid.gov/pubs/hiv_aids/childrenreport.pdf (accessed April 23, 2006).

USAID. "The Human and Financial Resource Requirements for Scaling up HIV/AIDS Services in Ethiopia." February 2005.

USAID. "The Impact of HIV/AIDS on Health Systems and the Health Workforce in Sub-Saharan Africa." June 2003, http://www.usaid.gov/ (accessed April 23, 2006).

U.S. Department of State. "Report on U.S. government efforts to negotiate the repeal, termination or withdrawal of Article 15(c) of the South African Medicines and Related Substances Act of 1965." February 5, 1999.

WHO. "Global Access to HIV Therapy Tripled in Past Two years, but Significant Challenges Remain." Press release, March 28, 2006, http://www.who.int/mediacentre/news/releases/2006/prl3/en/index.html (accessed April 23, 2006).

WHO. *Progress on Global Access to HIV Antiretroviral Therapy: A Report on "3 by 5" and Beyond, March 2006*. Geneva: WHO Press, 2006. http://www.who.int/hiv/fullreport_en_highres.pdf (accessed March 30, 2006).

WHO. *Progress on Global Access to HIV Antiretroviral Therapy: An Update on "3 by 5," June 2005*. Geneva: WHO Press, 2005. http://www.who.int/hiv/pub/progressreports/3by5%20Progress%20Report_E_light.pdf (accessed April 19, 2006).

WHO. *Resolution on Intellectual Property Rights, Innovation and Public Health*. 56th World Health Assembly, May 28, 2003, http://www.who.int/gb/ebwha/pdf_files/WHA56/ea56r27.pdf (accessed April 22, 2006).

WHO. *Scaling up HIV/AIDS Care: Service Delivery and Human Resource Perspectives*. Geneva: World Health Organization, 2004.

WHO. *"3 by 5" Progress Report, December 2004*. Geneva: WHO Press, 2006. http://www.who.int/3by5/ProgressReportfinal.pdf (accessed April 19, 2006).

WHO. "Tuberculosis." http://www.who.int/mediacentre/factsheets/fs104/en/index.html (accessed April 4, 2006).

WHO. *World Health Report 2005: Make Every Mother and Child Count*. Geneva: World Health Organization, 2005. http://www.who.int/whr/2005/whr2005_en.pdf (accessed March 30, 2006).

WHO/UNAIDS. " 'Accelerating Access' Initiative Moving Forward; 72 Countries Worldwide Express Interest." Press release, December 11, 2001, http://www.who.int/inf-pr-2001/en/pr2001-54.html (accessed April 21, 2006).

Congressional Testimonies

U.S. Congress. House. *What Is the United States Role in Combating the Global HIV/AIDS Epidemic?: Hearing Before the Subcommittee on Criminal Justice, Drug Policy, and Human Resources, House Committee on Government Reform*. 106th Cong., 1st sess., July 19, 1999, http://frwebgate.access.gpo.gov/cgi-bin/getdoc.cgi?dbname=106_house_hearings&docid=f:65308.pdf (accessed April 22, 2006).

U.S. Congress. Senate. *Halting the Spread of HIV/AIDS: Future Efforts in the U.S. Bilateral and Multilateral Response: Hearing Before the Committee on Foreign Relations*. 107 Cong., 2nd sess., February 13–14, 2002, http://frwebgate.access.gpo.gov/cgi-bin/getdoc.cgi?dbname=107_senate_hearings&docid=f:77846.pdf (accessed April 22, 2006).

SELECTED RESOURCES FOR ENGAGEMENT AND ADVOCACY

*Organizations with unique programs in the
front lines of the orphan crisis in Ethiopia:*

The Addis Ababa Muslim Women's Council
Bedria Mohammed
Educational and vocational programming for orphans of AIDS and other impoverished young people.

AHOPE
Sidisse Buli, project manager in Addis Ababa
Kathryn Pope Olsen, executive director in Vashon, Washington
A home for HIV-positive orphans in Addis Ababa; sponsorship programs for individual children; adoption increasingly an option through licensed agencies.
Web site: www.ahopeforchildren.org

Blue Nile Children's Organization
Selamawit Kifle, Founder and Director
A haven for orphans of AIDS in Bahir Dar, Ethiopia, focusing on both group care and the support of foster families.
Web site: www.bluenile.org

Barlow Clinic, World Wide Orphan Foundation (WWO)
Dr. Sofia Mengistu Abayneh, in-country medical director
Dr. Jane Aronson, founder and director, WWO
A wide range of support services for Ethiopian orphans, including Haregewoin's children and AHOPE's children. Medical, psychological, and nutritional interventions for HIV-positive and HIV-negative orphans, as well as educational, cultural, and sports activities. A community center for families and children impacted by HIV/AIDS is in the fund-raising stage. Qualified volunteers work as "Orphan Rangers" in Ethiopia, Vietnam, Bulgaria, and Azerbaijan.
Web site: www.orphandoctor.com

American Jewish Joint Distribution Committee (JDC)
Under resident medical director Rick Hodes, JDC provides emergency medical assistance to tens of thousands of Ethiopians of Jewish descent. Other aid includes food programs, parental care, and health education.
Web site: www.jdc.org

Medical Missionaries of Mary (MMM)
Outreach to the poor and sick, and medical training, under the auspices of the Ethiopian Catholic Church.
Web site: www.-medical-missionaries.com

Missionaries of Charity Sisters, Ethiopian Catholic Church
Founded in 1950 in Calcutta by Mother Teresa, this international religious congregation came to Ethiopia in 1973 and today operates fifteen branch houses around the country. Every region offers a home for the sick and dying destitute; a home for abandoned, mentally retarded, and physically disabled children; malnutrition centers; mother and child care units; kindergartens; dispensaries; and, in Addis Ababa, a home for women and children with AIDS.
Web site: www.ecs.org.et/Congreg/Missionaries%20of%20Caharity%20Sisters.htm#Miss ChaiSist

Rotarians for Fighting AIDS and the Orphan Rescue Project
Rotary International fields imaginative and generous programs throughout Africa, including Ethiopia.
Web site: www.rffa.org

Stephen Lewis Foundation
The Toronto-based nonprofit foundation of the UN Special Envoy on HIV/AIDS in Africa fields programs in fourteen African nations, including Ethiopia; focusing especially on the mothers and grandmothers bearing the brunt of the AIDS pandemic.
Web site: www.stephenlewisfoundation.com

Education, lobbying, research, activist, and medical organizations:

ACT UP/New York—AIDS Coalition to Unleash Power
332 Bleecker Street
Suite G5
New York, NY 10014
Web site: www.actupny.org

AVERT
4 Brighton Road, Horsham, West Sussex, RH13 5BA, England
Web site: www.avert.org

CARE International
A leading humanitarian organization fighting global poverty, with a special emphasis on working alongside poor women, active in Ethiopia since 1984. CARE's Ethiopian projects focus on development, emergency feeding, and education in addition to HIV/AIDS.
Web site: www.care.org

Bill & Melinda Gates Foundation
Underwriting medical innovation and front-line treatments across Africa.
Web site: www.gatesfoundation.org

Earth Institute at Columbia University
Professor Jeffrey D. Sachs, Director
Exploration of reducing poverty through science and technological tools, with collaboration between innovators from centers of learning and villagers in poor countries.
Web site: www.earthinstitute.columbia.edu

Elizabeth Glaser Pediatric AIDS Foundation
Funding research into pediatric AIDS and assisting HIV-positive children and families.
Web site: www.pedaids.org

Global AIDS Alliance
P.O. Box 820
Bethesda, Maryland 20827
Web site: www.globalaidsalliance.org

The Global Fund to Fight AIDS, Tuberculosis and Malaria
An umbrella organization channeling resources into front-line disease-survival strategies.
Web site: http://www.theglobalfund.org

Health Global Access Project Coalition (Health GAP)
511 E. Fifth Street, #4
New York City, NY 10009
Web site: www.healthgap.org

Make Poverty History
U.K.-based global campaign for trade justice, universal access to essential medicines, and responsible aid to foster true development of poor countries.
Web site: www.makepovertyhistory.org

Medécins Sans Frontières/Doctors Without Borders
Campaign for Access to Essential Medicines
Web sites: www.doctorswithoutborders.org, www.msf.org

One Campaign
Lobbying and education on behalf of the world's poor, especially those stricken with HIV/AIDS.
Web site: www.one.org

Physicians for Human Rights
Mobilizes health professionals, students, and the public against the global AIDS pandemic, starvation, and genocide.
Web site: www.phrusa.org

Student Global AIDS Campaign
An American student and youth movement with chapters at high schools, colleges, and universities, involved in education, advocacy, media work, and direct action.
Web site: www.fightglobalaids.org

The Task Force for Child Survival
Dr. Mark Rosenberg, Executive Director
Atlanta-based clearinghouse for innovation, collaboration, and funding of programs related to children's health, including campaigns against polio, malaria, river blindness, tuberculosis, HIV/AIDS, injuries, and violence; works in conjunction with WHO, World Bank, the Rockefeller Foundation, and UNICEF.
Web site: www.taskforce.org

Treatment Action Campaign (TAC)
P.O. Box 74
Nonkqubela, 7793, South Africa
Web site: www.tac.org.za

United Nations Children's Fund (UNICEF)
The UN agency devoted to children's survival and protection.
Web site: www.unicef.org

The William J. Clinton Foundation Anti-AIDS Initiative
Partnering with African governments with the goal of universal access to ARVs.
Web site: www.clintonfoundation.org/cf-pgm-hs-ai-home.htm

ACKNOWLEDGMENTS

I am indebted to *Waizero* Haregewoin Teferra, who opened her door to me no less than to the hundreds of children seeking entry, and who—despite difficult times—never shut me out. I am grateful to the many Ethiopians who patiently instructed me and invited me and showed me the heart of the matter; and to the Americans who shared their stories and the stories of their Ethiopian children. I am grateful especially to Selamneh Techane, entertaining guide, able translator, and tireless advocate for the poor.

My reporting from Ethiopia first appeared in the *New York Times Magazine*, assigned and edited by Katherine Bouton, and in *Good Housekeeping*, with editors Nancy Bilyeau and Evelyn Renold, under editor in chief Ellen Levine. The involvement of these editors kindled the interest of hundreds of readers, who have become child sponsors, adoptive parents, advocates, and donors.

Thank you to John Baskin, Susan Merritt Jordan, and Andrea Sarvady, who read early drafts of the book—phenomenally generous with their time, alarmingly honest with their criticism.

Professor Fekade Azeze, of Addis Ababa University, was a marvelous reader and gave me permission to quote from his unique archive of oral literature of famine survivors. Researchers Aubry D'Arminio and Hillina Seife in the United States and Helen Asemamaw in Addis helped uncover and interpret materials from ancient history to modern epidemiology. Azeb Arega was a constant in-house cultural adviser, assistant, and translator; and Matico Josephson an architectural consultant.

Thank you to Dr. Mark Rosenberg, Stephen Lewis, Dr. Jane

Aronson, and Dr. Sofia Mengistu for the lifesaving work you do every day and for your kindness in helping me to grasp it.

Thanks, once again, to the David Black Literary Agency—Susan Raihoffer, Leigh Ann Eliseo, Dave Larabell, Jason Sachar, Joy Tutela, Gary Morris, Jessica Candlin, and the ebullient David Black himself; and to Lucy Stille at Paradigm.

Karen Rinaldi, chief of Bloomsbury USA, Alexandra Pringle, editor in chief of Bloomsbury UK—and, in the New York office, Panio Gianopoulos, Maya Baran, Amanda Katz, Annik LaFarge, Colin Dickerman, Greg Villepique, Alona Fryman, Peter Miller, and Jason Bennett—have welcomed me to their amazing house. I'm honored to join the august ranks of their authors.

My husband, Don Samuel, and Molly, Seth, and Lee Samuel read and commented on early drafts of the book with keen discernment. The younger ones—Lily, Fisseha, Jesse, and Helen—were more likely to shove the paperwork aside to clear a path to the family computer but have shared in the book's evolution in every other way. All are the loves of my life.

INDEX

A NOTE ON THE AUTHOR

Melissa Fay Greene is the author of *Praying for Sheetrock*, *The Temple Bombing*, and *Last Man Out*. Two of her books have been finalists for the National Book Award, and *Praying for Sheetrock* was named one of the top 100 works of journalism in the twentieth century. She has written for the *New Yorker*, the *Washington Post*, the *New York Times Magazine*, the *Atlantic Monthly*, *Good Housekeeping*, *Newsweek*, *Life*, *Reader's Digest*, *Redbook*, Salon.com, and others. She lives in Atlanta with her husband, Don Samuel, and their seven children, two of whom were adopted from Ethiopia.

A NOTE ON THE TYPE

The text of this book is set in Centaur. Centaur was designed by Bruce Rogers in 1914 as a titling font only for the Metropolitan Museum of Art in New York. It was modeled on Jenson's roman.